EMPOWERMENT OF NORTH AMERICAN INDIAN GIRLS

CAROL A. MARKSTROM

EMPOWERMENT OF NORTH AMERICAN INDIAN GIRLS □ □ □

Ritual Expressions at Puberty

University of Nebraska Press | Lincoln and London

Publication of this volume was assisted by
The Virginia Faulkner Fund, established in
memory of Virginia Faulkner, editor in chief
of the University of Nebraska Press.

∞

Library of Congress
Cataloging-in-Publication Data
Markstrom, Carol A.
Empowerment of North American Indian girls:
ritual expressions at puberty / Carol A. Markstrom.
p.   cm.
Includes bibliographical references and index.
ISBN-13: 978-0-8032-3257-0 (cloth: alk. paper)
ISBN-10: 0-8032-3257-8 (cloth: alk. paper)
1. Indians of North America—Social life and
customs.   2. Indian girls—United States—Social
life and customs.   3. Puberty rites—United
States.   4. United States—Social life and customs.
I. Title.
E98.S7M24   2008
973.04′97—dc22
2007028811
Set in Adobe Garamond by Bob Reitz.
Designed by Ashley Muehlbauer.

Contents

Illustrations

Photographs

Tables

Preface

We were three days into the four-day ceremony. It was Sunday morning. I could feel the anticipation and excitement mount as the morning's events continued to unfold. There were the faithful who had been present from the onset—the girl and her family, her clan and extended family members, her co-sponsors (i.e., godmother and godfather) and their families, and a few other helpers and interested persons like myself. In addition, there were two hundred or so community members in attendance to observe the amazing events of this third morning. In spite of the early hour, the crowd was charged and alert with a shared energy—the Mountain Spirit dancers had finished painting the girl with the white clay solution, and this act had enraptured us. I surveyed the gathering casually; then I returned my gaze to the girl and was taken aback by a new image that met my eyes. No longer a girl, she was now an old woman. A transformation had occurred—a process that began a few days earlier and gradually had been building toward this moment. She was covered with white paint from head to toe—her buckskin dress, her feathers and all of her adornments, her hair, and her face. Every part of her was now covered with the solution that the Mountain Spirit dancers and her godfather had painted on her just minutes before. The weight of that paint must have compelled her to bend over or stoop somewhat. It was this posture—along with the cane that had been her constant companion up to this point on the third day—that gave the appearance of an old woman. She was no longer a girl, but a woman advanced in years. At that moment, the pieces fell into place for me—this is what it is all about—longevity—having a long life—a good life—living long enough to have gray hair and to need a cane. All the good things life has to offer people were now possible for this girl. She had the hope of a bright and promising future. As one grandmother cried to me on one of these occasions, "She is new again—born again." The crowd shared this realization. We were aware that we had just observed something truly astounding, beyond our capacity of understanding. Even though many of us had observed this same transformation weekend after weekend with different girls, each time it was if it had taken place for the first time.

This event, the Sunrise Dance, occurred among the San Carlos Apaches, but the theme of transformation of a girl into woman—into something qualitatively different from her earlier self—is common in North American Indian puberty ceremonies. It is believed that the quality of pubescence lends itself to the potential for girls to possess great power and to serve as those who have the capacity to bless others, to give life to others—to bring renewal, impart hope, and ensure the continuance of all of life and creation. I also observed these events among the Mescalero Apaches and the Navajos, and read numerous similar accounts among various North American Indian cultures.

As a developmental psychologist who specializes in adolescence, I was trained to possess the traits of an unbiased, aloof social scientist. Instead, I was amazed and humbled on my journey to understanding these unique cultural events of North American Indians. I had never encountered any cultural act whereby a pubescent girl is believed to be empowered to such a degree that she holds the potential to bring good things to others and to the Earth. Further, it is believed that this empowerment occurs by virtue of a developmental event, menarche, which predisposes her to become intimately connected to the spiritual realm and legendary figures of her culture's oral traditions. The proper performance of rituals is believed to complete the transformation at this critical juncture of development.

In my university class on adolescent development I teach that puberty is a highly transitional phase of the life span and that the human organism has not experienced change of this magnitude since infancy and will never again undergo such rapid change in the life span. It is known that hormones drive the maturational processes of adolescence and that the impacts extend beyond the biological realm to intellectual, cognitive, emotional, social, and other domains of development. Further, it is known that times of great change are critical periods of the life span. Periods of transition bring the potential for optimal outcomes for which all persons hope, but they also bring the risk that development can go awry. This is a fact of which North American Indians possessed implicit understanding, and one to which they gave expression in their puberty and coming-of-age rituals and ceremonies for both girls and boys. The research findings presented in this book have prompted me to conclude that North American Indian cultures had remarkable sensitivity to the realities of the transitional phase of adolescence, perhaps before similar realizations occurred among Europeans. While ancient Greek philosophers Plato and Aristotle recognized a stage of youth, and 18th-century writer Jean Jacques Rousseau demarcated stages of human development, it was not until the late 19th century that Western society incorporated their understanding of the unique needs of adolescents into educational and social interventions and, subsequently, the scientific study of adolescence was ushered in by G. Stanley Hall (1904).

In critical periods of development, one needs to "strike while the iron is hot." North American Indian cultures seem to have recognized such opportunities to maximize life potentials emerging from the critical point of pubescence. As I delved into the historical, anthropological, and Indigenous-based literatures, it became apparent that most North American Indian cultures had some form of coming-of-age observances for boys and girls. Girls' events were frequently linked to menarche and more public in nature—perhaps more ceremonial—but for boys as well, some kind of mentoring accompanied by physical challenges and a vision quest frequently occurred. These rituals served various functions, including the preparation of youths for their adult lives and instruction on their expected roles. As well, spiritual protection was always regarded as a necessity for success in life, and adolescence was a prime opportunity to acquire a personal protector in the form of a spirit helper that would accompany the individual throughout his or her life span.

This is a book about puberty according to its sociocultural expressions. Of specific interest is North American Indians' conceptions of the transition from childhood into adulthood and associated cultural expressions to recognize and celebrate this event. The female coming-of-age is most closely examined, for reasons delineated in chapter 1. To bring context and meaning to the topic, Indigenous perspectives on adolescence are presented, with comparable and complementary contributions from Western psychological and anthropological views. An attempt is made to integrate varying strands of knowledge that originate from very different worldviews in order to enlighten readers on important cultural expressions of the past that continue in the present.

There is lamenting of a loss of ritual and tradition among the melting pot of the broader, non-Native society in North America. The degree to which this connects to the problems of contemporary adolescents is unknown, but that such a connection exists is a reasonable speculation. A common response of non-Natives who attend North American Indian puberty ceremonies as well as various other types of ceremonies is a feeling of loss that their own culture does not offer such rich, life-affirming events. P. E. Goddard (1909) points to this response most aptly (ignoring the choice of his words reflective of his era): "Where one finds so much of rich art remaining under such adverse circumstances, he wonders how much of a similar or superior sort has forever perished through the indifference of man to any other art, literature, or religion than his own" (p. 394).

A few conclusions may be drawn from Goddard's remarks. First, many North American Indian cultures have retained ceremonial practices of rich, artistic forms in spite of the deleterious impacts of forced assimilation and colonization, the devastation of disease and warfare, and the perpetuation of derogatory prejudices and stereotypes from Western (i.e., European and European American) society. Second, the long-standing attitudes of preeminence that have dominated Western thinking regarding its own cultural superiority are drawn into question when it is observed that they have lost many of their own rich expressions of rites of passage. There are multifaceted reasons for this loss; society has certainly changed from earlier times, including a growing reliance on technology and less attention to community and ritual activities. The absence of ritual activity is apparently felt by European Americans I encounter who express regret for their own culture's forgetting of meaningful, ceremonial rites of passage. Indeed, some white mothers have told me of celebrations they create to acknowledge and affirm their daughters at menarche, such as a special mother-daughter bonding event that might include making an adult-like purchase for their daughters, such as an expensive piece of jewelry. In general, my motivation for writing this book was to bring recognition to these life-affirming rituals of North American Indian cultures, which continue to impress me as a developmental psychologist and a woman. It is hoped that readers will be enlightened, enriched, and intellectually stimulated through exposure to the concepts and practices presented in this book.

Acknowledgments

It is gratifying and exhilarating to reflect on family, friends, and colleagues who have contributed in various ways to this book. I have thought a great deal about those who have offered their time and support without fully understanding what might emerge in the final product. First and foremost, I thank my husband, Rick Sale, who understood my need for extensive travel to conduct research and to withdraw in solitude to write the results. Heartfelt gratitude is expressed for his encouragement and belief in this project.

I extend a deep thanks to the numerous Apache and Navajo young women who served as continual sources of inspiration. Friends on the Navajo Nation, San Carlos Apache Nation, Mescalero Apache Nation, and Grand Portage Ojibwa Nation opened their homes and hearts to me. I especially acknowledge my sister-in-spirit, Loreena Lynch, and her family, Emerson, Vivian, and Morgan Farley, who provided me with a home away from home on the Navajo Nation. Others on the Navajo Nation who have provided encouragement, support, and knowledge at critical times include Mitsie Begay, Ginnie Nez, Peterson Zah, Johnson Dennison, and Steve and Carole Semken. A special thank-you to Ronald Maldonado of the Historic Preservation Department of the Navajo Nation, who facilitated publication of the Kinaaldá work. As well, Eddie Tso's remark that "Changing Woman wouldn't give up" is a directive I continue to reflect upon. Thanks are expressed to Perry Charley, who critiqued my writing on the Navajo Kinaaldá. And to Linda Garcia for sharing an insightful personal experience that is used in this book. The seeds of this book extend back to the fall of 1999 when I was on sabbatical leave on the Navajo Nation, at which time Herbert Benally and Tony

Goldtooth of Diné College invited me to my first Kinaaldá. That event captivated my intellect and emotions, and from that point on there was no turning back. Thanks to both of you. Appreciation is expressed to Darrell Jumbo, who urged me to attend the Apache Sunrise Dance at San Carlos—a recommendation that ultimately led to extensive field-work for this book. For prayers and spiritual insights, I acknowledge and thank Greg Begay.

Several friends at San Carlos assisted in this work. Special recognition and thanks are extended to Herb Stevens, Director of the San Carlos Apache Cultural Center, who accompanied me to my first Sunrise Dance and validated this work. To Spike and Sadie Kniffen, thanks so much for your warm hospitality and sharing your home in San Carlos, and the same regards are extended to Elliot and Edna Sneezy. I am grateful, as well, to Hart and Sharon Preston and their family, who treated me as kin and gave critical insights into the Apache Sunrise Dance. Dr. John Bush, Superintendent of the San Carlos Public Schools, and other educators graciously supported this work. Thanks also to Mescalero Apache acquaintances who facilitated research efforts, most particularly Ellen Big Rope of the Mescalero Apache Cultural Center and Meredith Begay and her nephew Homer John.

Thank-you to my colleagues in the Division of Family and Consumer Sciences and the Native American Studies Program at West Virginia University for their encouragement of this project. Acknowledgment and thanks is extended to the various sources of funding for travel and research costs: the Judith Gold Stitzel Endowment for Excellence in Teaching and Scholarship in Women's Studies, the West Virginia University Research Corporation, the Anderson Faculty Enrichment Fund, and the West Virginia Agricultural and Forestry Experiment Station.

To my research assistant and frequent traveling companion, Elizabeth Compton, thanks for your creative insights as well as your diligence in those countless trips to the library and checking references for this document. Thanks are also extended to Stephanie King for secretarial assistance.

As I sit in the northern woods of Minnesota putting the final touches on this book, I want to thank Sue Riley, who generously loaned me her beautiful vacation home on the shores of Lake Superior. The solitude and the beauty of the surroundings turned out to provide just the inspiration I needed at this time. The budding leaves of this northern spring have caused me to reflect on the themes of renewal and regeneration that are implicit in the puberty ceremonies I have attended. Welcome surprises at the end of this journey are new friends from the Grand Portage Ojibwa Nation, Gilbert Caribou and Calvin and Margaret Ottertail, who shared their time and knowledge. Thanks to John Red Horse of the University of Minnesota at Duluth, who made these connections possible. To Cedric Sunray, thanks for describing your experiences.

Writing this book has been an intellectual and spiritual venture. One is ultimately changed from engagement in cross-cultural endeavors, and I thank the Creator God for the many blessings and for the privilege of sharing segments of the spiritual journeys of others in their celebrations of life and the Creator who is known to the Apaches as Usen, the Navajos as Di'yin God, the Lakotas as Wakan Tanka, and the Ojibwas as Kitchi-Manitou.

EMPOWERMENT OF NORTH AMERICAN INDIAN GIRLS

□ □

CHAPTER ONE

Contextual and Methodological Considerations

□   □   □

According to the beliefs of many North American Indian cultures, the transition from childhood to adulthood is regarded as a pivotal and empowering, as well as a potentially vulnerable phase of the life span. There are innumerable illustrations cross-culturally of ritual practices that occur at and around the physiological event of puberty, and for girls, especially at menarche. Whether coming-of-age rituals and ceremonies are temporally linked to menarche (a clear-cut marker for girls) or occur over a range of years, the rituals that make up these events possess strong sociocultural salience. In essence, biological processes provide the impetus for coming-of-age ceremonies, but of primary interest in this book are the complex meanings of rituals as they pertain to beliefs about the optimal development of North American Indian girls. Coming-of-age practices are embedded in broader belief systems of cosmological constructions, which include origin stories, explanations for the cyclical nature of creation and patterns of life, and the complex relationships between humans and the spiritual realm. Not only is proper adherence to puberty customs believed to ensure the well-being and longevity of initiates, but those positive impacts are extended to her group and to all of creation. These and other underlying meanings and functions of both historical and contemporary coming-of-age customs are probed to acquire insights into North American Indian beliefs about pubescence, adolescence, and the preparation of young people for adulthood. Of additional relevance to a broad understanding of coming-of-age in Native North America are perceptions of menstruation and menstrual customs, as well as attitudes and practices concerning women.

Conceptually, coming-of-age ceremonies are one expression of rites of passage, which, in a general sense, provide psychological comfort and reduction of anxiety at unstable, transitional times of life as well as offering assurances for the unknown future. Additionally, rites of passage serve to formalize the incorporation of new roles and statuses as the individual enters a new phase of the life span. Opportunities are provided to reinforce social connections and to acquire and express socially appropriate behaviors toward others. In essence, rites of passages serve to reinforce the customs, beliefs, values, and mores of a culture and, of particular relevance to coming-of-age rites among North American Indians, to facilitate connection to the spiritual realm. The spiritual significance of these events drives all ritual expressions and serves as the overarching factor that binds and integrates the numerous rituals into the totality of a coherent and holistic rite of passage.

In a pragmatic sense, cultural practices are more likely to endure when they serve functions for individuals and societies. It is evident that the functions of coming-of-age rites among North American Indians are multifaceted. For the female initiates, puberty ceremonies are designed to advance their optimal development and to secure strength and protection for the future. For instance, an aim of these ceremonies is to assign a socially appropriate identity within the context of connection to others. Identity ascription is a salient component of puberty rites, and in some cultures an identity is ascribed that reflects a primary female supernatural being of the initiate's culture. This personage becomes a significant role model for the initiate, as well as for the adult women of her culture. Character development of the young person is also emphasized according to the acquisition of various desired traits, such as endurance, honor, responsibility, and maturity. Various rituals at puberty also are included to have a physical impact on the initiate, such as to impress on her a tall and well-proportioned body and physical beauty. Additionally, coming-of-age rites are believed to serve protective functions from potential future harm or evil. In essence, over the course of coming-of-age events, rituals are believed to serve as mechanisms for the acquisition of desired personality, character, and physical traits in young women, as well as spiritually empowering them according to the beliefs of their cultures.

The optimal development of young people is certainly an inherent goal of coming-of-age rites. Furthermore, it is anticipated that these individuals will ultimately become contributing members of their social groups, and well-rounded individuals are always welcome participants in a society. In chapter 3 it is shown that North American Indian cultures possess well-articulated beliefs about the particular qualities of the developmental stage of pubescence, as well as other stages of the life span.[1] Girls and boys are thought to be especially impressionable in the transition between childhood and adulthood, and various rituals are observed to maximize the acquisition of knowledge and skills by pubescent-age youth and to facilitate the shaping of young persons into responsible members of society. Adults instruct pubescent young people according to expectations for their demeanor, behavior, and responsibilities now that they are no longer children. In societies that depend on the contributions of both men and women for survival, it is a necessity that the young comprehend expected adult roles and be reinforced for proper role performance. For instance, in the past, many cultures held special celebrations at the time of the young person's successful performance of their first adult task, such as a girl's completion of a complex piece of handiwork or a boy's first success in hunting large game (see chapter 5). While adoption of expected roles for physical survival of the group may have been more important in the past than in the present, coming-of-age rituals continue to emphasize role acquisition.

In North American Indian cultures, it is believed that girls are in special or sacred states at pubescence necessitating the expressions of particular behaviors on their parts, as well as mandating the cooperation and participation of their families, kin networks, and communities in coming-of-age events. Many North American Indian cultures of the past and some in the present day incorporate rituals that require girls at menarche to engage in acts of benevolence (e.g., blessing others) and to serve as mediators for prayer requests brought to them. It is the perceived power of menstruation and menstrual fluid, especially the particular quality of the earliest menstrual cycles, that serves to empower initiates. Due to the sensitivity of this stage of life, the continuance of the group and even the entire human race is deemed dependent on proper adherence to puberty customs. It would be erroneous to conclude that coming-of-age ceremonies at puberty are mere fertility rites. These and related ideas are more carefully explicated in chapters 3 and 4.

It is particularly noteworthy that the rite of passage at and around the time of puberty is not only a ceremony of transition from childhood to adulthood but also a transition to the spiritual realm, including newly acquired access to privileged knowledge and secrets (Wyatt, 1998a). In some cases, pubescence is regarded as the first time the young person possesses enough strength to be indoctrinated in the spiritual mechanisms of their culture. The vision quest experience, which sometimes coincides with puberty, is one obvious illustration of spiritual transcendence (it is discussed more fully in chapter 5). The spiritual implications of coming-of-age ceremonies also extend to the future well-being of initiates according to perceptions that a long and harmonious life can now be secured. Essentially, the spiritual significance of a wide variety of female coming-of-age rites cannot be understated.

Mechanisms of Impact in Coming-of-Age Ceremonies

It is apparent that coming-of-age ceremonies are regarded as life-enhancing events for initiates as well as for others. In this respect, it can be asked, What mechanisms of change or impact operate in formalized rites of passage at puberty? In the field of adolescent psychology, researchers and practitioners alike are currently espousing interest in positive youth development, which addresses identifying, understanding, and promoting factors that offer protection to youth and contribute to desirable outcomes in development. Protective factors are defined as "those personal, social, and institutional resources that can promote successful adolescent development or buffer the risk factors that might otherwise compromise development" (Jessor, 1993, p. 121). In short, protective factors mediate risk factors to enhance the likelihood of resilient and adaptive outcomes in development. The present work contends that the protective functions of coming-of-age ceremonies facilitate the potential for socially desirable impacts on the development of initiates. This assertion is reinforced throughout this book in review of the literature and reports of findings from fieldwork.

As will be discussed in chapter 2, some contemporary North American Indian youth experience high levels of poverty, substance abuse, violence, and other social and behavioral problems with corresponding hopelessness in their tribal communities. However, not all youth succumb to these risk factors, and it is reasonable to consider what might make the difference for them. It is known that, in general, a variety of personal trait, familial, and social support factors protect against risk. In more specific consideration of North American Indian coming-of-age ceremonies, it is suggested that operative protective factors encompass three broad domains of activity: the engagement of young people in meaningful tasks and responsibilities; the provision of social support and affirmation; and explicit cultural socialization. Ultimately, the solidification of purpose and meaning in life and identity are derived as adolescent girls come to a greater understanding of themselves according to their placement in their cultures and the broader society.

In the coming-of-age ceremonies addressed in this book, it is evident that young people are engaged in meaningful tasks and responsibilities. A contention by Reed Larson (2000) on the importance of initiative in positive youth development has some bearing on this discussion. Initiative is a necessity for membership in adult society, but an apparent lack of continuity in Western society relative to socialization of children for adult roles is regarded as a prohibiting factor in its development. Accepting Larson's arguments, initiative and positive youth development are then fostered through adolescent engagement in forms of adult-sponsored and community-endorsed activities. Further, social capital, which is understood as a force that builds cooperation, trust, understanding, and empathy (Newton, 1997), is derived. Those with the most social capital are said to be more deeply involved in their families, social networks, and communities (Coleman, 1988; Furstenberg & Hughes, 1995). Further, it is during adolescence that people are most likely to internalize the benefits of participation in adult-endorsed activities (M. K. Johnson, Beebe, Mortimer, & Snyder, 1998).

While the writings of Larson and others centered on adolescents' involvement in conventional adult-sponsored structured activities (e.g., extracurricular activities at school), these arguments have applicability to the cross-cultural realm. North American Indian puberty ceremonies can be approached as adult-sponsored and culturally endorsed activities in which the values of the social networks and tribes of these young people are incorporated. Initiates learn of their place and value in the social order through engagement in adult-like tasks and responsibilities. While coming-of-age initiations are embedded in long-standing oral traditions, it is suggested that immersion in meaningful ritual activities are as relevant to contemporary North American Indian adolescents as they were to their ancestors.

Adolescent engagement in meaningful task performance operates in concert with a further protective function of North American Indian coming-of-age rites, namely, social support. Pubescent girls are engulfed in atmospheres of support and affirmation prior to, during, and after their actual ceremonies. The attention and social reinforcement linked to the rite of passage may endure for months or years after menarche. The female initiate is firmly fixed within the sanctuary of kin and community, and her place and importance are continually bolstered in numerous forms through rituals as well as in spontaneous social interaction. The outpouring of social support has been one of the most impressive components of North American Indian coming-of-age ceremonies that I have observed.

Additionally, female initiates undergo explicit socialization at their coming-of-age ceremonies according to the traditions, beliefs, values, and practices of their cultures. As will be discussed in later chapters, socialization occurs through direct instruction of initiates by medicine persons or spiritual advisers, adults, and elders. Enactments of meaningful rituals serve to reinforce oral traditions, expected task performance, and personal responsibility. The pubertal rite of passage is significant as a culminating event that augments lessons and tasks taught in childhood. Impressed on pubescent girls are the expected responsibilities that they will assume as adult women; and cultural lessons are emphasized by ritual role performance that occur over the course of the coming-of-age event, with the anticipation that such behaviors will continue from that point forward.

Through engagement in meaningful activities, the provision of social support, and explicit cultural socialization, meaning and purpose in life are solidified. Taken together, the three operative mechanisms of change or impact at coming-of-age ceremonies serve to strengthen ethnic group identification, advance pride in culture, foster feelings of belonging, and promote understanding of traditions, beliefs, values, and practices. These and other ethnic outcomes encompass what Jean Phinney (1992, 1995) defined as ethnic identity. Further, for North American Indian adolescents, spirituality, as a component of culture, plays a strong role in ethnic identity formation, as asserted by Gattuso (1991): "religion is the cornerstone of American Indian identity" (p. 69). Ethnic identity is a component of one's social identity relative to group membership. For ethnic adolescents it is thought to be a highly meaningful aspect of the self-concept, and one that is related to more desirable adjustment outcomes (Phinney, Lochner, & Murphy, 1990). Indeed, Indian and Northern Affairs Canada (1996) stated that the failure to establish a meaningful identity and resulting identity confusion has been linked to various social and behavioral problems of some Aboriginal youth.

The rich array of rituals implicit in coming-of-age ceremonies appears to shape four outcomes of optimal identity formation as delineated by noted psychosocial theorist Erik Erikson (1968, 1987). First, optimal identity formation should be indicated according to a sense that one is becoming and feeling most like the self; in other words, a subjective sense of comfort is experienced. While some physical and psychological discomforts may be experienced during coming-of-age ceremonies, transition yields to transcendence through accomplishment of complex and challenging rituals; in this respect, see the discussion of the Dunham, Kidwell, and Wilson (1986) Ritual Process Paradigm in chapter 6. Second, optimal identity is characterized by a stronger sense of direction in life. Again, rituals serve as the channeling mechanisms for the advancement of purpose and direction in life. Third, there should be a perception that strands of sameness and continuity connect the self from the past to the present and to the anticipated future. Continuous socialization processes reinforce these strands of continuity, and ultimately the initiate begins to understand the purposes of the rituals according to the totality of the life span. Fourth, the optimal identity that is being formed is affirmed by a community of significant others. The social support and affirmation that are experienced by the initiate compels the individual forward with confidence in a future that is relatively unknown at the present. The implications of coming-of-age ceremonies for identity formation are pervasive and receive continued discussion throughout this book.

Why Coming-of-Age, and Why Females?

What is known as coming-of-age is a pivotally important and significant phase in the life span. Many North American Indian groups regard the maturation of the child to an adult as a central developmental transition in the life span. Certainly this belief can be historically observed, and it is still overtly acknowledged in beliefs and practices by various Indigenous North American cultures. Performance of puberty customs, rituals, and ceremonies are frequently regarded as critical for lifelong success of young people. In my conversations with individuals from a variety of tribes—both those who continue to observe puberty customs and those who do not—this imperative seems to ring true. In Western theoretical thinking as well, the adolescent years are perceived to cover a highly transitional phase in the life span, and times of change introduce greater stress to the human organism. The transitional nature of adolescence is particularly profound, especially with respect to puberty (Flach, 1988; Petersen, Leffert, Graham, Alwin, & Ding, 1997; Schulenberg, Maggs, & Hurrelmann, 1997). The child has not experienced biological change of this magnitude since infancy, and the impacts reverberate into social and psychological domains (Petersen et al., 1997). Consider that adolescence is the only time in the life span after birth in which the rate of growth actually increases (Spear, 2000), and the individual gains about 50% of his or her adult weight (Rogol, Roemmich, & Clark, 2002)!

In additional examination of the unique developmental patterns of the years that encompass pubescence, it is interesting that an apparent long-standing and universal belief associates early adolescence with the "age of reason." This phrase dates back to the ancient Greeks but is echoed in various forms across cultures and centuries. In essence, the age of reason signifies society's expectation that during the transition between childhood and adulthood, or what today is called early adolescence, young people are capable of greater maturity in decision making, behavior, and commitments in comparison to earlier years. Younger children are not held as accountable for their actions and are granted some flexibility for their limitations in comprehending right and wrong. At early adolescence, however, it is thought that the individual should now be capable of grasping the more complex matters of morality and social responsibility. While contemporary society permits a longer adolescent moratoria that can continue well into twenties, the expectation endures that the young adolescent should demonstrate some allegiance and commitment to the beliefs and values of their culture and engage in more socially responsible behavior.

Since the cross-cultural belief is that young adolescents can, for the first time, understand the complexities of life and engage in critical thinking at more adult levels, their allegiance is often required in some form. Ceremonies of commitment, confirmation, or initiation are found in numerous forms and are suggestive of underlying beliefs about the capabilities of these youth. The requirement to exhibit fidelity and commitment to religious and cultural beliefs can be observed in contemporary Western religious and/or culturally based formalized rites of passage at early to middle adolescence, such as Jewish bar mitzvahs and bat mitzvahs, Protestant and Roman Catholic religious confirmation ceremonies, quinceañera ceremonies celebrated for Latina girls at 15 years of age, and sari ceremonies experienced by pubescent Hindu girls. The common theme across cultures and history, therefore, is that early adolescence is a critical period of the life span for initiation of members into systems of belief and rituals, religious organizations, and cultural practices. There is an implicit sense of developmental urgency that this is the optimal time to require demonstrable commitments on the parts of young persons.

An understanding of the qualities of commitment ceremonies of early adolescence, according to the reinforcement of adult-supported ideals, values, and behaviors, can be extended to coming-of-age ceremonies of North American Indians. However, the practices of North American Indians are distinguished because they are typically all-encompassing events. Indeed, Schlegel and Barry (1980) explained that North American Indian coming-of-age ceremonies are total social transformations that exclude certain types of religious initiations that occur in modern ceremonies (e.g., bat mitzvahs and confirmation ceremonies). It is illu-minating to contrast the rather focused and compartmentalized aspect of educational and religious rites of passage found in Western society to the totality of the adolescent rite of passage of North American Indian cultures. Puberty ceremonies of the latter are designed to pervade all facets of existence of young persons and encompass the totality of their life experience, both in the present and the future. The impacts are not restricted to one component of life (i.e., spiritual or religious) but are pervasive within the person and actually extend to the community and, in some cases, to the entire Earth. These are spiritual events, indeed, but all of existence is perceived as spiritual; therefore the impacts are all-per-vasive. In summary, the kinds of coming-of-age ceremonies addressed in this book are more demanding in form and more all-encompassing in impact than those that may be more familiar to some readers, such as those found in Western religious confirmation ceremonies. Perhaps all of us can learn something from culturally instituted ceremonies that recognize, celebrate, and affirm the multiple changes occurring in girls at pubescence and the broader impacts of these events for the initiates and their families and societies.

While this book is about cultural traditions and their purposes and meanings, both in the past and present, it is essential to recognize that processes of colonization have significantly diminished North American Indians and their customs. As discussed in chapter 2, Duran, Duran, and Brave Heart (1998) argued that the lack of connection to culture, particularly linkages that are strengthened through coming-of-age initia-tions, is a contributing factor to current high levels of problematic be-haviors among some contemporary North American Indian adolescents. In the absence of formalized adult-sponsored coming-of-age rituals and initiations, youth develop their own rites of passage, and these frequently involve engagement in behaviors that adults view as either premature (e.g., consumption of intoxicating substances, etc.) or not acceptable at any age. Unfortunately, such behaviors do not embody the values that facilitate preservation of traditional cultural practices. Interestingly, the loss of coming-of-age ceremonies is also lamented by Western society, and for similar reasons. Certain types of transitional rites of passage oc-cur in Western-based societies of today, but they are attached to a more specific change of status, such as graduation from an educational institution (Schlegel & Barry, 1980), or are socially endorsed by adolescents but not by adult society.

A primary reason for this book's focus on females is that adolescent initiation or coming-of-age ceremonies were more frequently practiced for girls than for boys in North American Indian cultures (Schlegel & Barry, 1980). One potential reason for this distinction is the more obvious pubertal marker of girls, namely the onset of menses, as opposed to less specific indicators of transition in boys. The traditionally matrilineal and matrilocal characteristics of some North American Indigenous cultures and the incorporation of the feminine in virtually all of their belief systems are related factors that may account for the more ritualized female puberty ceremonies.

The focus in this book on the female experience is not intended to discount the validity and utility of male coming-of-age experiences. Indeed, a section in chapter 5 highlights the historical practices of boys' coming-of-age. This delineation offers a basis of comparison relative to the ceremonies and practices of girls' pubertal rites of passage. All contemporary youth may benefit from socialization experiences that affirm and celebrate their maturational milestones within the parameters of socially endorsed cultural events.

Clarifications on Labels

Explication about the selection and use of particular labels is necessary for the purposes of this book. Labeling is a multilayered construct, and there is no perfect label that encompasses all Aboriginal or Indigenous people of North America. For instance, a person may self-identify as American Indian, Native American, Alaska Native, First Nation, Aboriginal, his or her tribal or band designation, and/or other labels. In short, ethnic self-labeling, which is an implicit component of ethnic self-identification, can vary by choice on the part of Indigenous persons. Trimble (2000) observed the multiple identifications of American Indians: "within a tribe an American Indian may self-identify as a member of a clan, outside the tribe among other American Indians as a member of a particular tribe, among non-Indians as an Indian, and outside the country as an American" (p. 199). As a rule of thumb, when applying labels it is always preferable to use the more specific designation a tribe or band has devised for itself (e.g., Lakota, Nakota, or Dakota for the divisions of the Sioux Nation). But, it is not always possible to do so, especially when general statements are made that apply to several groups. The term *Indigenous* is increasingly being used to refer to the broader global sphere of First Peoples, as is the term *Aboriginal*. In this book, the phrases *North American Indians* and *Indigenous North Americans* are employed interchangeably as general referents to these peoples of the United States and Canada. Relative to the United States, the labels *Native American* and *American Indian* are currently both acceptable and used more or less interchangeably. However, the label *Native American* is more inclusive and also encompasses Natives of the Arctic region and Native Hawaiians, both of whom are generally not considered American Indians. In 1977 the National Congress of American Indians and the National Tribal Chairman's Association issued a joint resolution that, when it is not possible to use a specific tribal designation, the preferred term is *American Indian* and/or *Alaska Native*. The scope of this book does not include Native Hawaiians, but Arctic cultures are included in the discussion of cultural practices in chapter 4. However, because most of the book focuses on North American Indian cultures, and for purposes of brevity, the label *Alaska Native* is generally not applied. One final clarification regards the use of the labels *Ojibwe*, which is more commonly applied in the United States; *Ojibwa*, which is more commonly applied in Canada; *Chippewa*, which is sometimes encountered in the literature; and *Anishinabe*, which is used more so by members of the culture and translates as "first people" or "original people." These labels refer to the same group but may vary according to local custom. For the purposes of this book, *Ojibwa* will be employed because the informants in chapter 8 had strong connections to Canada.

Canada's Aboriginal peoples are collectively known as Natives, First Nations, or Indigenous Peoples. The Canadian Constitution of 1982 delineated Aboriginal people of Canada as Indian, Inuit, and Métis. The Indians had their origins in North America long before the Europeans and represent a broad range of cultures and languages. The Inuit are the Natives of the Arctic and were previously known as Eskimos. The

Métis are a group that evolved from unions between Indian women and European fur traders. This book is primarily written about Indians, with some inclusion of Inuit customs.

Individual Indigenous groups are referred to as tribes (more common in the United States) or bands (more appropriate in Canada). In recent years the trend has been for tribes and bands to refer to themselves as nations. It must be recognized that the European colonizers of the original North Americans applied the English terms *tribes* and *band*, which are laden with political connotations. In this book, the terms *group* and *community* are used interchangeably with *tribe* and *band*. Regardless of the label, historically, a tribe or band was a group of people associated with a particular region or territory, shared and spoke the same (or dialects of the same) language, practiced the same lifestyles and customs, and had linkages through blood, marriage, and other ties. There is such great diversity across Native North America, and broad range in the size of tribes, that this definition will not be applicable in all cases. Nonetheless, groups or tribes experienced some degree of organization around social, political, economic, subsistence, and spiritual parameters. In the United States there are currently 561 federally recognized tribes and numerous other state-recognized and self-recognized tribes. These tribes include at least 200 village groups in Alaska. In Canada there are 604 bands.

According to the 2000 U.S. decennial census, 2,475,956 people, or 0.9% of the population, self-identified solely as American Indian or Alaska Native. A total of 4,119,301, or 1.5% of the population, indicated American Indian or Alaska Native alone or in combination with one or more races (U.S. Census Bureau, 2002). The American Indian and Alaska Native population grew more rapidly than the nation's population as a whole between 1990 and 2000, and is projected to grow faster than whites or African Americans. It is eight years younger than the population as a whole, with an estimated median age of 27.8 years (U.S. Census Bureau, 2001b).

Statistics Canada (2001a) reported that 4.4% of the population, or 1.3 million people, reported at least some Aboriginal ancestry. However, that number drops to 3.3% according to those who explicitly identified with one of the three groupings of Aboriginals in Canada (North American Indian: 608,850; Métis: 292,310; Inuit: 45,070). With a median age of

24.7 years, the Aboriginal Canadians are 13 years younger than the non-Aboriginal population, but trends indicate that Aboriginals are an aging population.

For this volume, a deliberate choice was made to not use the term *myths* to refer to North American Indian oral traditions that tell of their origins, their cosmological structures and functions, and other aspects of their belief systems. Rather, the terms *origins* or *creation stories* or *beliefs* are used. A myth connotes a fable and minimizes the impacts of oral traditions on a group of people connected by a common culture. The point is that if an individual or group of individuals behaves as if their stories are real, for all practical purposes, they are real for them. Accordingly, people behave, organize their lives, and find meaning and purpose according to oral traditions that have been maintained and perpetuated for generations.

Terminology Used in this Book

It may be helpful for readers to have clear working definitions of various developmental and anthropological terms that are used in this book. *Adolescence* is a stage of the life span that, in current times, is said to begin around age 10 and continue to the early 20s. According to Schlegel and Barry (1991), "An anthropological definition of adolescence, in common with psychological and sociological definitions, recognizes adolescence as a social stage intervening between child and adulthood in the passage through life" (p. 8). *Pubescence* is embedded early within the span of adolescence and is frequently used as a marker for the beginning of adolescence. In times past it was treated as the bridge to adulthood; however, for contemporary adolescents the stage of adolescence continues for some years after the biological processes of puberty have been completed.

Puberty is a physical process that involves maturation of the entire body, and it can span 5 to 7 years. It begins at the end of childhood and conveys the child to adult size, shape, and sexual potential. For girls it begins as early as 7 years of age and as late as 13, and begins 1.5 to 2 years later for boys than for girls (Petersen, Leffert, & Graham, 1995). The increased secretions of hormones drive pubertal processes. It is a common misconception that puberty applies only to sexual maturation; in actuality, it refers to maturation of the entire body. Puberty events include maturation of reproductive capacity; the development of secondary sex characteristics (e.g., breast development) and the sex drive; and maturation in shape and size (i.e., height and weight) (Petersen et al., 1995). Whereas puberty is frequently linked to the growth spurt and sexual maturation, changes are actually occurring simultaneously in all domains of development—endocrinological, physical, psychological, cognitive, social, emotional, and so forth. *Menarche*, or the first menstrual cycle, is the marker of reproductive capacity occurring during puberty that is of central interest in this book.

The terms *sex* and *gender* are related but separate. *Sex* refers to the biological state of being male or female, but possesses very powerful social connotations. *Gender* refers to the cultural components of being male or female, for instance, what does it mean to be a girl/boy or a woman/man in a given culture? Both terms are used in this book according to what is appropriate for the discussion. *Gender-typed behavior* refers to specific roles and responsibilities that are attached to men and women in a given society. In saying that a society is gender-typed, it is assumed that the roles and expectations of women are different from those of men.

Rites of passage are ceremonies occurring at various transitional periods of the life span that validate, dramatize, celebrate, and affirm major life events, such as birth, coming-of-age initiations, marriage, and death (Markstrom & Iborra, 2003). Taxonomies of rituals have been proposed by various writers (e.g., Bell, 1997; Grimes, 1985; Turner, 1967), and rites of passage always appear as one of the categories. Meaning and direction are brought to a life-stage transition, and, through a series of rituals, social conveyance to the next social role or status is provided (Turner, 1967). There is strong psychological salience derived from the social conveyance (that occurs through rituals), because ultimately the initiate's self-perception is transformed as well as society's perception of the initiate.

The classic model of rites of passage was proposed by van Gennep (1908/1960), who delineated three major sequences: separation, transition, and incorporation. *Separation* refers to some type of removal of initiates, either in groups or individually, from their societies, and it can be expressed in both symbolic and physical terms (Fasick, 1988). In the

physical sense, historically, many North American Indian cultures practiced seclusion of girls at first menses (see chapters 4 and 5). The symbolism of separation represents the disentanglement of initiates from their
former familiar occupied states and attachments, but without the security of a bona fide new state. Rituals are then performed that facilitate
transition to the next stage of life, and, as explained by Turner (1967),
people "are at once no longer classified and not yet classified" (p. 6). At
the coming-of-age ceremony, the initiate is no longer a child but not yet
an adult. The phrases "betwixt-and-between" and "liminal" have served
to signify this phase of transition. Dunham et al. (1986) defined *liminality* as "the marginal or uncertain status of the individual who is being
forced out of an old identity but has not been accepted into a new one"
(p. 146). The third phase, *incorporation,* involves the reassimilation of the
individual back into society along with his or her new roles and statuses.
The passage has been concluded, and the individual is once again in a
stable state (Turner, 1967).

Any single rite-of-passage ceremony will consist of a series of *rituals.* It is the ritual component of rites of passage that is of particular
interest in the present work. The symbolic nature of ritual practices are
closely examined relative to their expressions and functions in girls' puberty ceremonies. The Apache Sunrise Dance serves as an illustration of
ritual activities and their meanings (chapters 5 and 6). Early in this 4-day
coming-of-age ceremony for Apache girls, a micro-ceremony occurs that
involves dressing the initiate. On this first day of the ceremony, a trajectory is established that makes it possible for later rituals to complete the
process of transformation of the initiate into the primary supernatural
being of Apache culture, namely, White Painted Woman. The initiate's
costume is adorned with numerous items—each bearing symbolic meanings that reflect important Apache values. For instance, an eagle feather
is fastened to the initiate's hair. The symbolic nature of specific rituals
is usually not understood through superficial examination; for instance,
one would not know by observation that the white and gray in the eagle
feather symbolize the color of hair that comes with old age (reflecting the
hope of longevity for the initiate). Careful probing of the perspectives
of cultural informants is required to ascertain the meaning of symbolic
objects and behaviors (e.g., Turner, 1967).

Rituals are highly symbolic, and *symbols* are the smallest elements of rituals. In other words rituals consist of symbols and, together, a series of interconnected rituals contains the larger rite of passage. Then, the rite of passage actually connects to the broader life span of the person; that is, rites of passage are embedded within the life span and are part of the overall developmental scheme of the person. Many events through the life span contribute to the individual's self-perception and identity, and socialization processes and experiences that occur both prior to and after the rite of passage embed that ritual event within the totality of the person's existence.

In advancing the topic more specifically to the adolescent rite of passage, it is useful to consider Schlegel and Barry's (1980) definition of this term: "some social recognition, in ceremonial form, of the transition from childhood into either adolescence or full adulthood" (p. 698). When a rite of passage is spoken of as a *coming-of-age* ceremony or celebration, the allusion is specific to the transition from childhood to youthhood or adulthood—very likely the most prevalent rite of passage. Coming-of-age practices frequently encompass the phase of puberty relative to performance of rituals that surround menarche in girls, but such practices can occur prior to or after menarche. Menarche receives the most attention in this book, but coming-of-age rituals encompass other aspects of maturation, particularly when the development of boys is addressed.

Rites of passage at the time of coming-of-age are sometimes referred to as *ordeals* or *tests of manhood* or *tests of womanhood*. Chapter 5 discusses numerous girls' and boys' coming-of-age rituals according to their qualities as physical and psychological ordeals. For example, Kawaiisu adolescents, in a ritual designed to prevent future difficulties, were required to swallow live ants, and then later were induced to vomit the ants (Zigmond, 1986). Numerous other ordeals and their meanings are described in chapter 5.

Initiation ceremonies can encompass multiple experiences across the life span whenever an individual is being incorporated into a new group or organization within society. Schlegel and Barry (1980) specifically defined the adolescent initiation ceremony as indicative of the transition from childhood into either adolescence or full adulthood. In some non-

Western cultures, adolescence may be very short-lived, lasting only the time of the initiation ceremony (Schlegel & Barry, 1980). Adolescent initiation ceremonies occur anytime during late childhood or adolescence (anytime between 8 and 18 years of age), with most occurring around puberty. At minimum, two individuals must be involved in the experience—the initiate and an initiator. In this book, the term *adolescent initiation ceremony* is used interchangeably with *coming-of-age initiation* or *coming-of-age ceremony*, wherein, around puberty, the young person or initiate is required to perform and experience various tests and challenges that can serve many functions, including strengthening him or her for adulthood, proving his or her ability to assume the responsibilities of adulthood, and being privy to knowledge and secrets that are confined to adults.

Methodological Considerations

Prior to proceeding further, it is necessary to situate the content and conclusions of this book within the methodological processes by which they were derived. There are strengths and limitations of any research methodology, including some element of error relative to the collection and interpretation of data. Objective and unbiased science has been the aim of the empirical method that has relied on carefully constructed and controlled experiments with dissection of variables according to their impacts. In recent years, with the rise in contextual approaches to understanding and interpreting phenomena, some social scientists have become interested in obtaining and presenting data according to the perspectives and interpretations of participants of a culture who serve as the research informants. Such an orientation typifies the present study, which applied tools of qualitative research methods to the collection and interpretation of data on puberty ceremonies of North American Indian girls. Perceptions of cultural informants were queried in order to acquire understanding of both the psychological and societal impacts of contemporary coming-of-age practices that are embedded in ancient beliefs and traditions. Participant observation augmented the phenomenological reports of informants in an attempt to enter into their experiences and impressions, albeit in a very limited sense. Of preeminent importance in this research has been obtaining cultural knowledge from the perspectives of informants and according to their interpretations of the meaning of rituals. As such, those reading the book from the cultures represented may have been taught a different interpretation of a ritual or event than what an informant shared with me. Indeed, varying interpretations of rituals were sometimes disclosed by different informants and I attempted to either obtain a consensus or present the various interpretations. In conducting the field research for this book, an ongoing point of consideration and discussion with key leaders and members of the cultures represented was their value for and interest in the subject of this book. Without their support and facilitative efforts, which I found to be overwhelmingly affirmative, this research could not have been conducted.

It is the expression and reassurance of these guiding attitudes that I believe facilitated my gaining entry into the cultures among which fieldwork was conducted. It is an absolute necessity to be genuine, trustworthy, open-minded, and respectful toward others and their customs. The researcher should possess preexisting knowledge on the history, customs, and beliefs of the group, as well as their contemporary lifestyles and concerns. For example, customs vary across cultures concerning how one should approach a medicine man or medicine woman for any form of assistance, including research-related assistance. In many cultures, an offering of tobacco should be given, but this is not a uniform practice; for example, among Apaches certain ritual items must be assembled and presented in the proper manner (see chapter 6). Of course, proficiency in the language is also highly desirable when attempting to gain entry into a culture; when this is not possible, some knowledge of common expressions of the language is helpful.

It must be acknowledged, however, that somewhat of a "snapshot" approach has been used in some aspects of the present work. That is, data-collection processes were specific to the topic of this book, namely, girls' puberty ceremonies. This method does have its limiting qualities, because the broader cultural context of any culture can only be partially accessed. Hence, data and interpretations are somewhat restricted as opposed to a more intensive field method that would require years of living in a culture, acquiring the language, participating in the customs, and so forth. An in-depth field approach can provide greater breadth of understanding according to a specific broader cultural context and its many components. Hence, the present work does not provide the breadth of examination of specific cultures. However, this work does aim to provide breadth relative to cross-cultural examination of puberty customs across North American Indian cultures.

In addition to breadth, analysis according to depth is another way to approach the topic, and again, years of immersion in a specific culture can provide a certain depth to understanding and interpreting ritual practices. This is not to diminish the depth of understanding of the present work, but it was very specific to certain cultural phenomena, namely, puberty customs. The most extensive analysis in the present work is evidenced in the case study of the Apache Sunrise Dance. The meanings of puberty rituals were ascertained according to the interpretations of research informants who were cultural participants. Meanings were corroborated through participant observation, interviews, prior published works, and feedback from participants on the investigators' interpretations. Certainly the Sunrise Dance (like puberty ceremonies of other cultures) is embedded within a broader cultural environment, but it was beyond the scope of this study to provide a complete ethnographic portrayal of Apache culture. Numerous works are cited that provide varying glimpses into aspects of Apache culture, both past and present.

Regarding the transmittal of knowledge from cultural informants, the present work was limited owing to the fact that communication occurred in English. Some ritual events and their interpretations are not easily translatable, and are most completely comprehended by cultural insiders. However, most of the initiates in this research spoke only English, as was true of some of the adults. The point is that limitations imposed through language barriers were shared by the researcher and many of the cultural informants. It must be acknowledged, however, that even with the use of a common language, the investigator was an outsider who most certainly could not grasp subtle cultural expressions: such a barrier is posed even when a researcher (if also an outsider) acquires the language of the group under investigation. That is, regardless of the degree of proficiency in a language, if a researcher has not been reared according to the customs of a culture, understanding of both verbal and nonverbal communication is inhibited.

A further acceptable limitation of the data, as is the case with any cultural study, is that the investigator is limited to the knowledge and perceptions that participants are willing to share and/or were previously reported in the literature. Some knowledge must be protected, and it would not be permissible to disclose it to the uninitiated, whether that person is from inside or outside a culture. For instance, one medicine man stated that he would only share knowledge with me that could be published. In addition to the special quality of certain information, informants may be reluctant to share cultural knowledge with outsiders due to the historical experiences of their tribe with non-Natives, such as earlier prohibitions against ceremonial practices imposed by the European or Western colonizers, as well as the destruction of North American Indian ritual paraphernalia by these same sources (see chapter 2). The point is that researchers base their studies on the knowledge that is accessible to them, and it must be accepted that a full and complete portrayal is lacking. An investigator must employ scientific methods to obtain accurate knowledge, construct understanding according to the available pieces of information, seek corroboration, and acknowledge the element of error.

In addition to the field methods used in this research, historical, anthropological, and Indigenous-based documents were accessed. What might be called an ethnohistorical critical approach was applied to the study of written documents. In reading various descriptions and interpretations of North American Indian cultures, it is imperative to always be alert to the filters operative in the conclusions that are derived. That is, was the writer Indigenous or Western? What academic discipline was represented in the writer? What was the historical era in which the document was written, and what historical factors might have influenced certain interpretations? It was found that many of the earlier historical and anthropological works were primarily descriptive with little or no interpretation of meanings. When interpretations were derived, they usually were embedded in the Western worldview of the investigators as opposed to the perspectives of the cultural participants. It is not until more recent years that North American Indigenous-based works written by cultural participants can be more readily located. An aim of the present work was to access the writings of North American Indians according to their perceptions and interpretations of cultural practices. In some cases, such as in the understanding of menstrual customs, very different conclusions were presented by Indigenous-based writers than by earlier works of Western-based anthropologists and historians. In the present work, preeminent status was given to North American Indian sources of knowledge relative to theories of human development, including the stage of pubescence as well as interpretations of menstrual customs and the experiences of women.

In summary, the tools of data collection and analysis in the present work encompass critical approaches to ethnohistory as well as qualitative field methods that included interviews and participant observation. The present work is multidisciplinary, according to the interpretation of the data, but encompasses tendencies of my own academic discipline of developmental psychology because the primary focus is the developmental event of puberty. As previously observed, it is the sociocultural aspects of a biological event that are of interest according to the meanings of customs that are believed to produce desired outcomes in the development of North American Indian young women.

Purposes of this Book

Coming-of-age ceremonies symbolize the hope for the eventual contributions of youth to the social order and to the perpetuation of their cultures. This book is unique in its attempt to provide both an overview of historical practices relative to coming-of-age at or around puberty among North American Indian females as well as to present more detailed examination of current practices among four cultures (Apache, Navajo, Lakota/Nakota/Dakota, and Ojibwa). A further distinctive aspect of this scholarly work is the preeminent status given to Indigenous sources of knowledge relative to theories of human development, including the stage of pubescence. Further, Indigenous feminist interpretations are offered on topics that have been misinterpreted in earlier written works, such as the meaning of menstruation and menstrual taboos, the feminine in cosmology, and the purposes of puberty customs and rituals for females.

The purpose of this chapter was to familiarize readers with various concepts that receive greater expression in the following chapters. Chapter 2 reviews the processes and impacts of colonization to advance understanding of historical trauma on the cultures of North American Indians. These topics are included because they offer insight on high levels of social and behavioral problems experienced by some contemporary North American Indian adolescents. As well, the diminishment of cultural practices, including coming-of-age ceremonies, can be understood according to policies of assimilation that led to greater acculturation to Western culture.

Prior to delving into later content illustrative of contemporary coming-of-age customs, it will be helpful for readers to have acquired appreciation for the complex worldviews and beliefs of Indigenous peoples of North America, particularly with respect to the topic of this book. Chapter 3 begins this line of inquiry with presentation and discussion of conceptions of spirituality and human development of some North American Indian cultures. It is shown that North American Indians have well-developed models of life span development. Nine beliefs about pubescent girls that appear to be characteristic across several cultures are summarized according to research conducted for this book. A further purpose of chapter 3 is to interpret the functions and meanings of North American Indian puberty rituals and ceremonies for girls according to a multidisciplinary perspective that draws primarily on Indigenous ways of understanding, with some contributions from Western theoretical approaches to the study of adolescents within their social contexts.

It also is important to address the complicated corollary of ideas that are inherent to the topic of this book, specifically, beliefs about menstruation and the practice of menstrual customs, such as seclusion, and the incorporation of the feminine in North American Indian belief systems. Chapter 4 brings light to these controversial topics according to more culturally relevant interpretations, rather than according to Western-based writings of the past, in which conclusions were oftentimes misinformed and misleading. Western and Indigenous feminist views are elucidated to dissect topics more carefully related to female and feminine concepts.

Chapter 5 provides a historical overview illustrating the breadth of coming-of-age practices; for purposes of comparison, a discussion on coming-of-age rituals for boys is included. At this point, it is sufficient to say that if any puberty ritual is observed, there is a reason for its performance—no custom is random or irrelevant relative to the important event of puberty. The scope of this book encompasses North American Indigenous cultures north of Mexico.[2] This widely varying geographical and cultural region encompasses 10 areas—Plains, Northeast, Southeast, Southwest, California, Great Basin, Plateau, Northwest Coast, Subarctic, and Arctic. Of immeasurable use in preparing the historical content of this book was the series *Handbook of North American Indians*, which was prepared and published by the Smithsonian Institution. These volumes represent the most recent comprehensive effort to identify and delineate the cultures of North American Indian groups across all cultural areas according to a variety of historical and anthropological works. Other primary and secondary documents were used in compiling the historical content on girls' and boys' coming-of-age experiences. Chapter 5 concludes with a delineation of salient themes according to the review of coming-of-age customs.

While chapter 5 is historically embedded, chapters 6, 7, and 8 include illustrations of coming-of-age ceremonies for girls in the present day. These traditions have been carried on from the past and continue, in some form, into the present day. In chapters 6 and 7, my fieldwork on girls' puberty ceremonies of San Carlos Apaches and Mescalero Apaches brings substance and depth of understanding to these cultural events with deep historical roots. This research illustrates the significance of coming-of-age rites for contemporary Apache young women. Chapter 8 presents Navajo, Lakota/Nakota/Dakota, and Ojibwa cultural practices, with my fieldwork among the Navajos supporting the discussion as well as interviews with Ojibwa adults.

In chapter 9, the broader meanings and implications of coming-of-age in Native North America are considered in the light of content from previous chapters. The significance of female coming-of-age events for contemporary North American Indians is considered, as is the future of these ceremonies.

This book is about cultural strengths relative to coming-of-age ceremonies. Descriptions of the problems that North American Indian adolescents face are readily apparent in the literature, but cultural strengths also exist and are frequently overlooked. Culture is an integral element that permeates all aspects of life, and greater understanding of cultural practices as protective factors may ultimately serve to be advantageous for youth and their cultures.

Contemporary Youth Concerns in Historical Perspective

□   □   □

The overall focus of this book is on coming-of-age ceremonies and celebrations, their meanings and significance, and the perceived impacts of these types of cultural activities on outcomes of optimal development among North American Indian adolescents. Nonetheless, these practices of considerable cultural importance were severely undermined through colonization, and they subsequently disappeared among numerous North American Indian cultures. Prior to proceeding more fully into the topic of this book, we will consider the significance of this loss by examining the crisis of youth that currently exists among some North American Indian groups. High levels of social and behavioral problems can be understood according to a multiplicity of causal factors that link to historical trauma stemming from long-standing colonization processes. This chapter reviews some of the more destructive colonial practices in the United States and Canada, particularly as they pertain to the well-being of youth and families. It is shown that social activism and subsequent progressive legislation of the past 30 to 40 years have served to advance Native rights and spark more concerted efforts of empowerment and decolonization.

Current Levels of Social and Behavioral Problems

The approach of this book is a departure from much of the literature on contemporary North American Indian adolescents, which is dominated by statistics on their inordinately high rates of substance abuse, mental health problems, suicide, and school dropout (see Beauvais, 2000, and LaFromboise & Low, 1998, for reviews of these and related outcomes). Nonetheless, it is useful to review the problem-based statistics to acquire a broader framework of understanding relative to North American Indian youth of the past, the present, and the factors that have contributed to their widely discrepant situations. Poverty is probably the single greatest jeopardizing factor for any group in society, and on most indices, North American Indians rank as one of the most poverty-stricken. According to the U.S. Census Bureau (2001a), American Indians and Alaska Natives experienced an average poverty rate of 24.5% across the years 1999–2001. This figure was higher than poverty rates for non-Hispanic whites (7.6%), Asians and Pacific Islanders (10.3%), Latinos or Hispanics (21.9%), and African Americans (22.9%). Consistent with these data and averaged across the same three years, the median household income of American Indians and Alaska Natives was one of the lowest, at $32,100, but was higher than that of African Americans, slightly lower than that of Latinos, and lower than that of non-Hispanic whites and Asians and Pacific Islanders. These are disturbing statistics when it is considered that unemployment, one index of poverty, is often associated with high levels of crime and substance abuse, and the unemployment rate was 15.1% for American Indians and Alaska Natives compared to the national average of 5.9% in 2003 (National Center for Education Statistics, 2003).

Similar statistics on unemployment and income are found on Canadian Aboriginals. As reported by Indian and Northern Affairs Canada (INAC, 2000) for 1997–98, the unemployment rate of Natives on reserves was 29%, compared to non-Native Canadians at 10%. Data from the 2001 Census revealed that the unemployment rate for the total Aboriginal population (reserve and non-reserve) was 16%, compared to 7.1% for the total non-Aboriginal population (Statistics Canada, 2001b). Median household income for all Aboriginals was $35,365, compared to $46,752 for the total non-Aboriginal population (Statistics Canada, 2002a, 2002b).

Some, but not all, North American Indian communities experience high levels of alcoholism and other forms of substance abuse. This topic warrants considerable examination according to the multifaceted causal factors, but it is beyond the scope of this book to include such an inquiry.

However, it is significant to illustrate the degree of substance abuse problems among American Indian and Alaska Native youth when comparisons are made against the national averages. In 2002, among persons age 12 or older, the rate of substance dependence or abuse was highest among American Indians and Alaska Natives (14.1%), while the lowest rate was among Asians (4.2%). The rate was similar among African Americans and whites (9.5% and 9.3%, respectively) and was 10.4% among Latinos (Substance Abuse and Mental Health Services Administration, 2003). It was shown in statistics from this same source that among 12-to-17-year-old American Indian and Alaska Native adolescents, illicit drug use was 20.9%, compared to 11.6% for all youth of this age bracket. Rates of binge drinking by underage youth were similar for whites (22.7%) and American Indians and Alaska Natives (22.6%), compared to rates of 16.8% among underage Latinos, 9.8% among underage African Americans, and 8.6% among underage Asians (Substance Abuse and Mental Health Services Administration, 2003). The use of methamphetamine is a growing problem among American Indians, as it is in the broader U.S. society.

According to the First Nations and Inuit Regional Health Survey (1999), data on substance use among Canadian Native youth are lacking. It was reported, however, that levels of alcohol consumption may be similar between Native and non-Native youth, but the usage of other substances by First Nations youth was higher, with special concern for the high rates of inhalation of toxicants in geographically isolated Native communities. Indeed, in comparison to non-Aboriginal inhabitants, Aboriginals age 15 and older in the Northwest Territories had higher usage rates of marijuana or hashish, LSD, speed, cocaine, or "crack," and heroin. Of particular concern was the finding that the Aboriginal population in the Northwest Territories was 11 times more likely to have sniffed solvents or aerosols (Health Canada, 2003).

The at-risk nature of North American Indian adolescents is especially alarming when causes of death are examined. Motor vehicle and other accidents are the leading cause of death among American Indians and Alaska Natives in the 5-to-14 and 15-to-24 age brackets, and at rates that are 2.3 and 2.9 times higher, respectively, than the rate for all races in the United States within these age groupings (Indian Health Service, 1998/99). Particularly disturbing are statistics showing that the suicide rate among

American Indians and Alaska Natives is 3.0 times higher for the 5-to-14 age bracket and 2.5 times higher for the 15-to-24 age bracket than among all races in the United States within these age brackets (Indian Health Service, 1998/99). Indian males of these age groups, especially, are at high risk for death by accidents and suicide. Similar findings are found among Canada's First Nations youth (Assembly of First Nations, 2000). In the 15-to-24 age bracket, the suicide rate was 4.0 to 8.0 times the national average over the years 1989–1993. Among 10-to-19-year-old First Nations youth, suicide and self-inflicted injury was the leading cause of death, followed by motor vehicle accidents (Health Canada, 2003). Consistent with U.S. findings, First Nations males in Canada are at greater risk for completed suicide than females (Health Canada, 2003).

As stated, it is not the purpose of this book to dwell on these statistics indicative of the high levels of problem behaviors among some North American Indian youth. Nonetheless, a book of this type would not be complete without some mention of the problematic circumstances present in the lives of some of these youth. Current rates of poverty, especially, must be considered an implicating factor in all high-risk behaviors of youth—regardless of ethnic or racial group affiliation. Groups that have been marginalized in society due to prejudice and discrimination are especially at risk for high poverty rates. Indigenous societies in North America were not perfect societies prior to European contact, but such a crisis of youth did not exist. What, then, accounts for these problematic circumstances? Numerous causal factors must be considered, beginning with the multiple facets of historical trauma that were highly destabilizing to cultures and peoples. Disconnection from cultural practices, such as coming-of-age ceremonies, served to remove sources of constancy and groundedness that brought meaning and purpose in life. The next section addresses the specific facets of colonization that affected the well-being of Indigenous youth, families, and their cultures.

The Trauma of Colonization

Despite the multiple functions of coming-of-age ceremonies for girls, impacts of forced acculturation for over 500 years have threatened and undermined the continuation of these and other cultural practices to the point that countless North American Indian cultures have lost their puberty customs. With exposure to European cultures, conflicting sets of customs were observed with traditional practices, such as those occurring at birth, puberty, and menstruation, disappearing and either not replaced or replaced by Europeans customs. Speaking on this topic in a work on the Native American holocaust, Duran et al. (1998) state:

> Particularly damaging has been the systematic destruction of the initiation ceremonies of many (though not all) tribes. Among the Apache, there were ceremonies for every step of child development, used to invoke the assistance of supernatural powers to protect the child. A lack of such ceremonies contributes to problems faced by contemporary Native American youth. Traditional initiation ceremonies have given way to other undifferentiated methods of initiation, conducted away from family and tribe and sometimes involving unhealthy activities. One of the major initiations for Native American youth has involved the use of alcohol, with devastating effects. (p. 68)

To acquire appreciation of the fact that somehow some cultures have maintained their coming-of-age rites in spite of colonization, it is instructive to consider the numerous assaults against North American Indians and their customs.

It is estimated that, prior to European contact, there were 8 to 12 million (some estimates range up to 18 million) Indigenous people in North America. After European contact in North America, it is estimated that populations diminished to 95% of their original numbers before the downward trends reversed. For instance, the all-time low of American Indians in the United States was 228,000, in 1890 (Sutton, 2004), and in Canada was estimated to be 102,000, in 1871 (INAC, 1996). It is essential to understand that the overall diminishment of Indigenous people and their societies resulted from a combination of assaults. If numbers alone are considered, the most destructive impact can be attributed to exposure to the numerous diseases carried by Europeans of which Indigenous peoples of North and South America did not possess immunities. Diseases such as smallpox, measles, influenza, the bubonic plague, cholera, typhoid, diphtheria, scarlet fever, whooping cough, malaria, yellow fever, some venereal diseases, and other diseases (see Sutton, 2004) served to decimate entire villages, and cultures were lost forever without opportunities to perpetuate oral traditions. Consider the alarming statistic that by the early 17th century about 75 percent of the Iroquois peoples had been killed due to European-based diseases (Sutton, 2004). Other destructive factors included warfare and military domination, genocide, slavery and exploitation, growing reliance on European technology, depletion of game and the means to practice traditional livelihoods, and forced displacement and migration, among others. Cultural practices were lost forever, as there were no survivors of some cultures, or no elders and other cultural experts to transmit traditional knowledge for others. Further, confidence diminished in traditional healing practices and ceremonies—as well as in those who conducted these spiritually based practices—because they were seemingly incompatible with and ineffective against the new types of diseases and problems that arose through European contact.

Particularly disturbing was forced assimilation through Western-based educational practices, which effectively removed Indigenous children from their homes and cultures and sought to educate them in residential contexts that encompassed the Western worldview. Clearly, institutions of formal education in North America have not regarded the protection and perpetuation of Indigenous cultures as part of their curriculum. European efforts to educate North Americans Indians began quite early in the colonial period (early-17th-century educational efforts occurred by French, English, and Spanish alike) (Noriega, 1992). Primary motives for education of Indigenous peoples were to diminish and eradicate their cultures and lifestyles and to pave the way for colonial settlement, which would establish European values and lifestyles in the Americas (Noriega, 1992; Tippeconnic, 1999). Indeed, it is apparent that the colonial strategy of dismantling cultures in order to colonize Indigenous peoples and dominate local resources was used in other parts of the world as well.

Boarding or residential schools were established to remove North American Indian children from their families, because those families were perceived to pose barriers to proper formal education (Reyhner & Eder, 1992). Since one of the aims of boarding schools was to disrupt traditional cultural practices, parents and tribes did not have input into the education of their young. The strong pressure toward assimilation by non-Indian educators, missionaries, and government officials was a prohibitive factor in the continued expressions of traditional culture, in numerous forms. Because a pubescent girl would be away from her kin and culture at the onset of menses, the prime opportunity for the practice of appropriate coming-of-age customs would be missed. Further, since girls would not learn about these important rituals, they would not be suitably empowered and informed to perpetuate such practices among their own offspring. For instance, Libby (1952) conducted fieldwork on puberty rituals among the Northern Athabascans in the 1940s, and by that time many of her informants were not practicing the rituals because they failed to see their functions.

No educational system is value-free, and education is the universal means by which a society transmits its values. However, the values perpetuated in formal education were in stark contrast to and frequently contradictory with those of Indigenous cultures. For instance, in 1611 French Jesuits opened boarding schools along the St. Lawrence River; situated away from their villages, children were instructed in the three R's, French language and customs, French history, and some skills (Noriega, 1992). The students were exposed to knowledge not relevant or meaningful to them and were separated from their own forms of education. Religious conversion—an aim of organized religion—was frequently a component of missionary-based education and was also an effective means of realizing government policies. In short, education served as a means to meet dual goals—conversion was the goal of religious groups, and land acquisition and domination was the goal of governments and colonists. On both accounts, it was deemed useful to instill European-based values, beliefs, and lifestyles to subdue a hemisphere of peoples who were not understood—nor sought to be understood—by their colonizers.

While the education of American Indian children was an activity of the European colonizers that began centuries earlier, in the latter half of the 19th century it became an even stronger institutionalized means of assimilation. Treaty making had ended in 1871, and most tribes had come under the control of the U.S. government. It was determined by the mid-1870s that day schools permitted too much contact between children and their families and cultures and interfered with the assimilationist strategies of formal education, as summarized by Noriega (1992): "Hence, by the end of the decade [1870s] an increasing emphasis was placed upon the more costly but far more efficient boarding school model wherein Indian children could be isolated from the 'contaminating' influences of their societies for years on end" (p. 380). With such concerted efforts that undermined family and cultural integrity, the General Allotment or Dawes Act of 1887 served to severely undercut Indian landholdings in the United States and undermined the collective power of tribes. While physical genocide had been practiced in various forms in earlier decades and centuries, in the late 19th century the assaults on American Indians occurred through acts of cultural genocide and the erosion of tribal power and identity.

The U.S. Congress advanced its agenda for Indian education even further, and by 1887 it was appropriating more than a million dollars every year to Indian education (Reyhner & Eder, 1992). The Carlisle Indian Industrial School, which opened in 1879 in Pennsylvania, was the first government-run off-reservation boarding school and served as a model for other schools of its kind. The institution was governed by Captain Richard H. Pratt, who had been the commandant at the Fort Marion Prison in Florida, where many American Indians had been confined (Nabokov, 1999). At Carlisle, students were both ideologically and geographically isolated from their cultures. Apache children and youth were transported from the Southwest by train, and youth ages 12 to 22 with Geronimo and other Chiricahuas in prison in Florida were likewise sent to Carlisle. Distraught parents resisted these efforts and attempted to hide their children from the removal. According to Debo (1976), "They would have been still more unwilling to part with them if they had known Carlisle was a death trap, an even more deadly center of tubercular infection that the crowded camp at Fort Marion" (p. 318).

While a range of boarding school experiences are reported, the Carlisle Indian School served as the prototype for the most severe educational and lifestyle practices of these residentially based educational institutions, of which the descriptions are chilling to read (e.g., Nabokov, 1999; Noriega, 1992; Reyhner & Eder, 1992; Tafoya & Del Vecchio, 1996; J. Wilson, 1998). These institutions were militaristic in their operation—strict, severe, and punitive. Indian agents, government-appointed officials assigned to control reservation life, acted as dictators and aggressively facilitated the process of removal of children, who, as young as 5 years of age, were sometimes surreptitiously and forcibly removed from their homes for extended periods (years in many cases). Relocation at some distance from one's familiar people was the established practice, with geographic barriers sometimes encompassing nearly the width of the country as was the case of Apaches as previously described. English-language immersion was required from the onset, with accompanying punishment for speaking tribal languages. Upon arrival children were assigned English names, and traditional clothing was destroyed and replaced with unfamiliar, Western-style clothing. Braids and traditional hairstyles were shaved and replaced with Western-style haircuts. These losses were significant, since hairstyles are a cultural practice and many tribes believe long hair to embody power and strength of the individual. Traditional religious practices were forbidden, and children were immersed in teachings of formal Western-based religions. They were withdrawn from their traditional structures of habitation and reestablished in buildings, dormitories, campuses, and furnishings of Western design. While acquiring European American society's forms of knowledge was one goal of education, children also were forced into physical labor in the kitchens, stables, gardens, and shops to maintain the running of schools. Compliance to regimented, timebound schedules replaced a more relaxed practice of time management these children had experienced in their cultures, and corporal punishment was common for rule violation of any sort. In short, there was complete immersion in a Western-based educational curriculum and lifestyle embedded in values and goals not of the children to whom they were directed.

While the Carlisle experience may represent one extreme, American Indians tell of a range of experiences at boarding schools, and it should be acknowledged that some even spoke highly of their education, as stated by Nabokov (1999): "Some youngsters flourished under these regimes and grew into eminent Indian spokespeople who would credit their success to this training" (p. 216). Nonetheless, the general consensus is that the negative impacts of forced assimilation through Western-based educational practices are immeasurable, as asserted by Oswalt (2006): "The boarding schools in the United States and residential schools in Canada were *the most powerful institutions for the systematic destruction of traditional Native American cultures*" (p. 47, emphasis in source). Through extended separation, children became strangers to their families and cultures. For instance, Sun Elk was the first child from Taos Pueblo to attend Carlisle, and after seven continuous years away from home, he returned to Taos. In the following account, published in Nabokov (1999), he told of his homecoming:

> The governor of the pueblo and the two war chiefs and many of the priest chiefs came into my father's house. They did not talk to me; they did not even look at me. When they were all assembled they talked to my father. The chiefs said to my father, "Your son who calls himself Rafael has lived with the white men. He has been far away from the pueblo. He has not lived in the kiva nor learned the things Indian boys should learn. He has no hair. He has no blankets. He cannot even speak our language and he has a strange smell. He is not one of us." (p. 223)

Languages and cultures were diminished as children no longer acquired their customs, including coming-of-age ceremonies. Due to rearing in unnatural day-to-day institutional living environments, children did not establish models for normative family life and parent-child relationships. Hence, they did not gain knowledge of parenting skills and, years later, were uninformed in rearing their own children or establishing functional and stable home lives. Owing to the historical trauma of boarding schools and other factors, a variety of social and behavioral problems are evident in some American Indian communities of today, such as poverty, learned helplessness, alcohol and drug abuse, suicide, and violence. In short, the impacts of formal Western-based education and especially boarding schools extended far beyond the intent to assimilate children into European American culture and served to perpetuate trauma among generations of people.

A related practice that received momentum from the Bureau of Indian Affair's (BIA) 1957 Indian Adoption Act involved the removal of American Indian children from their homes to be placed in foster care or adoptive circumstances in non-Indian homes. Governmental agencies and institutions ignored individual, child, and parental rights as well as the legitimate rights of tribal governments relative to the welfare of their children. Indian children were placed in foster care at a rate 20 times that of Anglo children (Select Committee on Indian Affairs, 1977). Parents had little knowledge of their rights to protect their children from removal, and feelings of helplessness were common. Like the boarding schools, this destructive practice weakened traditional family structures and tribal cultural practices. Indian children were removed from their homes according to nonsignificant factors, such as a child walking barefoot and playing in a mud puddle or a family not having enough bedrooms in their home (Select Committee on Indian Affairs, 1977). In short, decisions were made by those unfamiliar with American Indian cultures, and the European American middle-class standard was regarded as the ideal for rearing all children.

The adoption of American Indian children by non-Indians was deemed desirable by some because children would then be reared in more affluent households and, presumably, would be in a better situation due to their material advantages. Perhaps a latent function was the available market of Indian babies and young children for a ready pool of recipients, predominantly white adults seeking to adopt. However, the detriments for children were ultimately determined to outweigh the supposed benefits. Further, cultures cannot be perpetuated if there are no young to acquire the language and customs; hence the adoption practices were assaults, as boarding schools were, upon the stability and viability of American Indian children, families, and cultures. American Indian children who were reared in non-Indian (predominantly white) families were socialized according to European American culture and, as a result, grew to identify with this culture. However, they faced a rude awakening at adolescence, when they were expected to somehow possess an "Indian" identity. Likewise, these young people experienced discrimination according to their physical dissimilarity to white society. It became evident that these children were at risk in their later development, especially in terms of identity issues and substance abuse problems (Select Committee on Indian Affairs, 1977).

Numerous federal actions occurred in the 20th century—many with destructive impacts for American Indian children and families. Another federal strategy that proved to be disadvantageous for American Indians was the 1953 Termination Act, which aimed to terminate federal services to tribes—indeed, by the early 1960s, 109 Indigenous nations were dissolved by congressional action (Churchill, 2002). Likewise, the 1956 Relocation Act advanced assimilation efforts by facilitating the movement of American Indians off their rural reservations into urban areas according to the justification that there would be greater opportunities for their advancement. By 1980 nearly half of American Indians in the United States lived in urban areas (Churchill, 2002). There were many problems with relocation, including lack of continued economic and other forms of support for individuals and families making the transition to the unfamiliar and frequently hostile urban environment (Nabokov, 1999). Traditional systems of social support were absent, and cultural identity was weakened. Ultimately, relocation efforts did not turn out to be economically viable for the federal government; reservation poverty was replaced by urban poverty, and many Indians ended up on welfare rolls and other forms of federal assistance. In many respects, urban poverty presented more disturbing consequences for American Indians, because the buffering impacts of traditional, reservation-based mechanisms of support were absent. Eventually, urban Indian centers began to emerge to provide sources of support and material benefits, as well as cultural perpetuation (frequently pan-Indian in nature), among relocated American Indians from various tribes (Oswalt, 2006).

A particularly insidious covert practice was the involuntary surgical sterilization of American Indian women by the Indian Health Service during the 1960s and 1970s (Jaimes & Halsey, 1992). In the climate of the American Indian protests and calls for justice, in 1972 a large contingency of American Indians from across the country came to the BIA in Washington DC, with a 20-point program to redefine federal-Indian relationships, including a call to reassert full rights of sovereignty. The intent of the "Trail of Broken Treaties" was to be peaceful, but the group became provoked by delays in responses from the BIA. The result was that the group occupied the BIA building for several days and ultimately removed many documents from the building that were taken back to reservations and examined (Nabokov, 1999). From some of these documents the practice of sterilizing American Indian women—without their consent—became known. A study in 1974 by Women of All Red Nations (WARN) stated that as many as 42% of American Indian women of childbearing age had been sterilized without their consent (Jaimes & Halsey). According to Lawrence (2000), "Various studies revealed that the Indian Health Service sterilized between 25 and 50 percent of Native American women between 1970 and 1976" (para. 31). In a recent critical retracing of the political and social dynamics of forced sterilization, Lawrence (2000) offered the following remarks:

> Why did these sterilizations take place? In order to understand the reasons behind the sterilizations it is necessary to remember that physicians were performing large numbers of sterilizations not only on American Indian women, but also on African American and Hispanic women. . . . The main reasons doctors gave for performing these procedures were economic and social in nature . . . the majority of physicians were white, Euro-American males who believed that they were helping society by limiting the number of births in low-income, minority families. They assumed that they were enabling the government to cut funding for Medicaid and welfare programs while lessening their own personal tax burden to support the programs. Physicians also increased their own personal income by performing hysterectomies and tubal ligations instead of prescribing alternative methods of birth control. Some of them did not believe that American Indian and other minority women had the intelligence to use other methods of birth control effectively and that there were already too many minority individuals causing problems in the nation, including the Black Panthers and the American Indian Movement. (para. 30)

The numerous routes of forced assimilation, including cultural genocide, did not entirely produce the intended effects of dismantling cultures, but they did serve to severely undermine tribal cultures and disconnect generations of people from their cultures. Not until more recent years, with large-scale movement toward self-determination, do we see much more concerted efforts, supported by policy and funding, to strengthen American Indian cultures on numerous levels. Today there is a much greater sense of empowerment across Indian country. Individuals and tribal governments possess greater savvy regarding their legal rights as citizens and as Indigenous peoples. A glance at changes in education strategies is illuminating. In 1966 the Rough Rock Demonstration School on the Navajo Nation was the first of its kind to elect an all-Indian school board to direct and control education of its young people (Tippeconnic, 1999). Since that time, tribal self-determination has become the theme relative to education and multiple other forms of self-governance. As noted by Tippeconnic: "Contemporary Indian control is rooted in efforts to involve parents and other tribal members in the education of their children" (1999, p. 35). With schools working in concert with families and cultures in the socialization of culture and language, positive outcomes can be anticipated relative to both cultural preservation and ethnic identity formation of youth. As stated by Tippeconnic: "Mainstream schools interested in exploring alternative ways of teaching and learning will have new opportunities to establish mutually beneficial connections with tribally controlled schools that emphasize Indigenous knowledge and 'Native ways of knowing'" (1999, p. 33).

From the climate of social activism, civil rights, and the Red Power movement of the 1960s and 1970s, several progressive federal acts were passed in the United States. Key organizations, such as the National Indian Education Association and the National Congress of American Indians, mounted pressure for the passage of legislation supportive of tribal self-determination (see Tippeconnic, 1999, and Warner, 1999, for a review of some of this legislation). In 1972 the Indian Education Act appropriated funds for the educational needs of Indian children and included specifications that funds be directed toward the education of Indian children from early childhood to graduate school. Parental involvement in children's education was encouraged, and it remains a strong priority. The 1975 Indian Self-Determination and Educational Assistance Act underscored the importance of tribal and familial control in the education of Indian children. The 1978 Tribally Controlled Community College Assistance Act provided funds to support higher education at tribal colleges, and the Tribally Controlled School Act of 1988 provided funding to school boards to operate schools. The 1990 Native American Languages Act was enacted, in part, to preserve, protect, and promote use of Native American languages, to support use of language in instruction, and to encourage educational officials to work with Native communities to develop language instruction programs. This act recognized that language is essential for tribal survival and self-determination. It offers a stark contrast to earlier years when children were physically beaten in boarding schools for using their tribal languages. In 1991 the 1934 Johnson O'Malley Act was reaffirmed according to the initial mandate that the secretary of the U.S. Department of the Interior was authorized to provide educational and other services to American Indians. In association with both the 1994 Title IX of the Improving America's Schools Act and the Goals 2000: Educate America Act, funds are designated for the advancement of education of American Indian children.

Other federal legislation that served to strengthen cultural identifications of American Indian people included the 1978 Indian Child Welfare Act and the 1978 American Indian Religious Freedom Act. The Indian Child Welfare Act was passed to grant tribal control over child welfare when it was deemed a necessity to remove Indian children from their homes, to make foster care and adoption placements, and to terminate parental rights. It reestablished the rights of tribes and families to rear their children in the traditions of their cultures and, most importantly, was designed to stop the destructive practice of removing Indian children from their homes to be placed in foster care or adoptive circumstances in non-Indian homes (Markstrom, 2002). The American Indian Religious Freedom Act supported Indians' rights to believe, express, and practice their traditional religions. In 1885, a ban was imposed prohibiting the practice of traditional Indian ceremonies; indeed, the Sun Dance, an important ceremony associated with Plains tribes, was banned in 1881 (Reyhner & Eder, 1992). In Canada as well, the government banned Aboriginal ceremonial practices, such as the potlatch of the Northwest Coast cultures of British Columbia (Muckle, 1998; Nabokov, 1999). People were imprisoned for practicing potlatches, and sacred ceremonial items were confiscated. This ceremony was not legalized until 1951. In spite of these and similar bans in both countries, traditional ceremonies became covert and continued to be practiced in secrecy until the time when they could be practiced without fear of repercussion.

Aboriginals in Canada

Strikingly similar strategies of assimilation were imposed on Aboriginals in Canada to undermine their traditional cultures. The Canadian government deemed that the removal of children from their homes for purposes of education in residential settings offered the best means of assimilation of First Nations people (Muckle, 1998). The government provided the funding, and formal religious groups operated the schools. The practices were similar to those in the United States, with children being assigned new names, required to follow rigid schedules, punished for speaking their own languages, and so forth. Several disturbing first-person accounts are related in the *Report of the Royal Commission on Aboriginal Peoples* (INAC, 1996), including the following: "After a lifetime of beatings, going hungry, standing in a corridor on one leg, and walking in the snow with no shoes for speaking Inuvialuktun, and having a heavy, stinging paste rubbed on my face, which they did to stop us from expressing our Eskimo custom of raising our eyebrows for 'yes' and wrinkling our noses for 'no,' I soon lost the ability to speak my mother tongue. When a language dies, the world it was generated from is broken down too" (vol. 1, chap. 10, para. 26).

Of particular concern in the present day are reports of physical, sexual, and emotional abuse experienced by children in residential schools in the 19th and 20th centuries. These events and their consequences have led to a statement in the *Report of the Royal Commission on Aboriginal Peoples* that residential schools caused the greatest damage to Aboriginal families, their cultures, and their identities.

In spite of the widely known reports of abusive treatment in residential schools, it is important to acknowledge that Aboriginals possess varied perceptions of the impacts. As is the case with some American Indians in the United States, some First Nations in Canada credit these schools with teaching them the necessary knowledge and skills to function in European Canadian society (Muckle, 1998). However, the general consensus is that residential schools were disastrous in their impacts and failed miserably in their attempts to assimilate Aboriginals (First Nations and Inuit Regional Health Survey, 1999; INAC, 1996). Many churches that operated residential schools have apologized for the abuses imposed on Native children

(Muckle, 1998), and in 1999 the Canadian government expressed regret and apologized for its role in developing and administering these schools, which were ultimately so damaging to Natives (First Nations and Inuit Regional Health Survey, 1999). The harms caused by residential schooling encompass four forms: physical, emotional, and sexual abuse; inferior education; loss of culture and language; and harm to family structures (First Nations and Inuit Regional Health Survey, 1999). Numerous deleterious impacts continue to afflict survivors, including identity struggles due to years of listening to disparaging remarks about their cultures. Disruptions in the perpetuation of parenting skills have damaged people's ability to parent their own children. Sadly, some of the attendees of these schools learned to use and exert abusive forms of power, and abuse has been perpetuated to their own children (INAC, 1996).

Another parallel practice in Canada was removal of Aboriginal children from their families and cultures and their placement in non-Aboriginal homes (INAC, 1996). Additionally, migration to cities in search of employment and economic stability was and continues to be a disruptive factor on family and cultural life. In 2001 nearly half of the self-identified Aboriginal population in Canada lived in urban areas (Statistics Canada, 2001a). While the perception may be one that urban areas offer increased educational and employment opportunities, the transition to urban life is not as unproblematic as might be anticipated. With the loss of a support system, Canadian Aboriginals may face prejudice and discrimination, unemployment, and barriers to receiving public service, as was experienced by their counterparts in the United States.

The late 20th century was a time of growing empowerment of Canadian Aboriginals, similar to experiences of American Indians in the United States. The results were numerous changes in the nature of the relationship of Aboriginals with the federal government. In the historical perspective, the Royal Proclamation of 1763 defined the nature of the relationship between Aboriginal and non-Aboriginal people. This proclamation recognized the autonomy of the Aboriginal nations and offered them certain protections. It attempted to establish policies for protecting the rights of Aboriginals while allowing for European settlement. However, in the 19th century certain Indian Acts emerged that were controlling and confining of Aboriginal rights. For instance, the Indian Act of 1876, characterized as paternalistic and assimilationist, formalized restrictive policies affecting First Nations people, while on the other hand intending to offer them protection. In 1969 the Canadian government presented the White Paper on Federal Policy, which proposed a radical restructuring of federal–First Nations relationships. However, this proposition was deemed unacceptable by First Nations because it essentially would terminate all government responsibilities to this segment of the population (McMillan, 1988). The 1876 Indian Act has continued, but it has moved away from its original paternalistic nature. For instance, bands now have greater autonomy in governing themselves.

In 1991 the Canadian government established a Royal Commission to investigate events and policies and the impacts on Aboriginal people. The release of the findings in 1996 acknowledged that federal policies affecting Aboriginals for the past 150 years had been wrong and that an Aboriginal parliament and increased spending on programs for Aboriginals was needed to improve economic and social conditions (Muckle, 1998). In 1998 the federal government offered an official response of regret for its past treatment of Aboriginal people in Canada and created a healing fund (INAC, 1996).

In the current climate of Aboriginal rights and sovereignty in North America and beyond, the Canadian government's *Report of the Royal Commission on Aboriginal Peoples* (1996) presents three overarching goals relative to Aboriginal youth. First, youth desire greater recognition and involvement in their communities and in their nation in working with other Aboriginal youth on common concerns. Second, youth desire empowerment in political life in order to have their voices heard at all levels of government. Empowerment in economic life according to meaningful livelihoods also is desired. Healing was identified as the third goal according to the need to address the total person in the spirit, the mind, the emotions, and the body.

Historical Trauma, Decolonization, and Empowerment

While recent actions supportive of tribal self-determination in both the United States and Canada are critical steps in the process of decolonization, the cumulative impacts of disease, genocide, forced displacement, loss of traditional means of livelihood, military domination, boarding schools and adoption practices, and other factors are still evident. To account for the pervasive impacts from the trauma of colonization, descriptive phrases such as "the Native American holocaust," "historical trauma," "intergenerational trauma," "cultural genocide," and "the soul wound" have emerged. As Duran et al. (1998) explain: "Colonization of the life world occurs when the colonizers interfere with the mechanisms needed to reproduce the life world domains—culture, social integration, and socialization—of the colonized. Here, the creation and expansion of America produced an inevitable disintegration of the rationality of everyday Native American life" (p. 62).

Clearly, cumulative assaults to cultures and lifestyles for more than 500 years have perpetuated trauma that is not easily escaped. Intergenerational posttraumatic stress disorder (PTSD) is understood as the transmission of trauma from generation to generation without subsequent generations having experienced the trauma firsthand. Hence, young people of today might not have personally experienced the assimilationist strategies of boarding and residential schools, but they may experience residual impacts through older generations who struggle to overcome the severe trauma and physical and emotional abuse they experienced. Further, effective traditional coping and parenting skills were undermined through boarding schools' practices, and the next generation then suffers various forms of parental deprivation that can then become perpetuated to their own offspring. When I talk with older American Indians about the problems of youth today and loss of language and culture, one of the most frequent causes named is boarding schools. Some of these older adults still struggle with the pain of their separation from families and the lack of nurturance they experienced in boarding schools as children.

Progressive changes over the past 30 to 40 years, particularly through Indigenous-directed education, are huge empowering steps in dismantling processes of colonization and halting the perpetuation of intergenerational PTSD. Nonetheless, trauma continues to be instigated through current forms of prejudice, discrimination, and assaults on the integrity of cultures throughout North America. One priority for many Indigenous nations in the United States and Canada is the repatriation of cultural and human remains that were taken decades ago by anthropologists, collectors, and government officials and placed in museums and in private collections (Muckle, 1998; Sutton, 2004). The protection of sacred places is another ongoing concern in both countries. Some interpret the widespread misappropriation of Native ceremonial practices and ritual objects by non-Natives as the culmination of "taking" of intellectual and cultural properties from North American Indians. The misappropriation of Native images for mascots of sports teams serves to continue to reduce these complex and vital cultures to clichés. Of considerable current concern in the United States is the threat to tribal sovereignty that has been brought by all branches of government, most recently shown in U.S. Supreme Court rulings that have undermined the power of tribal governments. In short, North American Indians must maintain vigilance as they seek to not only become decolonized peoples but those who are self-determined in creating their own destinies. As an illustration of empowerment and decolonization, many groups are reclaiming their original names in replacement of labels that had been assigned to them through colonization. For instance, Chippewas or Ojibwas refer to themselves as Anishinabe, and the name Diné is becoming increasing popular among Navajos. In many cases, the names that tribes apply to themselves translate to phrases, such as "The People," "The First People," or "The Original People."

It is truly astounding that some North American Indian cultures have maintained coming-of-age practices in spite of the disruptive effects of processes of forced assimilation. The fact that, for some tribes, coming-of-age ceremonies have endured over time indicates that members found ways to keep their customs alive in the face of intense pressure to the contrary. Also, these customs have maintained relevance and continue to serve important functions that are recognized and valued. It has not been until the more recent passage of progressive legislation that tribes have acquired a degree of self-determination relative to child rearing, education, and family life. Interest in rekindling coming-of-age and other ceremonies has emerged in recent decades across Indian country. This certainly has been my observation in numerous discussions of coming-of-age practices with North American Indians in the United States and Canada. The reinstatement of cultural traditions serves as one mechanism in the process of decolonization.

CHAPTER THREE

North American Indian Perspectives on Human Development

□   □   □

Throughout history and across cultures, humans have been intrigued by the particular changes that occur in individuals during the life span and, of interest in this book, at pubescence. Cultures have devised various explanatory models of the human life span, and implicit in these models are the beliefs held about human development in general and about pubescence and adolescence in particular. This chapter scrutinizes North American Indian views of pubescence and adolescence according to how they are situated within broader conceptions of spirituality, personality, and life span human development—all of which are indicative of a distinctive worldview. A worldview is a paradigm or mode of understanding that serves as a core approach to perceiving, understanding, and explaining social and natural phenomena in the world. It is an abstract construct, but is certainly observed in the philosophies and behaviors of its adherents. Relative to discrepancies between European and Indigenous worldviews, Kidwell, Noley, and Tinker (2001) stated: "Reginald Horsman argues for a distinctive Native American history . . . he suggests that a global comparison of the impact of European colonization on Native cultures will reveal the fundamental differences in world view that underlay the results of European conquest" (p. 132). This statement is consistent with the underlying orientation of the current chapter, which attempts to present North American Indian–derived constructs of human development. In some cases it is useful to offer comparisons with Western conceptions of the same phenomena; while the conclusions reached according to both worldviews are not necessarily always contradictory, they are indicative of a different frame of reference or lens applied to interpretations of the meaning and purpose of pubescence and adolescence.

North American Indian belief systems regard the human experience as an integrated component of all of creation. It is essential to discuss views of the personality and life span development with particular delineation of pubescence and adolescence relative to beliefs about the sacredness and interconnectedness of human existence within the totality of creation. The notion of critical periods of development, common to both North American Indian and Western theories of human development, is of particular interest. This and related concepts are explicated relative to pubescence according to the rituals of Native cultures that are believed to maximize the positive outcomes of this influential stage of development. In general, the purpose of this chapter is to introduce concepts and forms of understanding that have greater expression in subsequent chapters.

The Spiritual Expressions of Existence

Prior to entering discussions on North American Indian theories of human development in general, and pubescence and adolescence in particular, it is useful to examine the larger perspective within which these notions are embedded. Specifically, it is imperative to consider the broader context of understanding relative to North American Indian spirituality, with perhaps the most illustrative comment being that spirituality cannot be compartmentalized from other facets of existence, because it is regarded as all-encompassing (Lum, 1996; Martin, 2001). The spirituality of existence is recognized as pervasive throughout all of creation—the Earth and its human and nonhuman inhabitants with whom it is shared. All components of life are valued and believed to be due their proper respect. Gattuso (1991) summarized the experience of Native spirituality in the following statement: "Today, as in the past, Native American religions are more than a collection of old ceremonies, prayers, and rituals.

They are a living faith, a way of seeing and understanding the world. For many Indian people, religion touches all aspects of human experience, from the spiritual to the mundane" (p. 66).

To understand this all-encompassing quality of Native spirituality, it must be acknowledged that it is most typically associated with the traditional beliefs of cultures that are embedded in oral traditions. Nonetheless, among contemporary North American Indians there is a range of expressions of faith within any particular tribe or band; and as is the case with any group in society, there are those that adhere to no faith tradition. Three broad categories of beliefs among Native persons are traditional practices that are based in and perpetuated through oral traditions of a culture; various forms of Christianity; and the Native American Church, a hybrid religion that combines traditional practices, Christianity, and other components. Certainly there are other beliefs and expressions of faith and spirituality among North American Indians, but these are three illustrations of pervasive expressions. Some persons practice their faith exclusively within any one of these traditions, while others may practice some combination of these and other expressions of faith. For example, forms of Christianity may vary from culture to culture according to the degree to which it is adapted to the customs and beliefs of a culture, and vice versa. Coming-of-age ceremonies fall within the category of traditional beliefs and practices. In some cases, however, Christian elements have found their way into some components of these ceremonies. For example, the figure of the Virgin Mary has been equated with the Apache personage of White Painted Woman, who is integral to the Sunrise Dance for pubescent girls (see chapters 6 and 7).

The edicts of traditional beliefs include values for responsibility in human behaviors and interpersonal relations. Many North American Indian cultures place a high value on maintaining harmonious relationships between oneself and others in one's family, clan, tribe, and the broader society (Anderson & Ellis, 1995). Such harmony is achieved through exhibitions of cooperative, courteous, modest, and respectful behavior; displays of generosity; avoidance of interpersonal aggression, or "pushiness"; and avoidance of excessiveness. The beliefs, traditions, and practices that have been passed on by ancestors are regarded as worthwhile and are considered as relevant today as in the past. While these comments are being stated in a general sense relative to North American Indian cultures, these and other themes of spirituality appear to have some universal applicability, at least among Indigenous peoples. For instance, in an interview, David Risling Jr., a Native American advocate of Indian religious freedom, noted many similarities among Indigenous people globally: "They all have creation stories. Their spirituality communicates with nature and beauty. There is always one Creator, one Great Spirit. There are always sacred places, such as mountains. They all have spiritual ceremonies. For most Native people, spirituality is a major part of their culture and part of their everyday life" (Risling & Boyer, 1994, p. 21).

This discussion of the value of tradition among North American Indians has direct implications for the ritual practices that occur for pubescent girls. Puberty rituals and ceremonies are clearly embedded in broader complexes of beliefs that are embedded in the oral traditions of cultures. Values held by a culture are reinforced in the rituals of puberty ceremonies; that is, any particular ritual practice is highly meaningful and reflective of underlying cultural beliefs. This notion is clearly illustrated in the case studies of later chapters. Conceptions of the human personality and stages of human development are meaningful topics in this chapter's focus on an Indigenous psychological view of adolescent development.

Conceptions of the Human Personality

Humans from all cultures have been interested in explicating models to account for the complex and multifaceted human personality. In particular, there are four components that have some universal application in respect to North American Indians' conceptions of the personality: wholeness, harmony, and balance; moderation and containment; complementary constructs; and the coexistence of values of interdependence and cooperation with individualism and personal autonomy. These conceptions are reflected in values that ultimately serve to direct behaviors. Further, they have applications to puberty rituals of North American Indian girls, most particularly in respect to personality development.

Wholeness, Harmony, and Balance

Wholeness, harmony, and balance are concepts that contribute to an orientation common across many North American Indian cultures; specifically, the entire person is regarded as a complex, integrated unit. In this respect, the personality is not compartmentalized from the totality of existence. Not only is there value for harmony within the person, but harmony with others and all of creation is to be pursued, for instance, as has been written about Navajo culture (Csordas, 1999; Eichstaedt, 1994; Woody, Jack, & Bizahaloni, 1981). The most common conceptualization of the self is that it comprises physical, emotional, psychological, and spiritual domains—all of which have implications for well-being and health. The medicine wheel and the circle serve as metaphors for the wholeness or completeness of the human experience according to these four elements. The characteristic of wholeness is also demonstrated in a comparison between North American Indian and Western worldviews according to, respectively, circular and linear constructions, with *worldview* defined as "the collective thought process of a people or a cultural group" (Cross, 1998, p. 144). Temporal associations of cause and effect are determined in the linear worldview, and a specific intervention is provided to produce a desire outcome. The drawback of this approach is that it tends to be discipline-focused and, subsequently, fails to take into account a more comprehensive evaluation of a phenomenon. In contrast, the circular or cyclical worldview is typical of Indigenous cultures and strives to account for many contextual variables influential in an event or situation, as stated by Cross: "It is intuitive, non-temporal, and fluid" (1998, p. 147). The circular worldview presents a more inclusive approach to understanding human experiences because numerous potential sources of influence are considered. Such a holistic orientation yields to harmony when all components of the person (i.e., physical, emotional, psychological, and spiritual) are in balance, as well as when a balance exists between the person and others and the surrounding environment.

A holistic view of interaction between the domains of existence finds expression in various healing practices of North American Indians, ranging from traditional practices embedded in ancient oral traditions, to the Native American Church, and to forms of Christianity that have been adopted by some Native persons (Griffin-Pierce, 2000). Traditional North American Indian beliefs and practices provide useful illustrations of concepts of wholeness and harmony. Healing is regarded as a spiritual exercise conducted by shamans, healers, or medicine men and women (Waldram, 1994). Illness is not compartmentalized from other facets of existence, nor is it solely relegated to the scientific medical establishment. Rather, illness is regarded as an extension of events that may have occurred in any domains of existence that have had an adverse impact on the individual, for example, physical or psychological illnesses resulting from environmental contamination. In short, interpreting illness and health according to a holistic orientation provides underlying reflections of social definitions according to the beliefs of a culture.

Navajos possess a well-articulated and complex system of beliefs about notions of wholeness, harmony, and balance with implications for dysfunction, diagnosis, and intervention. Traditional Navajos adhere to the concept of *hózhó*, a state indicative of "beauty, perfection, harmony, goodness, normality, success, well-being, order, and ideal" (Woody et al., 1981, p. 24). Health and wellness, which are reflected in the state of *hózhó*, also referred to as "Walking in Beauty," occur when there is balance between all domains of existence identified by Navajos (i.e., physical, emotional, psychological, intellectual, and spiritual) and essentially within the universe. Navajo ceremonials are designed to restore order in the universe, which has been disturbed through evil sources: "Improper contact with inherently dangerous powers like ghosts of the dead, certain animals or lighting, breaking taboos related to spiritual powers, or excesses in gambling, can lead to rupture of the natural harmony" (Hirschfelder & Molin, 2001, p. 200).

When Navajo adherents of the traditional belief system are out of harmony—which is evident through physical and/or psychological symptoms—they may seek out a culturally based healer. As a first step, a diagnostician may be consulted who uses various tools of discernment and ultimately prescribes for the patient one of the scores of Navajo healing ceremonies. Ceremonies may occur for 1 to 9 days and require elaborate rituals, such as sand painting, singing or chanting, and the use of holy objects (Connors & Donellan, 1998; Hirschfelder & Molin,

2001). By way of illustration, a major goal of the Yeibichai or Night Way healing ceremony, held over 9 consecutive evenings, as explained to me by a Navajo *hataali* (singer or medicine person), is not always the physical healing of the patient but rather the restoration of balance and wholeness within the totality of the person and his or her restoration in an orderly, harmonious universe. The Navajo Blessing Way—a complex of ceremonies that celebrates and shows appreciation for all forms of goodness—also leads to *hózhó*. As an invocation of blessing, it is a significant ceremony for key transitional phases of the life cycle (Markstrom & Iborra, 2003) and, of particular interest in this book, at puberty when the Kinaaldá ceremony is held for girls (see chapter 8).

Moderation and Containment

Connected to values of wholeness, harmony, and balance are those of moderation and containment. Excesses in personality and behavior tend to be suppressed and discouraged among Native peoples. Communication processes serve as excellent illustration of the values of moderation and containment. T. W. Cooper (1998) identified the communication ethics of Navajos as reflective of respect, balance, containment, moderation, and reverence. Thought and speech processes are intertwined, and one must carefully weigh one's words prior to speaking. The underlying belief is that persons are responsible and accountable for what they speak—words have consequences. For example, in Navajo communication patterns, pauses are comfortably permitted in order to allow the speaker time to gather his or her thoughts. In essence, language is not to be wasted, and when something is spoken it is regarded as meaningful and worthy to be heard.

Moderation is also seen in the observance of speech patterns that are not excessive, sensational, or flamboyant. For example, in speaking more generally about North American Indians, J. W. Lee and Cartledge (1996) identified several communication characteristics, including a tendency to avoid open-faced eye contact, suppression of emotion in facial expressions, minimized public displays of affection, and more sparing use of gestures. It must be cautioned that these characteristics do not apply to all tribal cultures, but overall they are believed to link more to North

American Indians than to European North Americans. It also must be emphasized that displays of moderation and containment as shown in these illustrations are suggestive of underlying values of respect for others (e.g., it is rude to stare in the face of another person, especially an elder), as well as a certain form of humility to not unnecessarily draw attention to oneself (e.g., demonstrating restraint in public situations).

The reinforcement of moderation and containment in the personality and behavior of pubescent girls is observed through various instructions given to them at the time of their coming-of-age. For instance, Hodge (1912) observed that, in the past, pubescent Haida girls were not to eat too much or risk being greedy later in life and to not smile too much or be inclined to hilarity. As discussed later in this chapter, one of the major North American Indian beliefs about pubescent girls is that they are particularly impressionable and malleable at this stage of the life span. Hence, adults, particularly adult female mentors, must maximize the opportunity to instruct initiates on expected decorum of young women. Such instruction frequently centers on the proper display of reserved behavior now that they are young women and no longer children. For example, chapter 8 presents a case study of an adult Ojibwa woman who discussed her instructions at puberty to not engage in boisterous play with her brothers, but rather to display only reserved and modest behaviors.

Complementary Constructs

Of further relevance to this discussion, particularly when notions of balance are considered, is the practice of North American Indians cultures to distinguish complementary constructs within conceptions of the personality, in the sphere of human relations, and in the natural world. Indeed, the notion of complementary constructs is a philosophy that underlies conceptions within the creation stories of Native groups as well as their stories about themselves and the world around them. Beck, Walters, and Francisco (1996) exemplified such pairings according to "cardinal directions, night and day, moon and sun, moist and dry, dark and light" (p. 15). The principal illustration for the dynamic interplay of complementary elements is found within the cosmology wherein the Sun or

Sky is regarded as the male counterpart of the female Earth and their relationship serves as a metaphor for a bi-gender Creator who is sometimes addressed as Grandfather or Grandmother (Kidwell et al., 2001). Indeed, the inclusion of both male and female supernatural beings and cultural heroes and heroines in the beliefs systems of North America Indian cultures is a further reflection of the value for complementary entities that serve differing functions but together bring completion, balance, and wholeness, such as White Painted Woman or Changing Woman in Apache and Navajo cultures and her sons Born from Water and Slayer of Monsters. In Navajo culture as well, male rain is described as heavy and torrential, while female rain is gentle and can be absorbed by the earth to cause life to flourish. The male-female duality is expressed in other forms in Navajo culture (e.g., Beck et al., 1996; Reichard, 1977; Schwarz, 1997) as well as numerous other Native cultures and ultimately denotes qualities of humans, plants, animals, geography, colors, and natural phenomena.

As a theme throughout this book and discussed more fully in chapter 4, traditional North American Indian cultures were generally gender typed, and men and women performed specified roles that contributed to the maintenance of their societies and survival of their kin and tribes. However, this complementary arrangement of male and female task distribution did not necessarily lend itself to inequality of power, as occurs in Western society. Rather, it was understood that the contributions of both men and women were essential for survival; hence, roles and the individuals who fulfilled these roles were valued. Native Americans had powerful models for complementary gender dualities that permeated their belief systems and the surrounding creation; hence, perhaps a regard for and value of both entities contributed to more egalitarian human relationships. This discussion of gender roles employs the past tense because traditional lifestyles and roles were severely undermined through colonization. Nonetheless, the regard for gender duality is still evident in various expressions of Native people; for example, Beck et al. (1996) tell of the half-red and half-blue blanket that is still worn today among tribes of the Plains region: "The blue side, like the blue arteries of blood in the body, signifies the male and the red side, like the blood veins, signifies the female" (p. 15).

The logic of complementary constructs has applications to understanding the domain of the human personality. In many Native cultures, men and women are viewed as possessing both masculine and feminine sides, and a balanced personality embraces both aspects of the self (Beck et al., 1996). In puberty rituals, feminine aspects of the personality are clearly impressed on girls, such as being nurturing and caring toward others, but masculine traits are also required, such as strength and endurance. Interestingly, there are illustrations from over 130 Native cultures of individuals, commonly referred to as two-spirits, who bridged the sexes by adopting the dress, behavior, and lifestyle of the other sex, forming a third, alternative gender (Hirschfelder & Molin, 2001). Perhaps because of a belief in their unique insights into the worlds of both men and women, two-spirits often served in important ceremonial and spiritual capacities. For example, in Lakota and other Plains tribes this individual was known as a *winkte'* and was thought to possess special powers relative to childbirth and child rearing and experienced the honor of being called on to name a child (W. K. Powers, 1977; St. Pierre & Long Soldier 1995).

The phenomenon of trickster or sacred clowns found in numerous North American Indian cultures provides an additional illustration of complementary constructs and, in this illustration, encompassing opposing, yet coexisting qualities. The sacred clown is found in some Southwest cultures, including the clown who is the leader of the Mountain Spirit dancers at the Apache girls' Sunrise Dance (chapter 6). The clown or trickster is well known as Raven, Coyote, and Iktomi the spider in various American Indian cultures (Kidwell et al., 2001). This figure is the rule breaker of society, not held to human standards, and in ceremonial settings may flaunt the solemnity of the moment. He is a paradox and contradiction, displaying both good and evil, innocence and wisdom, male and female, young and old, while essentially reminding people of the illogic and lack of control in their own lives. Nonetheless, these contradictory figures serve important functions, as explained by Beck et al. (1996): "Fundamentally, the sacred clowns portray the Path of Life with all of its pitfalls, sorrows, laughter, mystery, and playful obscenity. . . . They show the dark side; they show the light side; they show us that life is hard; and they show us how it can be made easier" (p. 298). Hence, the paradox is that while they appear to disdain and disrespect ritual and protocol, they may be regarded as the most sacred and powerful members of the ceremony (Hirschfelder & Molin, 2001). The theme of complementary constructs has many expressions in North American Indian cultures, and this discussion continues in the next section with examination of the compatibility of values for and expressions of interdependence and individualism.

Coexistence of Interdependence and Individualism

Complementary constructs also find expression in another ostensible contradiction of North American Indian culture, that is, the coexistence of values of interdependence and communalism along with those of individualism and personal autonomy. This is a particularly complex topic that requires careful dissection. The survival of human beings depends on their cooperative relationships with one another. North American Indian cultures serve as remarkable illustrations of the maintenance of complex kinship networks that serve to meet emotional, psychological, and survival needs of all group members. Hence, these cultures are frequently described as interdependent, communal, connectional, and cooperative, in contrast to European American culture, which is described as individualistic, independent, and autonomous. However, it should be noted that this false dichotomy of interdependence versus individualism is an exaggeration of Native and Western cultures alike. It has been used in the literature, however, to delineate a core difference between these cultures.

Within a relationship-based context of North American Indian cultures, young people are socialized for optimal identity formation according to their expected assumption of roles and responsibilities relative to family and kin. This point is demonstrated in a story that a Navajo woman related to me about a major event in her life. This woman was a promising high school student and had prospects for a college education to be supported by a scholarship. Before she could pursue this opportunity, her sister experienced a serious car accident and was left paralyzed. The family of the college-bound woman told her that she must suspend her own ambitions and assume responsibility for the care of her sister.

She acquiesced to their directive with the knowledge that responsibilities toward family and kin took precedence over personal aims and ambitions. Some years passed before she could actualize her dream for a college education. This example points to a value discrepancy between North American Indian and European American cultures. In the latter, personal aims and ambitions are of high value, particularly relative to education and the potential for career development and advancement. According to values characteristic of many North American Indian cultures, such individualistic pursuits are considered secondary to the mandate of responsibility toward family and kin.

It is important, however, to not approach this topic in completely dichotomized terms, because it can be reasoned that an interdependent/ relational orientation can operate conjointly with exhibitions of independence, individualism, and autonomy. Torrance (1994) observed the coexistence of highly individualistic hunting traditions in Algonquian cultures that were embedded in the communal structures of their societies. In the past and the present, it is permissible for individuals to gain personal recognition according to feats of bravery, tests of endurance, and personal accomplishments. For example, as discussed more fully in chapter 5, there are illustrations from many groups in Native North America, such as in the Plains cultural area, of individual competencies that served to bring status and recognition. Respect for individuality was observed in the Santee Sioux's belief that children should not be forced to comply with the demands of adults because it was not desirable to break the will of children. On the other hand, collective responsibility was encouraged with admonitions against selfishness (Albers, 2001). It can be further observed among this group that, historically, fur trapping was a privatized activity in which sharing was not required, while buffalo hunting was communal and the products were shared. In respect to Otoe and Missouria cultures, Schweitzer (2001) summarized the work of Whitman (1937) and concluded: "The emphasis on the individual, especially the child's place in the family and clan, provided identity with a large social group without losing a sense of the importance of the person" (p. 451). Hence, a social identity was ascribed, yet the integrity of the individual person was valued. To the Blackfeet, personal autonomy was of high importance for children and adults as well as for both men and women

(Kehoe, 1995). The acquisition and demonstration of competence was a manifestation of the autonomy of the individual.

In ceremonial life as well, the value of personal autonomy is prominent. For example, individuals from numerous North American Indian cultures of the past and the present seek personal power through rituals and ceremonies designed to connect the individual to the spirit world (see chapter 5). Vision quests and various other coming-of-age practices for both girls and boys serve as excellent illustrations of this point. Coming-of-age is an event that occurs at a given time in the life span and is a personal experience; hence the ritual events are experienced, in part, in isolation. Even with the accompaniment of public ceremonies to bring recognition to the change of status, individual adolescents must complete the complex rituals designed to direct the course of their life. An amazing degree of pressure and attention is placed on the young person at this time of the life span; while social support is usually available, the individual is still required to draw on his or her store of psychological and physical strength. In some cases, the ultimate goal of the various endeavors at puberty is the acquisition of spiritual power or a spiritual helper to acquire protection and permit smooth passage through the remainder of life. As discussed in later sections of this chapter, based on my own research and that of others, it is concluded that many North American Indian cultures believe that pubescence is a time of the life span when individuals are especially impressionable and malleable and are open or porous to the spiritual realm. For instance, vision quests, physical tests of endurance, and other demands and restrictions placed on adolescents are designed to facilitate their personal connections to the spiritual.

The false dichotomy between interdependence and individuality is overcome through the realization that individual accomplishments and achievements serve the welfare of the entire group (LaDonna Harris, personal communication, February 24, 2004). For instance, the medicine person who attains power during a vision quest uses that power to enhance the well-being of others in the group. Or, the young man who demonstrates accomplishments and bravery in hunting shares his bounty with others in the village. The young woman who acquires strength at her puberty ceremony is being prepared for future sacrifices in which endurance will be needed to help sustain others. Hence, individual achievements and accomplishments are acknowledged and the individual can be singled out for positive personal recognition, but first and foremost this individual is embedded in a connectional system and uses his or her personal strengths and accomplishments to the betterment of family, kin, and the group.

The coexistence of values of interdependence and individualism has profound implications for identity formation, because these and other values of a culture are supported and affirmed at coming-of-age ceremonies. The value of interdependence is affirmed according to reinforcement of social identity, with its corresponding mandate to become a responsible member of one's family and tribe. Ethnic identity, in particular, as a form of social identity, is enhanced through expression of numerous cultural beliefs, practices, language, and so forth at the coming-of-age event. Hence an implicit, perhaps latent, purpose of coming-of-age ceremonies is to impress on the initiate a socially endorsed identity. The rituals that make up these ceremonies are tools employed by a cultural community in the socialization of its young. Through participating in ritual activities, young people acquire greater understanding of the values, roles, and beliefs of their group, and a socially appropriate identity is shaped and reinforced. This point is significant in consideration of the idea that an optimal identity is one that is affirmed by the significant social group (chapter 1).

Markstrom and Iborra (2003) reported that in the Kinaaldá—the Navajo puberty ceremony for girls—a social identity is ascribed that is embedded in the desirable traits of the primary supernatural being of their culture, namely, Changing Woman. It is important to observe, however, that girls who experience Kinaaldá or any other rite of passage are not passive recipients of this ascription. They must cooperate and perform the rituals in order to bring about positive outcomes for their lives. For instance, Navajo girls are to engage in a running ritual—three times a day for four days—and their performance of this ritual is believed to ultimately influence their longevity.

As previously stated, values of independence and individualism are endorsed in North American Indian cultures. Relative to identity formation, then, in addition to ascription, identity can also be construed according to its achieved or personally pursued domains. I have observed instructions given to girls relative to their personal pursuits and accomplishments at both the Navajo Kinaaldá and the Apache Sunrise Dance. For instance, girls are frequently admonished to acquire an education and seek a career prior to making interpersonal commitments of marriage and childbearing. At one particular Kinaaldá, the family of the initiate shared with pride the fact that their daughter desired to become a veterinarian. They reinforced this personal aim by decorating the hogan with pictures of animals and placement of stuffed animals. The initiate's occupational identity of this sort reflects individual interest and will require personal achievement. However, Markstrom and Iborra (2003) note that this particular occupation (i.e., veterinarian) is highly meaningful and useful in Navajo culture and received clear social endorsement from the initiate's family and clan. That is, personal identity was formed, but it was identity that encompassed valued traits of a culture. This brings the discussion back to the earlier conclusion; specifically, societal values of interdependence/communalism and individualism/personal autonomy and their varied expressions are intertwined and extend to the processes by which identity is formed. Identity formation is implicit in coming-of-age ceremonies, because clearly the young person is being prepared for incorporation in adult society. The high regard for culture in North American Indian societies is reinforced according to ethnic identity ascription; however, an accommodation is made for the needs of the individual relative to his or her interests and pursuits. Ultimately, however, identity construction—whether ascribed or achieved—occurs within the social context of a communal culture in which the individual is valued and singled out, but is first and foremost a son or daughter, a future spouse, a future mother or father, and a member of his or her tribe. In summary, individualism and personal autonomy are not independent from the social milieu of the young person, but are most strongly realized with social endorsement and approval with the expectation that pursuits of the individual will ultimately benefit others.

Conceptions of Human Development

Values concerning esteemed human personality traits and behaviors were presented in the previous discussion according to conceptions of wholeness, harmony, and balance; moderation and containment; complementary constructs; and coexistence of values of interdependence and individualism. Of additional interest in a broad discussion of Indigenous approaches to understanding the person are models concerning the development of humans across the life span. Western-based psychological theories of the person are the dominant forms of understanding in the scholarly community of today. It is not generally known that North American Indian cultures possess their own complex theories of human development. For instance, ritual practices at puberty are embedded in broader theories of human development and are intricately linked to other stages in the life span. Of specific interest in this section are three fundamental conceptions of human development that are illustrative of many tribal cultures: child-rearing values according to patterns of socialization, stages of the life span, and critical periods of development. The last point is introduced in this section, but is addressed more fully in the next section relative to pubescence.

Patterns of Socialization

For successful passage through childhood and adolescence to adulthood, it is a society's responsibility to socialize or prepare its young. Continuous and discontinuous distinctions are two processes that societies may use to accomplish the task of childhood socialization. Generally these are regarded as divergent processes; however, in examination of North American Indian socialization patterns, both processes are applicable. To begin this discussion, it is necessary to define the terms *continuous* and *discontinuous* as they relate to patterns of socialization. The discussion then moves to illustrations of continuous patterns of socialization found in North American Indian societies. Finally, it is concluded that while continuous socialization is highly pertinent in traditional North American Indian cultures, illustrations of discontinuous socialization also are apparent, especially in examination of girls' coming-of-age rites.

The topic of continuous versus discontinuous socialization received attention in cross-cultural writings on childhood and adolescence from various noted anthropologists, such as Margaret Mead and Ruth Benedict. When the Western scientific view of adolescence was introduced in the late 19th century by G. Stanley Hall, biological determinism was the core defining concept and adolescence was characterized as a time of conflict and stress. There were those who challenged this conclusion, among them Margaret Mead, who argued that the norm of a tumultuous adolescence was not universally applicable and that culture was a defining feature of adolescent development. According to Mead, the storms and stresses of adolescence could be avoided through continuity of roles from childhood to adulthood and, of interest in this book, through rites of passage at puberty that recognized the change in status of the young person (Lambert, Rothschild, Atland, & Green, 1978). Ruth Benedict, as well, was interested in cultural forms of socialization in the development of the human personality and asserted that, through the age-graded system, children's development in Western society occurred in a more abrupt, discontinuous manner (Muuss, 1988). In contrast, in non-Western cultures, growth was described as more gradual and continuous, with children naturally evolving into adult roles. For instance, through continuous socialization, children were simultaneously immersed into the worlds of play and work, and adult responsibilities gradually evolved as play was transformed into work. Barry and Schlegel (1980) also were interested in this topic, and they actually linked the practice of adolescent initiation ceremonies to societies that practiced continuous forms of socialization (as measured according to high degree of social solidarity and sexual differentiation). In short, these writers concluded that continuous patterns of childhood socialization are characteristic of non-Western cultures and that rites of passage at puberty are associated with this form of socialization.

Illustrations of continuous forms of socialization are prevalent in writings of traditional socialization practices of various North American Indian cultures. For example, Pacific Eskimo girls as young as age 6 began weaving, and the play of boys involved throwing toy spears. Eventually, these activities evolved into full-blown adult activities (D. W. Clark, 1984). Upper Tanana girls would learn to sew by first sewing clothes for their dolls, and young boys would be given bows and arrows with which to play (McKennan, 1959). Ojibwa girls were kept very close to their mothers and observed them engaged in a variety of useful tasks. At young ages, girls would mimic the behaviors of their mothers and construct little birchbark rolls like those that covered wigwams, construct small buckskin clothing, and decorate the clothing of their dolls with beadwork (Densmore, 1929/1979; Hilger, 1951/1992). Densmore told how Ojibwa children were instructed to collect and gather every kind of flower they came across and, in the process, learned useful knowledge about the medicinal value of plants. V. O. Erikson (1978) wrote of the socialization of Maliseet-Passamaquoddy children according to informal socialization wherein they were given toy bows and arrows and acquired some proficiency in shooting at young ages. As boys grew older they obtained a full-size bow and accompanied their fathers on hunts. Fathers also provided small paddles to their sons and daughters, who subsequently learned to maneuver canoes by age 10. Delaware children, as soon as they were capable, were given tasks according to their biological sex and ages that prepared them for eventual adult responsibilities (I. Goddard, 1978). These and numerous other illustrations are indicative of the age-appropriate level of responsibilities given to children with the eventual evolution into adult-level performance of needed and useful skills.

Among the Western Apaches, Grenville Goodwin (1942) commented extensively on socialization practices of children. He observed that, around the onset of puberty, girls and boys were gradually introduced to a variety of adult-like tasks. Girls were required to assist their families in activities such as food preparation, construction of wickiups, sewing, and basket making. It was not uncommon to observe girls around age 15 learning these tasks while still engaged in play with their dolls. Goodwin observed that boys were gradually given responsibility for care of the horses beginning around age 10, and it was expected that they would assist in planting agricultural products and hunting small game. In spite of an increase in their responsibilities, boys, well into their late teens, continued to play with other boys. They married later than girls and still engaged in play behavior up until that point. The play behavior of both boys and girls, which began in childhood and extended well into adolescence, was clearly reflective of future adult responsibilities. Goodwin's informants indicated that boys and girls played together up until age 10 or so but that they then engaged in their own gender-typed differentiated tasks after that point.

My fieldwork among the San Carlos Apaches (described in chapters 6 and 7) confirms the observations of Goodwin and left me with a lasting impression. At the girls' puberty rite (Sunrise Dance), drumming occurs by adult males who have constructed drums from pots filled with water and covered with a piece of buckskin stretched across the top. At any given Sunrise Dance, one or more prepubescent boys stand with the men and drum on their own drums. One particular Sunrise Dance stands out as I observed a boy of about 8 years of age thoroughly engrossed in this activity as he drummed and sang along with the adult men. His proud mother explained to me that he had a special inclination in this respect and drummed at many dances. Likewise, in the following quote from G. Goodwin (1942), it appeared that drumming was an activity of boys that provided socialization in a continuous manner: "At Gá'n dances the accompaniment to the singing was the beating of wooden switches on a dry cowhide, and almost always it was small boys of eight to twelve who were chosen to do this. They kept perfect time and were intently serious on their job. Thus, in one way and another, they picked up a considerable amount of knowledge concerning ritual form while they were still quite young" (p. 477).

Pubertal rites of passage serve as illustrations of continuous socialization in the past and the present day. The skills and lessons that are reinforced at the coming-of-age event are those that have been introduced, in various forms, in childhood. For instance, younger girls have observed their adult female caregivers perform a variety of tasks, such as preparation of traditional foods and acts of assistance for kin. The expected responsibilities of adult women are impressed on pubescent girls through reinforcement via role performance during the rituals of their coming-of-age ceremonies. For example, during their Kinaaldá, Navajo girls are to demonstrate hospitality by ensuring the comfort of the guests who attend their rite of passage. Even rituals designed to build strength and empowerment impress on initiates traits that have been modeled for them by adult women.

Up to this point it has been reasoned that the continuous form of socialization is characteristic of North American Indian societies. Nonetheless, discontinuous patterns are also relevant. Specifically, the next section identifies stages of human development and maintains that each stage presents unique features, characteristics, and challenges. In this respect, each stage of the life span is qualitatively distinct from other stages, and cultures will require ritual activity specific to the needs and demands of that stage. For instance, coming-of-age ceremonies incorporate rituals illustrative of discontinuous socialization. As discussed in chapter 5, the widespread practice of some form of seclusion of North American Indian pubescent girls indicates an abrupt separation and detachment from sources of childhood security and familiarity. This separation is indicative of a belief in the qualitatively different state of the initiate in comparison to her earlier self in childhood. The distinctiveness of pubescence and coming-of-age is also shown through stringent reminders of the change in status of initiates according to rituals in which initiates are dressed in new clothes, experience a name change, or are painted or tattooed. Additionally, new behavioral restrictions are placed on initiates at the time of coming-of-age, such as food taboos, sleep withdrawal, physical activity demands, and various other deprivations and challenges. These and other ritual activities are indicative of a perception of the distinctiveness of this stage of the life span. Specifically, ritual requirements placed on pubescents are not suitable for younger children, nor are the demands likely required at their same levels of intensity in adulthood. It is at pubescence that specific rituals have their greatest meaning and applicability, as is clearly shown later in this chapter relative to nine beliefs about pubescent girls.

Stages of the Life Span

The notion that pubescence is a distinct and unique phase of the life span is embedded in broader conceptualizations of human development. Through examination of specific life-cycle rituals of many North American Indian cultures, it is apparent that there were perceptions of qualitatively different capabilities and expectations according to life stages. Some cultures indicated four major stages of life—infancy/childhood, puberty or youth, the reproductive years, and old age or seniority. Osgood (1937) identified the Tanainas' major stages of life as birth, puberty, marriage, and death. Another Northern Athabascan group, the Gwich'in, divided the life span into childhood, youth, maturity, and old age or seniority (Slobodin, 1981). For the Gwich'in, both youth and old age were distinguished by periods of separation from the band, and youth was said to begin shortly prior to puberty and to end at marriage. Additionally, feasts were held at significant periods of the life span among Peel River and Crow River Gwich'in (or Kutchin per Osgood), which included a few weeks after birth, at the first kill of large game (for boys), and after death (Osgood, 1936/1970). Additionally, a puberty feast was held among the Crow River Gwich'in by the parents of a girl after her puberty seclusion. In Lakota tradition, the four directions of south, west, north, east, and again south correspond to five stages of life—newborn, childhood, adolescence, maturity, and old age, respectively (W. K. Powers, 2000). It is important to note that the beliefs about stages of human development in Indigenous models frequently are embedded in ancient oral traditions that offer explanations for origins, creation of humans, the strengths and weakness of humans, and the relation of humans with the supernatural beings. These ideas are explicated further in later chapters in which case studies of selected cultures are discussed.

Navajos have a well-articulated model of human development that includes stages of just born/newly arrived, babyhood, weaning to adolescence, adolescence, early married life, advanced maturity, and very old age/beginning of disintegration (Reichard, 1977). Relative to puberty, Navajo educator Shirley Begay (1983) labeled ages 8 to 12 as corresponding with *honitsékees nílíinii hazlį į́*, or "one begins thinking." This stage is characterized by the child's ability to think logically and organize information. Begay also noted that this is the time when Navajo children may begin to participate in certain ceremonials, such as the Yeibichai and Fire Dance, and these experiences can serve as foundations to the girl's impending participation in her Kinaaldá. These notions in the Navajo tradition concerning the cognitive acquisitions of early adolescence are consistent with those of Western psychology. The young adolescent, through the acquisition of formal operational thought, can, for the first time, seriously grapple with abstractions, possibilities, introspections, and the future, and can generally experience an expansion of thought (Inhelder & Piaget, 1958; Gordon, 1988; Keating, 1980; Piaget, 1972). Due to these apparent universal acquisitions at early adolescence, cross-culturally, societies have held implicit beliefs that this is the time of the life span to incorporate youth more fully into the adult sector, such as in religious initiations (as discussed in chapter 1). It is perceived that young adolescents are now capable of greater comprehension of the complexities of life as well as the abstract conceptions of faith traditions. Relative to rites of passage, then, young adolescents, for the first time, can grasp meanings of abstract symbols that are embedded within rituals. Subsequently, advances are made in their comprehension of the supernatural, the sacred, the application of creation and origin stories to their realm of existence, and their group's worldview. In short, they can move beyond concrete childhood representations of their faith and spiritual traditions to reflect on issues and concepts that are embedded in existential and transcendental realms.

Critical Periods of Development

Each stage of human development signifies unique changes and challenges to developing humans. As addressed in the previous section, specific rituals are attached to transitional phases to facilitate successful passage through the life span. Implicit to the concept of transitional phases of the life span is the notion of critical periods of development, which are special times when persons are more susceptible to influences on their developing selves (physically or psychologically). It is the presence of rapid change, in particular, that yields a critical period of development. Whenever the human organism is experiencing a period of rapid development (e.g., puberty), there is the potential for developmental processes to go awry. With unfavorable development, future outcomes that depend on earlier developmental successes are jeopardized. Certainly the concept of critical periods is well recognized by developmental psychologists in Western psychology, but it is also implicit in North American Indian theories of human development.

Critical periods also necessitate the actions of those in the young person's environment who can facilitate success through these transitional phases. In essence, it is the notion that one must "strike while the iron is hot" to have the greatest positive impact on the life of the young person. For North American Indians, life is often spoken of as a road, such as the Red Road, which is the good way, and the critical phases during this span warrant special recognition. Spiritual practices and rites of passage serve as mediators of important functions at key transitional points across the life span (Gattuso, 1991). It is the rituals of ceremonial life that bring meaning, connection, and purpose at these times. In general, the purposes of ritual observances and rites of passage at critical periods of the life span are multifaceted, but they frequently occur to provide protection and strength for the future. As stated relative to Navajos: "A major purpose of the ritual is to carry him safely and pleasantly along this road from birth to dissolution" (Reichard, 1977, p. 37).

There are various illustrations from Indigenous conceptions of life span human development and critical periods of development that can bring substance to this review. An all-inclusive discussion of these concepts is too ambitious, since virtually all cultures have beliefs about human development, but some examples can suffice for illustrative purposes. Critical periods identified by Navajos are said to occur prenatally, at birth, at puberty, and during pregnancy (Schwarz, 1997). Rituals for the protection of children actually begin during the prenatal period, at which time both mothers and fathers are to avoid exposure to dangerous or out-of-the-ordinary situations (Leighton & Kluckhohn, 1947). For instance, pregnant woman are to avoid looking on dead animals, because it is believed that the child could take on the characteristics of the animal (Schwarz, 1997). Additional violation of taboos by either parent could lead to difficult delivery, birth defects, or childhood illnesses (Leighton & Kluckhohn, 1947; Schwarz, 1997). A Blessing Way ceremony prior to birth will help ensure speedy and painless birth (Begay, 1983). In Lakota culture of the past, it was said that a pregnant woman should not be too lazy around her tepee or her child would grow up to be fat (M. N. Powers, 1986). She was to avoid eating rabbit meat so that her baby would not have a harelip; similarly, eating duck could result in webbed feet of her offspring. Cherokee culture, as well, also suggested adherence to rituals to bring smooth passage through the critical prenatal period. In the past, Cherokee women were taken to water at each new moon in order to pray and be purified (Mails, 1996).

At birth and infancy, special rituals also are required for the future benefits of the Navajo child (see Leighton & Kluckhohn, 1947). Umbilical cords are strategically buried to shape interests, activities, skills, or inclinations of the individual when he or she is older (Schwarz, 1997). It is believed that losing the umbilical cord can result in lifelong disorientation or antisocial behavior of the child. In Lakota culture of the past, it was the midwife's responsibility to place the placenta high in a tree so that animals could not find it and cast an evil influence on the child (M. N. Powers, 1986). To this day, Navajo families celebrate the first laugh of the infant as a positive expression of emotion that warrants celebration as an important milestone in the child's development (Schwarz, 1997). The first laugh actually represents a much greater promise—that the child is emotionally embedded and connected within the context of the family and in human relationships. Historically, Ojibwas held a feast at the occasion of a child's first several steps. Indeed, the feast was to be held by whomever the child approached during its first walk, and it very well could have been neighbors (Hilger, 1951/1992).

Relative to the Mescalero Apaches, Talamantez (1991) described numerous ceremonies within the first year of life alone, such as ear piercing and putting on the child's first moccasins, indicative of taking the first steps along the path of life. A first hair-cutting ceremony occurred in the springtime, and ceremonial activities occurred when a child was presented with his or her first solid foods, including traditional foods of yucca, mesquite, mescal, and sumac or chokecherry. Both boys and girls participated in childhood rituals, but the mandate for girls was to pattern their lives after White Painted Woman, while the role model for boys was found in the figure Child of the Water (see chapter 6).

Many North American Indian cultures practiced naming as a significant ritual observance at critical periods of development, and such customs continue to endure in some cases. Naming can occur at birth, during infancy, later in childhood, in adolescence, or in adulthood, and multiple names might be acquired across the life span. Naming at birth or shortly thereafter is the most frequent practice, as characterized by cultures such as Cherokee, Navajo, Crow, Hopi, Kootenai, Haida, Tlingit, Lakota, and Powhatan (Dempsey, 2001; Garrow, 1974; Kluckhohn & Leighton, 1948; Mails, 1996; Oswalt, 2006; St. Pierre & Long Soldier, 1995; Spencer & Jennings, 1965). Among the Iroquois, the name was selected at or prior to birth from a set of names owned or held by the maternal clan. However, the actual naming did not occur until one of two ceremonies—the Green Corn Festival or the Mid-Winter Festival

(Alford, 1988). When the Peel River Gwich'in became aware of the birth of a child, all would begin thinking about a name that connected to the character of the parents (Osgood, 1936/1970). Among the Ojibwas, a naming ceremony was held for the baby, and a feast of venison and wild rice followed the naming (Fox, 1999). Naming ceremonies occurred at or around birth for Tewa and Acoma infants during a sunrise naming ceremony (Mails, 1983). The Netsilik Inuit woman, who might be facing a difficult delivery while alone in the snowhouse, would recite personal names representative of name souls. If delivery followed the recitation of a particular name, it was believed that the name soul entered the new-born (Oswalt, 2006).

Clearly, rituals and ceremonies during infancy and childhood were prevalent among numerous North American Indian cultures, and occurred for multiple purposes. Prior to pubescence, there may have been little differentiation in the form of ceremonies for boys and girls, as Reichard (1977) stated was the case among Navajos. However, coming-of-age observances commonly had different forms for girls and boys (Reichard, 1977; Talamantez, 1991). Presumably, young people were being prepared for the assumption of gender-linked adult roles and responsibilities, and, accordingly, different forms of initiations were required. In some cultures gender-linked socialization frequently began around age 8, 9, or 10, slightly prior to the onset of puberty (Fox, 1999). It is apparent that, in North American Indian societies of the past and the present, provisions are made for the integration of children and adolescents into broader human and spiritual communities. Practices that facilitate connection to other people, to one's ancestors, and to the broader physical environment foster the development of a communal orientation that accentuates relatedness and social responsibility as well as the development of personal strengths.

Puberty as a Critical Period of Development

Among North American Indians, the transition from childhood to adolescence or adulthood is viewed as a critical passage that deserves special recognition, especially for girls at menarche (Hultkrantz, 1980). It is this particular sex at this stage of the life span that is of specific interest in this book. The meaning of menstruation and menstrual customs among North American Indians is given much fuller discussion in chapter 4, while the goal of this section is to address the beliefs surrounding pubescence as a critical period of development. The pubertal years encompass a highly transitional phase of the life span, and transitional phases bring change and destabilization that introduce greater stress to individuals that, in turn, heightens risk and can aggravate developmental progressions (Flach, 1988; Werner & Smith, 1982). In short, pubescence is associated with biological and psychosocial sensitivity. It is interesting to note that North American Indian cultures, of the past and many of the present, recognize this sensitivity. In speaking of the numerous puberty ceremonies for girls found across Native North American, Hodge (1912) remarked on the significance of the special status of girls at this time of the life span: "It was believed that whatever she did or experienced then was bound to affect her entire subsequent life, and that she had exceptional power over all persons or things that came near her at that period. For this reason she was usually carefully set apart from other people in a small lodge in the woods, in a separate room, or behind some screen" (p. 314). In speaking more specifically of the Tutchones, McClellan (1981d) noted their strong adherence to ritual behavior at various times of the life span and, in particular: "The most stringent observances were associated with attainment of puberty, for at this critical juncture the boys and girls had to become fully capable and responsible adults in a small society where every individual counted" (p. 500).

Based on my review of a variety of sources of literature—Indigenous and Western—as well as my field research, I have derived several statements on beliefs about pubescent girls that appear to have been held by many North American Indians (see Table 1). In this respect, Driver (1941) indicated three generic beliefs: (1) that the girl is unclean and may harm other people or nature; (2) that she is especially susceptible to harm if she does not strictly observe the various taboos; and (3) that her actions at first menstruation predetermine her behavior throughout life. With the exception of the first belief, which is reinterpreted in my analysis, the second and third beliefs also are discussed in this section. It must be observed that these are general statements and do not apply to all cultures. Further, these beliefs and their associated practices were far

Table 1. Beliefs about Pubescent Girls Held by North American Indians

1. Menstruation and menstrual fluids are powerful in general, and the first menstrual cycles are particularly powerful.
2. Feminine representations in cosmological constructions, including origin stories, are instructive to the pubescent girl, as well as to all women.
3. The special quality of menarche is a necessary (but not sufficient) event for connection of the initiate to the spiritual realm (rituals complete the process).
4. The proper performance of rituals ensures the initiate's successful transition into adulthood and influences her life course.
5. The initiate's performance of tests of endurance will subsequently affect her life course.
6. The malleable state of the initiate at puberty necessitates her subjugation to the instruction and influence of adults, particularly an adult female mentor.
7. Due to her empowered state, the initiate's behavior at puberty will have an impact on her future; hence, taboos and behavioral restrictions must be followed.
8. Due to her empowered state, the initiate can influence the welfare of others.
9. The coming-of-age event is not only a transition from childhood to adulthood but also a transition into the world of the spiritual.

more common in earlier times, having been lost to some degree along with numerous other aspects of traditional culture through processes of colonization. Nonetheless, it is appropriate at this point to provide an overview of the major beliefs about pubescent girls that seem to undergird or provide a source of philosophical support to countless puberty rituals practiced across Native North America. Illustrations of actual ritual practices are discussed more fully in later chapters according to both description and interpretation of various sources of literature and my field research.

Belief 1: Menstruation and menstrual fluids are powerful in general, and the first menstrual cycles are particularly powerful.

A belief found throughout Native North American is that menstruation and menstrual fluids encompass a form of power and, like all powers, must be properly managed. A related belief is that the first or first few menstrual flows are exceptionally powerful and require certain observances at puberty. The most common menstrual custom, at puberty or any other time, is seclusion (see chapter 5). While earlier historical and anthropological writers seemed to assume that menstrual seclusion occurred because of a belief in the contaminating quality of this substance, the Indigenous meaning of menstrual customs is that menstruation and menstrual fluids are powerful forces that require certain forms of containment so as not to overwhelm other forms of power necessary for various activities, such as hunting or curing.

Through research I have conducted on Navajo and Apache puberty ceremonies for girls and examination of customs of numerous other cultures, I have concluded that, for many North American Indian cultures, menstrual blood is regarded as an extension of the same power responsible for all of creation and annual rejuvenation of the Earth. In cultures where a female supernatural being is central in the girls' puberty ceremony, menstruation then represents the creative essence of this personage, and it is perceived that the power of this menstrual flow transforms the girl into something qualitatively very different from herself as a child.

Belief 2: Feminine representations in cosmological constructions, including origin stories, are instructive to the pubescent girl, as well as to all women.

Traditional North American Indian beliefs systems incorporated feminine components in their cosmologies. Relative to the girls' puberty ceremony, a female supernatural being is sometimes identified and the girl is compelled to emulate her in character and form, as are all woman of a particular culture. Navajos call her Changing Woman, as do Apaches, who also call her White Painted Woman or White Shell Woman. Among the Lakotas she is known as White Buffalo Calf Woman. In various cultures of the Southeast and Southwest there is the personage of the Corn Mother, who appears to be similar in character and purposes as these other figures. These women of oral tradition have also been linked to the Virgin Mary of the Christian tradition, an association evident among Apaches, as discussed in chapters 6 and 7. In short, there is commonality of character and functions of these beings. For example, in speaking of the character of Changing Woman, Markstrom and Iborra (2003) indicated her multiple purposes as being born to be the mother of the Hero Twins, who would ultimately rid the world of monsters or evil; to create the Navajo people; to give Navajos the Blessing Way rite; to regulate all of life and to ensure fertility of humans and nature; and to cause the change of seasons and annual rejuvenation. Likewise, the identity of Changing Woman speaks to her endorsement of traits of creativity and nurturance according to her role as the ultimate mother; her association with the Earth; her representation of the universal life cycle; her character as being always good, giving, and nurturing; and her exhibition of traits of the ideal woman.

Belief 3: The special quality of menarche is a necessary (but not sufficient) event for connection of the initiate to the spiritual realm (rituals complete the process).

Beliefs 1 and 2 provide a logical flow into this particular belief. The special powers associated with the first few menstrual flows are believed to place the pubescent into a special status that will never again be encountered in her lifetime. This state is not sufficient in and of itself to connect the initiate with the spiritual realm or, in some cases, to facilitate her transformation into the primary female supernatural being of her culture. Such a potential can only be realized through the proper performance of rituals that are supervised by knowledgeable adults from her culture. Likewise, the rituals are not meaningful unless they are applied to a pubescent girl. Hence, mutuality is evident between the pubescent girl and the traditional knowledge and rituals that are provided by informed adults of her culture. This particular belief is of exceptional importance to the remaining beliefs, because it has implications for the proper performance of rituals by the initiate and by those who will impose rituals upon her. A broad range of expression of pubertal coming-of-age rituals, in predominantly a historical sense, is reviewed in chapter 5. The deeper meanings of rituals of various cultures are discussed throughout this book; but all rituals are meaningful and relate somehow back to the well-being of the initiate, her community, and ultimately the world.

Belief 4: The proper performance of rituals ensures the initiate's successful transition into adulthood and influences her life course.

The formula is complete with a pubescent girl and the proper performance of rituals. Puberty is a key transitional phase in the life span, and has the potential for desired outcomes for the life of the initiate, such as a profitable, healthy, and long life (Beck et al., 1996; Bol & Menard, 2000; Hirschfelder & Molin, 2001). Conversely, the absence of rituals and ceremonies at this stage of the life span is believed to withhold a certain protective factor for the initiate and to make her life more precarious and uncertain. For instance, among the Tohono O'odhams it was thought that if puberty customs were not observed, the girl might bring sickness and death to herself or her relatives (Joseph, Spicer, &

Chesky, 1949). It was believed that pubescent girls had strong powers of good and evil and were in dangerous conditions at this time of their lives with impacts that extended from themselves to others. Likewise, the Subarctic Ahtnas believed puberty to the most critical time in the life span for girls and boys (de Laguna & McClellan, 1981). Hence, detailed prescriptions were to be followed at this time to ensure success in future endeavors.

The following beliefs build upon Belief 4, as well as the belief that puberty is a critical period of development. Belief 5 addresses those rituals the initiate is required to perform during her coming-of-age sequence of events, while Belief 6 focuses on rituals performed on the initiate by others. In either case, rituals are to be followed to maximize the likelihood of a long, healthy life and all other good things that may come to the initiate. Beliefs 7 and 8 are embedded in the notion of the empowered state of the initiate and the implications of this state for herself and others.

Belief 5: The initiate's performance of tests of endurance will subsequently affect her life course.

It is quite common to subject initiates to tests of physical endurance. There appear to be two major purposes of these tests: to build strength for her life and to demonstrate that she is a strong person. In terms of the former, the performance of rituals such as running and dancing ensure that patterns are formed and strength is acquired that will serve the initiate well throughout her life span. As discussed in later chapters, both Navajo and Apache cultures require running rituals as part of the girls' pubertal coming-of-age event. Historically, Havasupais required the pubescent girl to run to the east and to the west so that she would always perform her work quickly and untiringly (Schwartz, 1983). The Kawaiisus of the Great Basin believed, as did numerous other cultures, that behavior at puberty was linked to later life. Hence, Kawaiisu pubescent girls were urged to rise early, run in the mornings and the evenings, and generally be industrious (Zigmond, 1986). The endurance activities also serve as tests, of sorts, to prove the strength and character of the young initiate.

Belief 6: The malleable state of the initiate at puberty necessitates her subjugation to the instruction and influence of adults, particularly an adult female mentor.

The basic notion behind this belief is that the initiate's mind and body are especially impressionable and that adults must therefore subject her to certain rituals specific to the capabilities and potential of this stage of life. Certainly the basis for this belief bears some commonality with the cognitive and socioemotional advancements at puberty. The Chilkats and numerous other Indigenous cultures emphasized the pubescent girl's acquisition of knowledge and skills at this time of the life span, because it was thought that her mind could easily grasp and remember what she was taught (Shortridge, 1913). Similarly, the Navajo Kinaaldá ceremony is embedded in the notion that the body and psyche are malleable at menarche, similar to a newborn, and that it is desirable to maximize such an opportunity to set the girl's future life course (Lincoln, 1981; Schwarz, 1997). This notion is found in other rites of passage, such as the Apache puberty rites (Talamantez, 2000) and the Lakota Išnati Awicalowanpi[1] (Bol & Menard, 2000; M. N. Powers, 1986).

An adult female mentor, and not necessarily the girl's mother, often performs various actions related to both instruction and physical manipulation to shape the initiate. Instruction and teaching were components of virtually all coming-of-age practices of the past, and they frequently centered on the girl's responsibilities toward others as well as her learning of gender-linked tasks. In some cases, girls were instructed on how women are to take care of themselves or seclude themselves during their monthly cycles.

In addition to instruction, in both the past and in the present day it is common to assign a female mentor to conduct physical manipulations on the initiate. For instance, by massaging the initiate it is thought that physical and psychological traits of the mentor are passed on to the initiate. Navajos continue these practices, and it is believed that through the bodily manipulations the girl is affected in the four areas of her being (i.e., spiritual, emotional, intellectual, and physical) and that she will be shaped into the image of Changing Woman (Beck et al., 1996; Schwarz, 1997). It is believed that the barrier between the physical body and the psyche is weak—the physical has an impact on the psychological. Physical manipulation of the initiate also may be thought of as a form of role modeling—but it is a physical action that provides the momentum for shaping the physique and psyche of the initiate. The initiate is encouraged to identify with the adult female mentor, who is selected for her admirable traits, and a major mechanism of identification is physical action. Clearly, the adult female mentor is perceived as possessing the power to reshape and remake the girl into her image, and as Markstrom and Iborra (2003) suggested relative to Navajos, the identification extends to the female holy person, Changing Woman. In a matrilineal culture such as Navajo, the lineage extends from Changing Woman to the adult female mentor to the initiate. The desired physical and psychological traits of Changing Woman should be evident in a well-chosen mentor and subsequently physically impressed on the initiate. A similar interpretation is offered for the Apache Sunrise Dance as discussed in chapters 6 and 7.

Belief 7: Due to her empowered state, the initiate's behavior at puberty will have an impact on her future; hence, taboos and behavioral restrictions must be followed.

This belief has found various expressions in a variety of cultures. It reflects the underlying notion that the behaviors engaged in by the pubescent girl during her puberty observances will represent her future activities. In short, her behavior at puberty is believed to affect the remainder of her life (e.g., Hodge, 1912; Shortridge, 1913). It is not an exaggeration to say that, historically, puberty was regarded as the most important time in the girl's life, as was the case of the Chilkats, who believed that the pubescent's future welfare depended on her care at that time (Shortridge, 1913). Similarly, McKennan (1959) observed that the Upper Tananas believed that, for girls and boys, pubescence was a critical stage of development and that behaviors at this time could affect later life. This thinking also was associated with the Nez Perce people, who believed that anything the pubescent girl did at this time of life would influence her later life (Walker, 1998b). Hence, during their puberty isolation, Nez Perce girls were to think good thoughts and keep busy. Tlingits also thought that the girl's conduct during pubescence would determine her future (de Laguna, 1990b). This could include the well-being of her future children, as was also the case of the Teslin girl whose actions at puberty were believed to link to the future arrival and activity of her children (Libby, 1952).

In the Pacific Northwest, the display of wealth surrounding the pubescent girl was thought to ward off poverty and to signify future wealth (Hodge, 1912). The degree of industriousness of the pubescent also was thought to reflect on her adult life. On the one hand, some Pacific Northwest Coast cultures discouraged activity in order that the pubescent might become a chief's wife and not be a slave. However, it was more common to engage the girl in industrious activities in order that she not be lazy in the future, as Hodge (1912) noted occurred among the Ntlakyapamuks. This value is certainly shown among contemporary expressions of the puberty ceremonies of the Apaches and Navajos.

Pubescent girls were subjected to a variety of taboos and behavioral restrictions (see chapter 5) that were deemed necessary because they were believed to have a direct bearing on future wealth, health, and personality. For instance, a widespread practice across Native North America was to forbid pubescent girls from touching themselves—a scratching stick was the substitute for fingers and hands when it was necessary to touch the self. The meanings behind this custom varied across culture, but Western Apaches believed that girls were so empowered at this time of the life span that they could scar themselves through their own touch. Food taboos required of pubescent girls in Teslin culture were thought to build strength and so they would not eat too much later in life (Libby, 1952). The Tlingit girl could not handle a knife for the first eight days of her seclusion because it was thought that her life could be cut short. Additionally, her hair would be washed in blueberry juice, signifying hopes for good luck, acquisition of a good husband, and permanently black hair (de Laguna, 1990b; Fried & Fried, 1980).

Belief 8: Due to her empowered state, the initiate can influence the welfare of others.

Power is a multifaceted concept in North American Indian beliefs, but it is always regarded as a force to be approached with caution and prudence. Power has the potential to offer blessings and help, but if not managed properly it can be a dangerous entity. Therefore, the empowered pubescent must take care in her behavior, as must those who are in contact with her. But it is also believed that the girl at her earliest menses possesses the power to bless others and is capable of curing and healing (Beck et al., 1996; Martin, 2001). Such beliefs were widespread in the past, and they continue to be recognized in some cultures.

Concomitant with the notion of an empowered pubescent who can offer blessings to others is the recognition that she also presents a certain sort of danger due to the power attached to her earliest menstrual cycles. For instance, as is summarized in chapter 5, some cultures, such as many of the Subarctic, required pubescent girls to be in seclusion, sometimes up to 2 years, and, when in public, they wore a large hood or bonnet that shielded their face from others. Those from Carrier culture thought that misfortune would occur for a man, especially a medicine man, who looked on a pubescent girl, potentially leading to his death (Libby, 1952). Various Pacific and Northern Athabascan cultures, such as Hupa, Sinkyone, Ingalik, and Tanaina, required that the head or eyes of pubescent girls be shielded from others to not cause them harm (W. J. Wallace, 1978a; Elsasser, 1978a; Osgood, 1940; Osgood, 1937, respectively).

On the other hand, the empowered state of the pubescent meant that she was in a position to offer blessings to others. Several illustrations of puberty rituals that utilized the power of the pubescent for the good of others are provided in chapter 4. In contemporary practices of Apache, Navajo, and Lakota puberty ceremonies, rituals occur that permit others to approach the initiate in some manner to obtain blessings.

Belief 9: The coming-of-age event is not only a transition from childhood to adulthood but also a transition into the world of the spiritual.
The spiritual significance of ritual practices at and around puberty should not be underestimated. Both boys and girls, but especially girls, are thought to be in special empowered states that are attractive to the broader spiritual powers of the universe. In some cases, pubescence is regarded as the first time the person possesses enough strength to encounter these powers. For instance, among Western Apaches of the past, boys and girls were not to take serious roles in curing ceremonies until after puberty, because the power attached to these ceremonies was deemed to be too strong for their hearts (G. Goodwin, 1942). The role of a medicine person, then, was critical to facilitate entry and introduction of the young person to the spiritual realm. Hence, special singing and prayer rituals occurred in conjunction with other puberty observances in various cultures. In essence, puberty is not regarded only as a rite of passage to adulthood but is also a rite of passage to the spiritual. In some cultures of the past, it was mandated that young people engage in a vision quest at this time of the life span. The success in such an endeavor ensured the

future welfare of the person and ultimately was thought to have benefits for the entire group. For example, the person who acquired special powers during his or her quest in childhood or adolescence would develop these powers further in adulthood and be expected to contribute to the welfare of others in his or her group.

Purposes of Coming-of-Age Practices

The previous section on beliefs about North American Indian pubescent girls contained implicit clues on the purposes of puberty ceremonies. It is useful at this point to engage in more explicit discussion of these purposes, which are certainly multifaceted in both historical and contemporary considerations. Relative to the purposes for celebrating the phase of coming-of-age, it can be asked, what specific domains of female development are targeted, or what components of the self are to be affected or transformed by ritual activities? Pubertal rites of passage aim to connect physical changes to expected changes in social roles (van Gennep, 1908/1960; Weisfeld, 1997). While the Western view of psychology has focused on maturation in cognitive and intellectual domains at coming-of-age (Scott, 1998), Markstrom and Iborra (2003) asserted that the biological stimulus for pubertal rites of passage compels correspondence with other domains of development. However, physiological and social puberty seldom converge (Sebald, 1992). Nonetheless, rituals performed at the event of physiological puberty are designed to advance maturation in other domains of development, such as the psychological, social, and emotional selves. Some puberty rituals build on gender-linked tasks performed in childhood accompanied by instruction of initiates to exhibit proper care and responsibility toward family. For example, in the Apache Sunrise Dance, initiates are required to bake four kinds of traditional breads; hence the initiate demonstrates adult female role performance. Successful ceremonies are expected to produce changes that have far-reaching and long-term impacts in the lives of initiate and ultimately her associates.

Markstrom and Iborra (2003) summarized the purposes of the Navajo Kinaaldá according to celebration, recognition of reproductive capability, instruction on social roles, tests of physical endurance, performance of rituals to develop desired physical and character traits, to develop strength and harmony for the future, and to reinforce an identity embedded in Changing Woman. Similarly, it is discussed in chapters 6 and 7 in this book relative to another Southern Athabascan group, the Apaches, that the Sunrise Dance is expected to provide girls with longevity, strength for the future, desired physical and character traits, and blessings, the latter especially providing benefits for the initiate and others. Also, in Navajo and Apache societies the puberty ceremony is an opportunity to bring the personage of Changing Woman or White Painted Woman into the midst of the gathering. The rituals performed, both by the pubescent girl and by those who perform rituals directed toward her, are believed to facilitate her transformation into the important female supernatural being that subsequently becomes accessible to the gathering. The initiate, then, becomes the channel for blessing and renewal of others.

In examining puberty rituals among Northern Athabascans, including the practice of separation or seclusion of the initiate, Libby (1952) cited the primary reason for these customs as "to control the mysterious power in the female and as an attempt to insure her not disrupting settled traditions and ways of life or of spoiling the men's hunting luck" (p. 3). Additional purposes noted by Libby were "to prepare the girl for her future life as a contributing member in the community as a wife and mother; to insure her bodily strength and well-being and that of her future children; and to mold, channelize, and to instruct her in the mental and spiritual attitudes of her group" (p. 3).[2]

There is a strong expectation that pubescent girls should acquire desired social roles of women of their cultures, as is evident in chapter 5 in the examination of puberty rituals of a variety of cultures. Rituals of instruction and shaping compel initiates to assume characteristics that will facilitate their performance of expected responsibilities. Historically, North American Indians societies tended to be gender-typed according to the assignment of specific roles and responsibilities to men and women. Women were distinguished for their childbearing and child-rearing capabilities, as well as their critical roles in social maintenance through the fulfillment of responsibilities toward family and clan. To this day, puberty ceremonies are performed, in part, to reinforce generative contributions of women to the good of others and to the perpetuation of their cultures. This theme is further displayed in groups, such as Navajos and Apaches, among whom rituals are designed to connect initiates to the primary female being in their cosmologies that represent life and creation.

The previous comments must be understood in context and warrant clarification. Gender-typing connotes something very different in North American Indian in comparison to European American societies (chapter 4). In the former, the contributions of women to the continuation, maintenance, and well-being of the group are valued, as opposed to Western constructions of gender, which link women and femininity to reduced power. Additionally, while the roles of women are reinforced in girls' coming-of-age ceremonies, stereotypically masculine traits such as physical strength and endurance are also impressed on initiates.

As evident in this discussion, it is erroneous to make a superficial assumption that the functions of girls' puberty ceremonies center on sexual maturation, reproduction, or fertility. Indeed, the conclusions of this chapter confirm those reported by Schlegel and Barry (1980) in their examination of data from the Standard Cross-Cultural Sample (Murdock & White, 1969) on initiation ceremonies according to the most common themes or foci. While it was reported that across all world areas and for girls, fertility was the primary focus, followed by responsibility and then sexuality, in more specific examination it was found that responsibility emerged as the most important focus of girls' initiation ceremonies in the North American world area (which was made up of Indigenous societies). Schlegel and Barry defined *responsibility* as "impressing upon the initiate the importance of taking adult duties, usually productive ones" (1980, p. 708). Indeed, North America was the only world region in the Standard Cross-Cultural Sample in which responsibility was the dominant theme or focus of the adolescent initiation ceremony for girls. As discussed in chapter 5, instruction on responsibility relative to adoption of appropriate social roles and their associated tasks was a major event of girls' puberty ceremonies across countless North American Indian cultures. In addition to the major emphasis on responsibility, Schlegel and Barry also found the promotion of future physical and spiritual well-being of initiates to be an important emphasis of puberty ceremonies in North America.

A related finding was that among those societies where responsibility (rather than sexuality or fertility) was the major focus of girls' initiation ceremonies, sexual egalitarianism was the norm, as summarized by Schlegel and Barry (1980): "This predicted relationship indicates that females' productivity is highly valued along with procreativity in the sexually egalitarian areas" (p. 709). A further finding was that in food-collecting societies (in the worldwide analysis) the major focus to emerge was protection of the girl for her future physical and spiritual well-being. The linkages between societal types and girls' puberty ceremonies are more carefully examined in the next chapter.

In short, Schlegel and Barry's (1980) findings reinforce the notion that purposes of puberty rituals among North American Indians center on benefits for both initiates and their social groups, with fertility not emerging as a focus. Rather, the encouragement of female initiates to assume social responsibilities that ultimately contribute to the well-being of their families and groups is of prominence.

It is concluded from this review of various authors on the topic that, concerning North American Indian puberty rites, purposes can be delineated according to two broad themes: those dealing with the well-being of initiates and those for the benefit of their social groups. These are certainly not mutually exclusive categories, and considerable overlap is evident. Relative to purposes for initiates, as previously discussed, puberty is recognized as a critical period of development, and rituals are performed to facilitate smooth transition through this phase and into adulthood; hence the purposes or functions of puberty ceremonies encompass several categories:

- Socializing the initiate according to the roles she is expected to perform in adulthood.
- Inculcating physical and psychological traits of value to her social group.
- Impressing on her an optimal identity reflective of the values of her culture.
- Building and providing strength and protection for her future, including longevity.
- Facilitating spiritual transcendence.
- Instructing her in how to control and manage the power that she has acquired.

- Celebrating her change in status or transition from childhood to adulthood.

Summary

The purpose of this chapter was to situate the reader within the framework of a general North American Indian worldview, particularly according to perspectives on the personality, human development, and pubescence and the phase of coming-of-age. The spiritual nature of all facets of human existence was stated to be preeminent in the Indigenous worldview. The phase of coming-of-age was shown to receive strong consideration to the degree that special rituals are required for success in the transition from girlhood to womanhood. Several beliefs about pubescent girls were delineated according to their derivation from review of the literature and field research conducted for the present work. These beliefs are foundational to the remaining chapters of the book. Clearly, puberty rituals and ceremonies are multifaceted within any culture, and purposes can be delineated according to beneficial outcomes for initiates and their social groups.

CHAPTER FOUR

Menstruation, Cosmology, and Feminism

□　□　□

When it comes to the broader society's understanding of the cultures and histories of North American Indians, including attitudes and practices toward women and menstruation, misunderstanding and misrepresentation are central concerns. Within the broader scope of this book on female coming-of-age ceremonies at puberty, it is essential to explore the underlying beliefs surrounding menstruation, as well as the feminine components that are incorporated in the broader cosmological structures of many Native cultures. Through examination of these cultures' beliefs about menstruation in general and the earliest menses in particular, the significance of ritual observances at puberty becomes apparent. It was shown in chapter 3, for instance, that pubescence is regarded as a critical period of development. Expressions of this belief are evident in the puberty rituals and ceremonies that are described in the following chapters, especially in the case studies of Apache, Navajo, Lakota/Nakota/Dakota, and Ojibwa cultures. An examination of rituals reveals a prevalent belief in the susceptible quality of the first menstrual cycles which situates the initiate in a state that permits connection to the supernatural realm and, in some cases, facilitates transformation into the primary female supernatural being of her culture.

The purpose of the present chapter is to introduce readers to concepts salient to this book, specifically, North American Indian beliefs about menstruating girls and women and toward menstrual fluids, as well as the resultant practices and ritual observances. Further, the significance of feminine elements in North American Indian cosmologies is elucidated. An attempt is made to present culturally relevant views of these notions according to the beliefs of the cultures of interest. Ultimately, issues of power and the status of women come to the forefront when concepts of biological sex, gender roles, and menstruation are addressed. Very different interpretations can be offered on North American Indian menstrual customs depending on the particular feminist orientation that is considered (i.e., Western or Native). This chapter is about female concerns and corresponding interpretations of female experiences and their implications for the well-being of both North American Indian men and women. A major goal of this chapter is to dispel myth and misunderstanding in an attempt to advance viewpoints that are reflective of many of those from within these cultures. In this regard, writings from Indigenous scholars and cultural participants were sought for this topic, including Paula Gunn Allen, Marilou Awiakta, Vine Deloria, Charles Eastman, Mary Jo Tippeconnic Fox, Theresa Halsey, M. Annette Jaimes, Tilda Long Soldier, Devon Mihesuah, Le Anne Silvey, George "Tink" Tinker, and Shirley Hill Witt.

Beliefs about Menstruation

Menstrual taboos and restrictions reflect underlying attitudes about menstrual fluids and the symbolic nature of menstruation. While not universal, they are ancient practices and are found in traditional cultures (Knight, 1991). In cultural analyses of menstruation, Knight (1991) and Buckley and Gottlieb (1988) reviewed various theories of menstrual symbolism—none of which have had a large number of adherents but are informative to examine for comparative purposes. From a psychoanalytic perspective, at the core of menstrual customs is castration anxiety, in which it was argued that, with greater male fear of castration, the greater the menstrual restrictions imposed by a society (Stephens, 1962). Bettelheim (1954) offered an opposing explanation, also from a psychoanalytic perspective, that men were not afraid of castration but rather that they envied the ability of women to bleed from their genitals. As a result, some societies engaged in initiation rites that involved male self-mutilation and bleeding in order to emulate the power of women's menstruation. In a very different psychological approach, it was explained that, among women in hunter-gatherer societies, menstruation was a less frequent event due to poor nourishment. Hence, the rarity of the event of menstruation resulted in certain suspicious attitudes and menstrual taboos (Frisch, 1975).

A utilitarian view of menstruation labeled *menotoxicity* focused on the perception that menstrual blood was toxic; therefore, menstrual restrictions were said to have emerged for scientific reasons—specifically, to protect food and other substances from biological contamination (Buckley & Gottlieb, 1988; Knight, 1991). Still another explanation centered on the odor of menstrual fluid and explained that menstrual taboos associated with male hunting activities were to prevent the spread of these odors through hunters and their implements, since it was believed that these odors could subsequently result in aversive avoidance behavior on the part of game (Buckley & Gottlieb, 1988). Buckley and Gottlieb (1988) also asserted that menstrual taboos link to culturally based spiritual or mystical foundations: "menstrual taboos are cultural constructions and must first be approached as such—symbolic, arbitrary, contextualized, and potentially multivalent whose meanings emerge only within the contexts of the fields of representations in which they exist" (p. 24).

The following discussion examines views of menstruation and menstrual taboos according to the cultural understandings of North American Indians. Native conceptions of menstruating women and menstrual fluids are controversial topics that have led to speculations on the perceptions of women and the degree of power women held in their societies. Depending on the characteristics and orientation of the writer (i.e., Native or non-Native, historical or present-day or disciplinary basis), there are various terms, albeit contradictory terms, that have been used to describe the special state of menstruating girls and women, ranging from "unclean" all the way to "sacred" (Lantis, 1984a). The question becomes, do North American Indians regard menstruation as a source of contamination or as a source of power? In either case, the practices of a variety of menstrual customs suggest that the state of menstruation and menstrual fluids require treatment apart from the ordinary and mundane. For numerous reasons, menstrual taboos are reflections of the perceived special status of women during these times in her cycle. The remainder of this section presents examples of menstrual taboos, followed by thoughts of various writers on the meanings of North American Indian conceptions of menstruation and the functions of menstrual customs. Ultimately these thoughts are suggestive of underlying attitudes toward women.

The most common menstrual taboo was seclusion of girls and women beginning at menarche and frequently continuing throughout all monthly cycles until menopause (although the past tense is used in the present discussion, it is important to recognize that some of these menstrual customs occur in the present day, albeit in a more limited sense than in the past). Physical seclusion could range from living in a separate space in the home to the requirement that girls and women remove themselves to a menstrual hut placed at some distance from the group (see chapter 5). At pubescence, in the past, seclusion might range up to 2 years, but it was more common for shorter spans of seclusion. With female adult menstrual cycles, seclusion was commonly for the length of menses. In the past and present, pubescent girls also can be required to observe food and other taboos, and are instructed by adult women. Sometimes, adult menstruating women also were required to adhere to food and related taboos (more so in the past). Another set of menstrual customs that were sometimes quite elaborate surrounded the separation of menstrual fluids and menstruating women from anything relating to successful procurement of animals or fish. These and numerous other practices at puberty are more carefully described in the next chapter according to 10 cultural areas in North America. Of particular interest in this chapter is exploration of the reasons for the various menstrual customs and taboos.

A range of customs and rituals were to be followed relative to pubescent girls and menstruating women across a variety of tribal cultures; however, less clarity is apparent when interpretations of these customs are considered. The contradictions and ambiguity surrounding the meaning of menstrual fluids and menstruation are clearly represented in the following quote by McIlwraith (1948) on the Bella Coolas: "Although the menstrual blood which appears at the first discharge is considered more baneful than that emitted on later occasions, it is always regarded as uncanny or unclean. It is the most human of all substances, and therefore, a potent protection against supernatural beings. It is valuable as a defence against evil monsters, but it is equally deadly to shamans and other human beings with supernatural powers" (p. 373). An aim of the present chapter is to decrease some of the ambiguity on the topic as evident in this quote.

Societal-Based Explanations for Menstrual Customs

While it is common to read historical accounts in which it was concluded that menstrual customs were required because menstruating girls and women were regarded as "unclean" or "contaminated," there are alternative explanations for these customs that are actually more societal-based, in some cases, and more spiritually based, in other cases. For instance, there are correlates between menstrual customs and societal organizational patterns, including male dominance, female autonomy, and subsistence patterns (Schlegel, 1972). Relative to subsistence patterns, a connection is apparent between menstrual customs and societies dominated by hunting and fishing. An additional dimension that is implicit throughout this discussion is the perceived power of menstruating women. Indeed, the previous quote from McIlwraith, while suggesting the "unclean" nature of menstrual fluid, also is suggestive of the perceived power associated with this substance. The two themes of societal and spiritual explanations for menstrual customs are examined more carefully in the following sections.

Schlegel (1972) was interested in patterns of male dominance and female autonomy relative to worldwide menstrual customs. The Standard Cross-Cultural Sample (Murdock & White, 1969) was used to assess these patterns worldwide, including non-industrial Indigenous societies of North America. Societies in which women were dominated by men were classified as "husband dominant" or "brother dominant," and societies in which women experienced relative autonomy were labeled "neither dominant." It was shown that in husband-dominant societies women faced a range of menstrual restrictions, while in brother-dominant and neither-dominant societies, menstrual restrictions involved seclusion only. This finding and others reported by Schlegel (1972) relative to beliefs about blood endangering ritual objects, the food supply, or men make it difficult to ascertain any meaningful trend due to a small sample size. Nonetheless, there is the suggestion that patterns of dominance of females by males (especially husbands) were associated with more rigorous and demanding menstrual requirements placed on women.

In extending the topic of societal characteristics to the practice of female adolescent initiation ceremonies, several points merit discussion. The Standard Cross-Cultural Sample was analyzed by Schlegel and Barry (1980), who reported that female adolescent initiation ceremonies occurred more frequently at first menstruation—a finding that was particularly true for food-collecting societies. Additionally, more adolescent initiation ceremonies occurred for girls than for boys in North American cultures, as summarized by these authors: "the preponderance of ceremonies for girls rather than boys is particularly striking in North America, where the hunting-gathering or hunting-horticultural subsistence pattern is widespread. This suggested that girls' ceremonies are most widely represented at the lower levels of efficiency in subsistence techniques" (p. 699). Specifically, those societies that practiced female adolescent initiation rites possessed certain characteristics found in many North American Indian societies of the past—less control over food sources, which necessitated food-collection activities; less sedentary; smaller in size; and having fewer jurisdictional levels. Further, female adolescent initiation ceremonies were related to societies with high female contribution to subsistence patterns and food-collection activities. Of particular interest, in these societies women were more valued for their productive and procreative activities.

Greater clarification is offered to this discussion by the finding that food-collecting societies that were heavily dependent on protein from wild animals more often had puberty ceremonies at first menstruation (Schlegel & Barry, 1980). Within these types of societies, connections between menstrual blood and hunting were commonly made. Hence, for the welfare of the entire group it would be expedient to manage menstrual fluids from the onset to not disturb the forces at work in the hunt. As explained by Osgood (1958), a woman of menstrual age was "responsible to the community and particularly to her household for not breaking taboos which, if broken, might endanger the health and economic security of the family. These restrictions which are concomitant to her position essentially involve the disassociation of herself as a menstruating woman—and more particularly of the menstrual fluid itself—from any uncontaminated person and especially a male involved in fishing or hunting. The restrictions extend quite logically to any weapon or other object involved in such pursuits" (p. 187).

Schlegel and Barry (1980) observed that different societies had various explanations for taboos against women, particularly menstruating women, in connection with hunters and hunting activities, but they went on to propose a pragmatic reason for menstrual taboos: "But we believe that there may well be an underlying adaptive rationale for this: the blood frightens away herbivorous animals, the kind usually hunted for food" (p. 711). Clearly, this was one of the reasons proposed by Buckley and Gottlieb (1988) for menstrual taboos, as discussed previously. Schlegel and Barry also stated that there could be social reasons for the separation of menstruating women when men prepare for the sex-typed behavior of hunting. In short, while hunting societies may have manifest rationales for menstrual taboos that are spiritualized in nature, there may be underlying pragmatic reasons to ensure the success of the hunt among peoples whose livelihoods depended on such activities.

The linkage of menstrual restrictions and customs to hunting societies has been discussed by other writers as well. In an argument similar to Schlegel and Barry's (1980), Bolt (1987) suggested that separation of women during menstruation was more common among cultures that subsisted on hunting because it was believed that menstrual blood could interfere with the power men needed for successful hunting expeditions. Indeed, as observed by Martin (2001): "These hunters assumed menstrual blood, associated with the positive forces of life, would overwhelm their power to kill" (p. 34). This belief was so strong that a hunter was not even to walk near a menstruating woman or swim downstream from where she bathed (Martin, 2001). Libby (1952) had earlier expressed similar thoughts in speaking of menstrual practices of Northern Athabascan tribes, among whom menstrual taboos and isolation at puberty were common. In summarizing data across several Northern Athabascan cultures, Libby (1952) concluded that "stringent puberty observances of the northern Athabascans is not horror of women, of menstruation, or of of menstrual fluid as such, but is, in part, a desire not to offend the game and fur animals on whose good will the natives still depend for much of their livelihood" (p. 2).

In considering the harsh northern climates of the Athabascans and other Subarctic cultures dependent on hunting or fishing for their livelihoods, strict taboos regarding menstruation acquire particular meaning and significance. The Ingaliks' menstrual avoidance behaviors, similar to other hunting tribes, were linked to anything related to male fishing or hunting activity (Osgood, 1958). For instance, a woman was not to step on a man's trail until at least 20 minutes after he had passed by. Blood was regarded as the essence of life, and a mystical connection was thought to exist between the blood of menstruating women and that of game. In generally summarizing the stringent menstrual taboos of the Subarctic cultural area, Honigmann (1981a) observed that the rituals represented efforts to contain the power of menstruation, which could compromise the success of the hunt engaged in by men. Hodge (1912) offered a very different explanation for the hunting taboos relative to pubescent girls, explaining that Alaskan Eskimos believed that menstruating girls were surrounded by a kind of film that, when transferred to hunters, would make them visible to their game.

It should be noted that menstrual taboos were not the only requirements relative to game animals. Elaborate rules existed for when and how certain animals should be hunted. Specified rituals were to be performed to ensure future harmonious relations with the natural world, as stated by Carmody and Carmody (1993) regarding Inuit hunting taboos: "we catch overtones of a millennial effort to establish good relations with the game on which the tribe traditionally depended. The relation between the hunter and the hunted was more mystical than that between a customer and a supplier" (p. 44). Menstrual customs, therefore, were part of a larger complex of behaviors that were to be observed to protect the critical subsistence source of a group.

As previously alluded to, menstrual taboos and customs were to be followed by both men and women, such as the Ingalik requirement that men and women follow numerous behavioral restrictions relative to menstrual fluid and women of menstrual age (Osgood, 1958). For example, it was explained that a man was required to properly dispose of his wood shavings in order to not risk a woman of menstrual age stepping on them, the consequence being difficulty for him in finding a good tree to work with in the future. The fathers of pubescent Ingalik girls also were required to observe taboos during their daughters' seclusion. In short, the taboos were to be observed by any woman of menstrual age or by any man in response to a woman of menstrual age. Niethammer (1977) noted an almost universal prohibition among American Indians regarding sexual intercourse with menstruating woman, as was noted in the Subarctic area by Honigmann (1981a). Also, Buckley and Gottlieb (1988) observed that menstrual customs could be more restrictive of the behaviors of those around the menstruating woman than for the menstruating woman herself.

Perceived Power of Menstruation

The presence of menstrual taboos and related practices of many North American Indian cultures should not be regarded as peculiar, particularly in consideration of the broader context of cultural understanding. For instance, Schlegel (1972) speculated on a parallel between menstrual restrictions of North American Indians and restrictions placed on men in states of heightened spiritual tension or danger (e.g., warfare, hunting, or participation in ceremonies). Implicit in this discussion is the notion that some kind of power was associated with menstrual fluids and menstruating girls and women. Power is to be managed properly and with respect, or risk is introduced for all of those involved. E. Wallace (1978) argued that the taboos and rituals surrounding girls at puberty and adult menstruating women were not derived from beliefs about the inferiority of women but rather from "magico-religious considerations" (p. 688). Indeed, the perceived power of menstruation and subsequent attempts to control that power were adopted for the benefit of men and women and the community at large. In essence, it is the spiritual concept of power that bears particular relevance to this discussion. It can be suggested that the practice of separating women during menstruation was a sign of respect relative to a form of power that wielded considerable influence in relation to other forms of power.

In writing about women and the power within them during the menstrual years, Libby (1952) stated: "It is this power that resides in a woman that is feared and guarded against rather than the woman herself" (p. 3). Bolt (1987) suggested that the power of North American Indian women was linked to their ability to bear children and that menstruation was regarded as the manifestation of that power. McClellan (1981b) discussed socialization of pubescent girls of the Subarctic Cordillera; during their lengthy seclusion they were taught that "as mature women they had the inherent power through menstrual and birth effluvia to offend the spirits of the game animals and other natural phenomena. They therefore had to learn how to manage this power through proper social restraints and ritual behavior, since people's livelihood depended on their behavior" (p. 385). The perceived enormous power of menstruation is reflected in the following comment in reference to the instruction of Tutchone pubescent girls about their newly acquired responsibilities: "her female physiology had now become a powerful force in relation to the pervasive spiritual aspects of the world about her. Her conduct could affect either favorably or unfavorably the state of the weather, mountains, rivers, and the animals and plants on which the welfare of the group depended. It could also affect the course of her life—the ease with which she would bear her children, her health, her social character" (McClellan, 1981d, p. 500).

In specific consideration of menstrual practices at puberty, it was discussed in chapter 3 that several North American Indian cultures had beliefs in the particular power of the earlier menses. For instance, the Navajo Kinaaldá, which is still widely practiced, ideally occurs during the first or second menstrual cycle, when it is thought that the girl's powers are greatest. The belief in the power of the earliest menstrual flow also is associated with the Lakota puberty ceremony (Išnati Awicalowanpi) (Bol & Menard, 2000) and numerous other North American Indian cultures that practice various expressions of seclusion during pubescence (Pritzker, 1998). Taboos at pubescence, such as those prohibiting girls from scratching and touching themselves, reflect the belief that menstruating girls could physically harm themselves with their own touch, hence necessitating the use of the scratching stick, as in Apache culture (Basso, 1970).

As further evidence of the special status of women during menstruation and, in particular, of girls at pubescence, many Native cultures believed that girls at this time possessed certain healing, purifying, blessing, and other forms of power. The Ingaliks had a ritual in which, while isolated in her "corner" for her year of seclusion, the girl could extend purification to boys with whom she was related or was friendly. This purification was needed for boys who had played with unclean substances, such as dirt, because their unclean states could ultimately compromise their hunting expeditions (Osgood, 1958). Hodge (1912) explained that it was believed that if a man was armed with the menstrual blood of a pubescent girl, he could assail hostile supernatural forces. As further evidence of the particular powers of menstruating girls, it was believed that if she scratched the place of pain on someone, the pain would stop (Hodge, 1912). Teslin pubescent girls practiced "weather magic" that consisted of picking lice off themselves, putting the lice in the snow, and telling them they would freeze if they did not bring warm weather (Libby, 1952). Additionally, the words of pubescent Teslin girls were perceived as especially powerful and could not be taken back once spoken to others. To this day, the Apaches incorporate blessing rituals in the 4-day Sunrise Dance, in which those desiring to do so may approach the initiate for particular prayers or blessings. Similar rituals are found in the Navajo Kinaaldá, in which others present personal objects that are blessed through their association with the initiate (Markstrom & Iborra, 2003). The conclusion to be drawn from these illustrations is that, in the past and the present day, pubescent girls are perceived as possessing special powers that enable them to benefit themselves and others. Alternatively, harm could ensue if they did not exhibit restraint relative to specified taboos.

Interestingly, the perceived power of menstruation and menstrual fluids often precluded female shamanism until after menopause (Bolt, 1987; Libby, 1952). In spite of the belief in equivalent male and female supernatural beings that is found across North American Indian cultures, men assumed primary responsibility for ceremonial activity. Nonetheless, it was not uncommon for women to become medicine women or healers after menopause, as stated by St. Pierre and Long Soldier (1995): "Beyond the childbearing years—beyond menopause—is when many opportunities for spiritual service to their people open up for Lakota women, . . . to help those who are suffering" (p. 25). However, it can be presumed that in earlier times fewer women reached the age of meno-pause. Hence, the roles of men in ceremonial activities as those respon-sible for the spiritual welfare of their group would be more apparent in historic accounts on the topic.

The present discussion on the perceived power of menstruation and menstrual fluids can be extended to the common practice of menstrual seclusion. The widespread perception is that menstrual seclusion is a restrictive activity. In contrast, in some cases it might be considered a monthly respite (Bolt, 1987)—a view certainly popularized in *The Red Tent*, in which Diamont (1997) fictionalized women's seclusion and so-cial networks in early Israeli tribal society. In speaking in the historical sense of Eastern Woodland groups, Martin (2001) stated that women's monthly seclusion "provided them with a regular, sanctioned break from the regular activities of tending crops, processing game, gathering wild foods, making pottery and baskets, counseling elders, consoling friends, romancing lovers" (p. 34). As well, the woman's extended family was re-sponsible for her children during the time of seclusion, which provided a relief from child-rearing tasks. However, there is an apparent absence of information on activities that occurred in menstrual huts of North American Indian women, and conclusions are speculative (Buckley & Gottlieb, 1988; Galloway, 1997). Nonetheless, it was likely that, due to a tendency for women of the same household to be synchronous in their menstrual cycles, the time spent in the menstrual hut was with other women (Galloway, 1997). Presumably, these women were provided with a lull from day-to-day demands and had opportunities for more leisurely activities relative to female companionship and socialization.

When culturally relativistic interpretations are applied to the topic of menstrual taboos and restrictions we arrive at conclusions at odds with earlier notions, in which it was assumed that North American Indian women were relegated to lower and exploited statuses in their group. It was shown in the previous discussion that such notions are faulty. Indeed, Marla Powers (1980) observed that anthropologists tended to in-terpret tribal taboos toward menstrual blood and menstruating women as misogynist. In contrast, a common view presented by North Ameri-can Indian writers is that menstrual blood represents power that is active in healing or curing (Beck et al., 1996) and reflects the creative forces of nature (St. Pierre & Long Soldier, 1995). Later in this chapter, in the section on feminist interpretations, it is shown that North American Indian women held power in numerous forms that were not readily apparent in earlier historical and anthropological works on the topic. The following comment by Buckley and Gottlieb (1988) on menstrual customs is thought-provoking and is suggestive of the necessity to probe underlying meanings of phenomena: "Many menstrual taboos, rather than protecting society from a universally ascribed feminine evil, explicitly protect the perceived creative spirituality of menstruous women from the influence of others in a more neutral state, as well as protecting the latter in turn from the potent, positive spiritual force ascribed to women" (p. 7).

The Feminine Element in North American Indian Cosmologies

In gaining a greater understanding on the status and roles of women in North American Indian cultures, it is useful to examine the pre-eminence of female personages in their cosmologies. It is apparent that these female and feminine-linked characteristics are intricately linked to puberty ceremonies for girls, as shown in the previous chapter. The seemingly equal importance of male and female supernatural beings in North American belief systems is in stark contrast to the patriarchal religion of the European colonizers (Bolt, 1987; Mihesuah, 2003). There are numerous illustrations of these figures across cultural areas of Native North America. In the Southwest, Navajos speak of several female holy persons, such as First Woman, Changing Woman, and White Shell Woman (the latter two sometimes being the same figure) (Reichard, 1977). Similarly, Changing Woman, also known as White Painted Woman and sometimes called White Shell Woman, is prominent among the Apaches (Mails, 1988). Spider Woman is connected with the Navajo, Hopi, Pueblo, and other cultures of the Southwest (Zak, 1989). Thought Woman is important to the Keresan Pueblos (Zak, 1989). In the Plains cultural area, White Buffalo Calf Woman is critical to Lakota culture (St. Pierre & Long Solider, 1995). The Northeast Woodlands cultural area heralds Star Woman in the Iroquois creation story, as well as Sky Woman in Algonquian traditions (Fox, 1999; Leeming & Leeming, 1994). A figure called the Corn Mother has importance, but perhaps somewhat different character and functions, in several cultural areas including those of the Southwest (Hopi and Pueblo), Southeast (Cherokee and Creek), and Northeast (Iroquois). Sedna is associated with Inuit (Gill, 1987; Leeming & Leeming, 1994). Sedna, the Old Woman of the undersea world, is regarded as a highly accessible spirit in shamanistic activities (Torrance, 1994).

Interestingly, European missionaries brought the figure of the Virgin Mary to the attention of North American Indians, and many could readily accept this female figure perceived to possess a holy status. Subsequently, she became incorporated as an important personage into the cosmologies of various cultures, such as the Yaquis, who came to center on the Virgin Mary in their religious traditions (Gill, 1987). As well, among contemporary Apaches it was widely reported in the research conducted for this book that White Painted Woman and the Virgin Mary are regarded as the same being. Some even view White Buffalo Calf Woman of the Lakotas as the coming of the Virgin Mary (St. Pierre & Long Soldier, 1995).

In a pan-Indian sense there is a tendency to regard female supernatural persons as the same being because of their similar character traits. Various tribal oral traditions tell of the female personage's intimate involvement in creation and the sustainment of humans and all facets of life on Earth. The label "Mother Earth" has become a popular all-encompassing descriptor for such persons, but, as shown in the following discussion, the richness of character and functions of individual female cultural heroines of oral traditions may be overlooked by collapsing these figures into one persona.

Mother Earth or Distinct Supernatural Persons?

A question can be asked at this point in this discussion: Can these supernatural female beings be conceived as really the same person with varying names, expressions, and purposes across cultures? Two different answers can be offered. Perhaps the most popular assumption is that they all are indeed the same being and all bear the persona of a "Mother Earth" figure. The conception of one figure with numerous expressions is found in Allen's (1986) description of this multifaceted being: "Old

Spider Woman is one name for this quintessential spirit, and Serpent Woman is another. Corn Woman is one aspect of her, and Earth Woman is another, and what they together have made is called Creation, Earth, creatures, plants, and light. . . . This spirit, this power of intelligence, has many names and many emblems" (p. 13).

It is certainly tempting to aggregate these various female supernatural beings, especially the fertility-linked figures, into the popular "Mother Earth" persona that has amassed adherents among Natives and non-Natives alike. The assumption of a Mother Earth figure has largely been unquestioned. For instance, in speaking of the world's first persons, Harvey and Baring (1996) stated: "In them is preserved our original human relationship with Mother Earth in all her wisdom, humility, and divine radiance" (p. 22). The counterargument is that to reduce them to the identity of one personage is to lose their uniqueness in character and functions. As noted by Gill (1987), Mother Earth is an unproductive and inaccurate depiction because tribes had their own names and associated traits and characteristics of their female supernatural beings.[1] To collapse these characters into one central figure diminishes their unique features that bring insight into the complexities and diverse expressions found in North American Indian cultures. Indeed, even while asserting the unity of the female beings, Allen (1986) conceded that collapsing these figures into one fertility goddess is demeaning.

A brief examination of the varied functions of some of the female supernatural figures speaks to their complexity. For instance, according to Navajo beliefs, Spider Woman brought humans the skill of weaving (Reichard, 1977); while in the Hopi tradition Spider Woman's character is described as benevolent, creative, and wise with prophetic abilities (Zak, 1989). Additionally, among the Hopis and other tribes of the Southwest, Spider Woman is said to be "either the assistant to the supreme creative power or the personification of that power" (Leeming & Leeming, 1994, p. 256). Indeed, the role of assistant to the Creator is found in various Native belief systems; for instance, her role might be to instruct people as a mother does her children. Such is the case of the Corn Mother in Arikaran culture, White Buffalo Calf Woman in Lakota tradition, and Star Woman of the Pawnees and other tribes (Leeming & Leeming, 1994). Legend tells of White Buffalo Calf Woman bringing the sacred calf bundle and the seven sacred ceremonies or rites to the Lakotas in order to provide them with structure and guidance in their lives (St. Pierre & Long Soldier, 1995). Similar purposes are apparent for the Navajos' Changing Woman, who was to create humans and furnish them with instructions on proper living and practice of ceremonies, including the girls' puberty rites (Begay, 1983; Reichard, 1977; Zak, 1989).

The female supernatural being also may be the Creator herself, as ascribed to Star Woman among the Iroquois and Pawnees (Leeming & Leeming, 1994). If the female supernatural being is not the one who creates, she may be the one who causes life to occur, as is the case with Thinking or Thought Woman of the Keresan Pueblos, whose mere thoughts are said to precede action and creation (Zak, 1989). There are Iatiku and Nautsiti of Acoma tradition—figures that plant seeds and breathe life into animals (Leeming & Leeming, 1994). Sacrifice is the theme in stories of the Corn Mother, who is an important figure in numerous cultural areas (Tinker, 1998). Pueblo peoples may seek help from Clay Lady to imbue their works of pottery with beauty (Zak, 1989). Stories of creation by emergence tell of a "creative female midwife," specifically, roles played by figures such as Spider Woman and Thinking Woman (Leeming & Leeming, 1994, p. 58). The female being may offer assurance to continual well-being of people and must be approached in the proper manner. For instance, the Iniut speak of Sedna, the governess of the animals, who lives at the bottom of the sea. When taboos or rules are broken (including violations of menstrual seclusion), it is the shaman's responsibility to visit Sedna to correct the wrongs (Carmody & Carmody, 1993; Torrance, 1994).

Are the two viewpoints contradictory—can these figures be aggregated into one Mother Earth characterization, or, by reducing all of these figures to the same entity, are the complexity and intricacies of their personalities and functions lost? Perhaps this question reflects a false dichotomy and both distinctions can be accommodated. The parallels in their personalities are certainly reflective of themes of creativity, nurturance, and sustenance and offer a unifying, pan-Indian modality to Indigenous people. But, each female supernatural personage must also be recognized according to her own personality and functions in order to acquire understanding of her place in the oral traditions of a specific culture, which is the more meaningful conceptualization for the purposes of this book.

Female Supernatural Beings and Pubescent Girls

In some North American Indian cultures, it is believed that the female supernatural beings play critical functions in pubertal coming-of-age events for girls, as well as in the formation of proper character and behavior of adult women. It is useful to examine the functions of these figures as role models for girls and women. For instance, in research discussed in later chapters, the most obvious linkages are between Changing Woman and the Navajo Kinaaldá, White Painted Woman (who is also called Changing Woman) and the Apache Sunrise Dance, and White Buffalo Calf Woman and the Lakota Išnati Awicalowanpi ceremony (all are puberty ceremonies for girls). The attributes of the female personage serve as archetypes of the kinds of outcomes to be emulated in pubescent girls and to be exhibited throughout their adult lives. The proper performance of rituals during puberty ceremonies is the mechanism by which inculcation of the traits of the female supernatural being by the initiate occurs. Specifically, the core desired attributes center on personality, character, disposition, physical strength (including a long life), and physical beauty.

Character formation is an especially important desired outcome of girls' puberty ceremonies, and the character traits of the female supernatural being—her altruism, goodness, generosity, and nurturance—are to be emulated by pubescent girls. The female supernatural personage is regarded as the ideal female in these respects and is a role model for the women of her tribe. Role performance relative to gender-linked division of labor characterized North American Indian cultures and, interestingly, these practices were sometimes linked to a female supernatural being. For example, among the Inuit of Quebec, gender-linked behaviors were human parallels to events of the universe. The activity of a feminine Earth Mother, who made all humans, animals, plants, and fruits, was a model for female-linked behavior of women (Saladin d'Anglure, 1984).

As part of the female being's altruistic caring for others, there frequently is a sacrificial theme in her creative activities or in her preservation of humans. For instance, Changing Woman of the Navajos is said to have created humans with peelings or rubbings of her own skin. She is also the one held responsible for the continuous growth and renewal of all life on Earth (Zak, 1989). Similar attributes are associated with White Painted Woman of the Apaches. The theme of altruistic giving of self develops additional meaning in the linkage of the female personage to sources of human sustenance, such as corn or buffalo. Since corn is held in high esteem by numerous tribal cultures that practice some form of agriculture, it is discussed in greater detail.[2]

To many North American Indian cultures, corn has attained a sacred status and is an integral component of their oral traditions and rituals. It continues to be of vital importance to the lifestyles and ceremonial activities of many groups to this day, including various cultures in the Southwest such as Navajo, Hopi, and Pueblo groups, as well as tribes in the Northeast and Southeast cultural areas, such as the Iroquois and Cherokees. Along with beans and squash, it is one of the "three sisters" of the Iroquois. The Hopi people, more than any other, perhaps have shown the greatest interdependence with corn in the many ways it is integrated into their lives (Rhoades, 1993). In Hopi oral tradition, blue corn was embraced as their own, with other tribes selecting various other colors of corn. Corn is integrated in numerous ceremonies, such as the naming ceremony, in which a perfect ear of white corn is passed over the 20-day-old Hopi baby four times while the child is being fed blue corn mush (Rhoades, 1993). At adolescence, Hopi girls experience the coming-of-age corn-grinding ceremony, during which they grind corn for 4 days (Stanislawski, 1979). Likewise, pubescent Navajo girls grind corn and make a corn cake (*'alkąąd*) as part of their Kinaaldá (Frisbie, 1993; Schwarz, 1997).

The notion that the human race was derived from corn or maize is found in various Indian cultures (Rhoades, 1993). For instance, Tinker (1998) wrote that some version of the story of the Corn Mother is found among Indigenous cultures throughout eastern North America from Canada to Florida, as well as among Keresan Pueblos of the Southeast. In essence, this story tells of the Corn Mother who ultimately sacrificed herself to ensure the survival of humans (see Awiakta, 1993, for the story of the origin of corn). This female supernatural person is sometimes represented as ears of corn, which may explain the sacred status that corn has acquired in numerous North American Indian cultures. As noted by Markstrom and Iborra (2003), corn is symbolic of food, fertility, and life, and among horticultural peoples, "corn was variously seen as a gift from the mother-creator, mother corn, the spirit of corn, corn maidens or corn women" (Bolt, 1987, p. 264). In telling a version of the story of the Corn Mother, Galloway (1997) explained that wherever her blood touched the earth, corn sprang up. She offered this insight on the story: "This is as clear a connection as could be desired between female fertility, of which blood is the sign, and agricultural fertility, of which female blood is the cause" (p. 58).

For the Lakotas, the central item was not corn but rather buffalo (*tatanka*). The female personage, White Buffalo Calf Woman, is associated with the buffalo, the most important historical food source of this group. The buffalo was not only the primary source of food but also contributed to clothing and shelter needs and most accurately represented the totality of all of life. The buffalo continues to be held in high esteem by the Lakotas, as is White Buffalo Calf Woman, who is perceived as a manifestation of the buffalo (Zak, 1989). Indeed, in Black Elk's telling of the first puberty ceremony of a girl, named White Buffalo Calf Woman Appears (J. E. Brown, 1953/1989), the initial officiator of the event, White Buffalo, received a vision of a buffalo mother cleaning its calf and equated this act with the preparation of a girl for womanhood (see chapter 8).

Returning to the feminine in cosmology, the interconnecting threads among the various female supernatural beings are their femininity, their linkage to fertility (in the broadest sense), and their creative and re-creative processes in the Earth's annual renewal. Indeed, Koehler (1997) asserted that the presence of the "Earth Mother" figure in North American Indian cosmologies extends to conceptions of women as the "creative agent, reproductively, productively, and cosmologically" (p. 211). It can be speculated that because of the quality of connection between the feminine in cosmology and women's traditional roles, the matrilineal form of descent has been the most common among North American Indians. For instance, in oral tradition, Changing Woman of the Navajos is associated with the Earth, and in that capacity she is believed to regulate all of life and is responsible for the annual rejuvenation of the Earth through the changing of seasons. Her creative capacities extend to humans, to whom she ensures fertility.

However, fertility, which may appear to be the obvious linkage between the female supernatural person and the female pubescent, is actually a more distant connection when the functions of girls' coming-of-age ceremonies are considered (as discussed in chapter 3). This point was further delineated relative to Schlegel and Barry's (1980) finding that the reinforcement of responsibility was the primary focus of girls' puberty ceremonies among North American Indians, with the promotion of future physical and spiritual well-being of initiates as additional foci. In short, it would be erroneous to conclude that the primary function of the female supernatural being relative to female pubescence and adulthood is fertility, even in those societies where pubertal coming-of-age practices occur. The important focus is the pubescent girl's connection with the spiritual realm in terms of her welfare and that of her social group. That is, the pubescent, at that time of life, now becomes part of the universal life cycle that includes all facets of existence and the continuation of all forms of life as well as a certain quality of life for herself and her associates.

Nonetheless, pubertal coming-of-age ceremonies coincide with menarche or occur shortly thereafter, and the feminine components in cosmology are believed to play critical roles in the girl's coming-of-age. Menstruation is a physical marker of a developmental transition, but it signifies much more than reproductive capacity. As discussed in chapter 3, North American Indians regard pubescence as a critical stage of the life span. Further, early adolescence, across cultures and time, has been associated with the age of reason according to advancements in the cognitive capacities of young persons (chapter 1). Hence, a female role model that embodies desired traits as expressed in oral tradition has something to offer the adolescent girl at this pivotal time of the life span. Of particular value in some North American Indian cultures, then, is the shaping of the initiate according to the female being's character and physique, and the opportunity for empowerment offered to the initiate. These desired outcomes are perceived to advance positive development of adolescent girls, propelling them forward on a promising trajectory of life. The numerous examples of puberty rituals in subsequent chapters certainly illustrate more specifically the desired outcomes. In the instruction of initiates according to their responsibility toward others, the oral traditions speak of caretaking, nurturance, and sacrifice—traits that women will be required to exhibit in life as daughters, partners, and mothers. The major point of this section is that, for some cultures, the feminine elements associated with tribal oral traditions and beliefs are intricately linked to the optimal development of adolescent girls, and puberty is deemed the best time to facilitate connection between the female initiate and her role model of oral tradition.

Feminist Considerations

The overall purpose of this chapter is to provide understanding on the status of women in North American Indian cultures, particularly in respect to practices and beliefs that affect pubescent girls. The previous sections on the perceptions of menstruation and the feminine in cosmology advanced knowledge on the topic. In essence, this chapter is interested in feminist topics—the status of women, perceptions of women, and women's experiences. In this last section of the chapter, a more specific attempt is made to answer the following question: What contribution does a feminist perspective make to an understanding of menstrual customs, the feminine in cosmology, and girls' puberty ceremonies of North American Indians?

From the onset, it is necessary to acknowledge the multiplicity of feminist viewpoints (e.g., liberal feminism, radical feminism, socialist feminism, etc.). In short, there is not one unitary feminist theory. Many of the feminist frameworks, particularly in the earlier phase of this current era of feminism, were generated according to the experiences of mainstream, middle-class white feminists. In contrast, in recent years approaches to feminist concerns have been developed explicitly to reflect the experiences of women of color. Feminist concepts and frameworks related to topics of gender roles and public and private spheres, cultural feminism, and women of color offer some basis for consideration relative to the topic of this chapter. These frameworks are presented and analyzed according to the kinds of interpretations they might offer on menstrual customs and puberty observances, as well as gender roles and other matters of concern relating to North American Indian women. Following discussion of these mainline Western approaches, an attempt is made to present a more culturally relevant analysis of North American Indian feminist approaches to the topics of interest.

Gender Roles and Public and Private Spheres

Gender roles are social constructions, as opposed to biological givens, which are ascribed to individuals based on their biological sex. Works by psychologists, sociologists, and family scientists of the mid-20th century dichotomized men and women according to masculine versus feminine traits or instrumental versus expressive traits and further promoted the idea that distinction in gender roles was innate, normal, and desirable. Complementarity in men's and women's roles was valued and thought to be a sustaining force for the entire community (e.g., Fox, 1999). In a critique of the fallacies of gender-role constructions, Trebilcot (1984) explained that society encouraged the appropriate adoption of men's and women's roles because innate psychological differences were believed to exist between the two groups. The argument continued that because of innate psychological differences, gender roles were inevitable, and individuals would be happier and better adjusted if they adopted the appropriate gender roles according to their biological sex. Then, tasks would be performed in more efficient manners. In Western society, the ascription of gender roles according to sex has been one mechanism used to diminish the power and status of women.

A further elaboration of conceptions on gender roles was the notion that men and women were distinguished according to their natural proclivity toward public or private domains (an idea that originated in the 19th century) (Osmond & Thorne, 1993). Women's domain and sphere of influence was centered in the privacy of the home, within which domestic and affective roles prevailed. Men, due to a perception of their possession of innate instrumental characteristics, were argued to be best suited for activities in the more brutal public world. This thinking has received sharp criticism from feminist scholars, in part due to the nature of characteristics ascribed to men and women and the power dynamics implicit in such inscriptions, as stated by J. M. White and Klein (2002): "The idea that women's and men's experience is divided into fairly distinct sectors is viewed by feminists as a means to organize people into social classes based on gender" (p. 181).

If these thoughts from the non-Native feminist movement were applied without regard to the power constructions and their meanings in North American Indian societies, girls' puberty ceremonies and menstrual seclusion of women might be abhorred. In short, the ceremonies would likely be viewed as institutionalized attempts to reinforce expected roles for women, thereby keeping them marginalized in society with restricted options. Puberty ceremonies might be regarded as glorifications of the feminine gender role in order to encourage women to accept their expected domestic roles with the associated diminishment of power. The leadership roles of men in puberty ceremonies of girls—as medicine men, singers, fathers, and other helpers—might be viewed as attempts of patriarchal control over the destiny of women. Men would have a vested interest in ensuring that women accept their place in the social order and adopt their expected roles, since the survival of male supremacy would depend on such outcomes.

There are several obvious problems with the previous interpretation relative to North American Indian culture. Most notably, it is important to recognize that this type of feminist response to ascribed gender roles and public and private distinctions of the home and broader society evolved from predominantly mainstream white feminists responding to a patriarchal society. In contrast, North American Indian societies are highly represented by matrilocal residence patterns and matrilineal descent patterns (Jaimes & Halsey, 1992). It would be erroneous to conclude that North American Indian societies are matriarchal (signifying women have greater power than men), but matrilocal and matrilineal characteristics provide women with a certain degree of power. True, gender-linked roles were the norm in North American Indian societies, but the meanings relative to perceived power associated with these roles cannot be compared to the diminished power associated with the feminine/expressive role in the patriarchal European American society. As stated by Maltz and Archambault (1995) in respect to Native North America, "it is a region in which gender is central to the cultural system but not closely linked to either biology or power" (p. 231). As explained by Witt (1984): "Although the lives of Native American women differed greatly from tribe to tribe, their life-styles exhibited a great deal more independence and security than those of the European women who came to these shores. Indian women had individual freedom within tribal life that women in more 'advanced' societies were not to experience for several generations" (p. 25). It is significant to consider that North American Indian women subsequently lost power through disruptions in their traditional societies due to contact from European patriarchal colonizers (Allen, 1986; Mihesuah, 2003). In short, gender relations in North American Indian societies must be assessed without the bias of non-Native frameworks. A culturally relativist interpretation of gender-typed behavior in North American Indian societies is more fully explored in the last section of this chapter.

Cultural Feminism

Another expression of Western feminism, cultural feminism, essentially argues for the elevation of the status of women according to reevaluation of the value of women's character and attributes. In contrast to the previous view of feminism, this approach promotes the celebration of women's culture, spirituality, and sexuality, with diminished value on traits of masculinity and, in some cases, male biology (Alcoff, 1995). In its most radical form, cultural feminism proffers the idea that society should be reorganized around women's values, with maleness and testosterone appearing as the antithesis of such values. A problem of cultural feminism in its extreme form is that the elevation of the female experience operates in a manner similar to patriarchy by separating men and women through an exaggeration of differences and further asserts the superiority of the feminine over the masculine. The rhetoric of this movement is utopian in form, for instance as promoted by McKee (1989), "envisioning one world civilization based upon the ideals of unity within diversity, the integrity of all life-forms, and interdependence for our mutual well-being" (p. 253).

On the surface, cultural feminism may appear to offer some application to analysis of the experiences of North American Indian women.

The inclusion of the feminine in North American Indian cosmologies could serve as an argument for the elevated status of women within these societies. The female puberty ceremony, which is frequently regarded as a celebration, and in some cases connects the initiate to the female supernatural being, appears consistent with cultural feminism. Certainly, current New Age attraction to the cult of the goddess and associated attempts to misappropriate the female supernatural beings of North American Indian creation stories fits this type of pro-woman agenda and has some appeal among adherents. The female supernatural beings of North American Indian traditions, then, become linked to a cultural feminist agenda that is biased in favoring the feminine with diminished regard for the masculine.

The elevation of the female over the male is highly contradictory to North American Indian cultures, which are notorious in their value for balance in character, including masculine and feminine traits, within both males and females. A further problem occurs with misapplication and sometimes misappropriation of North American Indian cosmic beliefs in that selected components are taken out of the larger cultural contexts within which these beliefs are embedded and have their most complete meaning. There may be a tendency to overly exaggerate and reframe the connection of the female supernatural person to the female puberty ceremony. Certainly, it cannot be ignored that in the beliefs of groups such as the Apaches and the Navajos the initiate is identified with and believed to be actually transformed into the primary supernatural female being of her culture. Further, the female puberty ceremony frequently is a celebration and reinforcement of positive feminine traits. Nonetheless, the ceremony is not just for the initiate and for women. The functions are believed to have broad implications for the ongoing survival and maintenance of all men and women in the initiate's group and, in many cases, to the entire world. Further, while the feminine appears to be emphasized in female puberty ceremonies, masculine traits are also accentuated, as discussed in this book.

Another erroneous portrayal of North American Indian women that is promoted perhaps by Indian and non-Indian alike is a representation of traditional Native culture as matriarchal and, to an extreme, a female utopia, ideas that Maltz and Archambault (1995) disputed and

J. M. Cooper argued as far back as 1932 that there was no evidence in the world for matriarchies. Depicting North American Indian societies as women-centered is an exaggeration of the historical and cultural facts. It misrepresents these cultures and peoples, and it fails to recognize the realities of human error, harsh living conditions, warfare, conflict, and the realities of family life (Maltz & Archambault, 1995). It also minimizes the existence of between-group diversity, specifically, the varied statuses of women across North American Indian tribes.

The elevation of the female experience to levels that are not reflective of the realities of life for women in a variety of cultures has also found some expression in new perspectives on menstruation discussed by Knight (1991). While the newer feminist interpretations of menstruation might be improvements over earlier ideas that concluded menstrual taboos were expressions of male dominance, it is not useful to overly elevate the status of women and misinterpret the meaning of menstruation. Ideas consistent with cultural feminism have found expression in the interesting but controversial writings of Allen (1986, 1991), in which traditional American Indian societies are portrayed according to their "gynocentric" social systems. While criticism of these writings on the feminine in cosmology and society may seem in contradiction to the previous portion of this chapter in which menstrual fluid was stated to be a power in the beliefs of North American Indians, the present discussion provides a cautionary note to not overly interpret the feminine in North American Indian cultures. While many of these cultures regarded menstruation and menstrual fluid as power, it was a power among other sources of power within a culture. Further, the notion of power must be understood within its cultural context as does the status of women.

Women of Color

Feminist writings in the 1960s and 1970s centered on the experiences of middle-class white women and attempted to unify women according to universal experiences of sexism. Women of color found little in these works that represented their own experiences, in which racism, sexism, and classism intersected. Additionally, lower-class white women had little to relate to in the writings of their middle-class counterparts. Hence, today's expressions of feminism are much more complex and diverse in form in an attempt to account for the multiplicity of women's experiences. Hood (1984) explained the issues at hand: "Racism and sexism (both of which include class distinctions) are then the intertwining oppressive structures operating under paternalistic patriarchalism" (p. 190). While sexism is the one unifying theme of all women in North America, racism and classism weigh heavily in the equation. Indeed, from the perspective of women of color, racism is regarded as the most insidious form of oppression, because not only do men benefit from the oppression of women of color, but so do white women (especially middle-and upper-class women) (Hood, 1984; Osmond & Thorne, 1993). For instance, women of color have played long-standing roles as paid domestic laborers for white families (Osmond & Thorne, 1993).

The literature on women of color has predominantly expressed the experiences of African American women, with little attention given to the realities of North American Indian women. Witt (1984) spoke of the "invisible Native women" (p. 23) due to the fact that portrayals of Native Americans in legend or through the media have tended to focus on male figures. Perhaps one explanation for this absence is that the early explorers and historians who had contact with Native cultures were male and would have experienced greater social inclusion within the male sphere. White men would not have had access to the multitude of formal and informal sources of women's interaction that would occur in the mundane experiences of work and home, as well as in the ritual and ceremony surrounding puberty and menstrual customs.

Scholarly works on North American Indian women have also been largely absent until recent years. Further, as in the case of scholarly works across all racial groups, the focus has tended to be on men, with generalizations of that knowledge to women. If North American Indian women are not being compared to their male counterparts, they are compared to white women (Silvey, 1999). Further, North American Indian women have typically been examined in respect to stereotypically expressive roles (e.g., child rearing, domestic tasks, and emotional links to the family), resulting in perhaps a distorted perception of their lifestyles and activities (Silvey, 1999). This issue receives some elaboration in the last section of this chapter.

In further applying the perspective of women of color to an understanding of North American Indian women, it is useful to deconstruct some of the long-standing myths that have proliferated about North American Indian women and gender relations. A common myth is of the sacrifices willingly made by the Indian woman to aid and join the white man—the assumption being that her situation in life would improve and that she would be treated with greater kindness. North American Indian women did form various forms of unions with white men, such as occurred for Pocahontas and Sacajawea, but these historical figures are perhaps perceived differently by Natives and non-Natives (Witt, 1984). A related myth was that Native men exploited and abused their women and that women were drudges. But, as pointed out by Bolt (1987), the construction of this myth served to justify efforts to transform American Indian males into farmers, to turn their wives into homemakers, and to sell surplus lands to white settlers. A common myth was that North American Indian women were passive and peaceful and that men were the warlike members of tribal societies. In reality, Indian women did engage in warfare, such as was found among the Blackfeet (Kehoe, 1995; also see Jaimes & Halsey, 1992). Women also encouraged men to pursue warfare to avenge the loss of relatives, as was the case with the Iroquois (Prezzano, 1997). A complement to the myth of the passive Native woman is that of the Indian princess, which, as Vine Deloria (1969) explains, European Americans have an inclination to claim in their ancestry.

In summarizing this section of the chapter, it can be stated that it is not appropriate to analyze North American Indian puberty rituals of girls, menstrual customs, and experiences of Native women according to European American–based feminist approaches. Gender-role theory interprets gender-role distinctions according to patriarchal societal conceptions of power, and as a result, Native cultures may be misconstrued as misogynist. On the other hand, cultural feminism can overly inflate the inclusion of the feminine in North American Indian cultures and oral traditions and further misinterpret the meanings of cultural practices. The major source of contention for women of color is that the white feminist movement has not adequately addressed the additional impacts of race and class to the oppression of women. This form of feminism has the most to offer in consideration of the realities of life for North American Indian women both in the past and the present. The next task at hand represents an attempt to construct a more culturally sensitive and relevant interpretation of girls' puberty ceremonies and the status of North American Indian women.

Culturally Relevant Feminist Interpretations

According to Laguna/Sioux writer Paula Gunn Allen (1986), "A feminist approach to the study and teaching of American Indian life and thought is essential because the area has been dominated by paternalistic, male-dominant modes of consciousness since the first writings about American Indians in the fifteenth century" (p. 222). An underlying value of feminist work is to situate the voices of women in the forefront relative to conveying their experiences, perceptions, and modes of understanding. Such a philosophy is of particular importance in writings on North American Indian women, because their experiences have generally been presented in the literature from both non-Native and non-female perspectives (Silvey, 1999). Virtually all aspects of North American Indian life were adversely affected by European contact (as discussed in chapter 2), as was certainly the case for the status of women. For instance, problems experienced today in some Native communities, such as intimate partner violence, are believed to be influenced in part by diminished status and loss of respect of women, the loss of men's traditional roles, substance abuse, and other factors related to colonization. These contributing factors should not be used to excuse the violence, but they do contribute to an understanding of it. The traditional roles of North American Indian men and women and the status afforded women (particularly in comparison to that of European women) were challenged by the European colonizers. Hence, Native women's traditional influence and power was undermined (Jaimes & Halsey, 1992). As stated previously, J. M. Cooper (1932) concluded, based on a global assessment, that the status of women was higher than what was commonly thought to be the case in the so-called primitive societies and that the status of women had actually been diminished with the rise in material culture. A Native viewpoint on the topic, also from the early 20th century, is from Dakota writer Charles Eastman (Ohiyesa) (1911), who described the empowered status of women of his culture and the subsequent destruction of it along with the traditional matrilineal household: "Thus she ruled undisputed within her own domain, and was to us a tower of moral and spiritual strength, until the coming of the border white man, the soldier and trader, who with strong drink overthrew the honor of the man, and through his power over a worthless husband purchased the virtue of his wife or his daughter. When she fell, the whole race fell with her" (p. 42).

It is useful to examine the status of North American Indian women in their traditional societies and the utility and meaning of gender-typed socialization and expectations for behavior. These topics have direct bearing on girls' puberty ceremonies; for instance, a common practice at these ceremonies is socialization of young women for full incorporation in their cultures and in adult roles. The emphasis on the content of this instruction can easily be misinterpreted. Hence, it must be remembered that traditional socialization of young women toward adoption of prescribed gender-linked behaviors and roles does not represent patriarchal control of women; rather, this represents an effort to promote efficient social organization for the overall well-being of the kin group and tribe. This present form of socialization is reflective of values and practices of the past that still have relevance in these largely communal cultures. For instance, the Blackfeet believed, as did numerous other cultures, that men and women were necessary pairs that ensured survival of the group through their performance of complementary roles (Fox, 1999; Kehoe, 1995). In particular, in Native North America there was recognition that the roles of women were necessary for the continuance of the people in a cultural context (Fox, 1999; Jaimes & Halsey, 1992). Even in North American Indian societies that were patrilineal, women were recognized for their roles as mothers and keepers and carriers of the culture (Fox, 1999).

From the reading of earlier European-based historical and anthropological accounts of the status of women in North American Indian societies, one acquires an impression that women were suppressed in power and exploited in practice. The practice of polygyny, which was fairly common, was sometimes cited as evidence for the low status of women. It also was observed that heavy demands of physical labor expected of Native women indicated their oppressive condition. In consideration of polygyny, a fair number of Native cultures engaged in this practice, and Europeans assumed that this marital form placed women in inferior positions. When practices of polygyny and female hardship are interpreted from culturally relativistic points of view, very different conclusions can be reached from those previously mentioned. For instance, examination of polygyny within its appropriate cultural context reveals that multiple wives were commonly sisters or related women who preferred not to be separated (Bolt, 1987). These women, presumably, shared in household and child-rearing tasks (Fox, 1999). Shimkin (1986) observed that the position of Eastern Shoshone women was paradoxical because their social position was thought to be subordinate to men due to polygyny and related practices, but these women possessed survival skills of value to the group and obtained individual successes later in life through midwifery, curing, or gambling. The Subarctic Chipewyan culture is another in which women were thought to be especially subject to male dominance and abuse, but Sharp (1995) challenged this notion and stated that the sexes operated as asymmetric equals; that is, men and women had separate but equally valued roles.

Relative to the Gwich'in, Osgood (1936/1970) offered an interpretation that accounted for the realities of life for men and women. Earlier explorers and writers had commented on subservient roles of Gwich'in women; for instance, they would carry the heavy items when the band was in transit, while the men seemed to be at leisure and carried only their guns. In reality, in this hunting society, men were always alert for prey and would have been encumbered in their role to meet subsistence needs if laden with heavy materials. These people frequently lived on the edge of survival, and the procurement of food was of utmost importance. A further erroneous conclusion on the perceived inferiority of women was based on the common practice of women eating after serving the men. This practice was found in many cultures, but relative to the Gwich'in, Osgood (1936/1970) noted that men would hunt for hours or days and frequently go without food. For this reason, upon their return they were the first to be fed. Women, as the domestics, had access to food and could break from work in their villages and homes to obtain nourishment when it was available.

Women held authority in the home, and this afforded them a degree of status and power. The home was the female domain, just as the outside world was the male domain (Osgood, 1936/1970). Of course, this hearkens back to the previous discussion on private and public domains of women and men; however, it must be remembered that the meanings of these private and public domains in North American Indian societies were not parallel to European American society. There was in the former a strong value of both home life and distant food procurement activities in recognition of the multiple roles needed for the survival of men, women, and children. Hence, in Native sex-segregated societies, men and women each had their sphere of influence and power. Further, Klein (1995) questioned the centrality of supposed influence of private and public domains and reasoned, instead, relative to Tlingit society, that kinship and wealth were the more powerful variables in power dynamics.

The assumption that North American Indian women were exclusively domestics (which frequently included gathering or agriculture) and not involved in hunting activities also warrants closer inspection. Pregnancy and child care were frequent explanations given for the constrained lifestyle of North American Indian women. However, Brumbach and Jarvenpa (1997) provided compelling evidence from Chipewyan culture (in both historical and contemporary times) that women were more heavily involved in hunting activities than was previously thought to be the case. In short, the assumption that North American Indian societies operated according to strict division of labor according to sex might have been exaggerated and warrants further investigation.

The acquisition of power was a major goal in many North American Indian cultures, and power came in various forms to men and women and could be of both secular and spiritual forms (e.g., see Patterson, 1995). For the Blackfeet an economic form of power was available to men and women, and women's economic power was reflected in myth and ritual, as explained by Kehoe (1995): "Women are seen as the intermediary or means through which power has been granted to humans. This crucial role appears in medicine bundled openings: only a woman should unwrap and rewrap a holy bundle" (p. 116). Blackfeet women were viewed as possessors of a greater degree of innate power due to their reproductive potential. In contrast, men had to vigorously pursue power through impassioned vision quests during which they would plead for power from spiritual helpers (Kehoe, 1995).

In both historical and current conceptions of women from various North American Indian cultures, women are regarded as innately possessing spiritual powers. Further, elderly women are regarded for possession of both spiritual and social authority (Jaimes & Halsey, 1992; Martin, 2001). A common perception is that women in Inuit society were particularly oppressed by their male counterparts; however, Guemple (1995) asserted that men and women of the Arctic shared equally in the shaman role. Ackerman (1995) observed that among tribes of the Plateau cultural area, male and female shamans were equal in number, or, in some cases, the number of male shamans outnumbered the female. Nonetheless, in either case their abilities were equal. Among the patrilineal Ojibwas, women were medicine persons and played roles in ceremonies and rituals, as well as curing sicknesses with herbal remedies (Fox, 1999). Also, Iroquois women, especially those of the Bear clan, were members of medicine societies and practiced the healing arts (Fox, 1999). In short, there are numerous illustrations for the spiritual authority of women, which is suggestive of their authority in social realms.

The power of women in North American Indian societies is also evident according to their activities in political realms such as in their integral roles in tribal decision making and the selection of leaders. Iroquois society is not a true matriarchy, but it is a society in which women held a great deal of power and considerable influence over the male hunt, warpath, and council (Bolt, 1987).[3] Residence was matrilocal, descent was matrilineal, and women owned the fields, crops, and houses (Bilharz, 1995; Fox, 1999; Niethammer, 1977; Prezzano, 1997). Perhaps more importantly, the matron of a lineage selected the male relative to serve as leader and represent the group at council and could remove this man from his position if she and others were not pleased with his representation. Iroquois women also had considerable influence in the determination of the fates of captives (Fox, 1999; Martin, 2001).

Political power among North American Indian women also was evident among the Cherokees, among whom women sat on council with the men. In speaking of the necessity of gender balance in society, contemporary Cherokee writer Marilou Awiakta (1993) related the following incident: "'Where are your women?' The speaker is Attakullakulla, a Cherokee chief renowned for his shrewd and effective diplomacy. He has come to negotiate a treaty with the whites. Among his delegation are women 'as famous in war, as powerful in the council.' Their presence also has ceremonial significance: it is meant to show honor to the other delegation. But that delegation is composed of males only; to them the absence of women is irrelevant, a trivial consideration" (p. 92). Various other cultures recognized women as leaders of the clan (e.g., Hopis), or a woman who might be called a "woman chief," as in the case of an Apache woman married to a chief (Niethammer, 1977). Even in the Subarctic cultural area, where the status of women was thought to be lower than in other areas, Osgood (1936/1970) commented that Gwich'in women did not generally attend council, but older ones could listen, and "If the men appear to be making fools of themselves, some old woman may get up and give them a piece of her mind. The old woman's right to do so is recognized and some are respected as very intelligent advisers" (p. 110).

In short, according to several writers the status of North American Indian women was greater than what has been presented in the literature, and certainly their status was higher than that of their European American female counterparts (Allen, 1986; Witt, 1984). However, this statement also needs to be approached with accuracy and precision. While some writers presented the viewpoint that at one extreme Indian women were exploited in their cultures, another belief is encountered at the other extreme, which misrepresents Indian societies as matriarchies—a term that is the counterpart of patriarchy and is in reference to the sex with the greatest power. There is no evidence of a female-dominated or female-controlled North American Indian society (i.e., matriarchy). Consistent with previous comments in this chapter, it can be more precisely stated that most North American Indian nations practiced matrilineal descent patterns and matrilocal residence patterns (Jaimes & Halsey, 1992), practices that afforded them greater power. Hence, traditional North American Indian societies might best be viewed as egalitarian—or, at the very least, as more egalitarian than the highly patriarchal European societies that they encountered. Indeed, this conclusion is similar to that of J. M. Cooper (1932) of some time ago regarding women in North American Indian and other traditional societies: "While, however, she seems not to have attained a markedly higher status than man, she is on the other hand rarely the abject inferior, slave, or drudge that she is so often pictured to be" (p. 42).

To bring some empirical support to this discussion, it is useful to further examine findings of Schlegel (1972) on the variable of domestic authority type (i.e., husband-dominant, brother-dominant, neither-dominant). It was found that North American nonindustrial societies (i.e., Indigenous) were strongly neither-dominant (i.e., women were not dominated by their husbands or brothers). When the domestic authority types were examined for worldwide data, the husband-dominant type was suggestive of less power of women, while the neither-dominant type was suggestive of greater power for women. For instance, in neither-dominant societies there was an apparent decrease in the practice of polygyny and a greater occurrence of the practice of matrilocal residence. Matrilocal residence was also associated with brother-dominant societies. Schlegel summarized her findings in the following way: "The Neither Dominant category is strongly associated with the variables related to high female autonomy, while women under the authority of either husband or brother tend to have less control over person and property and a less significant role in broader societal activities" (p. 106).

It is useful to expand this discussion further and consider sexual division of labor and social organization of societies, as studied by Schlegel and Barry (1986) in their analysis of societies represented in the Standard Cross-Cultural Sample. Their major finding was that in those societies with greater involvement of women in procurement of the food supply (i.e., food-gathering or-collecting, agricultural, or horticultural societies), women had higher status and were less likely to be perceived as objects primarily for male sexual gratification or reproduction. Schlegel and Barry further reported that North American nonindustrial societies fell somewhat in the middle relative to other world areas in female contribution to subsistence. While in many North American Indian societies women were engaged in horticultural and agricultural activities, many other societies were characterized as subsisting on the activities of males relative to fishing and hunting. This latter pattern is reflective more so among the northern areas where the climate is less conducive to agriculture and plant and fruit gathering. Relative to the Schlegel and Barry finding, then, the status of women is lower among those societies that rely on the fishing and hunting activities of men for subsistence. However, this conclusion is derived from worldwide data and was not analyzed separately for North American Indians. Further, the assumption that women were not involved in subsistence activities in societies dominated by hunting and fishing should be questioned, because women were involved in processing and preparing game. Sharp (1995) particularly noted the role of Chipewyan women in converting the raw meat brought by the men into food, and Brumbach and Jarvenpa (1997) concluded that the role of women in hunting activities in Chipewyan culture has been underestimated.

In summarizing various comments on the status of women according to societal characteristics, it can be stated that matrilineal descent was frequently an outgrowth of matrilocal residence (Bolt, 1987), and there is an association of both forms with agricultural societies in which women had considerable involvement with the land and held ownership of the fields (Witt, 1984). In reviewing several studies on Native women and power, Maltz and Archambault (1995) concluded that "women have more power when descent is matrilineal, residence is matrilocal, restrictions on female sexuality are limited, men are frequently absent due to involvement in activities such as warfare, or women have some veto power, if not control, over some formal political, military, or religious offices" (p. 236). An illustration of such a society is the Iroquois nation, which was described in precontact terms by Bilharz (1995) as having "complementary gender roles with matrilineal descent and matrilocal residence suitable for a horticultural society where males were often absent hunting or on the warpath" (p. 107).

The prevailing themes that emerge from a feminist reinterpretation of gender-related concepts among North American Indians are that although gender division of labor was broadly practiced, there was more role flexibility than previously thought, and it represented something very different among these cultures than in European American society. In examination of an edited volume by Klein and Ackerman (1995) on gender in Native North America, the authors use various terms that are best descriptive of the status of women and gender relations, such as "complementarity," "asymmetric equals," "complementary but equal," and "egalitarian." In short, it was most typical in North American Indian societies, relative to social and gender relationships, for organization to occur around kinship as opposed to patterns of dominance reflected in hierarchical power dynamics, Further, adoption of appropriate roles was an efficient mechanism to ensure survival of the group, in some cases where life and death weighed heavily on a daily basis.

Conclusions and Summary

In summarizing the content of this chapter, it is useful to examine implications relative to the girls' puberty ceremony. In more specific examination of the social characteristics of societies and their practice of puberty ceremonies from an evolutionary perspective, Schlegel and Barry (1980) observed that puberty ceremonies for girls were more common in food-collecting societies and that such a societal pattern predominated in Native North American, where women were "a scarce and valued resource" (p. 711). Further, the purposes of these ceremonies went far beyond a reproductive function. Schlegel and Barry cross-tabulated the variable "focus of puberty ceremonies" according to subsistence patterns, and they summarized the predominant theme of puberty ceremonies for girls in food-collecting societies in the following way: "the focus of the ceremony is the protection of the girl, and the ceremony is conducted for her future physical and spiritual well-being. The picture conveyed by initiation ceremonies in simple societies is one of high evaluation of females, who are given social recognition and possibly magical protection as well" (p. 711). This statement is quite consistent with my field research on Apache and Navajo puberty ceremonies (described in later chapters). Reproductive viability is a less central purpose of ceremonies of these and many other North American Indian cultures. Rather, the assurance of lifelong well-being for females is a major goal, and ceremonies at puberty are designed to impart power and protection to girls (as discussed in chapter 3). In short, the functions of puberty ceremonies are indicative of a high value of women and of the belief that women possess life-giving properties that encompass multiple dimensions of activity supportive of group maintenance and well-being.

As stated previously, an erroneous conclusion can be made that puberty rituals and ceremonies for North American Indian girls reinforce gender-typed roles of women that serve to oppress or control women's destinies. In contrast, as shown in this chapter, North American Indian women were afforded status and power as carriers and conveyors of the culture (Fox, 1999; Jaimes & Halsey, 1992; Silvey, 1999). Gender-linked tasks of both men and women were regarded as necessary for the survival of the group. Hence, women's tasks were not viewed as less important or weaker—attitudes that would diminish the status of women. It is not appropriate to impose European American models of feminism that could lead to misinterpretation of the status of North American Indian women and gender relations. Core problems are beliefs in white supremacy and white privilege and practices of colonialism—factors that have had adverse effects for all Indigenous people of the Americas (e.g., see Allen, 1986; Jaimes & Halsey, 1992; Mihesuah, 2003). Unfortunately, colonization practices have served to undermine traditional values that affirmed women, and in the process of becoming decolonized, Native peoples are faced with the task of reaffirming the status and value of women in their cultures.

In this light, puberty ceremonies that acknowledge and celebrate the contributions of women bring status and recognition to them by reaffirming their important traditional roles in societies. When the initiate is connected to a highly regarded female supernatural being of oral tradition, such as Changing Woman of the Navajos, her status and the status of all women is raised (Shepardson, 1995). There appears to be implicit recognition that all of life is sacred, and women, through their innate qualities and contributions to the maintenance of life, serve very sacred purposes. As demonstrated in this chapter, it is essential to probe meanings and interpretations according to the perspectives of the peoples and cultures in which beliefs, attitudes, and practices are embedded. The next chapter presents a range of puberty observances for girls according to cultural areas. The present discussion serves to encourage the reader to consider these customs within their appropriate cultural contexts.

CHAPTER FIVE

Historical Overview of Coming-of-Age Practices

□   □   □

The aim of this chapter is to provide readers with a greater appreciation of the diverse range of puberty and coming-of-age practices according to cultural areas. The content of this chapter consists of concrete illustrations in support of the beliefs about pubescent females discussed in chapter 3. This review is not designed to be systematically comprehensive or analytically scientific in nature; rather, the purpose is to provide readers with some substance to their understanding of the breadth of puberty customs. The review is compiled from a combination of primary source (historical and anthropological) and secondary source documents. As a secondary source, the Smithsonian *Handbook of North American Indians* has been of immeasurable use in this review, at the very least to acquire a cursory understanding of puberty and coming-of-age observances across a broad range of cultures.

This chapter is structured around 10 North American Indian cultural areas located more or less north of Mexico; examples are presented separately for girls and boys relative to the cultural areas. The inclusion of boys in this historical overview facilitates deeper understanding of the similarities and differences according to coming-of-age of both sexes. After a broad descriptive overview of girls' and boys' puberty rites, themes are identified and discussed according to some of the more compelling components of the review of literature.

The very useful organization scheme of the 10 cultural areas follows commonly used delineations in the literature (e.g., the Smithsonian *Handbook of North American Indians*). The underlying rationale of the cultural area scheme is that Indigenous groups within a particular geographical area share commonalities in culture more so than they do with groups in other cultural areas. Shared customs of groups within a cultural area certainly are a function of geographic propinquity, with related factors of climate, topography, and access to sources of subsistence. Nonetheless, between-group diversity exists within any particular cultural area. It is also apparent that many practices are shared across cultural areas, such as the seclusion or separation of girls at menarche. Four of the cultural areas include Indigenous groups located in the United States (i.e., Southeast, Southwest, California, and Great Basin), with Southwest and California cultures overlapping into Mexico. The remaining cultural areas (Plains, Northeast, Plateau, Northwest Coast, Subarctic, and Arctic) encompass groups located in both the United States and Canada. The construction of international boundaries is a phenomenon that has little meaning for individuals whose fellow tribal and band family members live across borders.

Illustrations of pubertal coming-of-age customs were limited for some areas (e.g., Southeast and Arctic), while there were much larger bodies of literature available on other areas (e.g., California). There are two potential reasons for voids in the literature: either there were few puberty customs actually practiced, or there was an absence of historical writings and anthropological studies among certain groups and/or cultural areas. Unless otherwise stated, the coming-of-age rituals reviewed are centered on historical customs and practices. Some of the rituals may continue to the present day, and mention is made in such cases when known.

Girls' Coming-of-Age

Plains

The Great Plains encompass a broad region from the Mississippi River valley of the East to the Rocky Mountains of the West, and extend from Texas into the prairies of southern Canada. Numerous tribes are associated with this area, and a wide variety of customs are apparent. Seclusion or confinement at first menses and sometimes for each subsequent menses was the most common puberty custom for girls of the Plains area, as well as those of other cultural areas. Interpretative analysis of the practice of seclusion was discussed in chapter 4 and is addressed more completely later in this chapter. Comanches practiced seclusion at menses (Kavanagh, 2001),[1] as did various groups of the Sioux, who required seclusion of the girl at her first and all subsequent menstrual cycles (DeMallie, 2001b).[2] Santee Sioux required girls to engage in ritual fasting and seclusion at the onset of menses (Albers, 2001). Pawnee girls moved into a small lodge accompanied by their grandmothers where, at each subsequent menstrual cycle prior to marriage, the girl and her grandmother would withdraw to this lodge (Parks 2001). Similarly, an older woman stayed with the Plains Cree girl during her seclusion at puberty (Darnell, 2001). Assiniboine girls were isolated in a small lodge near the family tepee (DeMallie & Miller, 2001). For a few tribes, such as Teton Sioux and the Cheyennes, girls were carefully chaperoned after their seclusion because virginity in single women was valued (DeMallie, 2001b; Moore, Liberty, & Straus, 2001; respectively). An exceptional case was the Cheyennes, who required girls to wear protective chastity belts from puberty to marriage. Girls were usually bathed and reclothed after their isolation, as occurred among the Pawnees, who also purified girls with cedar smoke.

Among the Plains cultures, as with groups in other cultural areas, the time in seclusion was accompanied by various other adherences and practices. During the 4-day seclusion of Assiniboine girls they were obligated to fulfill many dietary and behavioral restrictions (Pritzker, 1998). Consistent with comments by DeMallie, Greene (2001) explained that instruction in domestic skills was an important aspect of the seclusion for Teton Sioux girls, noting that, in general, among the Plains, "Girls' instruction in craft production was early, rigorous, and universal" (p. 1049).

Following the time of seclusion, it was common for parents who had the means to host a feast and distribute gifts. For instance, several weeks after pubertal seclusion, Lakota fathers who were able sponsored ceremonies (Pritzker, 1998). Indeed, it was found in other cultural areas that the degree of lavishness expressed at puberty and other ceremonies was associated with the family's wealth. A shaman presided over the ceremonies of both Lakota and Plains Ojibwa groups. The Cheyennes would give away a horse in honor of the girl's first menses.

Quests for visions and dreams were sometimes a component of the coming-of-age experience for girls of the Plains, but they were nearly a universal experience for North American Indian boys. Hence, a more complete description of the vision quest is found later in this chapter on boys' coming-of-age rituals. Kansa girls fasted and dreamed visions, but these dreams were usually not considered important (Bailey & Young, 2001). Cree girls acquired visions during their four nights of seclusion at puberty (Pritzker, 1998). Tattooing of the pubescent girl occurred among some groups, including the Otoe and Missouria tribes (Schweitzer, 2001). Wichita girls were tattooed as a form of social identification to distinguish them from female captives and women of other tribes (Newcomb, 2001).

Some groups did not observe detailed and involved puberty rituals, but nonetheless it was common to give some nod of recognition to the event of a girl's menarche. For instance, the Poncas might simply give the pubescent girl a horse accompanied by speeches from an elder (D. N. Brown & Irwin, 2001). While the Blackfeet did adhere to beliefs about the dangers of contact with women during menstruation, they did not have special female puberty ceremonies (Pritzker, 1998). However, the completion of a daughter's first quillwork or beadwork could result in her family's sponsorship of a feast (Dempsey, 2001).

In summary, seclusion was the most widespread pubertal practice among groups of the Plains area, and the time spent in separation was put to efficient use in skill development. Vision quests were important at puberty in some cases. Celebration and ceremony sometimes followed a girl's time in seclusion.

Northeast Woodlands

The Northeast Woodlands cultural area includes the eastern United States from the mid-Atlantic region northward into Canada. It is a heavily forested region and gradually becomes transformed into the Plains of the Midwest to the west and transitions into the boreal forest and tundra to the north. The common practice of menstrual seclusion at first menses occurred among several Northeast cultures, such as the Lenapes (Delawares), Micmacs, and Sauks (Pritzker, 1998). I. Goddard (1978) wrote of the seclusion of Delaware girls in a separate hut until after the second menstrual occurrence. They wore a blanket over their heads and observed certain behavioral restrictions, including not touching their hair or any food or utensils for eating. They were required to eat with a stick and drink from their hands. Some semblance of these customs accompanied all subsequent menstruation. Seclusion at all menstruations was also practiced by many Northeast cultures (Sutton, 2004). Kickapoos isolated girls for 10 days in the woods in a special hut set at a distance from her family's home (Callender, Pope, & Pope, 1978). An older woman advised the pubescent girl about expectations for her proper behavior as an adult. Similar to the Kickapoos, the Ojibwa girl was removed to a separate wigwam by her mother or grandmother at her first menstruation. She could be isolated for 4, 5, or even 10 days, during which time she was instructed on the responsibilities of womanhood (Fox, 1999; Torrance, 1994). A feast and celebration at her village, called the Womanhood Ceremony, followed the Ojibwa girl's time of seclusion. Southwestern Ojibwa girls were isolated in a small wigwam at puberty with the expectation that they fast for four days and nights. A vision might emerge, but it was not a necessity for girls as it was for boys (Ritzenthaler, 1978). Chapter 8 provides a more detailed description of various expressions of Ojibwa coming-of-age ceremonies for girls.

Vision quests for both pubescent boys and girls at puberty were linked to several Northeast cultures, such as Foxes, Miamis, Ottawas, Potawatomis, and Shawnees (Pritzker, 1998). Ojibwa girls and boys were instructed to fast and were sent to the forest to obtain their guardian spirit helpers (Fox, 1999). Indeed, fasting and isolation could occur as young as age 4 or 5 among Ojibwas (Hilger, 1951/1992). It also was observed that groups such as the Miamis and Menominees began preparing children for their pubertal fasts prior to puberty (Pritzker, 1998; Spindler, 1978). Illinois girls remained in a small lodge and fasted until they obtained a vision that would bring promises of power for their futures (Callender, 1978). Both Menominee boys and girls underwent puberty fasts (food and water) in order to receive dreams that would prescribe activities related to dancing, singing, engaging in games, and directing other aspects of life (Spindler, 1978). The young person was isolated in a small wigwam with his or her face blackened. The vision usually came in the form of an animal and would later be interpreted by the shaman concerning the specific powers and obligations that had been received by the young person.

There was reference to a particular rite of passage called *huskanaw*, which was observed for both girls and boys among the Iroquoian and Algonquian cultures of eastern Virginia and North Carolina. This rite was shown to be quite important to the Tuscaroras as late as 1755 and was described by Boyce (1978) as follows: "young people were taken to an isolated cabin where they were deprived of food and given what may have been hallucinogenic plants or beverages. They were kept in isolation for periods of two or three weeks to a few months. Upon returning to the village they did not speak for several weeks" (p. 285). Since this fascinating rite appeared to have been more intensified for males, it is discussed in the later section on boys' coming-of-age.

Beyond the practices of seclusion at first menstruation and vision quests, there is little mention of other pubertal coming-of-age customs relative to girls in the Northeast cultural area. There is minimal reference to ceremonies and celebrations in conjunction with puberty. However, several practices relative to Ojibwas, past and present, are explicated more carefully in chapter 8.

Southeast

This cultural area encompasses a range of landscapes of the Southeast, including the coastal regions, the piedmont, rolling hills, mountains, and forested areas. Unfortunately, there is a dearth of literature on puberty rituals among tribes of the Southeast. Indeed, Driver (1941) observed the paucity of public puberty ceremonies east of the Rocky Mountains. A question to pose is whether the cultures of the Southeast (and of the Northeast to some degree) actually were less likely to hold such practices or if there is rather a lack of literature on the topic. It must be remembered that Indigenous cultures of the East were seriously decimated as points of first contact by European explorers and colonists. Hence, systems for perpetuating oral histories and traditions were interrupted, and by the time historians and anthropologists were engaged in their research on North American Indians there had been significant diminishment of cultures and traditional practices in the East.

In speaking generally about the Southeast cultural area, Jackson, Fogelson, and Sturtevant (2004) concluded: "First menstruation was accompanied by restrictions imposed to contain and control their newly acquired power, which was viewed as having both generative and destructive potential" (p. 39). Indeed, Brightman and Wallace (2004) indicated that Chickasaw women were secluded at first menstruation and from that point on in life. Prior to returning to their homes, women purified themselves by bathing in running water and anointing themselves with oil. Creek women were secluded at menstruation, with non-seclusion bearing a capital offense (Pritzker, 1998), and menstruating Choctaw women secluded themselves in a separate house for women (Galloway & Kidwell, 2004). Catawba pubescent girls learned how to properly wear decorative feathers (Pritzker, 1998). Both Chitimacha girls and boys engaged in a type of vision quest in which they fasted for 6 days and performed a "fire dance" on the sixth night. Fainting ensued from the intense dancing, and relationships were formed with a type of animal spirit that would function as the initiate's spirit guardian from that point onward (Brightman, 2004).

Fogelson (2004) mentioned the isolation of Cherokee girls during menstrual cycles, and Mails (1996) spoke of the seclusion of Cherokee girls for 7 days at the time of first menstruation. Girls remained at a distant camp and could not be touched by others. It was required that they be fed by another woman, since they were not to handle food themselves. After the 7-day seclusion, the girl washed herself and her clothing and returned to her family. Eggan (1937) wrote of the taboos associated with menstruation of Eastern Cherokee pubescent girls: "A female must emphatically be avoided while menstruating; one must not eat anything cooked by her, or touch any object that she has touched, or even walk along a trail over which she has recently traveled. She must not be allowed to wade in the river near where the fish traps are set, or she will spoil the catch. If she should chance to walk through the cornfield, she will stunt and injure the crops. The husband of a woman in this condition is, by reason of her relation to her, compelled to avoid other people" (p. 301).

It appears that puberty, in and of itself as an event, was not the focus of girls' initiations in the Southeast; rather, it was their entrance into the world of menstruating women that necessitated the learning of important menstrual customs (Sutton, 2004).

Southwest

The Southwest cultural area is culturally quite diverse and encompasses a great number of tribes of this region of the United States and northern Mexico. It can be divided according to Pueblo and non-Pueblo groups, with the Eastern Pueblos surrounding the Rio Grande in New Mexico and the Western Pueblos lying west of the Rio Grande in New Mexico and Arizona (specifically, Lagunas, Acomas, Zunis, and Hopis). The best-known puberty observances for girls in the Southwest are the quite elaborate ceremonies of the Apaches and Navajos, both of which are addressed in greater detail in chapters, 6, 7, and 8.

Among the Pueblo cultures, initiation ceremonies were the most common form of coming-of-age events, and in some cases they continue to be practiced in the present day. Hodge (1912) noted that Hopi girls were spared some of the more rigorous puberty observances and taboos of other cultures. Schlegel (1973) wrote of the first initiation that occurred in childhood in which Hopi girls and boys were brought to the kiva and whipped (boys more severely than girls). Corn grinding was and continues to be a visible demonstration of coming-of-age among Hopi girls, but whether it occurs at puberty or later in adolescence appears to vary from village to village (Mails, 1983; Stanislawski, 1979). Corn grinding was supervised by paternal aunts, and the girl was engaged in this task continuously for 4 days (Beaglehole & Beaglehole, 1935). During this time she was required to adhere to certain taboos, including avoiding the outdoors during daylight hours, abstaining from meat and salt, and refraining from touching herself (which necessitated the use of a scratching stick). On the fifth day the girl would be given names by her paternal aunts and a ceremony would ensue. At that time, her hair would be arranged in the traditional butterfly whorls of maidens.

Corn grinding also was required by the Zuni girl, who, at first menses, was led from the home by an older female relative on the paternal side of the family and engaged in this task. The purpose of corn grinding among the Zunis was to bring ease to menstruation and to reinforce industrious behaviors in the pubescent girl (Curtis Collection, 2004).

At San Juan Pueblo, girls and boys of age 10 and older experienced a finishing rite in which the two sexes were separated and whipped by the head kachina god. As in the case of the Hopis, the whipping was more severe for boys (Mails, 1983).

Of non-Pueblo cultures in the Southwest, Maricopa girls were secluded at puberty in circular huts that were also used at birth and for the purification of warriors (Harwell & Kelly, 1983). Tohono O'odham (Papago) girls spent time in a menstrual hut at first menstruation and faced dietary restrictions (Joseph et al., 1949). In Seri culture, the girl's mother selected a sponsor, and the girl was in seclusion for 4 days in her sponsor's home (Bowen, 1983). The Seri girl's face was painted, and she was not to look at herself during her time of seclusion.

In addition to seclusion at first menses, a wide range of pubertal events occurred in the non-Pueblo Southwest. Wearing of special clothing frequently marked this time of the life span; for example, Havasupai girls were given a special buckskin dress that was stained with powdered ocher (Schwartz, 1983). This dress was worn for 4 days and nights, during which time girls would lie on a bed of sand heated by rocks. Yavapai girls also were heated at pubescence by resting on a pit of cedar branches placed over warm coals for 4 days (Khera & Mariella, 1983), and Walapai girls laid on hot stones that were covered by a blanket (McGuire, 1983). Cocopa pubescent girls also were required to lie in a trench that was warmed with fire (de Williams, 1983), as were Yuma girls who were to lie in a shallow pit heated with stones (Forde, 1931). During their 4 days of part-time "roasting," Yuma girls had their hair washed each morning and plastered with mud prior to returning to their heated beds.

Girls of the Southwest were required to perform tests of physical endurance and industry. The Yavapais practiced a variety of arduous rituals in connection with girls' coming-of-age experiences. For 4 days, girls had to rise in the morning prior to others and bring in water and firewood and engage in other tasks. Likewise, Tohono O'odham pubescent girls were required to be industrious at this time and fetch wood and water for the family. Hard work on the part of initiates was emphasized among the Walapais. The Havasupai girl was required to run to the east at sunrise and to the west at sunset, which appears to bear some similarity to the running of the Navajo girl to the east 3 times a day for 4 days (as explained in chapter 8). Fasting from various food and liquid items also was common among the non-Pueblo cultures of the Southwest. For instance, Seri girls were required to fast from meat for 8 days. Yavapai and Apache pubescent boys and girls were required to use scratching sticks and drinking tubes (see chapter 6), and Cocopa girls were required to use scratching sticks. Yuma pubescent girls faced food taboos and were prohibited from touching themselves.

Various forms of physical manipulation occurred among many groups; for instance, an older woman massaged the Yavapai girl in order to direct her future growth. Massage of the initiate by an adult female mentor was and is also practiced in the Apache and Navajo puberty rituals (as discussed in chapters 6 and 8, respectively). The Cocopa girl was required to have her back walked on by a female relative. Ritual bathing frequently occurred at first menstruation, as was the case for Tohono O'odham, Cocopa, and Walapai girls, who were bathed and shampooed by their mothers with root from the yucca plant. Ritual hair washing continues to occur among the Navajos as a purification rite (see chapter 8). Tattooing of the pubescent girl occurred among the Cocopas and the Karankawas and was apparently the only puberty observance of the Karankawas (Newcomb, 1983). Tattooing of the Yuma girl could occur sometime after puberty observances, but usually prior to age 16.

Feasting and celebration were common correlates of girls' puberty observances among the non-Pueblo cultures of the Southwest. Feasting went on every night for a month for the Tohono O'odham girl, and the Apache Sunrise Dance and Navajo Kinaaldá involved feasting and celebration. Seri girls experienced a 4-day puberty event with a fiesta representing the public aspect of the ceremony. The fiesta at the girls' puberty ceremony was stated to be the only major ceremonial event remaining in Seri culture.

The frequent practice of mentorship of female pubescents by adult women was found in the non-Pueblo Southwest (e.g., Tohono

O'odhams, Apaches, and Navajos). Additionally, special prayers by a medicine man might occur at some point in the complex of puberty observances, as was the case for Tohono O'odham girls, who, after a month of puberty rituals, would be purified with an eagle feather and drink a special white clay mixture. Girls also might be given a new name at this time. The influence of a medicine person was and continues to be a significant component of Navajo and Apache coming-of-age ceremonies, as well.

In summary, initiation ceremonies typified puberty observances for girls among the Pueblo Southwest, corn grinding occurring in some cases. For the non-Pueblo groups in the Southwest, pubescent girls were engaged in a wide variety of rituals, such as seclusion, but also rituals were designed to shape initiates, such as warming or heating and massaging. Physical activity and exertion, instruction, and celebration were commonly practiced ritual activities, as well.

California

There was an impressive array of puberty observances among Indigenous groups located in what is now known as California. According to Kroeber (1922), "Probably every people in California observed some rite for girls at the verge of womanhood: the vast majority celebrated it with a dance of some duration" (p. 311). Driver (1941) explained the pattern of puberty observances of this region as follows: "In general, puberty rites are most rigidly observed and most highly publicized in the north, gradually thinning out southward to the minimum of ritual expression in the southern San Joaquin Valley" (p. 27). The discussion that follows, while not comprehensive in nature, gives indication of the variety of practices in this cultural area.

One of the most common puberty customs in the California cultural area was confinement or seclusion at menses. Seclusion practices could occur for only the first menstrual cycle, for several of the first cycles, or for all menstrual cycles throughout the life span, as was the case for the Lake Miwoks (Callaghan, 1978). The length of the seclusion was quite variable, ranging from 4 days to 2 years. The least-restrictive practices required 4 days of seclusion, as was practiced by the River Patwins

(P. J. Johnson, 1978). Coast Miwok girls also were secluded for 4 days, but were occasionally led outside with their faces covered (I. Kelly, 1978). The Wappo girl was confined for 4 days in a special menstrual room in her family's house (Sawyer, 1978). She was required to cover her head with a deerskin when she left the room. After 4 days she could leave the room, but was more or less restricted to her house until after her second menstrual cycle. Eight days of confinement in the house was required for Lake Miwok girls.

In addition to 4-and 8-day seclusions, some tribes required 10-day seclusions, such as the Tolowas, in which ritual fasting and bathing also occurred (Gould, 1978). Shasta girls were confined to a menstrual hut for 8 to 10 days for their first or second menstrual cycles, and for 1 or 2 days at subsequent cycles (Silver, 1978b). Hupas required pubescent girls to remain secluded for 10 days, and when they ventured outdoors they covered their heads with deerskin (Pritzker, 1998; W. J. Wallace, 1978a). Several Athabascan tribes in the California region also required that pubescent girls cover their eyes or head when in public (Elsasser, 1978a), a characteristic shared with some Subarctic Athabascans, as discussed in a later section.

Among some groups, confinement may have been a matter of a month or as long as 2 years. Wintu girls could be secluded in a specially built brush hut for 1 to potentially several months, and were restricted to the hut except at night (Du Bois, 1935; LaPena, 1978). A head covering was required if they left the hut during the day. They experienced sleep deprivation and certain protections against evil spirits—practices that were linked to a concern for their safety. The Kitanemuk girl was secluded in an isolated hut for 4 months after undergoing various rituals (e.g., being lashed with nettles, washed with hot water, painted, and required to run while being chased by an industrious woman) (Blackburn & Bean, 1978). Chimariko girls were secluded for 2 years in a separate hut either alone or with a female relative, after which a public event was held (Silver, 1978a).

In addition to the number of and length of confinements, the place of seclusion also varied. Sometimes confinement was merely in the house of the girl's family, as was practiced by the Southern Valley Yokuts (W. J. Wallace, 1978b). Or, it could be in a special room attached to the house. In other instances, a separate menstrual hut or shelter was required, as was the case of the Nongatls and Lassiks (Elsasser, 1978a). The Yana pubescent girl was required to camp by herself in a hut away from the village, gather her wood, build a fire, and get along with little sleep (J. J. Johnson, 1978). For many tribes, when a separate hut was used for the pubescent, it was commonly used for all menstrual cycles when required. The Eastern Pomo girl was confined in a separate room of the house where she: "was isolated in a small tule structure attached to her house, where she lay on a bed of coals covered with fresh tules, purifying herself with a sort of steaming, during the whole period" (McLendon & Lowy, 1978, p. 314). After the fourth or fifth night of the puberty observances, she was bathed and given good clothes and prepared an acorn mush.

The pubescent girl in the California cultural area did not pass the period of confinement in leisure; rather, this was a prime opportunity for instruction of the initiate by her family members and elders, as was practiced by the Wintus. Hupas adhered to the common belief that the girl's behavior at this time of life would influence her future endeavors; hence, her mother and other female relatives visited her daily to remind her on matters of cleanliness, keeping a good temper, and being industrious. Gabrielino girls were lectured and instructed on proper conduct and personal care (Bean & Smith, 1978a). A ceremony was held and included a sand painting that served to educate the young woman on her proper place in the larger scheme of life. Serrano girls were instructed on how to be good wives (Bean & Smith, 1978b). During their 2-month confinement, pubescent Chimariko girls were instructed and taught songs, moral conduct, and mythology by older female relatives. The Athabascan groups of the California cultural area had special puberty schools where both boys and girls might be instructed (Elsasser, 1978a). Coast Miwoks had doctoring specialists, one who sang over girls at menses. At the conclusion of the puberty observances, the girl jumped in cold water.

The onset of puberty was a major life event for Western and Northeastern Pomos, and during their confinement girls were instructed on their future roles as women (Bean & Theodoratus, 1978). Luiseño girls were taught many lessons at puberty, such as "to respect their elders, to listen to them, to give them food, not to eat secretly, to refrain from anger, to be cordial and polite to in-laws, to follow rituals exactly and respectfully or be subject to punishment and death by the messengers of

Chingichngish (rattlesnake, spider, bear, and sickness)" (Bean & Shipek, 1978, p. 556). Gill (1987) summarized the images and themes of death that surrounded the Luiseño girls' puberty ceremony: "The initiates were buried up to their necks in heated sand for several days. This practice combines the death and rebirth imagery of entering and emerging from the grave with that of cooking the initiate, both common initiatory motifs" (p. 97).

Konkow girls experienced the support of an attendant during their puberty rites (Riddell, 1978), and elderly persons would give instructions and sing and dance around the pit at the Tipai girls' coming-of-age rites (Luomala, 1978). A peer companion also might partner with the initiate during her puberty rites; for instance, among the Konkows an older girl experienced several of the rites along with the pubescent girl, such as being set on fire and running. Tapai girls also had the company of two or more other girls while confined for a week in a pit with fragrant branches covering heated rocks.

The use of a special stick to scratch oneself during puberty rites was a widespread practice across cultures, such as Southern Valley Yokut, Hupa, Yana, Coast Miwok, Wintu, Lake Miwok, Foothill Yokut (R. F. G. Spier, 1978a), Nisenan (N. L. Wilson & Towne, 1978), Maidu, Kitanemuk, Sinkyone (Nomland, 1935), Monache (R. F. G. Spier, 1978b), and numerous other groups, including several additional Pacific Athabascans (Elsasser, 1978a).

Food restrictions (e.g., meat and salt) were to be observed by pubescent girls from most groups in the California region, such as Southern Valley Yokuts, Costanoans (Levy, 1978), Yanas, Chumash (Pritzker, 1978), Coast Miwoks, Kitanemuks, River Patwins, Wintus, and Hupas. Sometimes these restrictions continued for each menstrual cycle, as was the case for the Tubatulabals (C. R. Smith, 1978). Among the Mattoles, Nongatls, Sinkyones, Lassiks, Wailakis, and other Athabascan groups, as well as some tribes in the Klamath River region, Elsasser (1978a) noted several taboos, including prohibitions against eating meat and drinking cold water, as well as not eating with others, social confinement (in a menstrual hut among the Nongatl and Lassik), sleep restrictions, not touching oneself (requiring the use of a special scratcher), and covering of eyes or head in public.

Tattooing was another menstrual custom practiced by some tribes, such as the Southern Valley Yokuts and the Tolowas, who tattooed girls prior to puberty. Lassik girls were tattooed at puberty or shortly thereafter. Tipai girls and their female companions were tattooed during the puberty rites. Sinkyone girls were tattooed at the end of their puberty rituals. Wintu girls had their ears pierced and chins tattooed sometime in early or middle adolescence.

In some cases, girls (and more frequently boys) drank the powerful drug *datura* (or *toloache* in Spanish), derived from a root and capable of producing visions. It also yielded unconsciousness for several hours, which necessitated guarding the initiate so that she would not harm herself while under the influence of this substance. Tubatulabal boys and girls consumed datura shortly after puberty to produce long and healthy lives. Monache adolescent girls and boys also could drink datura at a spring ceremony to ensure a good life and spiritual knowledge.

Ritual bathing often followed the completion of various puberty rituals among groups such as the Wintus, Chimarikos, and Kitanemuks. Some parents of Monache girls sponsored a cleansing ritual for their daughters during which time girls were washed and adorned with new clothes and ornaments. Lake Miwok pubescent girls were bathed and provided with new clothes after 8 days of seclusion. Nisenan girls were bathed on the 16th day of their puberty observations, and a ceremony was held.

In addition to private or personal menstrual customs of seclusion, fasting, and special behavioral restrictions, some groups observed public ceremonies, dances, and celebrations. Such was the case of the Western and Northeastern Pomos, who celebrated with gift giving by relatives and instructing girls in methods of food preparation and basketmaking. A menstrual dance was observed for the Yuki pubescent girl and was regarded as a necessity for the good fortune of the girl and her tribe (V. P. Miller, 1978). In addition to numerous pubertal rituals and restrictions for individual Wintu pubescent girls, a dance was held for several girls in the fall of the year. Neighboring villages attended, and dancing and feasting lasted 5 days or longer. The Gabrielino's puberty ceremony was a cause of joy and happiness, and girls underwent a purification ceremony that included dancing and singing.

One of the main dances of Chimariko culture was the puberty dance that served as a public recognition after a girl's 2-year seclusion. The pubescent girl danced with her mother in the center while men and women danced around them. The Karoks observed a flower dance during the summer for girls who had begun to menstruate (Bright, 1978). This was a nocturnal ceremony that involved painting the face of the girl while she carried a deerhoof rattle, and both men and women participated in singing and dancing. Karok girls were told that the behavior they exhibited during their puberty ceremony would reflect their behavior later in life. For the Maidu girl, after journeying to the mountains with her mother and observing various food restrictions, dancing ensued for several nights interspersed with various rites, including ear piercing and body painting. Women, children, and older men of the tribe sang over pubescent Sinkyone girls for 5 nights. These were serious occasions that were thought to have an impact on both the girl's future and that of the entire group.

The female puberty ceremony and dance was the most important public event for the Shasta peoples. It commenced on the night of the onset of the girl's menses and continued for 8 to 10 nights. It was repeated for 1 or 2 subsequent menses. Like the Shastas', the Atsugewis' puberty dance was the most important, if not the only, ceremonial dance of the group. At first menses, a girl wore special clothing that could include an old buckskin dress and moccasins, wristlets, a headband, a belt, anklets, and a cloak. She ran to the mountains for good luck, and then the dancing commenced (Garth, 1978). Three different dances were performed with great community involvement. The girl ran to the east at dawn and worked hard during the day. The ceremony could last 4 to 6 days and could be repeated at several subsequent menstrual cycles. The ceremony ended with the girl's earlobes being pierced.

The higher-status family of a Hupa girl might hold a public celebration of her coming-of-age. Similarly, the Chilulas required only a 5-day confinement, which was followed by a public dance. The Patwin girl, while secluded, was sung for and danced around for 3 to 4 nights by men and women (Kroeber, 1932). After this time she was washed and painted, and she and another girl traveled about inviting everyone to a dance.

Some groups, such as the Wiyots, did not observe any of the usual menstrual customs, such as seclusion to menstrual huts, but their puberty ceremony for girls was more elaborate than that of the Yuroks to the north (Elsasser, 1978b; Pritzker, 1998). The Achumawis appeared to have the most elaborate social puberty observances for girls. At her first menstrual cycle, the girl and the community sang, danced, and feasted for 10 days and nights. She was required to dance until dawn, facing east, but was supported by men on either side when fatigued. This ritual was repeated for 9 days at her second menstrual cycle, 8 at the third, and so on. After 10 months she was considered a woman (Olmsted & Stewart, 1978).

In summary, the puberty customs for girls in the California cultural area were quite extensive and included practices that were found to varying degrees in other cultural areas, including seclusion, adherence to food and behavioral taboos, instruction by adult women, body modifications (tattoos), songs, and celebrations. A curious practice found in the California cultural area was burying girls in hot sand, which bears some similarity to heating of pubescent girls, in various forms, in Southwest and Great Basin cultural areas. Puberty, as a cause for celebration, was certainly a component of the customs of many groups in the California cultural area. In short, girls' puberty dances were common throughout northern California, but they were of greatest social importance to the Athabascans of this region, who held a number of other dances, such as those dedicated to fish, animals, and other food sources (Elsasser, 1978a). The puberty rites for girls were quite celebratory in comparison to those of some of the other cultural areas, such as the Subarctic and Arctic. Perhaps the mild climate and year-round access to food in the California region permitted the luxury to develop more elaborate cultural practices, such as those dealing with girls' coming-of-age.

Great Basin

The Great Basin encompasses the present-day state of Nevada and surrounding regions of a large geographic depression in the western United States. Puberty customs of tribes of this region, as with those in California, were widespread and encompassed both private and public components. Privately, Ute girls were secluded in separate huts and were subject to eating and drinking taboos and required to use a wooden scratcher (Callaway, Janetski, & Stewart, 1986). Additionally, they were required to avoid hunters, gamblers, and the sick. Western Shoshones practiced individual puberty rites that required girls to be in near isolation for a few days, during which time they were instructed on proper behaviors by their mothers (Thomas, Pendleton, & Cappannari, 1986). Likewise, Eastern Shoshone girls were isolated in the family menstrual hut and observed meat taboos as well as restrictions against daytime sleeping (Shimkin, 1986). Fowler and Liljeblad (1986) mentioned that menstrual huts were present for only some of Northern Paiutes. Washoe girls were not secluded, but they did sleep in a shallow pit warmed by ashes (d'Azevedo, 1986).

Many of the Great Basin groups observed food taboos; for instance, Southern Paiute girls refrained from eating meat or salt and from drinking cold water (T. Kelly & Fowler, 1986). Kawaiisu girls were required to abstain from meat, fat, and salt (Zigmond, 1986). Meat, fish, and salt taboos were to be observed by pubescent Northern Paiutes, who could only drink warm water. Meat and fish taboos also were required for Washoe pubescent girls.

Southern Paiute girls experienced various additional pubertal rituals, including sleeping on a hotbed at night, employing scratching sticks, and having their faces and bodies painted red. Kawaiisus exhorted girls to rise early, run in the mornings and evenings, and generally be industrious. Such actions were believed to link to their behaviors later in life. Northern Paiute pubescent girls engaged in morning runs for 5 to 10 mornings. In such cases an older woman would accompany the pubescent girl, and after the run the older women of the camp bathed the girl.

A few years after puberty, Kawaiisu girls and boys took the intoxicating datura root from which visions would emerge. Another ritual was performed around age 14, when adolescents would swallow live ants and then later be induced to vomit the ants. These rituals were regarded as preventative of future difficulties.

An interesting expression of female adolescent ceremonies was thought to exist in a petroglyph sites at Mono Craters that represented female genitalia (Schaafsma, 1986). It was said that similar icons were used in Diegueño initiation rituals and were believed to protect the initiates from evil as well as to secure safe childbirth.

The Washoes had a very complex and important puberty ceremony for girls that, according to various authors as summarized by d'Azevedo (1986), continued into the late 20th century. The Washoe girl was instructed by her mother on the duties of womanhood and was required to observe various food taboos. Physical activity was expected, and the initiate had "to run daily, fetch firewood, help with domestic chores, sleep only briefly, not lie down in the daytime, and avoid gambling and the sick as well as hunters and their equipment" (d'Azevedo, 1986, p. 486). The pubescent girl was required to use a scratching stick, and she carried an elderberry staff for support. The Jumping Dance also accompanied the Washoes' puberty ceremony beginning on the third day with the singing of puberty songs. At that time, the initiate, being supported by another girl, danced while the adult women swayed back and forth while facing the east and a fire. This segment was followed by the Round Dance in which men and women would dance together, and a feast followed at midnight. The girl was painted with ashes or ocher just prior to sunrise. The entire ritual was performed again a month later. The Ute performed a Bear Dance that served a variety of purposes, including serving as a public announcement of the end of the girl's puberty rituals (Jorgensen, 1986).

In short, puberty observances for girls were important among some groups of the Great Basin. Menstrual seclusion and instruction by older women occurred, as did physical challenges related to running and dancing. Food taboos were observed. In some cases it was important to induce an altered state of consciousness through the ingestion of datura. Potentially, rock art could have been incorporated into Great Basin initiation rituals for girls.

Plateau

The Plateau region includes portions of northern states in the United States (Idaho, Montana, Oregon, and Washington) and provinces in Canada (Alberta and British Columbia) located between the Rocky Mountains to the east and the Coast and Cascade ranges to the west. Seclusion of girls in a special hut or shelter at first menstruation was found in many groups of the Plateau area, including Lillooets (Kennedy & Bouchard,

1998a), Thompsons (Wyatt, 1998b), Shuswaps (Ignace, 1998), Northern Okanagans, Lakes, Colvilles (Kennedy & Bouchard, 1998b), Middle Columbia River Salishans (J. Miller, 1998), Spokanes (Ross, 1998), Coeur d'Alenes (Palmer, 1998), Yakimas (Schuster, 1998), Wascos, Wishrams, Cascades (French & French, 1998), Western Columbia River Sahaptins (Hunn & French, 1998), Nez Perces (Walker, 1998b), and Klamaths and Modocs (Stern, 1998b). Walker (1998a) stated that characteristics of puberty rituals in this area included secluding pubescent girls in menstrual lodges, binding their hair up, requiring them to use scratching sticks and drinking tubes, painting their bodies, and the wearing of special clothing. In comparison to tribes in other regions, such as the Subarctic, the puberty confinement was short, usually lasting less than a week. However, the Lillooets could practice puberty seclusion for up to 4 years, but 2 years was a more typical time frame for an extended seclusion. Girls would wander at night to make childbearing a possibility in the future and to build industry and good health. Similarly, Thompson pubescent girls ran about at night to build strength and also engaged in a variety of time-consuming tasks to learn discipline. Umatilla and Walla Walla tribes secluded 12-to 16-year-old girls in groups (Stern, 1998a).

Instruction was implicit during the puberty rituals, and seclusion was a prime time to captivate the girl with exhortations on her proper conduct. Frequently one woman or several women stayed with the girl during her seclusion, during which time she acquired new skills and performed various tasks. Shuswap girls, under the supervision of older women, practiced crafts and skills and kept their lodges as if they were married. Umatilla and Walla Walla girls, while in group seclusion, were instructed by older women on various skills such as sewing and coiling baskets. When Middle Columbia River Salishan girls gathered their first roots or berries, a feast was held for the old women. Girls of Wasco, Wishram, and Cascade groups presented their first picking of huckleberries to elders.

Girls from various tribes in the Plateau cultural area employed scratching sticks, and some also used drinking tubes (e.g., Lillooets). Kalispel girls were painted with white clay (Lahren, 1998), and faces of Lillooet and Nicola girls were painted (Wyatt, 1998a). Kalispel girls had to wear a conical hat during pubescence, and Lillooet girls wore headgear of goatskin. The headdress of Thompson girls consisted of fir branches.

The wearing of special headgear is also characteristic of cultures in the Subarctic.

Another form of withdrawal or seclusion that occurred in the Plateau cultural area was the vision quest. Both prepubescent boys and girls engaged in this experience, which required them to withdraw to remote areas in order to enter into a relationship with a spirit and obtain its song and power (Ackerman, 1995). Girls from a variety of Plateau tribes participated in vision quests, but usually prior to puberty. The pattern of the vision quest in the Plateau was similar to that of other cultural areas and involved preparation with an elder followed by isolation in a remote location for several days and nights. Girls would fast and wait for a visit from a spiritual helper (Olsen, 1998), but the power was often not manifested until adulthood as was the case for the Northern Okanagans, Lakes, and Colvilles. Among the Middle Columbia River Salishans it was stated that, by puberty, girls should have acquired a guardian spirit from their quests through visions obtained after dark or from diving into deep pools. Rock art was an interesting addition to the puberty rituals of Northern Okanagan, Shuswap, and Thompson adolescents (Boreson, 1998). The Thompson girl might draw a record of her nightly wanderings and training on rocks.

Ceremony, singing, and dancing accompanied puberty observances of girls in some cultures of the Plateau. Social status of the girl's family was sometimes reflected in the quality of the puberty observances, such as with gift giving and ceremonies. Northern Molalas celebrated the girl's coming-of-age with a 5- or 10-night dance. The girl would be elaborately dressed and would dance while others sang and danced (Zenk & Rigsby, 1998). In general, girls were usually considered ready for marriage after the completion of menstrual seclusion and celebrations. Lillooet girls ended their seclusion with a purification ritual by a shaman. During the evenings of their confinement, Klamath and Modoc girls danced by a fire with one or two other girls. L. Spier (1930) observed that among the Klamaths it was only the daughters of chiefs and the wealthy that had puberty dances. Specifically, the 5-day puberty dance would be repeated four more times, but only for those who were wealthy. The Nespelem pubescent girl danced and prayed each evening and morning for 10 days while in seclusion (Olsen, 1998).

Songs were implicit to many Plateau puberty events and served various functions. Pubescent girls composed laments and love songs and practiced them with the aim of perfecting the songs (Olsen, 1998). During their vision quests, Plateau girls and boys awaited a personal song from their spirit helper that would be publicly revealed some years down the road. It was described that the Southern Okanagan girl, while in isolation, would sing one song in the evening while facing west and another song at first light while facing east. She would dance for several nights during this period of isolation. During the 5-night Klikitats' puberty dance, women's songs and love songs were sung (Olsen, 1998). The Klamath and Modoc songs were embedded in beliefs related to personal power and shamanism and were sung at girls' puberty ceremonies and at many other ceremonies.

A variety of puberty observances occurred in the Plateau cultural area, including the typical elements of seclusion, taboos, and fasting. The vision quest also was a prominent practice. Puberty celebrations that involved singing and dancing were integral to several cultures, and social status was sometimes a factor in the degree of elaborateness of these practices.

Northwest Coast

The Northwest Coast is a geographically broad area stretching from the Oregon coastline through the Washington and British Columbia coastlines to southern Alaska. Most of the puberty customs in this cultural area overlap with those of other areas, beginning with the typical seclusion. Eyak practiced seclusion several months at pubescence (de Laguna, 1990a). Tsimshian girls were secluded at first menstruation (Halpin & Sequin, 1990). Bella Coola girls were secluded for 4 days in an enclosed area within which it was required that their knees be tightly held against their chests (Kennedy & Bouchard, 1990a). Bella Coola girls also were required to adhere to restrictions in activities and diets for 1 year. Following a major ceremony, Nootkan girls observed a light seclusion with accompanying restrictions for 4 to 10 months (Arima & Dewhirst, 1990). Northern Coast Salish girls were secluded in a cubicle in the family home for 16 days and faced severe food and behavioral restrictions (Kennedy &

Bouchard, 1990b). Southern Coast Salish girls were isolated in a mud hut and faced various taboos with encouragements to perform tasks (Suttles & Lane, 1990). Chinookan girls of the Lower Columbia were secluded for 5 months and faced numerous taboos (Silverstein, 1990). The Chilkat (Tlingit) pubescent girl and her attendant stayed in a small room near her parents, and the pubescent was kept engaged in sewing, basket weaving, or plucking feathers of swans (Shortridge, 1913). After her seclusion, the Chilkat girl's "coming out" required that she wear a cape with an attached hood with long fringes sewn on it. Upper Coquille girls were secluded for 10 days on a bed platform. They were adorned with special clothing and used a shell scratching stick and moss menstrual pads (J. Miller & Seaburg, 1990).

Puberty was the most important life event for Tlingit girls, for whom confinement could last for 2 years; during this time they were supervised by female relatives who also taught them traditions of the clan (de Laguna, 1990b; Fried & Fried, 1980). The initiate's grandmother would rub a stone on her mouth eight times and then the stone would be buried. The purpose of this rite was to prevent the girl from becoming a gossip, and burying the stone signified good luck for the girl. Additionally, a Tlingit girl's seclusion could be spent in a dark hole under a platform of a house—after the confinement her translucent complexion was admired. Haidas also practiced seclusion at the girl's first menses: the higher rank of a family, the longer the seclusion. She might be secluded for a month or longer in a partitioned area of her parent's house, during which time she was not to talk or laugh (Blackman, 1990). Her father's sisters, who received property after the seclusion, attended the Haida girl. As shown with the Tlingits and Haidas, a common practice in the Northwest Coast area was for an older female relative to supervise girls during their confinement.

Fasting was a frequent accompaniment of seclusion. Tillamook girls were secluded and fasted 4 to 5 days at puberty and were required to lie very still and be painted with red paint (Seaburg & Miller, 1990). Nehalem Tillamook girls were secluded about 15 days and were to adhere to various food and behavioral restrictions. The Chilkat girl would fast during her separation, typically for 4 days. There were additional taboos required for the following 2 to 5 years. The onset of menarche for a Tlingit girl required 8 days of fasting, and fresh foods were taboo during her long seclusion. During the initial 8 days she was not to handle a knife, or it was thought that her life could be cut short.

A variety of additional interesting puberty observances were required of pubescent girls in the Northwest Coast. Tututni girls had to wear a deerskin over their heads when they left the house, and wore a tiny basket around their necks with various apparatus to slash their bodies to encourage blood flow (J. Miller & Seaburg, 1990). Tututni girls also swam 10 times, which was repeated for the next two menstruations. Eyak girls were required to use bone scratching sticks and sucking or drinking tubes. Haida pubescent girls were subject to many taboos, including avoidance of hunting, fishing, and gambling equipment. Chilkat girls adhered to a variety of complicated rules, including the use of a bone drinking tube. They also practiced neatness in all of their behavior and manners and were to exhibit numerous forms of personal care. The coming-of-age rite of the Tillamook girl was the first gathering of food, which was subsequently given to the elderly.

Upon first menstruation, Kwakiutl girls experienced a 4-day seclusion, without severe restrictions, that was followed by ritualistic washing on several occasions by an elderly woman (Boas, 1966). Then, numerous physical restrictions ensued regarding seclusion in the home, the wearing of special clothing and adornments, food taboos, and limitations on expressions of speech and behavior. The restrictions were linked to some expected future positive outcome for the pubescent. For example, it was thought that the use of a copper scratcher prevented her skin from always being rough, and the use of a drinking tube ensured that she would not have a stout belly.

In addition to adherence to other puberty observances, Southern Coast Salish girls would quest for a vision before menses and directly after their first menstruation. The seeker was said to experience some manifestation of the spirit that might then appear in animal form. The quester would fall into a trance and ultimately receive power and a song that would be used in later life. After her initial seclusion, the Tillamook girl was sent on a vision quest. She might acquire a spirit, but it would remain inactive until she reached middle age.

The rich ceremonial lives of the Northwest Coast groups were reflected in their puberty observances. Driver (1941) noted the linkage of the potlatch to puberty ceremonies of girls of the middle North Pacific Coast area. Rank of family was a salient variable, and the potlatch essentially served as the girl's social debut. Additionally, potlatches were associated with a variety of other occasions among the Northwest Coast peoples. Haida girls were ritually cleansed and then a feast was held. Kalapuyans gave ceremonies at the girl's first menses (Zenk, 1990a). The Tsimshian peoples gave first names at puberty ceremonies and received gifts from relatives in their lineages. A higher-status Bella Coola father might put up a feast at the end of his daughter's year of puberty observances. Contemporary Kwakiutl pubescent girls can be ceremonially recognized at puberty and be given a new name at the time. Gifts to be distributed at this time are toys "to symbolize the end of childhood, and soap and combs to portray purification after the onset of menses" (Webster, 1990, p. 388). While not identifying a specific culture, Hodge (1912) noted that, among Pacific Northwest groups, as much property as the family could afford would be hung on the girl while she was fasting in order that she might be wealthy in her life. Further, she was not allowed to work at this time so that she might become a chief's wife and not be a slave.

When a Tlingit girl broke her 8-day fast, celebration followed with sharing of foods by her family. The girl's hair would be washed with blueberry juice, which signified hopes for good luck, a good husband, and perpetual youth. She also was ornamented with new clothes and jewelry, was tattooed, and a stone ornament was inserted in her lower lip to enhance beauty. Her old clothes were burned and the ashes placed in a tree stump to ensure long life. Tlingit girls were required to wear a hood from that point until they were married. The father of a Kwakiutl girl conducted a potlatch after his daughter completed the arduous puberty observances (Boas, 1966). The potlatch involved the typical giving of property to others, and the girl received a name from her mother's family.

The pubescence of the Nootkan girl of Vancouver Island was associated with the greatest potlatch of her family, and the potlatch of a Nootkan chief's daughter might warrant the building of a new house. The well-born Nootkan girl "stood outside between two masked dancers representing thunderbirds or whales, great torches flaming on either side. . . . Guests improvised songs satirizing sexual relations and requested gifts. Feasting, announcement of the girl's new name and potlatch distribution followed" (Arima & Dewhirst, 1990, p. 405). Apparently, the Northern Nootkans were continuing the girls' puberty potlatches in the 1970s. The family of a Central Coast Salish girl might celebrate her first menses with a feast and a public display of gifts (Suttles, 1990). After her seclusion at first menstruation, a Southern Coast Salish girl's family, especially if they were higher status, might give a feast to announce her marriageability. Siuslawans and Coosans held elaborate ceremonies for girls' puberty celebrations that involved the participation of a shaman (Zenk, 1990b).

In summary, seclusion, fasts, supervision, and instruction were important components of coming-of-age practices for girls in Northwest Coast cultures. What perhaps reflects the uniqueness of these cultures is relative to social stratification and the linkage of puberty ceremonies to potlatches. Cultures of the Northwest Coast were known for their emphasis on material wealth and social stratification; hence it is not surprising that these elements would be reflected in some forms in girls' puberty customs.

Subarctic

The Subarctic cultural area includes numerous cultural groups and covers a great expanse of territory, stretching from northeastern Canada to the interior of Alaska. With few exceptions, the cultures of the eastern part of this region are of the Algonquian linguistic family (e.g., Northern Ojibwa and various branches of Cree), and the Athabascan linguistic family dominates in the west. The Subarctic cultural area was characterized by rigorous puberty and menstrual restrictions and taboos—extreme measures taken relative to seclusion at the onset of menses particularly stands out for this cultural area. Separate shelters were used for isolation at first menstruation by such groups as the West Main Cree (Honigmann, 1981c), Western Woods Cree (J. G. E. Smith, 1981b), Hare (Savishinsky & Hara, 1981), Mackenzie Mountain (Gillespie, 1981), Slavey (Asch, 1981), Sekani (Denniston, 1981), Dogrib (Helm, 1981), Tutchone

(McClellan, 1981d), Carcross (Tagish) (Libby, 1952), Klukshu (Tutchone) (Libby, 1952), and Gwich'in (Slobodin, 1981). For instance, Peel River Gwich'in girls lived in a specially constructed shelter up to 1 mile away from the main camp for 1 year (Osgood, 1936/1970), as did Teslin (Inland Tlingit) girls (Libby, 1952). Groups of girls from the Cordillera could be secluded for up to 2 years (McClellan, 1981b), as could Inland Tlingit girls (McClellan, 1981a). Carrier girls also could be secluded up to 1 to 2 years in a small, isolated hut (Tobey, 1981). The seclusion of Koyukon girls could occur in a hut as far as half a mile away from her family and village (A. Clark, 1981). McClellan (1981c) suggested that the Tagish isolation of pubescent girls for 2 years was symbolic of fetal life and rebirth.

Upper Tanana girls followed many of the typical puberty customs of the Subarctic. Their seclusion occurred in a separate hut for 3 to 4 months (McKennan, 1959). The first month was spent in complete seclusion; after that time the pubescent could sometimes leave the hut, but only with a face covering to prevent her from looking at the sun and at men. The seclusion continued in other forms for a year in respect to adherence to food taboos and ensuring one was not exposed to the sun. The seclusion of the Teslin pubescent girl introduced additional challenges when the group was in transit. For instance, the girl was required to stay at some distance behind the group and, with the help of her mother, break her own path through the snow.

The time in seclusion was not completely spent in solitary pursuits. Mothers or other female relatives would provide pubescent girls with food and engage them in useful tasks. Chilcotins emphasized character development of pubescent girls, especially patience and diligence (Lane, 1981). Pubescent Chilcotin girls also could acquire spirit power. Tagish girls were instructed on proper moral and social behavior during their time of seclusion, and they acquired training in sewing. Carrier girls were instructed on the domestic arts by their female relatives, and Inland Tlingit girls were trained in sewing, as were Tutchone pubescent girls. The Dogrib girl was engaged in women's tasks to learn to be a hard worker. Teslin pubescent girls were to remain quiet and subdued but were also to stay engaged with industrious tasks in order to ensure that they would be industrious in adulthood. The education of pubescent girls of the Cordillera stressed their understanding of menstrual taboos and the tremendous power within that had to be properly controlled to not offend the spirit of game animals.

There were various taboos concerning consumption of fresh meat and other foods by pubescent girls in many of the cultures of the Subarctic. Carrier girls ate dried fish, dried berries, roots, and bark. The taboo against eating fresh meat was especially widespread, as observed among the Carcross. Han pubescent girls were required to eat dried meat, fish, and berries for a year (Crow & Obley, 1981). Peel River Gwich'in girls avoided fresh meat, with the exception of liver, and could only drink cold, clear water. The food taboos of the Teslin were required to build strength in girls and to prevent them from eating too much later in life. Along with the common practices of seclusion and food and drinking taboos, other requirements included the use of a special scratching stick and special drinking tube, as observed by the Teslins, Upper Tananas, and Tanainas (Osgood, 1937). Peel River Gwich'in girls were also required to use scratching sticks, and Crow River Gwich'in girls used bone drinking tubes (Osgood, 1936/1970). Koyukons required a drinking tube at puberty, and a special cup and bowl were to be used at first and all subsequent menstrual periods. The use of a special scratching stick and drinking tube (frequently made from a swan's bone) at puberty was widespread in the Subarctic.

After initial seclusion or sometimes concomitant with seclusion, puberty observances in the Subarctic included the wearing of special head coverings. The Western Woods Cree required girls to wear their hair disheveled and carry their heads hung low for a month or two after isolation. The Mackenzie Mountain Indians required girls to wear a special hat with fringes to hide their faces from view, and they used a special drinking vessel that hung from their belts. Carrier pubescent girls also wore a bonnet with fringes to hide their faces, as did Gwich'in girls. Carcross girls wore a large hood so that they would be pretty. Han girls also wore a special hood when outside that served to prevent them from looking anywhere except at the ground in front of them (Osgood, 1971), as did Teslin girls, whose hoods hung down their backs almost to the ground. For at least their first menstrual cycle, Klukshu girls wore a menstrual hood as well as a string of porcupine quills about their chest. Peel

River Gwich'in girls wore a hood with rattles that hung near their ears that would prevent them from hearing anything. A further rigor for Han girls who broke the taboo against eating fresh meat during their year of seclusion was to stay away a second year and wear a cap fashioned as a cape that prevented them from seeing any men. It was observed that the faces of Han girls were white after emerging from their long fasts from fresh food.

The Tanainas are another Northern Athabascan group that conducted rigorous puberty observances for girls (Osgood, 1937). The girl wore a hoodlike cap to adhere to the strict taboo that forbade her from looking at anyone. The Ahtna pubescent girl was called "the one in training" or "hood wearer" and wore a huge hood of moose skin with fringes falling over her face to shield others from the impacts of her glance (de Laguna & McClellan, 1981). Pubescent Ahtna boys and girls had their wrists, elbows, knees, ankles, and fingers tied with strings of caribou hide in order to have limber joints and small bones.

The dependence on hunting among groups of the Subarctic area yielded many of the elaborate taboos already mentioned as well as others to be adhered to by pubescent girls and menstruating women. Carrier girls would avoid trails used by hunters. Menstruating Sekani girls and women would only eat dried meat or dried fish so as not to ruin the hunt. Chipewyan peoples required girls to observe certain taboos, such as those related to hunting and game animal avoidance (J. G. E. Smith, 1981a). Likewise, the Dogribs practiced menstrual seclusion and hunting and game restrictions at puberty and all menstrual cycles. The significance and meaning of these types of menstrual taboos in hunting societies was examined in chapter 4.

For many of the Subarctic groups, separation at puberty often was the beginning of female separation at each subsequent menstruation. However, it was observed that puberty practices had certainly diminished over the course of the 20th century. Among the Koyukons, seclusion had been significantly reduced over time—by 1900 it was for 6 months, by 1960 it was for 2 months, and by 1970 it did not occur except for a blanket or partition separating the girl from the rest of her family. Nonetheless, A. Clark (1981) observed that, even in the 1970s, Koyukon women continued to wear kerchiefs on their heads and to walk separate trails during each menstrual cycle. It was said that for the Ahtnas the practices were already being abandoned by 1900 and that no one in 1970 observed them. However, the elderly persons did recall being subject to pubertal observances and tended to blame current problems, such as bad weather, food scarcity, and bad teeth of the young, on the failure to practice pubertal rituals. It was observed at the time of Libby's fieldwork in the mid-20th century that the Teslins still required seclusion of the pubescent girl at a special shelter located at some distance from the rest of the group. Further, adult menstruating women observed various menstrual customs. Among the Klukshus, the seclusion of girls had continued into present day with their confinement to their homes. However, canvas had replaced the traditional shelter of brush and logs, and shelters could be reused by women at the birth of their children or for their own daughters' seclusion. At the time of McKennan's (1959) writing, the seclusion of pubescent Tanana girls continued to the degree that their living space consisted of a corner of the tent with a blanket designating their separation. Numerous taboos also were observed.

Celebrations or banquets did not appear to be a major component of coming-of-age in the Subarctic, with a few exceptions. Osgood mentioned that the wealthy Crow River Gwich'in held a feast after their daughter's puberty seclusion was completed. The father of the pubescent Han girl would hold a banquet for the community. A small potlatch would be held in the village after the seclusion of Teslin and Carrier girls. Fathers would give small gifts and food to the community. As was typical in the tradition of potlatches or giveaway feasts, giving away more property was demonstrative of the higher social status of the girl and her family. In the case of the Teslins, the goal was for an adult to become a highly honored person, which was accomplished by giving presents to others on behalf of one's children from the time shortly after their birth and onward. If a family was short on resources during a child's younger years, they could make up for previous deficits at their daughter's puberty feast.

As already apparent in this discussion and specifically noted by Osgood (1937), puberty rituals for Northern Athabascan girls were very rigorous. Osgood (1958) provided a detailed account of the lengthy puberty rituals conducted by the Ingaliks, an Athabascan-speaking people of the lower Yukon River in Alaska. It is useful to examine the Ingaliks' puberty observances more closely to appreciate the multiple components of these events. A girl was conditioned to inform her mother at the time of first menstruation—to not do so was believed to potentially produce dire consequences. Once informed, the mother instructed her daughter to walk outside as much as possible, because it would be her last opportunity for some time to come. She also was given as much food as was available at the time.

For the Ingalik girl's seclusion, her mother would construct a separate room, and the pubescent was dressed in old clothes for this period of time. An older woman was asked to come and sing for the girl, and other rituals occurred interspersed with the singing. The girl was rubbed all over by the older woman. After turning sunwise four times, the girl went "into her corner" with her feet stretched out toward the corner. After everyone in the village had retired for the evening, the girl's mother allowed her to come out and use the toilet. During this brief release, she wore an old parka and a headband with long fringe. This headband was passed down in the family and was to be used every time she would go outside during her seclusion. According to Osgood (1940), the headband was worn "As a protection against the evil influence of the eyes of a girl at puberty" (p. 407).[3] She had to drink water through a swan bone drinking tube during her seclusion. After 10 days of seclusion she was told to rub charcoal on her face, and her mother painted her with red ocher at various times. The seclusion was expected to last a year, during which time the girl made new clothes for herself and engaged in other tasks such as tanning skins.

At the end of the Ingalik girl's seclusion, the old clothes were taken off and the girl was bathed in warm water. She then put on her new clothes. At that point, an older woman would return to sing songs again interspersed with various rituals. For instance, a headband of soft skin with fringes was ritualistically placed on the girl's head. This band was to be worn until her next menstrual period and, if worn, would protect her from headaches as she grew older (Osgood, 1940). She was instructed on her proper behavior at that time. A girl's father, if wealthy, would "put down" a gift of food and other gifts for other men in the kashim to publicly acknowledge his daughter's completed isolation (Osgood, 1958).

In summary, there are several intriguing puberty observances of the Northern Athabascan and other Subarctic groups. Girls were frequently secluded for long periods of time, up to 2 years, and sometimes the place of seclusion was some distance from their families. It was common for girls to wear large bonnets or hats with fringes covering their faces when it was necessary for them to exit from seclusion. Pubescent girls were required to adhere to strict food taboos. Avoidance of hunters and hunting implements were widespread practices. McKennan (1959) noted that retiring to menstrual huts, wearing hoods when leaving the hut, employing a scratching stick, drinking through a tube, and not eating fresh meat were found in various forms among numerous Northern Athabascan groups, such as the Upper Tananas, the Hans, the Gwich'in, the Tanainas, and the Ten'as. Such practices were heavily focused on the containment of female power at pubescence, especially, and all other subsequent menstrual cycles. The containment was necessary to not offend the power needed for successful hunting and fishing expeditions. The many rituals of the Subarctic emphasized the pubescent girl's development, relative to acquiring the necessary womanly skills to be a contributing member of her society and to ensure and protect the girl's lifetime success, safety, and health.

Arctic

Similar to the Subarctic cultural area, the Arctic spans a large geographic area from Greenland across the northern reaches of Canada to northern and western Alaska. There is a shortage of literature on Arctic puberty practices in comparison to most of the other cultural areas. Whether this reflects the absence of puberty customs or an actual lack of published literature on the topic is unknown. I speculate the former due to the harshness of the Arctic environment and the ongoing need to maintain survival, which would limit the possibility of practicing some puberty rituals. Nonetheless, the typical seclusion of the girl at first menstruation occurred for some Arctic groups, such as the Aleuts (Lantis, 1984a) and the Pacific Eskimos, who continued the practice for all subsequent menstrual cycles (D. W. Clark, 1984). Alutiiq women were secluded in huts during menstrual periods, and the initial seclusion could last several months or longer (Pritzker, 1998). Unangan (Aleut) girls at menstruation were confined for 40 days (Pritzker, 1998).

Some Arctic groups required girls to observe various taboos at puberty, such as the Yup'iks (Pritzker, 1998). The Nunivak Eskimos recognized life crisis patterns associated with physiological change, such as the female puberty experience. Change was regarded as unnatural and potentially dangerous; hence, the pubescent girl faced numerous taboos (Lantis, 1984b). Unangan girls were subjected to various food and behavioral taboos, and their joints were bound so that they would not ache in old age (Pritzker, 1998). The Unangans thought that, at puberty, girls could cure minor illnesses because it was believed they had special powers during this time of their lives (Pritzker, 1998). Tattooing the pubescent girl also was mentioned in the literature; for example, Iglulik girls were tattooed as soon as they reached puberty (Mary-Rousselière, 1984). Pacific Eskimo girls were tattooed on the chin to indicate that they had reached puberty.

In addition to recognizing the physiological nature of life crises, the Nunivak Inuit recognized change in status relative to obtaining food resources. Hence, the girl's accomplishment in female tasks of berry picking or gathering of grass was cause for public recognition and gift giving by parents. A young person's ability to contribute to the food supply was a skill from which the entire community would benefit.

Reinforcement of values for children and childbearing was found among the Saint Lawrence Eskimo puberty rituals. Girls had their bodies stroked and shaped by an older woman to instill beauty and attractiveness (Hughes, 1960). The pubescent girl was subjected to rituals of a pregnant woman to the extent that she held a doll representative of an infant. In summary, there are fewer illustrations of puberty rituals in the Arctic cultural area than most of the other areas, but clearly there was some adherence to these customs.

Summary of Girls' Coming-of-Age

In summarizing this section on girls' puberty rituals, it is useful to draw on Driver's (1941) conclusions relative to girls' puberty rites in cultural areas of western North America. As previously noted, Driver observed a lack of pubertal rituals east of the Rocky Mountains, and this observation was confirmed in this review of practices of Southeast and Northeast cultures. One exception, however, is Ojibwa culture, which is discussed more fully in chapter 8. Many Plains cultures practiced various forms of puberty rites and celebrations, including the Lakotas, who are addressed in chapter 8. Driver observed that puberty ceremonies were integral parts of Athabascan cultures of the Southwest, as was a belief in the girl's curing power. Certainly these conclusions are reflected in the elaborate puberty celebrations of Apaches and Navajos described in subsequent chapters. Driver also noted what he labeled a fear of menstruation to be more common in northern cultures. Certainly if the elaborate pubertal taboos of Subarctic cultures are indicative of this fear, this conclusion is apparent. However, it must be remembered that protective measures taken toward menstruation and menstrual fluids were reflective of perceptions of power, as opposed to perceptions of a contaminated or an unclean state of women, as was a common misconception by those from outside these cultures.

It was also noted by Driver (1941) that the puberty rites of southern California cultures were fairly distinct and different from the Athabascan Southwest, northern California, and Northwest Coast cultures than these latter three cultures were from one another. For instance, group puberty rites were more common than individual rites in southern California. Indeed, Driver speculated that the recognition of individual girls at puberty originated in the Northwest Coast and spread, perhaps entirely through Athabascans, to northern California and then to the Southwest. In such a pattern of dissemination, different patterns evolved independently in southern California. Another distinctive pattern of southern California was said to be the heating of female initiates; however, similar rites were found in cultures that were geographically close to southern California (i.e., Southwest and Great Basin).

Puberty rites of the Plateau were said to emphasize strenuous physical activity on the part of girls, and were said to be similar to boys' rites (Driver, 1941). It also was stated that there were no unique elements to the puberty rites of girls of the Great Basin; that is, all rituals were found in other cultural areas as well. There was little emphasis on puberty ceremonies or celebrations among cultures of the Pueblo Southwest—a conclusion also supported by Driver, who remarked on the greater emphasis on boys' initiations in these cultures. Nonetheless, female initiations did occur, and the corn-grinding ceremony of adolescent girls had and continues to have importance in some Pueblo cultures.

Additional historical speculations by Driver (1941) indicated the advancement of public puberty ceremonies as progressing from the Northwest Coast and probably carried through Athabascan migration patterns that ultimately reached the Southwest. Unfavorable environmental conditions of the Great Basin and Plateau were said to have curtailed expansion of puberty traits further east. Driver did not address the Subarctic cultural area in his work, but these cultures, which include the Northern Athabascans, did practice numerous puberty rituals that certainly were embedded in migration schemes. However, there were few similarities shown between Northern and Southern Athabascan puberty rites in the review in this chapter. In this respect, the very different geographical patterns between these regions must account for some variability in practice, as well as the influences of neighboring cultures in each region. Driver observed that public recognition of a girl's coming-of-age was more likely in areas of greatest population, with sedentary populations, and most favorable environmental conditions relative to subsistence. The warmer climate of the Southwest permitted events that could occur outdoors and accommodate a variety of rituals that included the participation of many individuals.

This review of pubertal customs relative to girls' coming-of-age was intended to be broad and descriptive. The next section on boys contributes to the overall discussion at the end of this chapter.

Boys' Coming-of-Age

In addressing the topic of coming-of-age ceremonies for boys, it can be noted at the onset that there is an absence of a definite physical marker of puberty, such as menarche. Nonetheless, the transition from childhood to adulthood for boys received special recognition among numerous North American Indian cultures. According to Hodge (1912), coming-of-age rites for boys may not have been specifically connected to puberty, but they did occur around that time of the life span. The belief in puberty as a critical phase of development was indicated in the value for proper expression of coming-of-age rites for boys with subsequent expected long-standing impacts on their lives.

Hodge noted that particular observances for boys included "isolation and fasts among the mountains and woods, sweat bathing and plunging into cold water, abstinence from animal food, the swallowing of medicines sometimes of intoxicating quality, and the rubbing of the body with fish spines and with herbs" (1912, p. 315). Additionally, boys were subjected to various regulations and taboos, and their coming-of-age events were frequently linked to initiation into some kind of male society. Hodge also observed that boys' coming-of-age rites were not as widespread as those for girls and that they deteriorated more quickly with European contact. The latter is an extremely interesting point, but it is beyond the scope of the present review. The following characteristics of boys' coming-of-age observances are arranged according to 10 cultural areas that were delineated in the previous section.

Plains

The coming-of-age experience of boys in the Plains area was most frequently exhibited through a vision quest or recognition at first success in hunting or battle, as opposed to formal puberty ceremonies. In short, the maturity of boys was observed according to their acquisition of spiritual power or their demonstration of adult male accomplishments. Torrance (1994) observed that the vision quest could be considered the boy's rite of passage to manhood in North America, rather than puberty rituals. Specifically, the vision quest accompanied the transition to manhood among groups in all cultural areas, and it was a ritual repeated throughout the life span among men of the Plains tribes. Vision quests are still prevalent among many North American Indians and may occur during childhood or pubescence later in adolescence, or in adulthood.

As a coming-of-age event, the vision quest typically began with a sweat bath, after which the boy would be brought to some sacred location to fast, pray, and seek a vision. He was commonly required to be alone for 4 days and nights without food and water, but the time could extend up to 10 days. In the Teton Sioux tradition, the person would seek pity from the supernatural beings (*wakan*), who would offer powers to recipients to be used in war or for curing. Preparation was integral, as an older man supervised this rite of passage from start to finish. In the Cheyenne tradition, after 4 days the boy returned to the council of elders or a shaman and discussed his obtained vision. The elders would then interpret his experiences and a new name (a medicine name) would be assigned (Foster & Little, 1987). The acquisition of a new name at this time offered the young person a source of power (Hirschfelder & Molin, 2001), as related by John Lame Deer of the Minneconjou Sioux, who told of his vision quest and subsequent name assignment: "Then I saw a shape before me. It rose from the darkness and the swirling fog which penetrated my earth hole. I saw that this was my great-grandfather, Tahca Ushte, Lame Deer, old man chief of the Minneconjou. I could see the blood dripping from my great-grandfather's chest where a white soldier had shot him. I understood that my great-grandfather wished me to take his name. This made me glad beyond words" (Lame Deer & Erdoes, 1972, p. 16).

Visions were also thought to emerge in dreams, a means that permitted direct communication with the spiritual world. Whatever the means of obtainment, a desirable outcome of a vision quest was the formation of a relationship with a guardian spirit who could make itself known in the guise of an animal. Subsequently, the individual became empowered through such a relationship. A personal medicine bundle was assembled according to the objects identified by the guardian spirit, and the person carried this bundle, which offered him protection. Interestingly, vision quests were a highly individualistic activity, but the cultures within which they occurred were communal in various other respects. This dichotomy was discussed in chapter 3 relative to the integration of communal and individualistic orientations in Native cultures.

Kansa boys engaged in a vision quest in an isolated spot with hopes to be contacted by ghosts of ancestors or animals or some type of supernatural spirit. Blackfeet boys could seek a vision between ages 15 and 20 and prior to marriage. Plains Cree boys experienced vision quests at puberty to obtain spirit power. A Comanche boy would begin to consider his need for power as an adolescent, but he would not search for it until about 20 years of age. Santee Sioux boys, as well, experienced the vision quest. For Otoe and Missouria boys, the vision quest was an appeal for power rather than an actual vision.

Boys in the Plains cultures would also come of age through a successful buffalo hunt or inclusion in their first war party (Pritzker, 1998). For example, Lakota boys could come of age through a vision quest, a first successful buffalo hunt, or a first war party. The first kill was significant for the Assiniboine boy, who would butcher it and leave it for animals to ensure future success in hunting. Likewise, the first kill of a Blackfoot boy was regarded as significant and could result in his family's sponsorship of a feast.

Among the Cheyennes, achievement rather than ceremony marked the transition from boyhood to adulthood. A new name could be given to the Blackfoot boy after earning it from going to war. Gifts were given in honor of the Comanche boy's first kill of game. The Lipan Apache boy was considered holy at the time of his first raid or warpath experience (Opler, 2001).

The Plains cultural area included two of the most common rites of passage for boys—vision quests and success at first hunt or battle. Variations of these practices are observed throughout all cultural areas.

Northeast Woodlands

Vision quest for boys, and frequently for girls as well, were common experiences among the Northeast Woodlands cultures, including Abenaki, Delaware, Illinois, Miami, Ojibwa, Ottawa, Potawatomi, Sauk, Shawnee, and Winnebago (Pritzker, 1998). Similar to the Plains experience, the vision quest was a means to attract a spiritual helper and might lead to the compilation of a medicine bundle. The spirit helper was said to appear as an animal and would be perceived as a lifelong helper to the individual. The vision quest was apparently practiced at some point in the past for boys of the various Iroquois nations, and was nearly universal for Algonquians, among whom these individualized rites occurred initially in early adolescence but could be repeated later at personal points of crisis (Torrance, 1994). Menominee boys and girls would fast and seek a vision to direct life endeavors. A similar experience was required for Ojibwa boys and girls, who, just prior to puberty, were encouraged to fast and go to the forest to seek their guardian spirit helper (Fox, 1999), and at even younger ages as well according to Hilger (1951/1992). Ojibwa boys could fast as many as 10 days and be carried from this experience to the sphere of the manitous or spirits. The vision quest was the most important stage of the Southwestern Ojibwa boy's life. Rogers (1978) deemed it to be of great importance among the Southeastern Ojibwas, among whom the boy would fast for several days in order to be visited in a dream or vision by his guardian spirit. A father would question his son to determine if a vision had been obtained; if not, the boy would continue the fast until success was attained. Rogers summarized the process of the vision quest based on reports in the *Jesuit Relations*: "An individual's guardian spirit might be a bear, a beaver, a bird, or similar creature. After having acquired his guardian spirit, the youth killed the animal or bird that had blessed him and placed a segment of it in the most conspicuous part of the lodge. He then made a feast in its honor during which he addressed it in a most respectful manner. Thereafter this particular species was recognized as his guardian spirit and the individual carried the skin of this animal or bird to war, on the hunt, or on a trip" (p. 763).

Virginia and North Carolina Iroquoian and Algonquian cultures practiced the huskanaw, which was relevant to the coming-of-age of both boys and girls. The Iroquoian huskanaw was described in the earlier section on girls' coming-of-age in the Northeast. Among the Virginia Algonquians, youths were ritually separated from their parents and were trained in the woods for 9 months by priests and advisers. After this time, they returned to their villages and were perceived to be reborn with knowledge and language having been relearned (Feest, 1978). Rountree (1989) provided a more extensive description of the huskanaw ceremony relative to Powhatan boys, who were trained from early in life to be stoic warriors who could withstand multiple hardships. Boys were initiated from 10 to 15 years of age and, once initiated, could become men with status and achieve leadership positions within the tribe. The ceremony began with singing, feasting, and dancing in the woods. After vigorous and exhausting activities on the part of the people, boys, who had been painted white, were brought into the circle and the people danced and sang around them. After a series of impressive violent acts directed toward the initiates (which were more aggressive in appearance than in actuality), boys experienced a series of abductions. Ultimately, the boys were held deep in the forest for several months by older, initiated men who subjected the boys to beatings and forced them to ingest an intoxicating but dangerous plant (possibly jimsonweed). After a state of imposed madness and confinement, boys were gradually withdrawn from the drug and returned to their homes. The stupor effect of the drugs was interpreted to mean that they had forgotten their earlier lives as boys and had been retrained as men. While boys were ceremonially killed and reborn through the huskanaw, some boys actually died from the rigorous rituals. This ceremony reflects two key components found in numerous other male puberty rites worldwide: "hazing to gain the victims' loyalty and a shared secret to cut the possessors off from others" (Rountree, 1989, p. 82). A further significant aspect of the Powhatan rite was the vigorous treatment designed to create a total break from boyhood. Indeed, if young men demonstrated connection or recognition of their past boyhood status, they could be required to undergo the huskanaw again (Garrow, 1974).

The rite of passage for Kickapoo boys was the killing of their first game, after which time a feast was held with songs and prayers. For Micmac boys as well, killing of the first large game was recognized as a rite of passage (Pritzker, 1998), as it was for Illinois boys. No pubertal rites were mentioned for Maliseet-Passamaquoddy boys, except that they could sit in council with the older men after killing their first moose and could participate in public feasts (V. O. Erikson, 1978).

In summary, coming-of-age rites of boys in the Northeast cultural area were consistent with those of the Plains relative to vision quests and recognition of success at first kill of game. The huskanaw ceremony that was practiced by some Virginia and North Carolina Iroquoian and Virginia Algonquian cultures represented one of the most severe rites of passage for boys.

Southeast

There is limited information available on coming-of-age rites for boys in the Southeast cultural area, but a few cultural practices have been presented in the literature. In general, boys were toughened by engagement in winter plunges and the taking of special herbs (Pritzker, 1998). As previously described, Chitimacha boys (and girls) engaged in rigorous initiation ceremonies that involved fasting, dancing to exhaustion, and acquiring a spirit helper (Brightman, 2004). Choctaw boys were tattooed at puberty, and some wore bear claws through their noses (Pritzker, 1998).

Yuchi boys were formally initiated at the Green Corn festival, and as explained by Speck (1909/1979), "Initiation was, in brief, the formal admission of youths into the privileges of the hereditary society, and into the rank of responsible manhood in their clan and town" (p. 96). Fogelson (2004) indicated there were no puberty rites for Cherokee boys comparable to the seclusion of girls. However, minor ceremonial recognition of the first kill of game occurred. Additionally, Eggan (1937) stated that Eastern Cherokee boys' coming-of-age emphasized dancing, hunting, and engaging in ball games. Among the Chickasaws, boys distributed the products of their first kill of large game among their kin but ate none of the meat themselves. This action was believed to bring favorable actions in future hunting endeavors (Brightman & Wallace, 2004).

Southwest

There were extensive and widely varying coming-of-age events for boys of the Southwest. In Pueblo cultures, coming-of-age for boys centered on initiation into societies, such as the assignment of a nonclan mother or father to Hopi-Tewa boys, who then experienced a whipping rite at about ages 8 to 10. As part of their initiation, boys were assigned a new name and could play kachina roles. In speaking of the Hopi in general, Schlegel (1973) discussed the first childhood initiation, which involved whippings for both boys and girls (more severe for boys) and their introduction to the secrets of the kachina ceremonies. Children experienced disillusionment when the identities of the kachinas were revealed to be their actual relatives who assumed the costumes and identities of these figures. An initiation occurred again at about age 14, when boys received a new ceremonial father from their clan's kiva group and were initiated at the Tewa's winter solstice ceremony. Similarly, boys of San Juan Pueblo were whipped and then the identity of the adult behind the kachina mask was revealed to them. Boys were instructed not to reveal this knowledge. The whipping ceremony was the last of three rites of childhood and served to embed the young person in the moiety to which they would belong for life. Santo Domingo boys were initiated at around age 10 (L. A. White, 1935). Pubescent Zuni boys were initiated into the *katikyanne* society and could subsequently perform in masked dances in which gods were personified.

In the non-Pueblo Southwest there were various coming-of-age practices for Apache boys. The famed war leader Geronimo apparently assumed responsibility for the rigorous training of young men, which included repeated plunges in icy streams in the winter (Debo, 1976). In his autobiography (as recorded by Barrett, 1906), Geronimo related that the training of young men to become warriors included the rigors of the warpath on four separate occasions. During such times, youth were to serve the warriors, endure various hardships, and adhere to various restrictions relative to food and speech. Those who proved themselves courageous, industrious, and capable of enduring the hardships without complaint were voted by the council to be incorporated as warriors. Nonetheless, the Apaches' warrior system was hierarchical and new initiates entered at the lowest ranks. The initiations into warfare also involved learning the sacred names of items used in battle, as explained by Geronimo: "War is a solemn religious matter" (p. 188).

In further elaboration of the Chiricahua Apache boy's coming-of-age, Opler (1983b) confirmed the significance of the first four raiding expeditions: "On these occasions the youth was addressed by the name of the culture hero, was subject to some of the same restrictions that had been placed upon the girl at the time of her puberty rite, and had to learn a special vocabulary to use during these ventures" (p. 414). Opler (1941) reported that the first four raiding or war expeditions occurred around age 16 and that boys were somewhat protected or shielded on these initial ventures. Certainly, in the process, they were sensitized to the challenges and dangers of warfare and raiding. A boy volunteered for such an experience when he perceived his readiness, and if one did not take part in this rite of passage he might never be accepted as a responsible member of a war party. Shamans frequently played a critical role in the socialization of boys for these endeavors, because the insights of shamans were necessary in strategizing against enemies (such as the strategic insights Geronimo obtained from his "power" relative to war). Boys would be identified with the male cultural hero of the Chiricahuas, namely, Child of the Water, and be called by this name. This practice is parallel to the Apache girl's identification with and subsequent transformation into White Painted Woman (see chapter 6). Boys also adhered to numerous taboos and restrictions, including limited sexual intercourse. Interestingly, during their apprenticeship boys were required to use drinking tubes and scratching sticks, but for reasons different than those for girls. If a boy did not use his drinking tube, it was stated, his whiskers would grow fast. Use of the scratching stick would ensure that he would not have soft skin (in contrast, girls used the scratching stick to protect their skin). After successful apprenticeship in four war parties, boys were expected to perform like men during their fifth and subsequent endeavors.

The Jicarilla Apache boy's coming-of-age event was the first hunt of big game, for which he was prepared for in advance (Opler, 1936). After the boy served a period as an apprentice, his grandfather brought him on a hunting expedition. If success ensued, the blood from the heart of the animal was rubbed on the boy's face and hands to signify accomplishment of this rite of passage.

For Western Apache boys, as well, G. Goodwin (1942) identified the war party as the significant coming-of-age event. At this time, a boy was subjected to restrictions and taboos and specified rituals were performed. Upon returning from the war or raiding event, he was no longer considered a boy.

Reagan (1931) reported on the adolescent rites of boys on the Fort Apache Reservation in Arizona based on his field notes from 1901 and 1902. Essentially, he described a form of a vision quest that required boys to go off alone or in groups to fast and pray under the instruction of a medicine man. The goals of this ceremony were to "make them strong, courageous men, to secure them a suitable wife and healthy offspring, and to receive instruction so they can choose their life occupation and guardian spirit" (p. 309). As is typical in a vision quest, a guardian spirit was expected to be encountered after extensive prayer and fasting. Based on such a manifestation, a miniature effigy was made of the spirit, and this was worn around the young man's neck from that point on. The boy was also given a medicine bag to be worn for protection throughout life. A closing ceremony followed with feasting and dancing.

The absence of boys' coming-of-age events is significant in present-day Apache culture. Norelli (1994) noted that such activities were previously forbidden by the U.S. government to minimize the warrior culture in Apaches, and these practices have never recovered from such prohibitions. Nevertheless, however, according to my observations and conversations in the field relative to the Apache Sunrise Dance, it was apparent that some boys and young men are initiated in the sacred rites of their culture through their assumption of roles as Mountain Spirit dancers, as singers at ceremonies, and through sweat bath rituals. Considerable ongoing socialization occurs as more experienced medicine men select and train these dancers and initiate younger men into other ritual activities.

In writing of Navajo culture, Reichard (1977) indicated that there was no clear physical indicator of the boy's transition to manhood, but in the past boys were subjected to rigorous physical training and were prepared for roles in hunting, trading, and warfare. It was further stated that boys gradually evolved into the responsibilities of manhood. In my fieldwork among the Navajos I specifically queried medicine persons and others on the practice of boys' coming-of-age events. It was confirmed that such traditions had diminished over time but that there were still some expressions of rites of passage for boys, such as a sweat bath ceremony. Also, boys (and girls) between the ages of 7 and 13 are initiated during the last night of the famed Yeibichai, or Night Way Ceremony, when young people put on the masks of the dancers after the identities of the masked dancers have been revealed to them (Locke, 1992). This is similar to the disillusion experienced by Pueblo boys relative to kachina societies.

There were a few additional mentions of boys' coming-of-age experiences in the *Handbook of North American Indians*. Changing of a boy's voice was the signal for the Yavapais' puberty observances. For four mornings, the boy had to rise before others. Various physical observances were required, such as sharpening his eyesight by watching the gray rocks of the fireplace, running, eating little food for days, and using a drinking tube and scratching stick. Cocopas' initiation into manhood involved having the nasal septum pierced (with accompanying dietary restrictions) and having footraces to a secluded spot where the boy painted symbols on rocks.

Joseph et al. (1949) stated that although there were puberty ceremonies for Tohono O'odham girls, there were none for boys. Instead, around age 11, boys entered the world of men and began to assume male adult responsibilities. Yuma prepubescent boys experienced nose-piercing ceremony from ages 6 to 10; engaged in ritual racing, bathing, and fasting; and were to avoid scratching themselves. Forde (1931) also noted that the Yuma boys' initiations were viewed as the male counterpart to girls' puberty rites. Certainly, this is a theme that is observed in other cultural areas, and it is discussed more fully in the last section of this chapter.

California

Elsasser (1978a) observed the less abundant and less complex puberty rituals for boys in this cultural area. It was further noted that boys' coming-of-age rituals were not important in northwestern California (Elsasser, 1978b). Perhaps they were not as important as those for girls, but there were varied coming-of-age events for boys in several cultures of the California area.

Achumawi and Shasta boys and boys of other groups obtained their spiritual power through the vision quest. Chumash boys were given strong liquor to seek visions. As well, various rituals surrounded recognition of a young man's coming-of-age through his first kill. Among the Shastan peoples, the game from an adolescent boy's first kill could not be consumed by his parents or by himself. The Nomlaki boy could not consume the kill of his first success in hunting (Goldschmidt, 1978). A feast was given by the parents of a Wintu boy after he killed his first deer or caught his first salmon. He was not allowed to eat this kill and was required to bathe after the hunt. Lake Miwok boys went on their first hunt at adolescence and fasted for the first time.

Initiation ceremonies that sometimes included instruction were another form of coming-of-age for boys. A male tribal rite was performed for Coast Miwok boys at ages 6 or 7. The boys endured training in song and dance for several days, after which they performed the skills they had acquired. Western and Northeastern Pomo boys were taught various dances throughout childhood and, around age 12, were presented with a hairnet and a bow and arrow. Additionally, around ages 10 to 12 they were initiated into shamanistic, ritual, and professional roles during the Kuksu ceremony. Eastern Pomo boys could be given a hairnet along with a toy bow and arrows at ages 8 or 10, accompanied by ritual bathing and a feast. Piercing the nose was a component of boys' initiations in Achumawi and Tipai-Ipai cultures. There was no puberty ceremony for Sinkyone boys, but they were tattooed at pubescence.

Konkow boys age 15 or older could be initiated into a secret society, as could Patwin boys at puberty. Patwin boys were brought to the hills to be trained and were shot at four times with a padded arrow at close range (Kroeber, 1932). The goal was for them to closely observe the actions of arrows and dodge them. Ceremonies and dance lessons went on for 8 days, at which time the new initiates were given new names and wands. Puberty schools for boys and girls were present in many Pacific Athabascan cultures, such as Lassiks.

Atsugewi boys underwent a puberty celebration when their voices changed. They endured a variety of challenging activities, including whipping and gargling with sand. Yana boys also were whipped with bow strings and would have their ears pierced and possibly their septums perforated. Foothill Yokut boys were strengthened through nightly swims in the winter. At age 12, Cahto boys were put in a dance house for the winter and were warned about dangers and instructed to be good (Myers, 1978).

The taking of datura by adolescent boys (and less frequently girls) was associated with several of the California tribes, such as Costanoans, Foothill Yokuts, Luiseños, Monaches, Salinans, Serranos, Tubatulabals, and Yokuts (see Grant, 1978; Hester, 1978; as well as previous citations for these cultures). Indeed, Kroeber (1922) noted that, along with the Kuska (a secret society into which boys were initiated), the taking of datura was the other signifying event of boys' initiation in the California cultural area. During the Serrano boys' puberty ceremony, called Tamonin, initiates ingested a datura-laden beverage and danced around a fire in the ceremonial house. After the ceremony they learned special songs, and this was followed by feasting and gift giving. Kitanemuk boys would be given datura during the winter months in order to acquire their spiritual helper. While in a comatose state, the boy was expected to see a vision, and he would subsequently report his experiences. Other restrictions followed including separation from others and various food taboos to solidify his new relationship with his spirit helper and to be considered an adult. The experience of Serrano boys was similar; after taking datura and being permitted to sleep, they "would have visions that were later interpreted by the shamans and used as sign posts for the boys' future lives" (Bean & Smith, 1978b, p. 572). Luiseño boys, 3 days after taking datura, had to leap from stone to stone over a pit with a net symbolic of the Milky Way. A misstep was taken as a prediction of an early death, while success was deemed an escape from the spirit of death.

Clearly, some kind of initiation for boys at or around puberty was important to several cultures of the California cultural area. However, boys' coming-of-age activities were not as extensive as those of girls. Some of the manipulations required for girls, such as warming or heating, also were not indicated for boys. In contrast, the taking of datura occurred in several cultures as well as in certain types of male initiations.

Great Basin

The practice of coming-of-age events for boys in the Great Basin was minimal. Among the Northern Paiutes, a ceremony occurred at the boy's first kill of large game in which his father, accompanied by another great hunter, stood on a pile of sagebrush and chewed the meat with sage. These items were then placed on the boy's joints to build strength. In the Pyramid Lake region, the Northern Paiutes would give boys a choice cut from their first large kill. It then became acceptable for their families to eat game of boys. Neither the Southern Paiute boy nor his parents would eat the game he killed until it was game obtained after he was of marriageable age. When he reached that status, he was bathed, his face and body were painted with red paint, his hair was trimmed, and he was required to run. The Utes did not have formal puberty ceremonies for boys, but they did adhere to the practice of many other tribes of not permitting boys to eat the meat of their first kill of large game. Kawaiisu boys faced similar puberty ordeals as girls; these involved ingesting datura, inducing vomiting, fasting from meat, and, potentially, experiencing the ant-eating ordeal previously described.

Plateau

Boys of a variety of groups in the Plateau area were required to engage in physically demanding activities as part of their coming-of-age experience. Vision quests were frequent requirements for boys (and girls), and it was believed that such experiences granted boys powers that would be useful to them as future hunters, warriors, shamans, root diggers, fishermen, and in other roles (Walker, 1998a). A successful vision quest for boys resulted in their admittance to the sphere of adult men. Fasting, praying, and sweat bathing accompanied the vision quest. It was believed that during the solitary and remote quest, Plateau boys and girls entered into a relationship with a spirit and obtained its song and power, which would be revealed more completely at a later time. Premature revealing of a vision was believed to result in a loss of power, as was described for the Kalispel.

A vision quest could be quite lengthy, as was the case of Kalispel boys, whose quest might last 7 to 20 days. The process could be quite taxing for individuals of some groups, such as the Lillooets, whose subsequent vision quests included purging with medicine. Spokane boys prepared for their vision quest by following a strict program of running and swimming. Coeur d'Alene boys sought guardian spirits and also endured a physical training longer than that of girls that included burning their skin.

The Lillooets believed it useful for boys to acquire a guardian spirit helper from their quests to provide protection, knowledge, and abilities. Impressions of these experiences were painted on rock bluffs, stones, or trees. Northern Okanagan, Shuswap, and Thompson adolescent boys and girls depicted their ceremonies and dreams in rock art as well as pictures of their future wives and husbands, respectively.

Many groups, such as the Nez Perces, required boys (and girls) to engage in several quests to seek a vision. The Shuswaps' series of vision quests could continue for 1 to 10 years until a guardian spirit was obtained. Sweat bathing and the taking of plants that induced dreams or hallucinations accompanied the vision quests. The prepubescent training of the Northern Okanagan, Lakes, and Colville boys and girls were described by Kennedy and Bouchard (1998b) as "physical activity, a daily regime of sweathouse and bathing using special herbal rubs, and observation of the natural world. Each day the trainee marked his or her face with red paint or charcoal, and supplicated the dawn and sunset, asking for good luck. At night, they wandered to lonely parts of the hills where they danced and implored spirits to protect them. Eventually an animal, bird, or other creature appeared in a dream or vision and offered its protection and a song to the pubescent child" (p. 249).

Middle Columbia River Salishan boys did not have formal puberty observances, but, in addition to the quest for a guardian spirit, they would receive a public pronouncement of being a young man after successful performance in a hunt or some other good deed. The Yakima child was instructed to seek a guardian spirit in a remote place. Beyond that experience, puberty was recognized for boys at about age 13 when they began to engage in men's work.

In addition to the quest for a guardian spirit, Wasco, Wishram, and Cascade boys would present to the elders their first catch of fish or results of a successful hunt. Among the Cayuse, Umatilla, and Walla Walla cultures, a family ceremony would be held and elders would be given the products of boys' first kill of game or fish.

Singing or the acquisition of songs was of prime importance in boys' coming-of-age events in some groups of the Plateau. Thompson boys would sing all night during their vision quest (Olsen, 1998). When the Klamath boy's voice changed, this was an indicator for the vision quest, which involved fasting until a song was revealed in a dream.

While few observances were associated strictly with puberty, coming-of-age experiences for boys were important in the Plateau area. Various arduous rituals accompanied vision quests, and quests could be repeated several times until successful attainment of a guardian spirit. The expression of these visions in rock art is interesting, and may be a component somewhat exclusive to Plateau cultures.

Northwest Coast

Relative to Northwest cultures, as with other cultural areas, it is sometimes more appropriate to address the topic as preparation toward manhood as opposed to puberty ceremonies. For Tlingit and Haida cultures, such observances began in childhood with boys being toughened with swims in icy waters and various other physically demanding tasks. Maternal uncles supervised boys in these tasks, as well as instructing them on their traditions and orienting them according to their clans and lineages. As well, Tlingit boys observed food taboos until their first successful hunt, which culminated in a feast.

Northern Coast Salish boys underwent both physical and mental puberty training. A major component of this was acquisition of a guardian spirit through a quest that involved solitude, cold-water baths, sweat baths, and little eating. The guardian spirit power could be received through a dream or trance from a bird, animal, or inanimate object. The powers were thought to yield useful skills in hunting, fishing, or canoe making. Southern Coast Salish boys also sought guardian spirits. Twana and Coast Salish boys began their training for adulthood at age 5 or 6, followed by solitary fasts with the goal of obtaining a guardian spirit. Once obtained, this encounter was forgotten until a much later time, perhaps as much as 20 years later (Torrance, 1994).

The Eyak boy's first kill of game was recognized with a presentation of gifts to members of the opposite moiety. Likewise, Nootkans recognized the boy's first kill of game with a feast. The first kill of Tillamook boys were given as gifts to the elderly. The Central Coast Salish boy also would be recognized at his first kill. His voice change, as well, could yield ceremonial recognition.

Among the Tsimshian peoples, boys (and girls) would receive their first names at puberty ceremonies, and gifts would be distributed by relatives of their lineage. The Bella Coolas did not observe puberty observances or initiations for boys. However, the belief that "a boy would have good luck in his life if he noticed blood in his urine during the time of puberty" was reported in the 1970s (Kennedy & Bouchard, 1990a, p. 331). A small feast was observed for the Bella Coola boy's first kill of game. Contemporary Kwakiutl boys were initiated as Cannibal Dancers or members of some other secret society linked to family rights. In short, coming-of-age rites for boys of the Northwest Coast cultural area included vision quests, various tests of physical endurance, and recognition at the first kill of game.

Subarctic

Pubertal rituals for boys in the Subarctic were not as prominent as those for girls, but coming-of-age observances did occur especially in respect to goals of building physical strength and engaging in vision quests for spirit helpers. Relative to the vision quest, Honigmann (1981a) stated that "Everywhere, except among the eastern Cree, Naskapi, and Atlantic Shore Algonquians, a boy at about puberty hoped to find supernatural helpers while in solitude in the forest, through a dream that conformed to the right type" (p. 719). It was highly desirable to be able to inform others that a successful vision quest had occurred. Western Woods Cree boys engaged in isolation and fasting to induce dreams that might bring spiritual powers from manitous. Mackenzie Mountain Indian boys withdrew and camped alone in order to dream and obtain "medicine" that would yield supernatural powers. Slavey boys would seek spiritual power for curing and hunting through dreams from animal spirits. More southerly Cordillera cultures stressed vision quests, as did the Sekanis and the Kaskas (Honigmann, 1981b).

In addition to vision quests, boys of the Subarctic were faced with rigorous demands at their coming-of-age. The Chilcotin boy engaged in intensive puberty training, which included a restricted diet for 1 year, exercise, hard work, and early-morning swims in cold water. After initial training, the boy would go to the mountains for several days and run, swim in cold water, and nap without the benefit of a fire or shelter. The goal was to build endurance, agility, and mobility. A feast would be held by his family after he endured these hardships. Similarly, Carrier boys experienced intensive physical training at adolescence along with food restrictions that could hinder their hunting and running abilities (Tobey, 1981). Carrier boys had their ankles, legs, wrists, and fingers bound with a cord (McKennan, 1959), as did Ahtna boys, with the purpose to produce limber joints and small bones. Simultaneous with their vision quest, Kaska boys would plunge into icy waters and were whipped with willow switches. Inland Tlingit boys underwent their rigorous training at puberty while living together and being trained by male relatives other than their fathers, who were thought to be too indulgent. Likewise, Tutchone boys lived together in separate camps and were rigorously trained by maternal and paternal kin. Gwich'in boys were "thrown out" of their parental lodge and sent to live with other boys in a special lodge where they would live until marriage. Mature men, specifically chosen for the task, supervised the training of these boys (Slobodin, 1981). Tagish boys were trained by grandfathers, fathers, and uncles who subjected the boys to strict physical training including their learning of patterns of subsistence, their moral obligations, and the characteristics of their matrilineages. At some point in childhood, Chilkat boys were given over to their uncles to be raised because it was thought that if they stayed in their homes they would be spoiled and not be strong men.

Another facet of coming-of-age of boys of the Subarctic was celebration of the kill of first large game, such as occurred among the Western Woods Crees, Slaveys, and boys from bands and tribes of the Cordillera. This was the only celebration for Hare boys at adolescence. The Han culture had minimal celebration at a boy's puberty (Crow & Obley, 1981), but a celebration usually occurred at the event of a boy's first kill of big game (Osgood, 1971). The father of the Peel River Gwich'in boy hosted a public feast at his son's kill of first game (Osgood, 1936/1970). The son was praised and publicly recognized by his social community at the time of this event. Osgood noted a certain correspondence or basis of comparison between puberty celebrations for girls and celebrations of boys' first successful hunt of large game among the Crow River Gwich'in. The Kachemak Bay Tanainas required boys to fast from food and water after killing their first large game (Osgood, 1937). The men celebrated by eating his game, and the boy could eat any small pieces left over. These customs were conducted to facilitate luck for the boy in hunting.

Adolescence was a time for Chipewyan boys to acquire hunting skills, but there were no coming-of-age ceremonies. Likewise, Dogrib boys experienced no puberty celebration or recognition, but their childhood associations with girls were expected to cease. McKennan (1959) observed that puberty rituals for Upper Tanana boys could go practically unnoticed. However, the Upper Tananas held a belief that, for boys and girls, this was a critical stage of development and that behaviors at this time could have an impact on later life. When their voices changed, boys were to refrain from eating ducks or porcupines, or it was thought that pimples could result. It also was believed that if boys pulled out their first few whiskers and tied them to trees they would grow to be rich men.

The Upper Inlet Tanaina boys practiced a set of coming-of-age events around age 15. They were isolated in the woods for 5 days and fasted from food and water during that time. They used a head scratcher, as girls did in their puberty ceremonies, and would drink through a bone drinking tube during a second 5-day stint in the woods. The male puberty rituals were conducted to make men rich and lucky in life. The Tyonek Tanaina boys also experienced a 10-day puberty ritual, but they stayed at home during that time and faced food and water restrictions.

Clearly, boys of several Subarctic cultures experienced various forms of separation, such as that which occurred through the vision quest experience or the requirement to live apart from their family of origin. Boys were subjected to physical demands designed to build strength. Although the rituals might not have occurred at puberty per se, they can be considered part of the coming-of-age experience.

Arctic

There is only minor reference to coming-of-age rituals for boys of the Arctic cultural area. From about age 12, instruction of the Pacific Eskimo boy by an adult, particularly an uncle, would ensue. By age 16 these boys would be in their own kayaks accompanying hunting parties. The killing of his first bearded seal served as a rite of passage for the Nunivak Eskimo boy. This event typically occurred after puberty, but it necessitated certain observances that mimicked those of girls' puberty ceremonies. The most important rite of passage for the West Greenlander boy was his first seal kill (Kleivan, 1984). Mackenzie Delta Eskimo boys at about age 12 or 13, ceremonially, had incisors filed down, earlobes perforated, and cheeks perforated for labrets. The boy's first kill of large game also was a cause for a ceremony (D. Smith, 1984).

Summary of Boys' Coming-of-Age

In summarizing this section on boys' coming-of-age, there were few observances specifically linked to a biological aspect of puberty, but boys' initiations can be conceived as counterparts to girls' puberty observances. The vision quest experience, at some time from childhood to young adulthood, was the most common coming-of-age rite for boys. Sometimes arduous rituals accompanied these quests, and they could be repeated several times until successful attainment of a guardian spirit.

Indeed, tests of physical endurance were frequent occurrences of boys' coming-of-age. A boy's first great accomplishment as a hunter or in battle also signified successful transition to adulthood. In short, the following quote by Kroeber (1923) is illustrative of boys' coming-of-age rites in Native North America: "The boys' rites come at the corresponding period of life, but their reference to sex and marriage is generally less definite. Fortitude, manliness, understanding are the qualities they are chiefly intended to test and fix. Privations like fasting, ordeals of pain, admonitions by the elders, are therefore characteristic of these rites" (p. 365).

Themes of Coming-of-Age Practices

Chapter 3 presented foundational concepts relative to North American Indian views of human development, notions of critical periods of development, and beliefs regarding pubescents, particularly girls. It was noted that, beginning in infancy and childhood, North American Indian cultures practiced rituals throughout the life span to bring recognition and celebration to transitional and potentially vulnerable phases of development. Further, the desired outcomes of these observances frequently centered on the protection of initiates and the inculcation of desired traits and abilities. This chapter brought substance to the theoretical and philosophical underpinnings by providing a broad historical overview of puberty rituals relative to both girls and boys.

It was also indicated in chapter 3 that, prior to puberty, there was little differentiation between the performances of rituals according to sex. However, by later childhood, and surely by puberty, distinctions in rites of passage for boys and girls were apparent. Various reasons can be offered for sex distinctions at this time. Certainly physical evidence of maleness and femaleness becomes apparent according to both sexual maturation and changes in physical shape and size, but it is perhaps the social significance of these physical changes that serves as an even greater impetus to sex-linked puberty rituals. As discussed in chapter 4, North American Indian cultures traditionally exhibited a strong value toward the expression of gender-typed behaviors. The roles of men and women and their associated tasks were distinct, but all gender-linked activities were valued for their contributions to the survival of the group and the good of the social order. Due to the maturational patterns of pubescence that are indicative of impending adulthood, pubescence was regarded as the prime time for proper socialization of young people into the spheres of men and women.

The transition from childhood to adulthood, therefore, is dependent on certain physical markers that possess strong psychological and social salience, which subsequently prompt the occurrence of gender-linked rites of passage. Girls possess the most obvious physical marker through the event of menarche; hence, coming-of-age rituals frequently surrounded this event to the extent that sometimes elaborate rituals and public celebrations occurred. In contrast, such a clear-cut marker is not apparent for boys, although a change in the boy's voice was sometimes used as a physical indicator of maturation. It was more typical in the past, however, to acknowledge and celebrate other indices of boys' coming-of-age, such as the first kill of large game or first success in battle. Indeed, for both boys and girls there were expectations that adult-like skills should be performed, and such accomplishments were socially reinforced and sometimes celebrated.

In addition to the markers of coming-of-age (e.g., menarche, accomplishment of an adult feat, etc.), in the past and in some present-day cultures, both boys and girls were situated in particular states to maximize their exposure to the spiritual realm at a time of the life span when they were believed to be highly impressionable and susceptible to such influences. For girls, the physical action of menstruation alone signified a special status that instilled them with power or made them more attractive to the spiritual realm. Since boys do not experience the empowering quality of menstruation, they were compelled into circumstances to alter their states of consciousness and expose them to the spiritual world (these rituals were sometimes applied to girls, as well). For example, young people were frequently subjected to various forms of isolation, fasts, sleep deprivation, and physical rigors of the vision quest in order to obtain their guardian spirit helper.

The vision quest experience was an almost universal coming-of-age experience and, as previously explained, could be considered the boy's rite of passage to manhood in North America, as opposed to puberty rituals per se. As an explanation for the preponderance of this activity for males, Barnouw (1950) explained: "a man's activities—hunting and warfare, etc.—involved unpredictable elements in which magical support was essential for success" (cited in Torrance, 1994, p. 243). Torrance went on to say, "Woman might be more open to spontaneous visions, but mastery of spirits through the disciplined quest was an overwhelmingly male prerogative" (p. 243). It was the cultures of the Great Plains that exhibited the height of individual achievement and among whom the vision quest predominated, as explained by Torrance (1994): "Yet few cultures have more emphasized individual achievement, and to none has the vision quest been more central" (p. 245). Nonetheless, this important individualized spiritual quest occurred across tribes of Native North America.

The vision quest was characterized by individuality and unpredictability and, as with other coming-of-age events, was largely individualized. Even in cases where ceremony accompanied the rite of passage, it was usually about an individual adolescent who had demonstrated some attribute of adulthood, such as menstruation, successful passage through rigorous rituals of a rite of passage, successful vision quest, or accomplishment of an adult feat. These individualized events were embedded within communal cultures and are further evidence of the coexistence and sometimes integration of communal and individualistic traits operative in North American Indian cultures.

Evidently, as is revealed in this review, a broad range of puberty customs occurred in the past and, as is shown in subsequent chapters, some continue into the present day. While it is beyond the scope of this book to conduct a thorough content analysis of these customs according to cultures or cultural areas, it is useful to discuss complexes of coming-of-age customs according to the following themes: various forms of separation or seclusion, industry and tests of physical endurance, adherence to taboos, accomplishment of adult feats, instruction/mentorship, physical manipulations and adornments, celebration, and spiritual transcendence.

Separation

According to van Gennep (1908/1960), separation is the first phase of a rite of passage, as discussed in chapter 1. Various forms of separation were shown to occur during coming-of-age rites, with perhaps the seclusion of females at first menses the most widespread practice. Seclusion could be required for the first menses only or for up to 2 or more years. Further, seclusion during menstruation could continue until menopause. The location of seclusion ranged from simply a separate space designated in the family's home to a shelter or hut constructed some distance from the group. Associated practices of seclusion could be quite extreme, as in the case of some Subarctic cultures that required seclusion for up to 2 years with adherence to strict food and behavioral taboos. In several of the northern hunting cultures, massive efforts were taken to maintain distance between pubescent girls and hunters, hunting implements, and the game of hunters in order not to jeopardize procurement of important and necessary sources of subsistence.

For boys the vision quest was close to a universal experience across North American Indian cultures, and it was sometimes important for girls as well, as was seen in the Plains, Northeast, and Plateau cultural areas. The phases of rites of passage are readily apparent in the vision quest beginning with separation. For instance, Sullwold (1987) illustrated the initiation of the Crow chief Plenty Coup according to van Gennep's model. Plenty Coup was first removed from the world of women at the age of 9 and given over to the care of his grandfather. This separation yielded transition during which time he was taught important skills of alertness, watchfulness, stillness, and agility. The huskanaw ceremony of some Algonquian and Iroquoian cultures of Virginia and North Carolina forced the separation of boys, who were subjected to a series of severe rituals. Separation began with removal from their homes to the woods for several months under the tutelage of priests and advisers. Subarctic cultures, as well, removed boys from the comforts of their homes to undergo rigorous training supervised by older men. For boys, the purpose of such severe separation was to build physical and psychological strength.

In addition to the vision quest and various other forms of separation, sometimes an altered state of consciousness was induced through the ingestion of datura or some similar substance to facilitate separation and provide avenues to the spiritual realm. While it is unknown if mood-altering substances are still used for ritual purposes at puberty, the

Native American Church uses peyote, a mild hallucinogen, to enhance the potential for connection to the spiritual realm and to obtain visions. It is unknown if the Native American Church has specifically identified pubescence a time in the life span to introduce the contemporary young person to peyote.

Separation readily yields to transition (the second phase in van Gennep's model), and these two phases frequently merge for initiates, who, while in their separated states, are subjected to rituals that serve to intensify their present state of distinctiveness. Further, coming-of-age rituals are explicitly designed to induce change and yield psychological or physical discomforts for initiates that correspondingly heighten a liminal or "betwixt and between" state. The following two sections include illustrations of actions of transition during the coming-of-age rite of passage.

Industry and Tests of Physical Endurance

Puberty rituals were typically demanding of the physical energy of youth. Whether it was the requirement to engage in challenging tasks to learn industry or to prove oneself through ordeals that tested one to his or her physical limits, a goal was to build strength and character. As indicated in chapter 3, a common belief among Indigenous groups in North America was that the behaviors of pubescent girls would have an impact on their future lives. Hence, it was necessary to subject them to physical tests to build endurance as well as to test their strength and character. Indeed, Driver (1941) stated that rites of physical exertion associated with girls' coming-of-age events were intended to build character more than to strengthen their bodies. At any rate, there is cultural variability in such functions; for instance, building both psychological and physical forms of strength is certainly a goal of contemporary Apache and Navajo puberty ceremonies (see chapters 7, 8, and 9).

During their separation, girls were typically required to maintain a level of industriousness and to stay engaged with female-linked tasks. Driver (1941) stated that industry was a universal trait across western North America in girls' coming-of-age events, an assertion that is supported in this chapter. While industry was universal, the content of instruction varied according to culture. For instance, Carrier pubescent girls built birchbark vessels, tanned hides, sewed, and wove rabbitskin blankets (Libby, 1952). Corn grinding was required of Navajo, Hopi, and Zuni girls and is still part of Navajo and Hopi coming-of-age events. Zunis believed that corn grinding at pubescence would bring ease to menstruation and reinforce industrious behaviors. Other physically demanding tasks required of girls included extensive physical activity such as running (e.g., Navajo, Havasupai) and dancing in the hot sun (e.g., Western Apache). Walapai pubescent girls were engaged in several tasks of industry, as explained by Kniffen, MacGregor, McKennan, Mekeel, and Mook (1935): "She should be busy all the time, rising early in the morning to bring wood and water, and cooking meals whether she previously knew how or not. This would make her a diligent and good wife. If she were sent on errands she must race to do them, so that she would become a strong and fast runner" (p. 139).

The requirements of physical challenges at pubescence extended to boys' coming-of-age and, in some cases, were quite severe. Boys of the Northwest Coast and Subarctic were subjected to plunges in icy waters. In some Pueblo cultures of the Southwest, boys were whipped as part of their initiations to kachina societies. The huskanaw ceremony of the mid-Atlantic region was an intense experience of separation from parents that included vigorous and exhaustive activities, beatings, and ingestion of a dangerous plant. The extreme actions of this rite of passage were designed to impress on boys a complete break from childhood as they transitioned into adulthood.

Adherence to Taboos

Taboos represent an extension of separation because they serve to create social and psychological distance required by initiates and sometimes by others. A range of taboos at puberty was noted in the review of literature. The underlying cause for taboos centers on the special quality of the young person that, if not properly contained or managed, could have deleterious consequences for herself or others. Indeed, Driver (1941) concluded that the most frequent set of reasons for taboos encompassed either the consequences of lack of obedience (e.g., premature death) or, alternatively, the benefits of adherence (e.g., longevity). It was further concluded that, in most cases, impacts of taboos manifested in the physical well-being of initiates, although the latent impacts of taboo violation occurred in the spiritual domain.

The actual objects or behaviors targeted according to taboos varied across cultures. There are two general categories of explanations for the multitude of taboos and behavioral restrictions: those for the well-being of others, and those for the well-being of initiates. These two functions are not mutually exclusive, since both may be applied to the same taboo in the same culture. By way of illustration, four types of taboos will be discussed: fasting from meat and engaging in hunting avoidance, concealing one's face or head, not touching or scratching oneself, and not drinking beverages in the typical fashion but using some kind of drinking tube.

Driver (1941) observed that initiates' avoidance of hunters, fishers, gamblers, and men in general was a nearly universal trait in western North America, and Libby (1952) remarked that various taboos were logical outgrowths of hunting cultures. Carrier culture offered a particularly complex and interesting set of explanations for the taboos prohibiting pubescent girls from eating fresh meat, fish, and berries (Libby, 1952). Specifically, if a pubescent girl ate fresh meat or fish, these animals would be insulated and her relatives could not catch them. In essence, these particular food items represented a form of "blood" in their own right. It was further believed that the blood of her parents was mingling and conflicting in her veins at puberty, and the pubescent should avoid these other sources of "blood" so as not to contaminate her own. The consequences for taboo violation of this type were severe for both her family (who could die soon) and herself (who could experience a premature death from a rabies type of disease). In addition to the taboos against eating meat, fish, or berries, Carrier girls were prohibited from even touching men's objects. Further, the pubescent girl had to be carried across animal paths, because walking on such a path was considered a form of contact that could lead to contamination of this important food source. An extension of this taboo occurred wherein pubescent Carrier girls could not wade or swim in streams or lakes or the fish would die or her relatives might not be successful in procuring this food source.

In some cultures, particularly those of the Subarctic and California,

the perceived power of pubescent girls necessitated behavioral requirements to encase their head or eyes while in public. Cultures such as the
Hupa, Sinkyone, and Tanaina required this ritual for the protection of
others. Many Northern Athabascan girls wore a head covering, referred
to by writers as a veil, bonnet, or mantlet that shielded their faces from
the gaze of others. As discussed in chapter 8, similar practice occurred in
Ojibwa culture, wherein pubescent girls wore hats and blackened their
faces with ash to subdue the impacts of their powerful gaze. Carrier culture believed that a misfortune would befall a man who looked on the
pubescent girl. Indeed, it was believed that the man might even die,
especially a medicine man who was particularly at risk in these events.
On the other hand, it was thought that the girl might die if the medicine
man was especially powerful (Libby, 1952). By covering their heads and
faces, initiates were offered some advantages; for instance, it was believed
that wearing a hood would yield beauty for Carcross girls. Ingaliks required that pubescent girls wear a headband of soft skin with fringes to
protect them from having headaches as they grew older.

Two of the most ancient (and therefore most widespread) customs required of pubescent girls and sometimes boys were prohibitions against
scratching or touching oneself (which necessitated the use of a scratching stick) and against drinking liquids in the normal fashion (which required drinking through a hollow reed or bone straw) (Driver, 1941).
This chapter provided numerous illustrations of both of these practices.
Relative to the scratching stick, it was thought that the power of menstruating girls could be directed toward themselves in an adverse manner
if they touched themselves directly. Therefore, the scratching stick served
to facilitate a means for the pubescent to touch the self without harm.
In some cultures it was believed that the pubescent girl could contract
fatal diseases or her hair might fall out if she scratched herself. Indeed,
an Ojibwa informant (see chapter 8) described how she had initially ignored this taboo at pubescence and subsequently lost a great deal of her
hair. In chapter 6 it is explained that during the 4 days of the Apache
Sunrise Dance girls are required to use the scratching stick to prevent
permanent scarring from touching themselves while in their empowered
state. As previously stated, Apache boys were required to use the scratching stick to ensure they would *not* have soft skin. Driver indicated that

perceived consequences from violation of the scratching taboo centered consistently on adverse impacts on the hair and skin of pubescents.

Use of the drinking tube or straw as a substitute for drinking in the typical fashion was found in numerous cultures, especially those of the Southwest, Plateau, Northwest Coast, and Subarctic. This action served several functions—for instance, to prevent stomach trouble in the girl, ensure that she would have a small mouth, or prevent hair from growing on her lips (Driver, 1941). In Carrier culture it was thought that the girl could contract throat diseases if she did not drink out of the tube (Libby, 1952). Kwakiutl girls used the drinking tube to prevent acquiring a heavy stomach. In the Apache Sunrise Dance, the drinking tube continues to be used by girls to prevent the growth of hair on their faces, among other reasons. Apache boys of the past were required to use drinking tubes to prevent whiskers from growing too fast.

Accomplishment of Adult Feats

Accomplishment of an adult feat was a signifier of coming-of-age, especially for boys. Such activities were representative of gender-linked behaviors that were valued and reinforced by a culture. This theme supports the notion that puberty was commonly viewed as a break from a more androgynous childhood to an adulthood in which one performs gender-specific tasks and one's social network was of one's sex. While girls were expected to perform adult female-linked tasks during pubescence, completion of these tasks was typically not the cause of celebration. One exception is among the Blackfeet, who, while not giving great attention to the girl's pubescence, sponsored a feast at the completion of a daughter's first quillwork or beadwork.

For boys, however, a common signifier of successful passage from childhood to adulthood was first success in hunting or fishing activities or in battle. In the framework of van Gennep's model of rites of passage, accomplishment of an adult-like feat is illustrative of phases of transition and incorporation. In additional consideration of Sullwold's (1987) illustration of Plenty Coup's rites of passage, it was explained that, when he was prepared, Plenty Coup joined the men on a buffalo hunt and was required to stand in front of the advancing buffalo. When a young man successfully accomplished this feat, which sometimes required many attempts, he was incorporated as a full member into the adult male community. In short, gender-linked skill accomplishments were highly valued and sometimes celebrated at the time of coming-of-age, particularly for boys.

Instruction/Mentorship

Adult mentors played a critical role in the separation and transition phases of coming-of-age rites for boys and girls. These mentors performed varied and multifaceted roles and assumed major responsibilities in supporting and guiding the young person through his or her coming-of-age event. It is perhaps in the transition from childhood to adulthood that the adult mentor played the most important role, in comparison to rites of passage at other transitional stages of the life span. The special quality of pubescence indicated that, developmentally, this was the best time of the life span for young people to comprehend and retain the knowledge they were taught (Shortridge, 1913). In the past, social education, as opposed to formal education, was the primary means of instruction in North American Indian cultures. Hence, while children and youths did not have schoolteachers per se, other familial and non-familial adults stepped in and assumed responsibility for instruction. As discussed in chapter 3, the cognitive and emotional advances that correspond to the physical changes of pubescence were recognized in North American Indian cultures as circumstances that established an especially crucial need for instruction.

While instruction at coming-of-age events appeared to be universal across Native North America, the content of instruction varied by culture and could encompass directives relative to behavior and decorum, dress, morality, character, and gender roles. Instruction for girls sometimes centered on understanding proper adherence to taboos that were to be followed at all menstrual cycles, as seen in the case of a mother's or grandmother's instruction of the Ojibwa girl. Instruction typically centered on learning and perfecting skills required of adult women. For example, the mother and other female relatives of a Hupa girl impressed on her qualities of cleanliness, a good temper, and industriousness, and Serrano girls were instructed in how to be good wives.

For boys, the mentor's role could include imparting spiritual information during initiation ceremonies that were to be maintained as secrets, such as those in Pueblo kachina societies. In vision quests as well, elders prepared the young questers and aided in interpretation of their visions. Adult men also supervised more arduous aspects of boys' coming-of-age, especially those rituals designed to prepare them for strength and bravery in their future roles as warriors.

The historical literature did not provide a great deal of information regarding why a particular mentor might be selected, the exception being that this person was typically an adult relative and not necessarily the mother or father of the initiate. It was common throughout Native North America for nonparental relatives to assume responsibility for more stringent or disciplined aspects of parenting in order to safeguard the emotional attachment between child and parent. Certain adults might be selected for the important role of mentor due to their particular skills or traits. For instance, it was reported how the eminent war leader Geronimo assumed responsibility for boys' rites of passage as they were trained for battle and war. In the Navajo Kinaaldá, a female mentor who is a relative is selected according to her demonstration of desired traits of womanhood; she is actually called the "Ideal Woman" (see chapter 8). She is regarded for her qualities of physical strength, health, beauty, ambition, and good character and for her display of skills of value to the Navajo people, such as weaving. For the Western Apaches this female mentor must be a nonrelative, and she is selected according to her demonstration of admired character, skills, and morality. The selection of a nonrelative mentor is a means to create fictive kin in cultures in which kinship is of high value. Regardless of how the adult is selected, an implicit assumption is that he or she possesses traits of value that can be imparted to the initiate through direct instruction, role modeling, or, in a more mystical fashion, through transference activities of massaging or physically manipulating the initiate.

Physical Manipulations and Adornments

The application of physical manipulations at puberty links to the belief described in chapter 3 of the malleable quality of pubescence. Physical manipulations are believed to have an impact not only on the physique but also to extend to the character of the young person. As noted previously, the adult mentor must be carefully selected because he or she must possess the desired traits of the culture that will be transferred to the initiate through the physical manipulations. It is believed that girls will be affected not only in stature and size but also in physical beauty, as is the case in contemporary Western Apache and Navajo puberty ceremonies.

Massage of initiates was a common form of manipulation, as exhibited in Navajo, Apache, Yavapai, and Cocopa cultures of the Southwest. Because the initiate is in such a malleable state at this critical juncture of the life span, physical manipulation serves to mold or shape the initiate according to the desired traits of her culture. In some cultures the physical manipulation took the form of girls actually lying in heated pits—in some cases for several days, as occurred among several cultures of the Southwest (Cocopa, Havasupai, Southern Paiute, Walapai, and Yavapai), California (Eastern Pomo, Luiseño, Tapai, and Yuma) and the Great Basin (Southern Paiute and Washoe). Diegueño girls had a large heated stone placed between their legs to soften their abdomen and prepare them for motherhood (Kroeber, 1925). Again, the assumption of malleability of pubescents and the need for shaping them likely served as the impetus for such actions.

Ritual bathing and hair washing, as well, represented forms of physical manipulation and served various purposes, depending on the culture. Ritual bathing frequently occurred among cultures such as Tohono O'odham, Cocopa, Walapai, Southern Paiute, Wintu, Chimariko, and Kitanemuk, and ritual hair washing occurred in Navajo, Hopi, Walapai, Southern Paiute, and other cultures. These rituals can be conceived as purification rites as well as serving a beautification function so that the girl would always have long hair and clear skin. The beautification functions of physical manipulation were more common for girls than for boys and certainly are suggestive of a universal value for female physical attractiveness. This point is discussed further in chapter 7 relative to rituals of the Apache Sunrise Dance, but it should be remembered that the development of character and lifelong strength were perhaps even stronger functions of physical molding and manipulation of initiates.

A practice related to physical molding or manipulation was that of adorning pubescent girls and boys with special dress, decorations, paintings, or piercings. Painting and tattooing were quite common and served a multitude of purposes, such as growing old with grace or to signify transformation, as in the case of Western Apache girls who, to this day, are painted with a white clay solution to signify their transformation into White Painted Woman and facilitate longevity. Girls in a variety of cultural areas were tattooed at puberty for reasons ranging from social identification, beautification, or to signify the rite of passage.

Driver (1941) found bathing and changing clothes at the end of menstruation or seclusion to be nearly universal in western North America, and the previous review of literature provided several illustrations. Change of clothes is a visible sign of a transition and entrance into a new stage of life, specifically adulthood. Hence, the clothes worn are those of adult women of the initiate's culture.

Celebration

In addition to the hard work, discipline, and commitment required on the part of initiates, there frequently was cause for celebration at coming-of-age events. Not all pubertal rites of passage included ceremonies, but for those that did, feasting and gift giving were important components. It was commonly the case that the ceremony's degree of lavishness was a reflection of the family's wealth. Certainly this belief was associated with the Northwest Coast potlatches, but it also occurred in other cultural areas.

While there are illustrations of celebrations occurring prior to or concomitant with other puberty rituals, it was most common for feasting and celebration to follow menstrual seclusion of the initiate. For instance, in both historical and contemporary times, Ojibwas hold a Womanhood Ceremony after seclusion, and Navajos practice gift gifting after the most demanding components of the coming-of-age ritual are completed. Giveaways were important components of Lakota coming-of-age celebrations for girls. Contemporary Western Apaches engage in feasting and gift exchanges at the onset of menarche, during the puberty ceremony and again a year later. When celebration occurred after the major coming-of-age rituals had been successfully completed, it was indicative of incorporation according to van Gennep's (1908/1960) rite-of-passage model. It was also common to hold a feast or celebration to signify incorporation of a boy after first success in hunting large game or in battle.

Spiritual Transcendence

By way of concluding this chapter, it is important to recognize the inherent spirituality of coming-of-age rituals and ceremonies practiced by North American Indians. These were and, in some cases, continue to be events that recognize the transition from childhood to adulthood; but perhaps more importantly, they were transitions into the world of the spiritual. As previously noted, pubescence was sometimes regarded as the first time the young person had the internal strength required to encounter spiritual forces. Additionally, pubescence, as a stage of the life cycle, was frequently believed to be a time when the person was especially disposed to the spiritual realm. However, it was sometimes believed that the power obtained at this life stage, such as from the vision quest experience, would not be manifest or made available to the initiate until adulthood.

In chapter 4 there were illustrations of the belief that menstruating girls were in special, sacred states and were empowered to provide blessings to others or perform other supernatural feats. In contemporary Navajo and Apache coming-of-age ceremonies for girls, rituals are included that permit onlookers to approach initiates with special requests or for blessings. In these cultures, as well as the Lakota culture, it is believed that blessings are available due to the empowered state of the initiate through her connection to an important female supernatural personage.

The ceremonial components of a coming-of-age event required the involvement of a medicine person or shaman to sing or pray over the initiate. Such an individual could also serve as a spiritual supervisor or guide in a vision quest or similar encounter of transcendence. The medicine person was recognized as the authority and the one who had acquired the spiritual wherewithal to encounter the spiritual powers required in the coming-of-age event. Prayers were spoken, chanted, or sung, and guidance and instruction were imparted to initiates.

As part of the ceremonial recognition of a successful rite of passage, a new name or sacred or medicine name could be assigned. The new name signaled a new social status, a new identity, and the expectation of a new role in society. The act of naming imparts a social identity, and the assignment of a subsequent name signifies to the person and his or her social network that an important transformation has occurred (Alford, 1988). The new name could serve as a replacement name or as an additional name. As discussed, a Cheyenne boy would receive a new name assigned by the elders after his successful vision quest. In this illustration, the new name provided the recipient with power. A new name also could be assigned after the performance of a great feat, such as in war. In general, sacred or medicine names are acquired at a rite of passage or some other ceremonial context; they are not to be broadly shared with others, but are to be maintained for ceremonial or sacred purposes.

Summary

One final point to make in this chapter concerns universal puberty traits, which Driver (1941) speculated were the oldest and most difficult to trace relative to dissemination. These traits include seclusion, the presence of an attendant or mentor, restrictions on food and drink, a scratching taboo, work at the time of menstruation or after, bathing and changing clothes at the end of seclusion or menstruation, instruction, and probably avoidance of hunters, fishermen, gamblers, or men generally. Certainly, these patterns were observed across a broad range of cultural areas in this review. For instance, Driver considered the use of some kind of scratching stick to scratch or touch oneself one of the most ancient and widespread puberty practices. Rationales for its use varied, but the overall belief appeared to link to the notion that, because of the impressionable state of girls at puberty, they could cause permanent scarring or wrinkling by touching themselves.

The purpose of this chapter was to provide a greater understanding of the broad range of puberty customs across cultural areas of North America. The breadth of analysis did not permit depth of analysis; the latter purpose is reserved for subsequent chapters on historical and contemporary coming-of-age practices among Apache, Navajo, Lakota/Nakota/ Dakota, and Ojibwa cultures. The themes raised in this chapter demonstrate their relevance in subsequent chapters and indicate the complexity and range of expression of coming-of-age events among North American Indians. One final conclusion to be drawn from coming-of-age rites of boys and girls is that parallel themes of separation, transition, and incorporation are relevant, but rituals illustrative of these phases differ in many ways for males and females.

CHAPTER SIX

The Apache Sunrise Dance

□   □   □

One of the best-known North American Indian puberty celebrations for girls is the Sunrise Ceremony, or as it more commonly called by Western Apaches today, the Sunrise Dance. It consists of numerous rituals that, together, form an event that is fairly unique among the puberty rituals and ceremonies of North American Indian cultures (Driver, 1941). The Apaches, known as Ndee, or "the People," are an Athabascan culture of the southwestern United States and are known for their observances of girls' puberty rites. The Western Apache term for the Sunrise Dance is *na ih es*, which is translated as "preparing her" or "getting her ready" (Basso, 1966).[1] The Mescalero Apache version is sometimes called the Sunrise Dance but more commonly referred to in English as the girls' puberty ceremony or puberty rites, and in Apache is identified as 'Isánáklésh Gotal, a term that encompasses the process by which the initiate is transformed into the female culture heroine 'Isánáklésh (Talamantez, 2000).

Practiced by Apaches of the past and those of the present day, the girls' puberty ceremony is the most important ceremonial event of the various Apache groups (L. H. Clark, 1976). Opler (1983a) classified the Apache puberty ceremony as a "standardized nonshamanistic ritual" rather than a "shamanistic ritual" (the latter requiring less preparation and expense). Lamphere (1983) identified three types of Apache ceremonials according to the attraction of supernatural influence, the removal of evil influence, and the identification of the individual with the supernatural. The puberty ceremony is clearly of the third type, because the girl becomes sacred by virtue of the physical events of pubescence, as well as through her subsequent engagement in rituals that connect her to the primary female supernatural person of the Apaches, referred to in English as White Painted Woman, but in the literature on San Carlos Apaches as Ests'unnadlehi (P. E. Goddard, 1918), and in the literature on Mescalero Apaches as Es dzanadeha (Nicholas, 1939), Isdząnatłees (Farrer, 1980), and 'Isánáklésh (Talamantez, 2000). Basso (1966) identified the female personage as Changing Woman or Ih sta nedlęheh based on his fieldwork among the Cibecues, a Western Apache group having much in common with San Carlos Apaches. Regardless of the label for the culture heroine, common themes are her role as the mother of the male culture heroes and as the central figure of the girls' puberty ceremony. Basso (1970) described the Sunrise Dance as the most elaborate of the Apache ceremonies and as characterized by a rich array of symbolism. Additionally, this ceremony affects the greatest number of Apache people in its cultural expression. As stated by Golston (1996), "*Na'i'es* is retained by the Western Apache as the strongest link to traditional life and values. Other ceremonies, briefer and more private, are still occasionally enacted, but the full community celebrates its heritage publicly when a girl comes of age" (p. 27).

The Apache girls' puberty rites begin at menarche and continue for several months after the highly ritualized 4-day Sunrise Dance. If the ceremonial gift exchange that occurs 1 or 2 years after the 4-day dance is considered, the entire sequence of events could last up to 2 to 3 years. Numerous rituals are performed from first menses to the climactic 4-day dance, which culminates in the transformation of the initiate into White Painted Woman (also called Changing Woman and White Shell Woman) and subsequently empowering the initiate with desirable qualities of this important supernatural being of oral tradition (Basso, 1966; Ganteaume, 1992; Mails, 1988; Stockel, 1991; Talamantez, 2000). Through her transformation and empowerment, the girl shares these blessings with others in rituals incorporated in the public ceremony. Because of her participation in the rigors and demands of the Sunrise Dance, the girl acquires a greater sense of her identity and purpose in connection with other Apaches.

The Sunrise Dance represents a critical juncture in the life span of Apache women and is likely the most important ceremony in their lives. Ceremonies designed to incorporate young people into Apache culture and to build Apache identity begin at birth, such as ceremonies associated with the first time a child is put in a cradle or when he or she first walks. According to Opler (1935), "No matter what your straits, if you are an Apache, you can be sure that there is some ceremony designed to meet the situation" (p. 65). Relative to the Mescalero Apaches, Talamantez (1991) described numerous ceremonies within the first year of life, such as ear piercing and putting on the child's first moccasins, which is indicative of taking the first steps along the path of life. A first hair-cutting ceremony occurs in the springtime, and ceremonial activities occur when a child is presented with his or her first solid foods, including traditional foods of yucca, mesquite, mescal, and sumac or chokecherry. Both boys and girls participate in childhood rituals, but the mandate for girls is to pattern their lives after 'Isánáklésh, while the role model for boys is the figure Child of the Water (Talamantez, 1991).

The expected benefits of the Sunrise Dance for adolescent girls have bearing on both physical and psychological realms to their preparation for the assumption of adult roles and responsibilities (Opler, 1983a). These perceived positive outcomes are more fully addressed in the next chapter. In extrapolating the functions of the Sunrise Dance, fertility might seem an obvious theme due to the ceremony's temporal association with menarche. However, this would be an unmerited and erroneous conclusion. The research conducted for this study did not yield an explicit connection between the Sunrise Dance and the girl's anticipated reproductive capabilities, nor is this point apparent in the literature.[2] The Sunrise Dance is a ceremony about life—in its numerous forms and manners. It is thought that the behaviors girls exhibit during the Sunrise Dance will influence the course of their life span. As one informant stated, during these dances, "girls are really living their lives . . . it represents their entire life." They are to exhibit good character at this time, because that will become their character for life (Hoijer, 1938; Nicholas, 1939). Certainly, there is the hope for longevity, strength, and well-being of initiates for years to come. However, the notion of life is broadened to a hope for perpetuation of the Apache people and to an assurance of continual expressions of renewal of life on the Earth such as occurs through the change of seasons. The Sunrise Dance facilitates continuation of processes involved in all of creation, and its positive outcomes are extended to the initiate, to those who contribute to the success of the dance, to those who attend the ceremonial events, and ultimately to the entire world.

The Apaches

The Apaches, like their Navajo cousins, are labeled Southern Athabascan. According to contemporary thinking, they arrived in the Southwest in the middle of the 14th century or slightly later from the interior of what is now known as Alaska and northwest Canada (Dutton, 1983).[3] The designations used for Apache groups are Western, Chiricahua, Mescalero, Jicarilla, Plains (also referred to as Kiowa Apaches), and Lipan. The Apaches are one of the 10 largest American Indian tribal groupings, and 57,060 people self-identified as solely Apache in the 2000 decennial census (U.S. Census Bureau, 2002). The Western Apaches are located in Arizona and consist of San Carlos, White Mountain, Cibecue, Northern Tonto, and Southern Tonto groups. Today the San Carlos Apaches occupy the San Carlos Reservation, and White Mountain and Cibecue Apaches are associated with the Fort Apache Reservation. However, some Apaches on the eastern side of the San Carlos Reservation near the Gila River recognize their lineage as White Mountain (i.e., the community of Bylas). As explained by P. E. Goddard (1919b), some White Mountain Apaches chose to remain on the San Carlos Reservation while others joined their relatives on the Fort Apache Reservation. The Chiricahuas and Mescaleros are found on the Mescalero Reservation in central New Mexico, and the Jicarillas are located on the Jicarilla Reservation in northern New Mexico. The Plains or Kiowa Apaches are in Oklahoma, and the Lipans are in Texas.

Apache groups of interest in this study are those on the San Carlos and Mescalero reservations. The San Carlos is of particular interest, because most of the fieldwork occurred among this group. The San Carlos practice the Sunrise Dance for girls on individual bases, while the Mescalero also hold individual ceremonies but are best known for a version of the girls' puberty ceremony that is held simultaneously for several girls or maidens in conjunction with the tribe's annual Fourth of July festivities. The San Carlos group comprises the Pinal, Arivaipa, San Carlos proper, and Apache Peaks bands (G. Goodwin, 1942). Since there is extensive kin relatedness and interchange between San Carlos and Fort Apache reservations, White Mountain and Cibecue groups also were of interest in the present study. The White Mountain group is divided into Eastern White Mountain and Western White Mountain bands, and the Cibecue group includes Carrizo, Cibecue proper, and Canyon Creek bands (G. Goodwin, 1942). Historically, bands had their own territories. Within a band, each individual belonged to a clan, had blood relations, and had affinal relationships (G. Goodwin, 1942).

Today, on the Mescalero Reservation, Apaches are of predominantly Mescalero and Chiricahua descent, with a smaller number of Lipans. It appears that, historically, the Mescaleros were a fairly unified group without discernible bands (Opler, 1983c). Traditionally, the Lipans consisted of Northern and Southern bands (Opler, 2001), and Chiricahuas comprised Central, Eastern, and Southern bands (Opler, 1983b). A sad account is told of the Chiricahuas' loss of land, continual pursuit by both American and Mexican military forces, and forced imprisonment first in Florida and then in Fort Still, Oklahoma, where Geronimo ultimately died. In 1913 the Chiricahuas were released from their imprisonment and given the choice of remaining in Oklahoma or joining the Mescalero Apaches on their reservation in New Mexico. Most joined the Mescaleros, and over time these two groups have combined their efforts in the practice of the girls' puberty rites (Opler, 1941).

L. H. Clark (1976) remarked that the San Carlos version of the Sunrise Dance is the most traditional among the Apache groups. All Apache groups with the exception of the Plains or Kiowa Apaches currently practice some form of a girls' puberty ceremony. Two informants whom I interviewed (one Mescalero and the other Plains Apache) concurred that the Plains Apaches of Oklahoma do not practice the girls' puberty ceremony, as was stated in Clark (1976). The Mescalero informant stated that her Plains Apache relatives were the last to experience the puberty ceremony and that was back in the 1920s. While there has been some question concerning the celebration of the girls' puberty ceremony among the Jicarillas, the fact is that it was historically important and continues to be practiced. Tiller (1983) stated that the Jicarilla tribal council began subsidizing this ceremony in the 1960s for purposes of cultural preservation. This 4-day puberty ceremony was noted to have many commonalities with the Western Apache version (Lamphere, 1983), and Dutton (1983) observed that the Jicarilla version of the puberty ceremony is similar to that of the Navajos who lie west of their reservation. The girls' puberty rites were practiced by the Chiricahua and Mescalero Apaches of the past (Tiller, 1983), and continue to be held on the Mescalero Reservation in New Mexico (which includes both Chiricahua and Mescalero Apaches). In addition to dances at San Carlos, I attended the annual Fourth of July puberty ceremony at Mescalero.

Apache Origin Story

The Apache girls' puberty ceremony is embedded within Apache cosmology, as explained by one informant: "The moon, the sun, the stars, and everything . . . are all made for their purpose. All of them are placed there by God. . . . Mother Earth was created . . . and according to the Apache belief, God created all people equal. . . . But then different people have their own ways. . . . That's what they sing about, and that's what they pray about. . . . So, as a tribe, we pray that the Mother Earth would stay and would carry on for everybody."

The central supernatural being of oral tradition who is foundational to the Sunrise Dance is known as White Painted Woman. She is a critical figure to Apache culture and quite comparable to the central holy figure of their Athabascan cousins, the Navajos, among whom Changing Woman is foundational to the Kinaaldá ceremony for pubescent girls. In fact, the names *White Painted Woman* and *Changing Woman* are used interchangeably by some Apaches and in the literature.[4] In speaking with Apache informants about the distinction between these two female supernatural beings, I was told unequivocally that they are the same person. As one informant stated, "Well, she [White Painted Woman] is Changing Woman. The girl becomes Changing Woman because she is changing from a girl into a woman." White Painted Woman or Changing Woman represents the universal life cycle and annual rejuvenation of the Earth. G. Goodwin (1938) described her purposes and character, stating: "She has control over fertility and fruition of plants; is kindly. She is the essence of long life, having the power to change from old to young and back" (p. 26). She is a Mother Earth–like figure, but one does not want to reduce her to this cliché. The Apaches, like the Navajos, believe that she is the one from whom they are created and who gave them their teachings, including the mandate to dress the girl in her image and to conduct the puberty rites (Opler, 1941, 1942). As well, girls are required to adhere to the same taboos as White Painted Woman and to have the same songs sung for them (Nicholas, 1939). By virtue of their identification with White Painted Woman, girls are to be referred to by that name rather than their own during their puberty rites (Hoijer, 1938; Nicholas, 1939).

The story of White Painted Woman or Changing Woman and her culture-hero sons is similar among the San Carlos, White Mountain, Jicarilla, Chiricahua, and Mescalero Apaches, as well as the Navajos. P. E. Goddard (1909), in particular, remarked on the similarity of some segments of the San Carlos and Mescalero origin stories. The legend usually begins with her creation by Usen (the Creator or One in Charge of Life) who sends White Painted Woman to live alone on the Earth, which was dominated by large monsters at the time.[5] This beginning of the telling of the story by G. Goodwin (1938) is somewhat different from other accounts, such as those of P. E. Goddard (1918, 1919a), which simply tell of a maiden leaving the other people and going off alone to the mountain. Various accounts also tell of a great flood (e.g., Opler, 1942) and describe how White Painted Woman floated on top of the water in a large abalone shell (Golston, 1996). In one account from the San Carlos Apaches, it is a vessel of turquoise in which she floats and in another account it was a hollowed-out sycamore tree (P. E. Goddard, 1918). What ultimately occurs in the story is that White Painted Woman (Changing Woman) or her daughter bears one or two sons (by either the sun or water) that serve as culture heroes for the Apaches. The names assigned to these sons are more or less parallel across Apache cultures. Nay en ez gane, or "Slayer of Monsters," is identified as the first son in Western Apache accounts (G. Goodwin, 1938, 1939; Basso, 1966, 1983), and the comparable figure in Mescalero, Chiricahua, and Jicarilla versions is "Killer of Enemies"

(Hoijer, 1938; Opler, 1938, 1941, 1942). The other son in Western Apache tradition is Tuh ba tes chine, or "Born-of-Water-Old-Man" (Basso, 1966) or "Born from Water" (G. Goodwin, 1938, 1939), and in somewhat variant stories from Mescalero, Chiricahua, and Jicarilla cultures is "Child of the Water" (Hoijer, 1938; Opler, 1938, 1942). In some versions the two brothers (or one son) are born not fully formed, possessing webbed fingers and toes, no hair, and absence of facial features and joints (P. E. Goddard, 1918, 1919a).

The key players and the processes by which these pregnancies occur vary across stories. White Mountain Apache culture tells of a maiden going to the top of a mountain; after four subsequent mornings of penetration by the sun's rays, she becomes pregnant and a son is born 8 days later (P. E. Goddard, 1919a). The woman then becomes pregnant by dripping water and bears a second son in the same time frame. In the San Carlos version of the story, the female figure (called Ests'unnadlehi) also becomes pregnant by the sun, but gives birth to a girl who becomes pregnant by water and bears a son (P. E. Goddard, 1918). Concerning the Western Apache origin story, in one version G. Goodwin (1939) tells of the sun's rays penetrating between the woman's legs resulting in pregnancy followed by the birth of Slayer of Monsters. Then, from penetration by dripping water, Born from Water is born. Interestingly, in another version of the story in G. Goodwin (1939), a wickiup where pregnancy occurs is described, and this structure is strikingly similar to that used on the third day of the contemporary Sunrise Dance. Still other accounts tell of a maiden who has a daughter by the sun, and this daughter then bears the culture-hero son or sons (e.g., P. E. Goddard, 1918; G. Goodwin, 1939). The Jicarillas' version tells of two girls who bear the culture heroes, and ultimately these girls become known as White Shell Woman and White Painted Woman (Opler, 1938). In Hoijer's (1938) Mescalero and Chiricahua accounts, the Creator and White Painted Woman initially existed, and then Child of the Water is born followed by the birth of Killer of Enemies (who, in some accounts, is the older brother but is always lesser in importance and even identified with evil). In contrast, Slayer of Monsters is the culture hero of White Mountain Apaches and is known for war power, being called "man's champion" (G. Goodwin, 1983, p. 26).

Hoijer (1938) describes the cultural variations in the discrepant statuses of the brothers: "For the Navajo, Western Apache, Lipan, and Jicarilla, Killer of Enemies is the principal culture hero and performs deeds and exploits comparable to those attributed to Child of the Water in this story. By the Chiricahua and Mescalero, however, Killer of Enemies is relegated to a subordinate position" (p. 141). It should be explained, however, that Killer of Enemies is identified in Chiricahua songs that appear later in this chapter, but, as noted by Opler (1941), his name is considered synonymous with Child of the Water, who is the actual culture hero of the Chiricahua Apaches. In the puberty ceremonies the name Killer of Enemies persists, but he is understood to be Child of the Water.

The story typically continues with the introduction of a giant and White Painted Woman's efforts to hide her sons from the giant, who would like to consume them (e.g., Hoijer, 1938; Opler, 1942). Accordingly, an informant from Mescalero related the following story: "She fooled the giant and got the giant who wanted to take those two little boys, and she put them under her campfire. She made a little hole under that, and that's where they stayed. They grew up. It's a beautiful story." In oral tradition of both the Apaches and the Navajos, a major accomplishment of these half brothers was to rid the world of monsters or evil (Basso, 1966; Markstrom & Iborra, 2003). While some accounts tell of two brothers taking on this role, others tell of one brother, such as G. Goodwin's (1939) account, in which it was the younger brother who pursued his father, the Sun. The boys experienced an escalated infancy and childhood and began to question their mother about the whereabouts of their father. After several escapades and encounters with various helpers along the way, such as the Raven and the Eagle, they came to the Sun's house. The boys were faced with challenges and tests presented by their father in order to prove that they were indeed his children (e.g., P. E. Goddard, 1919a; G. Goodwin, 1939). Then a sweat lodge was built, either by the Sun's wife or the sons, and the boys entered four times. Upon the fourth attempt, the Sun appeared and finished the formation of the boys by shaping their fingers and toes, muscles, joints, limbs, facial features, and every part of their body (P. E. Goddard, 1918, 1919a). Upon completion, the Sun gave his sons their names. It could be interpreted that the shaping of the boys' physique by their father, the Sun, was their rite of passage to adulthood. It is parallel, in some respects, to the Apache girls' puberty ceremony, wherein girls are massaged and molded by their adult mentor so that they may possess her physical and character traits.

It is stated in oral tradition that White Painted Woman gave the Apaches the girls' puberty ceremony and instructions on how to conduct it (Hoijer, 1938; Opler, 1942).[6] According to the oral tradition as related by Opler (1942), "White-Painted Woman said, 'From here on we will have the girl's puberty rite. When the girls first menstruate you shall have a feast. There shall be songs for these girls. During this feast the Gahe shall dance in front. After that there shall be round dancing and face-to-face dancing'" (p. 15). Additionally, the legend mentions that women who take care of the girl were to "make sounds when she ran and to mould her and pray for her" (Opler, 1942, p. 15).

The commonality of the central elements in the various versions of Apache origin and creation stories serves to link the cultures of all Apache groups. These slight variations in stories are not problematic, such as those found in the Judeo-Christian creation stories (e.g., two versions of a flood in Genesis). It is essentially the underlying meanings and impacts that are of greatest significance in imparting hope, purpose, and protection for life. The importance of White Painted Woman and her sons (or son depending on the legend) to the girls' puberty ceremony cannot be overstated. The initiate essentially impersonates White Painted Woman, and her son is a powerful presence in the prayers and songs in which he is named (P. E. Goddard, 1909). Indeed, Slayer of Monsters is thought to still appear as an animal or as the wind and is mentioned in nearly all of the ceremonial song cycles (G. Goodwin, 1938). In essence, White Painted Woman and her sons serve as role models and sources of identification. They represent male and female forces that bring balance and contrast as a mother and son rather than as a generative couple (P. E. Goddard, 1909). In the description of the San Carlos and Mescalero Sunrise Dances that follow, the reiterations of stories implicit to Apache culture are apparent. The performance of rituals serves to re-create these events that Apaches consider foundational to their culture.

Methodology

The greater part of my fieldwork among the San Carlos Apaches occurred from March 2002 to June 2004 and involved 8 visits to their reservation.[7] Four follow-up visits through 2007, including a 6-month sojourn on the San Carlos Reservation, facilitated clarification and expansion of earlier observations and interpretations. In 2003 I attended the Mescalero Apaches' annual Fourth of July festivities, of which the girls' puberty ceremony is the central event.[8] The San Carlos and Mescalero versions of the girls' puberty rites are similar, but they have a sufficient number of differences to justify separate descriptions. The San Carlos version receives the greatest discussion in this chapter because of the larger amount of field data collected.

The qualitative research traditions of ethnography and case study were used to conduct this study with respect to both the process of data collection and subsequent data interpretation, including the organization of data. Relative to the former, the study was ethnographic because culture was the central concept, an emic (insider's) perspective was adopted, and the study was conducted in the natural setting (Gall, Borg, & Gall, 1996). However, the ethnographic approach is frequently linked to an all-encompassing, holistic portrayal of a cultural group. In this respect the present study departed somewhat from ethnography, because its focus was a specific event of a cultural group—namely, the Apache Sunrise Dance. This specificity of a cultural event then leads to the applicability of the case-study approach to this research; as noted by Gall et al. (1996), "a good case study brings a phenomenon to life for readers and helps them understand the meanings" (p. 543). Certainly, interpretation of meanings was a central aim in this analysis and yielded comprehensive descriptions of events relative to chronology, the principal players, their interactions with one another, and performance of specific rituals.

The sampling strategy was perhaps most reflective of the case-study approach, because it was purposeful (Creswell, 1998; Patton, 2002) according to specialized selection of participants: girls who were currently undergoing the Sunrise Dance or who had experienced it in the past 18 months;[9] the parents (predominantly mothers) of these girls; and elders, medicine persons, and other cultural experts. Although the Sunrise

Dance is embedded within a broader cultural milieu, it was beyond the scope of this study to analyze the broader aspects of Apache culture, as might occur in an ethnographic portrayal.

There were several tools of data collection employed in this study that are consistent with strategies used in ethnographic and especially case-study research (e.g., Creswell, 1998; Gall et al., 1996), including the following: observations and field notes taken by the investigator and her research assistant who served as participant-observers at the ceremonies;[10] semistructured, audiotaped interviews of female initiates, the initiates' parents, female co-sponsors or godmothers of initiates, adult cultural experts, and medicine persons with particular knowledge of girls' puberty rites; numerous informal conversations with San Carlos and Mescalero Apache cultural experts and participants, both at puberty ceremonies and in other social settings; review of existing historical and anthropological sources of literature on Apache girls' puberty rites;[11] examination of physical artifacts used in the ceremonies; photographs; and existing videotapes. While both ethnography and case study utilize tools of interview and participant observation, the latter approach is more extensive relative to the use of multiple tools of data collection (Creswell, 1998), as occurred in the present study. To establish the validity of the findings, "triangulation" or the convergence of information (Creswell, 1998), or what is also called the verification of repeatability of the observations, was utilized. Sources of corroboration were sought among the multiple sources of data collected. Further, cultural informants read the prepared chapters on the Sunrise Dance and inspected them for cultural accuracy, a strategy labeled "member checking" (Creswell, 1998). Additional aspects of data analysis are reviewed in the next chapter.

Over the course of the fieldwork phase that began in 2002 at San Carlos, I attended all or part of 13 Sunrise Dances and an abbreviated 1-day version of an Apache puberty rite. I observed the leadership of six different medicine men who conducted these ceremonies, one medicine man six times, one three times, one two times, and the others one time each. While most of the rituals were common to all dances, no two dances were alike, and this impression was certainly confirmed by informants who attend numerous Sunrise Dances. I also attended the annual Fourth of July girls' puberty ceremony on the Mescalero Apache Reservation in

New Mexico in 2003. Six maidens were participating in that particular coming-of-age rite, which is described in a later section of this chapter. At both San Carlos and Mescalero, field notes were taken at the time of the ceremonies and were based on personal observation, participation, and information provided by informants at the ceremonies.

Of those formally interviewed at San Carlos, there were six initiates, five mothers and one father of initiates, four adult cultural experts (including two of the four who had served in co-sponsor roles), and one medicine man. One medicine woman was interviewed at Mescalero. Separate interview protocols were developed for categories of interviewee (i.e., initiates, parents, and cultural experts), but a great degree of variability was permitted in conducting the interviews in order to allow informants to express their thoughts on the Sunrise Dance and its impacts according to their own scheme of organization. The goals of the interviews were multifaceted, but primarily focused on the perceived purposes or functions of the Sunrise Dance for the initiates, the Apache people, and the world; the activities families engaged in to prepare for their daughters' Sunrise Dances; the significance of the Sunrise Dance for contemporary Apache young women, including the perceived positive outcomes and contributions to identity formation; and initiates' understanding of the meanings and symbolism behind the rituals. In addition to the formal interviews, countless conversations were engaged in with onlookers at Sunrise Dances. These reports were recorded in field notes at the time of the ceremonies. Utilizing the interview and observational data and, consistent with forms of analysis of qualitative data, salient themes were identified. The next chapter is interpretative relative to these themes. The purpose of the present chapter is to describe the versions of the girls' puberty ceremonies observed by the investigator on the San Carlos and Mescalero reservations.

The San Carlos Apache Reservation is located approximately 100 miles east of Phoenix, Arizona. The population on the reservation is 9,385 (U.S. Census Bureau, 2000c). The poverty level is high, with 52.6% of families with related children under 18 years falling below the poverty level, and the median family income being $17,585 (U.S. Census Bureau, 2000b). The San Carlos Reservation encompasses 1,853,841 acres, of which more than one-third is managed forest or woodland (Tiller, 1996b). Major employers are the federal and state governments (through various tribal agencies and schools) and the tribal casino. Other employment is found in cattle ranching and the mining of the semiprecious stone peridot. Traditional basket weaving and tourism-related endeavors also provide employment. Traditionally, San Carlos Apaches have practiced matrilineal descent patterns and matrilocal living patterns (G. Goodwin, 1942).

The Mescalero Reservation lies in the San Francisco Peaks in the central southern region of New Mexico and encompasses 460,679 acres (Tiller, 1996a). The population on the reservation is 3,156 (U.S. Census Bureau, 2000c) and comprises Apaches from Mescalero, Chiricahua, and Lipan descent (Tiller, 1996a). The major sources of employment at Mescalero include wood products, cattle grazing, a variety of government jobs, and tourism, which is accentuated by the tribal casino (Tiller, 1996a). The median family income is $23,163, and the number of families with related children under the age of 18 that fall below the poverty level is 34.5% (U.S. Census Bureau, 2000a). As with the San Carlos Apaches, Mescalero culture is traditionally matrilineal and matrilocal (Hoijer, 1938; Talamantez, 1991).

At the point of data analysis, the quandary for the qualitative researcher is meaningful organization and presentation of mounds of data sources, as stated by Patton (2002): "A skillfully crafted case reads like a fine weaving. And that, of course, is the trick. How to do the weaving?" (p. 450). There is no one right or perfect way to synthesize and report the findings of a qualitative study, and each researcher will organize the findings according to his or her own style and inclinations. It is here again that case study and ethnography can provide guidance on the tools to be employed for analysis of data. In-depth description, as evidenced through substantive narrative, is a data-management tool of both ethnography and case-study approaches (Creswell, 1998), and it was used to depict the data on the Sunrise Dance. Additionally, organization of data according to chronology and themes is linked to the case-study approach, as were the analytic strategies employed in the present analysis (Patton, 2002).

This chapter presents the events of the Sunrise Dance in chronological format to provide an organizational structure to the data. The Ritual Process Paradigm (RPP; Dunham et al., 1986) also facilitates organization and presentation of data. Within these frameworks, rituals and events are de-

Table 2. The Ritual Process Paradigm (RPP) (Dunham et al., 1986), Psychosocial Conceptions, and Sunrise Dance Applications

Steps of the Ritual Process Paradigm	Psychosocial Conceptions	Sunrise Dance Applications
	Preparation	
1. Old support group—Significant others have prepared her for this ceremony.	Principal socialization figures. Introjection and identification.	Family socializes girl to anticipate her Sunrise Dance.
2. Old identity—Previously acquired social roles, personal traits, and affective or cognitive features that will be transformed.	Ethnic group awareness and identification.	Continued socialization, and heightened anticipation by initiate.
3. Old identity completion—Cues that the initiate is ready for the ceremony.	Cognitive advancement (formal operations). Affective and social maturation.	Menarche is the cue for the ceremony. Select co-sponsor and medicine man. Extensive preparations for several months prior to scheduled date of ceremony.
	Separation	
4. New environmental demands—The initiate is pushed into the insecurity of new roles and requirements.	Role confusion.	Initiate and family build and move to encampment for 10 days. Initiate and partner live in separate wickiup. Initiate is dressed by her godmother. No bathing/use scratching stick/use drinking tube.
5. Liminality—Marginal, "betwixt and between" status.	Disequilibrium, dissonance, confusion/uncertainty lead to:	Continuation of previous demands. Phase 1—All alone, she dances. Phase 2—Sitting or kneeling. Phase 3—Lying. Phase 4—Cane set out for her, she runs around it. Phase 5—Running.
6. Activation—Emotional responses of anxiety and fear due to new demands.	Motivation for active involvement in identity formation and accelerated psychological maturation.	Continuation of phases 1 to 5.

7. Agony—Feelings of helplessness, depression, and inner crisis.	Continuation of motivation (above)	Continuation of phases 1 to 5.
8. Numinosity—Respect and awe and openness to learn and to be guided.	Transition Developing comfort with new self and circumstances.	Phase 3—Lying. Instructions from medicine man, godmother, and other adults. Dancing with Mountain Spirit dancers.
9. Accommodation—Cognitive change as initiate begins to incorporate new roles.	Industry Developing connection to new identity.	Physical actions bring psychological changes through role performance—baking four breads; carrying food in burden basket; praying for others.
10. Ecstasy—Relief and joy as the liminal state diminishes.	Assigned/ascribed identity.	Painting of initiate on third day. Transformation into White Painted Woman.
11. Transcendence—The initiate and the community recognize that the old identity has been abandoned and the new identity is emerging.	Reincorporation Affirmation from social group. Comfort with oneself.	Phase 6—Candy, it is poured. Phase 7—Blessing her.
12. New identity—New roles, commitments, and responsibilities expected for oneself and demanded by the community.	Role enactment. Having direction in life. Perceived sameness and continuity of self.	Praying for others. Phase 8—Blankets, she throws them off.
13. New support group—Mentors assist the initiate's understanding of and mastery of new roles.	Affirmation of identity by others.	Identification with godmother and other adult women.
14. Identity reinforcement—Social reinforcers from new support group, as well as intrinsic reinforcers.	Equilibrium. Feelings of accomplishment.	Reflect on previous events for 4 days after the ceremony. Anticipate mature behavior in girls after ceremony.

scribed along with their meanings and functions. According to Dunham et al., rites of passage occur as "formalized social interactions with a phasing which separates individuals from their previous identities, carries them through a period of transition to a new identity, and incorporates them into a new role or social status" (1986, p. 140). The four-phase (preparation, separation, transition, and reincorporation), 11-step RPP model addresses identity transformations during a rite of passage and is an expansion of Arnold van Gennep's (1908/1960) classic model of separation, transition, and incorporation (described in chapter 1). Preparation encompasses childhood events leading up to the rite of passage. Separation encompasses rituals that disentangle initiates from their former secure occupied states, with an understanding that they have not yet acquired the next state. Transition is an insecure state also referred to as "betwixt-and-between" and "liminal." Reincorporation involves the reassimilation of the individual back into society along with her new roles and statuses. At that point, the passage has been concluded and the individual is once again in a stable state (Turner, 1967). The 11 steps of the RPP do not necessarily follow a strict linear sequence of rituals of the Sunrise Dance. For example, the initiate's transformation into White Painted Woman begins in separation and continues through the remaining phases of the RPP, and rituals of separation are also indicative of transition. Table 2 presents the major rituals of the Sunrise Dance according to their placement in the RPP. The application of the RPP in this manner is consistent with Markstrom and Iborra's (2003) analysis of the Navajo Kinaaldá.

In the next major section of this chapter, the Western Apache version of the Sunrise Dance is carefully described utilizing the multiple data sources previously articulated, with the RPP serving as a conceptual scheme. The description of the Mescalero version of this ceremony follows. Themes that emerge as salient relative to the descriptive content are identified and interpreted in the next chapter to bring greater depth of understanding to the meanings and impacts of the Sunrise Dance.

The San Carlos Sunrise Dance

It became apparent early in this research that rituals of the Sunrise Dance are highly meaningful. With questioning and probing, underlying meanings of many of the rituals were obtained. It also became apparent in the observations and interviews relative to the Sunrise Dance as well as the literature that there are variations in the inclusion of various rituals, in the performance and timing of rituals, and in the participants in the rituals. Certainly, variations exist among branches of Apaches (e.g., San Carlos, White Mountain, Mescalero, etc.). As well, it became evident that there are variations even among those rites conducted on the San Carlos Reservation. As explained by informants, some medicine men conduct the ceremony according to styles that evolved in geographical areas (e.g., Whiteriver, San Carlos, or Bylas) and according to how they were trained by their mentors. However, these variations were relatively minor as observed among the San Carlos Apaches.

The San Carlos Sunrise Dance is conducted for girls on an individual basis beginning in the early spring of the year (i.e., March) and extending as late into the year as early November. It is a rare weekend during this time frame (with the exception of the exceedingly hot months of July and August) in which fewer than two dances are being held somewhere on the San Carlos Reservation. No dances are held in the winter, as one informant explained, because nothing grows in the winter. Presumably, the inactivity of growth in nature during this time extends to the initiates, who are thought not to benefit from their Sunrise Dances if held in the winter. Some informants noted that it is best to conduct the Sunrise Dance in the hot summer months to build the strength of initiates for the years to come; if the girls can successfully endure the hot desert weather, it is believed, they can survive subsequent challenges in life. An informant also explained that because many of the foods used in the ceremony are harvested during this time (e.g., berries and acorns), it is desirable to hold the Sunrise Dance in the summer, an observation confirmed by Goseyun (1991). Basso (1966) was told in Cibecue (of higher elevation and cooler temperatures than San Carlos) that the months of July and August were desirable because the evenings were warm for social dancing and because more students were home from boarding schools and could attend the ceremony. The latter reason may not be applicable today, as the vast majority of students attend schools in their communities.

At the first dance I attended, which happened to be in the pleasantly

Table 3. Sequence of Events of the Sunrise Dance

Day	Time of Day	Event
Within first 4 days of menarche	Early morning	Girl's parents meet with extended family (*ndeh guhyaneh*, or "wise people") to strategize. Co-sponsor or godparent (*na ihł esn*, or "one who prepares her") is identified and approached within 4 days. If accepted: • Female co-sponsor accepts stone and massages the initiate. • Initiate's family (sponsor) prepares breakfast for co-sponsor and family.
	Early morning	Medicine man (*dí yin*, or "one who has power") is identified and approached within 4 days. If accepted, medicine man accepts turquoise stone.
Within first few weeks after menarche		Ceremony scheduled for a later date.
Day 1 of Encampment		Initiate, her partner, and her family move to encampment. Co-sponsor and family build and move to separate encampment.
		Initiate and her partner build wickiup.
Several evenings prior to Sunrise Dance	Evenings	Nightly singing at camp (*bi goh ji tał*, or "half-night dance").
Day 1 of 4-day Sunrise Dance	Morning	Medicine man and his helpers conduct sweat bath and bless ceremonial items to be worn by initiate (*gish ih zha ha aldeh*, or "cane, it is made").
	Noon (approximately)	Food is exchanged between families (*nił sla ih ka*, or "food exchanged").
	Noon (approximately)	Initiate and others bring food to medicine man and helpers.
	Late afternoon	Initiate is dressed by her godmother (*bi keh ihl ze'*, or "she is dressed up").
	Evening	Social dance is held (*bi til tih* or "night before she dances").
Day 2 of 4-day Sunrise Dance	Morning (begins prior to dawn)	8 phases: 1. *bihl de nił ke* (all alone, she dances) 2. *niztah* (sitting or kneeling) 3. *nizti* (lying) 4. *gish ih zha ha yinda sle dił ihłye* (cane set out for her, she runs around it) 5. *nistan* (running) 6. *sha nał dihl* (candy, it is poured) 7. *ba na ihl dih* (blessing her) 8. *gíhx ił ke* (blankets, she throws them off)

Table 3. Continued

Day	Time of Day	Event
	Evening	Initiate dances with four other girls and Mountain Spirit dancers.
Day 3 of 4-day Sunrise Dance	Morning	Initiate is painted by Mountain Spirit dancers and male co-sponsor. Attendees, led by initiate and Mountain Spirit dancers, dance/pray through wickiup four times.
	Afternoon	Gift exchange between two families.
Day 4 of 4-day Sunrise Dance	Morning	Initiate is undressed by female co-sponsor in reverse manner.
4 additional days		Initiate is to reflect on the events that transpired.
Approximately 1 year later		Gift exchange between sponsor and co-sponsor.

Note: Apache terms and English translations are from Basso (1966, 1970).

cool month of March, I spoke with a visitor who was of Ojibwa descent. She remarked that I should attend dances during the hot summer months to acquire greater appreciation of the level of endurance required by the initiates. I concurred with her imperative and subsequently attended dances in much warmer months of June and September. A listing of upcoming Sunrise Dances appears in a local paper according to the date, the names of the initiate's parents (called the sponsors), the names of the co-sponsors (or godparents), and the location of the dances. Dances are somewhat accessible for outsiders, but there was considerable curiosity from others concerning my motives for attending. Community attendance is desirable to enhance the prospect of a successful dance (N. Goodwin, 2001), and it appeared that the dances were the major social event at San Carlos.

Preparation

"Apaches attach a great deal of importance to ceremonial preparations, and negligence in carrying them out is sternly rebuked. To a large extent, the effectiveness of a ritual is thought to be dependent on its being flawlessly performed, in precise coincidence with its established pattern" (Basso, 1966, p. 133). If non-Apaches are familiar with the Sunrise Dance, it is probably the ritual-filled 4-day sequence of events. However, careful preparations begin at menarche long before it culminates at an outdoor encampment for approximately 1 week or longer, of which the final 4 days garner large public attendance (see Table 3 for full sequence of events of the Sunrise Dance).[12] Excluding the preparations for the Sunrise Dance that begin about a year prior to the public event, preparation actually begins earlier in childhood as girls are socialized to be attuned to this important ceremony. The Sunrise Dance is the major ceremonial activity of the San Carlos Apaches, and certainly most children and adults in attendance appreciate its social importance if not its spiritual significance.

Years prior to their actual experience of menarche, girls are attuned to their eventual Sunrise Dances, and this is where the first step of the RPP, old support group, is applicable. Socialization by parents, grandparents, and other significant adults serves to influence the desired values, beliefs, and behaviors to be absorbed by the child. Some parents explicitly socialize their girls from a young age for their ceremonies, as described by Goseyun (1991), who wrote of her own daughter, Carla, undergoing the Sunrise Dance: "Early on, I readied my daughters for their Sunrise Ceremonials, and I taught them how important it was to prepare themselves in the ways and thoughts of our traditions" (p. 8). Similar preparations are observed in the literature relative to the Navajo Kinaaldá (Keith, 1964; Markstrom & Iborra, 2003) and the Mescalero girls' puberty rites (Talamantez, 2000). In a psychological sense, children are ready to absorb the content of socialization (i.e., values, beliefs, behaviors, etc.) due to processes of identification and introjection that operate to connect them to their families emotionally. Developmentally speaking, children desire to identify and model the significant adults in their lives, and they will incorporate or inculcate the preferences of their adult caregivers.

Mechanisms of observational learning enable girls to acquire greater awareness of the challenges required during the complex 4-day dance. In this respect, Apache informants of G. Goodwin (1942) related an amusing account of their 7-year-old daughter, who had attended a puberty ceremony 2 years previous:

This made a strong impression on her, and immediately afterward she started dancing as the pubescent girl does. Her father, noticing this, encouraged her and sang one of the songs from the rite for her to dance to. This became a regular occasion each evening before she went to bed, and sometimes when she arose in the morning. She danced on the blankets of the bed, pretending the woman who molds the girl's body danced beside her. Then she kneeled and, holding her hands up, swayed from side to side in time to the song, as the girl does. Then she lay flat on the blanket to be molded, as in the rite. (p. 449)

Those interviewed for this study were resolute on matters of preparation. As one informant explained, if girls have been properly prepared in childhood, they should be ready for their Sunrise Dances. Among other things, they should be taught not to be lazy and to maintain a positive attitude when demands are made of them without backtalk to their elders. They should also be learning household tasks, such as making bread. Informants noted that grandparents should take major responsibility in teaching girls the kinds of things that will help them in the Sunrise Dance and in life to come. In this respect, a medicine man explained: "Right away, grandpa and grandma teach us to get up early. Don't sleep, get up early, and the first thing you do is put on your shoes. We have been attacked by our enemy . . . so, when we get up, we put on our shoes and go get wood . . . and make her run . . . she'll be strong, you know."

In short, relative to the step of old support group, the girl acquires heightened anticipation for participation in the ceremonial aspects of her culture, especially her Sunrise Dance. However, she is still a child, and the expectations that she has for herself and that others have for her are consistent with her present life stage: she is not yet expected to behave as an adult or to possess the judgments of an adult. However, due to the Sunrise Dance at pubescence, not only will her self-perception be altered, but significant others will have greater expectations for maturity in her behavior.

The second step, old identity, is that aspect of preparation that is explicit to the social roles, personal traits, and affective or cognitive features that will be transformed through the Sunrise Dance. It is acquired ethnic and cultural sensitivity in childhood, in particular, that should be readied for deeper understanding. The content of socialization by the support group encompasses the initiate's ethnic awareness and ethnic identification as an Apache. Prepubescent children have the capability to self-identify as a member of their ethnic group and understand that their group membership is different from that of others. As part of their ethnic socialization, young Apache girls attend the Sunrise Dances of older girls and become attuned to meaningful dimensions of their culture that encompass belief, values, practices, and language.

When readiness for the rite of passage is imminent, the third step, old identity completion, becomes relevant. Menarche, a biological trigger, is the developmental cue that the ceremony is to be performed, and movement to the next phase of the RPP will ensue. The developmental context of pubescence includes rapid advances in virtually all domains of development (i.e., psychological, emotional, social, cognitive, etc.). It would be desirable to compel these domains of development to be in synchrony at menarche, but given the variability for the onset of menses and related components of maturation, it is unlikely. The implication is that girls may have physically experienced menarche, but in socio-emotional and cognitive forms of development they may not be prepared for the responsibilities required by the rituals of the rite of passage or understand the complex and abstract meanings behind the rituals. Piaget (1952, 1972) identified formal operational thought as the cognitive milestone of early adolescence. Acquisition of this form of thinking heightens the likelihood that the pubescent understands the rich abstract and symbolic meanings behind the rituals of the Sunrise Dance. However, formal operational thought may not be firmly established until somewhat later in adolescence; as a result, girls' application of these newly acquired cognitive skills are likely to be immature and inefficient at the time of menarche. Hence, understanding of the rituals may not fully occur until some years later.

Because of the financial costs and other inevitable sacrifices, the determination of whether or not to have a Sunrise Dance is not entered into lightly by families (Goseyun, 1991). Parents interviewed for this book generally wanted their daughters to undergo the ceremony, but they

were considerate of their daughters' preferences. Most initiates stated
that they had initially felt ambivalence on the subject. They did recognize it as an important cultural event, but they were unsure if they were
prepared to make the necessary sacrifices and engage in the demanding
rituals. Peer pressure to hold a Sunrise Dance was an important variable.
As girls observed their sisters and female cousins undergoing the Sunrise Dance there was mounting pressure to experience this same event.
As one initiate explained, "when all of my cousins had one, I was like,
'Okay, I want one, too.'"

There are actually four options regarding the Sunrise Dance. The first
option is basically to choose not to have any ceremonial acknowledgment of the girl's menarche. Of the three other options, the simplest
and least expensive is to arrange for an adult female to massage the girl
within 4 days of her first menstrual cycle. A massage during this time
frame should occur for the remaining options as well, while the girl is
still "hot," as one informant explained. One adult informant stated that
this was her experience at menarche; she was raised in the Christian
tradition, and there were some objections to her undergoing the Sunrise
Dance. It is believed that the massage alone still imparts desired traits
of the adult woman onto the girl, so it is regarded as a legitimate choice
for a family to make. The next option is to conduct a 2-day ceremony,
and the third option is to conduct the full 4-day ceremony.[13] Based on
his fieldwork in the 1930s, G. Goodwin (1942) spoke of an abbreviated
1-day puberty ceremony that poor families held, while wealthier families
conducted the full 4-day version. A family's ultimate decision depends
on several factors, including their acceptance of traditional ceremonial
activities, their finances, the support of their extended family, and the
desire of their daughter.

If a family opts to proceed with a Sunrise Dance (a decision that
may have been made prior to menarche of their daughter), at the onset
of the girl's first menses her immediate family calls together extended
family members, especially the older members (called *ndeh guhyaneh*,
literally meaning "wise people"), to make some important decisions and
to accomplish rituals that need to be performed during the first 4 days.
As probably already discerned by readers, the number 4 is sacred to the
Apaches; it is found in the cardinal directions, the 4-day Sunrise Dance,

the arrangement of songs during the dance, the 4 colors (i.e., black, blue or green, yellow, and white), and numerous other expressions (see P. E. Goddard, 1909, 1919b; G. Goodwin, 1938; Lamphere, 1983).

At this initial phase, a mother of an initiate explained, "We invite our close relatives, personal friends, and anybody we may know that we're close to. We have a planning meeting." Because of the numerous rituals to be performed during this first menses, Opler (1941) called the preliminary steps of the Chiricahua version "the 'little' rite" and "a much-reduced version of the full rite" (pp. 90–91). A major decision at this time is the selection of a co-sponsor, a term currently used at San Carlos, which is sometimes called the sponsor in the literature (e.g., Basso, 1966). At San Carlos, however, the sponsor is usually the girl's parents or guardians, who make the Sunrise Dance possible. It is the co-sponsor or *na iłł esn* (translated as "one who prepares her" or "one who gets her ready"), or, as commonly called among Western Apaches, the godmother, who is the focus of the present discussion, but the godmother's husband will be required to fulfill certain responsibilities during the Sunrise Dance.[14] One mother asserted that this was the most important decision to be made within the 4 days because the woman to be selected must be the kind of woman her daughter would become. Another mother explained: "in a sense, you're giving your daughter to this other family." In short, this is not a decision one makes lightly. The co-sponsors must *not* be related to the initiate and her family; that is, they must be unrelated to the girl's clan or her father's clan, with maternal clan of particular importance (also see Basso, 1966; Whitaker, 1971). This was determined to be a challenge for many families in the relatively small communities of San Carlos and Bylas (the principal towns of the reservation), in which many are related to one another. Further, as reported by informants, many San Carlos people no longer know their clan membership; hence the guidance of older family members is critical to select godparents not related by clan or otherwise. As well, the girl's family must consider co-sponsors who are living respectable lives and who will be good role models for the girl. Basso (1966) indicated that after mutual clan was ruled out, character and wealth were considered in making the final decision of *na iłł esn*. Pregnant women cannot serve as co-sponsors because, as one initiate explained, the girl might become pregnant at a young age.

One mother of an initiate described the qualities that are examined in potential godmothers: "First of all, we pick out a lady in the community that we highly respect . . . that works and does her household thing . . . never leaves her children alone . . . and that's strong and stands for her values and tradition and culture. . . . So, both, as a couple, are looked at strongly for their values and their personality, what family they come from, how their family values the tradition."

The solidification of the relationship with the co-sponsor or godmother, who is also known as "the attendant" in Chiricahua culture (Opler, 1941), constitutes a separate ceremony in itself. The responsibilities associated with the co-sponsor's role are simply learned from other women. She is someone who must provide the girl with moral support and instruction throughout her Sunrise Dance and also serve as a role model and guide in the years to come. There is an implicit understanding of a financial commitment to the girl should she have financial needs in the future. The couple, as the co-sponsor, really becomes surrogate parents to the initiate. For example, if something were to happen to the girl's parents, her co-sponsor should assume parental roles. In short, a lifelong commitment between the girl and her co-sponsor is created that extends to all relations between their respective families, and these obligations can be just as demanding as those of one's clan members (Basso, 1970; Whitaker, 1971). It was ascertained from the interviews that initiates and their co-sponsors formed strong connections that endured beyond the ceremony, and frequently co-sponsors extended their hospitality to their goddaughter's siblings. One mother stated that the relationship between her daughter and the co-sponsor had been such a good match that her daughter calls her co-sponsor "Mom." Of the ceremonies observed, the co-sponsors who were selected were observed to be similar in age of the initiates' parents.

Once a decision is made concerning the co-sponsor, the girl and her family must go to the co-sponsor's home—unannounced and prior to sunrise—as explained by a mother: "Because if you do it after the sun rises, it is like bad luck." An eagle feather and a blue turquoise stone—both sacred objects—are presented to the potential female co-sponsor with cattail pollen within the context of a specified ritual.[15] Like stones and feathers, cattail pollen is a substance from a natural source that plays a powerful role in the Sunrise Dance. The potential co-sponsor may accept these items at that time or take time to consider the implications of the request and discuss it with her husband and family, because their support and assistance are essential in this endeavor. If accepted, money, food, and other gifts are presented to the co-sponsor. The amount of money can vary ranging from $20 to $200, according to one informant, depending on the resources of the girl's family.

An important component of the transaction involves the massaging of the initiate by her co-sponsor within the 4-day time frame of first menses. Ideally, the co-sponsor performs this ritual, but another adult woman can substitute if a co-sponsor has not yet been arranged. At that time, the girl and her family prepare a breakfast for the co-sponsor and her family. This appears to signify the beginning of a long-term relationship and the onset of the transfer of desired qualities of the godmother (and essentially White Painted Woman, whom she represents) to the initiate. The massage of the initiate has implications for the physical and psychological state of the initiate, as explained by a co-sponsor:

> When you start massaging her, you go down to her face and to her mouth . . . you put your hand over her mouth to where she'll speak kind words. . . . Then you go down and you massage her face where she'll stay young and, in her mind, she'll have good thoughts . . . lovely thoughts . . . her mind would be clear. . . . Then you go down on her shoulders, so she'll be strong. . . . Then you go down and you massage her hair, for her hair will stay long . . . be healthy. . . . You just go all the way down her body . . . as you're going down . . . you pray for her . . . she'll be healthy and grow up strong and live a long life. . . . Get to her fingers and massage her fingers. . . . You tip up her fingers, where her fingers will not be so long. . . . You go down her back, where she'll be straight . . . have good posture. . . . Then you go down and you massage her legs, and you get to her feet, where you keep her feet straight . . . where it stays flat . . . where she won't start walking outward. . . . She'll walk straight . . . stand straight.

It is believed that each time a woman serves in the co-sponsor role she loses something of herself or her essence to her young initiate. Of a woman who was a co-sponsor five or six times, one informant said, "you can tell that when she did her first one, she was very, very young. But now she really looks old, because part of her has gone to the girls." In keeping with the sacredness of the number 4, some informants stated that once a woman accepts the co-sponsor role she is obligated to fulfil it four times in her life. However, others stated that the number of times was inconsequential, as is indicated in the previous example of the woman serving five or six times. Another informant stated that as long as a woman was strong she could continue in the co-sponsor role.

The co-sponsor not only mentors and supports the girl through the ceremony and becomes a surrogate parent; she also is instrumental in bringing two previously unrelated families together. In a culture such as the Apaches', where kinship serves as a foundation for all social relationships, fictive kin are created where previous relationships did not exist. Hence, the girl and her co-sponsor bring two kinship systems together by virtue of the Sunrise Dance. This union of families is demonstrated in dancing during the Sunrise Dance between both kin groups. One or more male or female relatives from the sponsor's side will dance across the ceremonial grounds to relatives of the opposite sex and of the co-sponsor's family and engage them in dancing, and vice versa. An informant stated that this action represents forming new relationships between the two previously unrelated families.

Another major decision facing the family soon after their daughter's menarche is the selection of the medicine man (*dí yin*) who will sing the Sunrise Dance. Apparently, the right to sing this ceremony is not bestowed in the typical shamanistic manner of receiving a vision or having some other encounter with the supernatural beings, as stated for Chiricahua culture (Opler, 1941). Rather, one learns the ceremony through experience and memorization of the numerous songs, as I was informed at San Carlos. Assisting an experienced singer over the course of years is the common manner of acquiring this skill. Indeed, the son of one of the medicine men observed in this study was serving as his father's assistant to acquire the skills to conduct the ceremony himself, and at various points in the ceremony he assumed primary responsibility for the singing.

A medicine man might be selected because he is related through clan membership or marriage, or perhaps a family member had attended one of his ceremonies previously and could vouch for his expertise or effectiveness, as one mother explained: "And there's just a feeling you get during his dances that I really liked." This mother was particularly impressed because the medicine man remembered the 170 individual girls for whom he had conducted dances. She explained that at a time subsequent to this woman's daughter's Sunrise Dance, the medicine man remembered her daughter and inquired about her well-being. When a family makes a decision about a potential medicine man, he must be approached in the early morning, prior to dawn. A cross is drawn with cattail pollen on the palm of the medicine man's right hand, and on top of the pollen are placed an eagle feather with a piece of turquoise attached to it and a monetary gift. One family explained that once they secured the medicine man, he instructed them on the proper protocol for other necessary rituals during the first 4 critical days, as well as through all phases of the Sunrise Dance.

In short, preparations during the 4 days of the initiate's first menses can become frantic, as families must solidify commitments from a medicine man and the co-sponsor. The commitments are long-term, especially those of the co-sponsor. Any one of these individuals may refuse the request, including the potential co-sponsor. In such a case, the family must begin the process over again with another co-sponsor and ensure that an agreement is reached and the girl is massaged within the specified 4-day time frame.

The family also must select a peer of their daughter's who will be her partner for the duration of the ceremony. The partner is typically a relative of the initiate, and she must have recently experienced her own Sunrise Dance. A good partner will have the benefit of experience from her own recent dance and, along with the godmother, serve as a mentor to the initiate, as one mother explained: "Her little cousin who danced with her also helped guide her because she's been through a dance . . . 'this is going to happen to you' . . . when they painted her, she'd say, 'If you get it in your mouth, just swallow it.'" By serving as a partner, one has the opportunity to wear the elaborate buckskin costume that was worn previously at her Sunrise Dance. At the Sunrise Dances I attended, the initiates and their partners were viewed in nearly constant company with one another during informal occasions. Partners were observed to be very attentive to initiates as observed by their wiping the sweat off the faces of initiates with scarves tied to the initiates' dresses (it is taboo for initiates to touch themselves at this time) during pauses between songs. As well, partners and godmothers hold beverages for initiates to facilitate their use of the drinking tube (it is taboo for them to touch their lips to beverage containers during the 4-day dance). While Basso (1966) specified the significance of these ritual objects for 4 days after the ceremony, the scratching stick and drinking tube were used during the 4-day dance by initiates at San Carlos in this study and removed on the fourth morning.

Additional decisions to be made prior to the Sunrise Dance (but not in the initial 4-day time frame of first menses) concern the site where the dance will be held and selection of key camp personnel. An individual must be identified who can serve as camp boss and take responsibility for smooth functioning of all aspects of camp management. Relatives also are approached to manage food preparation, and a camp cook must be selected and approached with the request. Serving as camp cook was observed to be an exceedingly demanding responsibility that required rising about three or four o'clock each morning during the encampment to cook three meals a day for scores of people. Goseyun (1991) described the enormous amount of food preparation required during the encampment and mentioned that at least 50 different dishes are prepared many using traditional food items. People also must be identified who can ensure that the fire in the camp remains lit for the duration of the Sunrise Dance.

The Sunrise Dance will be scheduled for a later date in order to provide families with the time needed to prepare and to accommodate participants' schedules. Typically, it will occur several months after the onset of menses, but it should be within the first year. A lengthy time span of preparation was also noted by Opler (1941) relative to Chiricahua culture. During the interim, families are busy making the elaborate and costly arrangements, which are estimated to run as high as $10,000 in the present day. Those who must be paid include the medicine man and his helpers and the Mountain Spirit dancers and their leader. In the past, medicine men would be given horses, saddles, and blankets for their services (Golston, 1996). Today they will be given hundreds of dollars for a very substantial commitment of time and energy. The initiate's buckskin dress and moccasins are handmade at the cost of several hundred dollars. Opler (1941) stated that five skins were required to construct the girl's cape, skirt, and moccasins. The family must obtain several ceremonial items to conduct the Sunrise Dance. Food must be purchased for the encampment of the initiate, her partner, her immediate family, and some extended family members. As well, all helpers and guests must be fed. Firewood is required for bonfires at the nightly dancing, meal preparation, and the nonstop fires in the camp. One father expressed his concern about acquiring all of the needed wood and stated that his co-workers and extended family members rose to the occasion and helped cut and store the wood. In addition to all of the requirements for the Sunrise Dance, expensive gift exchanges will occur between the sponsors and co-sponsors, and families begin accumulating the needed items long before the actual event.

Initiates and their families also use the months prior to the Sunrise Dance to prepare themselves physically. One initiate reported that her preparation included running with her cousins to become physically in shape for her ceremony. As discussed in chapter 3, numerous North American Indian cultures regard first menses as an especially critical juncture of the life span. Girls are to be disciplined and busy previous to and throughout the Sunrise Dance, as explained by a San Carlos Apache mother: "she needs to start working for four days . . . it's very sacred . . . she has to get up before the sun rises, she goes to bed late, she cleans . . . then she has to cook three times a day . . . she has to learn how to make bread, not only inside but outside . . . she has to start her own fire . . . she has to walk clockwise and make sure she starts her fire that way."

Psychological and spiritual preparation is also critical. Sponsors, co-sponsors, and initiates are instructed by grandparents and other elders to be engaged in prayer throughout the months prior to the dance. Parents are told to make their daughters rise early and to pray. One mother explained that as soon as they gave the stone to the godmother, she and her daughter rose every morning at four o'clock to pray for her Sunrise Dance so that she would have strength during the dance and would dance as light as a feather. Indeed, many informants discussed the great deal of prayer that occurs prior to and during the Sunrise Dance. The medicine man and his helpers and the Mountain Spirit dancers pray as they make preparations for the ceremony. During the dance itself, the medicine man and elders instruct the godparents and initiates, as well as all of those who are closely involved, to continually pray for the dance. The onlookers or the public who are in attendance also are to be engaged in prayer throughout the event. The initiate, her family, the spiritual leaders, and the onlookers—all who are involved—are to think "good thoughts" throughout the Sunrise Dance, because it is believed that people's attitudes and thoughts will influence the likelihood of positive outcomes of the dance for the initiate, themselves, and others. Regarding prayers for initiates that occur at the Sunrise Dance, a medicine person explained: "we ask Usen to give this girl knowledge, wisdom, and love in her heart. And, it is not just a word, but it comes with spirit and power. She will get what the medicine man told her in the dance . . . good life . . . happy family."

Preparation to Separation

As chapter 5 demonstrated, some kind of physical or psychological separation of initiates at first menstruation is common to numerous North American Indian cultures in history. Separation is an imposed phase of the rite of passage representative of a break from the immaturity, dependence, and safety of childhood. Implicit in the separation are the new environmental demands that impose challenges that are not considered suitable for a child but are required of the pubescent without the benefit of her earlier sources of coping and comfort. For instance, many North American Indian puberty ceremonies—of the past and the present—place high physical demands on initiates, such as engagement in extensive fasting, adhering to taboos, and running. It is expected that, through the introduction of new demands, initiates will acquire strength through successful performance of rituals. The uncertainty that results from separation from the familiar and one's old identity induces the state of liminality in which the person does not yet have the security of a new identity. Activation is characterized by anxiety and fear that emerge from the state of liminality, and agony is composed of helplessness, depression, and inner crisis. Both activation and agony are emotional consequences of the insecurity induced by the separation phase.

Relative to the contemporary version of the Sunrise Dance, a psychological sense of the initiate's separated status really begins at menarche with the onset of rituals. The actual physical separation of the initiate occurs sometime later, at the time of the Sunrise Dance, and will extend up to 12 days: 4 days prior to the public ceremony, during which time the initiate begins staying at the encampment with her family and partner; 4 days during the ceremony; and 4 days after the ceremony, wherein the girl is still considered to be in a sacred state. During the first 4 days, the initiate, her partner, and her family move to an encampment they construct expressly for the purpose of her Sunrise Dance (see Basso, 1966, for a description of the construction of these camps). This temporary relocation of the initiate and her kin to a special camp represents a re-creation of earlier Apache village life (Norelli, 1994). The camp is blessed by the medicine man; in the case of Carla's Sunrise Dance described in Goseyun (1991), the parish priest also blessed the camp by conducting a special mass.

The initiate's co-sponsors or godparents build their own encampment in relatively close proximity to that of the initiate and her family. All the encampments of the Sunrise Dances I attended were located at one of three sites around the community of San Carlos, but there are other sites on the San Carlos Reservation where these dances are frequently held. The efforts of extended family members are critical to preparing the site, and work begins prior to the actual encampments. Areas for cooking, eating, sleeping, and dancing are constructed using large tin sheets to compartmentalize different living areas. While touring one such camp I was told that a family member had carefully drawn up plans for it, including separate sleeping areas, eating and cooking areas, and public areas. The setting was cool and comfortable with ample shading from the branches of the large trees above our heads. Cots and bedding in the sleeping areas of either traditional wickiups or conventional tents made for cozy lodgings.

The initiate and her partner, without the use of tools, are required to build their own sleeping structure, a wickiup, which is the traditional home structure of the Western Apaches. Long branches from willow trees are manipulated to create the domed structure and are tied together with strips of yucca leaves. Branches with leaves attached are placed as covering over the structure to provide shading and shelter. This structure, which becomes their home for the duration of the encampment, can be interpreted as part of the new environmental demands step of the separation phase. By virtue of the primacy of her own menarche and Sunrise Dance, the initiate's partner is permitted to share this separation with her. Close family members sleep in separate wickiups or tents in close proximity to that of the initiate and her partner.

Singing and social dancing, called *bi goh ji tał,* or "half-night dance" (Basso, 1966), occur for several evenings prior to the onset of the 4-day ceremony.[16] A camp singer who is often a medicine man (and may be someone other than the medicine man who will conduct the 4-day ceremony) is hired to bless the camp and lead singing in the evenings. These preliminary days serve to further heighten the liminal status of the initiate, and the new environmental demands placed upon her constitute an accelerated pathway in psychological maturation. At this time, the initiate is expected to behave responsibly and display discipline. She is to rise early, be helpful to others, and engage in the chores of an adult woman. She must listen to the instruction of the medicine man and others, talk less, and not talk back to her elders. She is instructed not to laugh during the Sunrise Dance, especially during the critical 4 days, or she will have wrinkles when she is older. The initiate is separated from her typical day-to-day activities and must adapt to a new environment—a transitional environment—that serves to separate her from her former existence. She will ultimately return to her home, her friends, and her school, but she will return as a more disciplined and mature young woman.

The final 4 days of the encampment are the culminating series of events that attract public attendance and constitute the Sunrise Dance proper. The first day begins with the initiate rising early and preparing four types of bread—fry bread, ash bread, donkey bread, and tortillas. Some initiates stated that they also made corn bread. It is interesting to read in Reagan's (1931) accounts from 1901–1902 of the preparation of Apache breads that bear strong similarity to the breads prepared today by initiates. The camp cook and her helpers are also quite busy this first morning in the preparation of foods that will be brought to the co-sponsor's camp in a food exchange (*nił sla ih ka*). The exchange of food symbolizes the newly formed kin relationship that will endure, with the premise that all is shared between the two families (Basso, 1966).

A significant event of the first day is the dressing of the initiate (*bi keh ihl ze'*, translated as "she is dressed up") by her godmother, which signifies the onset of the initiate's transformation into White Painted Woman. More precisely, the dressing prepares the initiate to assume the power that makes her holy (Basso, 1966).[17] This and other rituals performed throughout the next few days will reach the climactic painting on the third day, when the transformation into White Painted Woman becomes complete. In preparation for the dressing ritual, new environmental demands are placed on the initiate according to the requirement that she not bathe or take a shower during the critical 4 days of the ceremony. She cannot wash herself or come into contact with water during her dance, because it is believed that she would sacrifice her power. The taboo against bathing and the special dressing further heighten the initiate's liminal status.

In preparation for the dressing ritual, the medicine man, the singers, the drummers, and the initiate's father conduct a sweat bath (*gish ih zha ha aldeh*, translated as "cane, it is made") on the morning of the first day.[18] At this time they prepare and bless ritual items used by the initiate, including her cane, an abalone shell, feathers, a new buckskin serape on which she will kneel, lie, and stand at various points during her dance, and additional ceremonial paraphernalia that she will wear or use during the Sunrise Dance (Basso, 1966). The sweat bath is a third separate camp (the other camps being the initiate's and her family's camp and the co-sponsor's camp), and the medicine man and his assistants sing and drum the prescribed songs as the ritual items are assembled. Food is brought to these men at the sweat bath through the initiate's demonstration of role performance. The initiate wears the traditional Apache "burden basket" strapped across her forehead and resting on her back—another physical reminder of her separated status. Others from her camp carry stews and breads to the nearby location of the medicine man, and singers accompany this procession with songs. After the food is delivered, the initiate and her partner must run back to their own camp and the others walk.

Dressing of the initiate typically occurs in the later afternoon, but I know one medicine man who conducts this ritual in the morning. The difference in timing relative to dressing the initiate is an example of the kind of stylistic preference or orientation of medicine men. The initiate stands on a large white cloth and faces the east. Her godmother is instructed by the medicine man to place the necessary ceremonial objects on the girl in a specified manner. These are the items that were prepared and blessed earlier in the day by the medicine man at the sweat bath. Strict protocol dictates the sequence of placing the sacred objects, and the four sacred colors (i.e., black, blue or green, yellow, and white) should be incorporated in her costume. One informant explained that yellow and black, especially, should be worn by the girl, because yellow represents the sun and black protects from evil. The buckskin covering, cape, or serape is placed over the initiate's cotton camp dress. The buckskin is painted yellow—a color that is sacred because it reflects White Painted Woman (L. H. Clark, 1976). Yellow is also regarded as a sacred color because of its resemblance to cattail pollen, which is used as an offering and blessing during this ceremony and other Apache ceremonies.[19] Clearly, the symbolism of the color yellow is multifaceted and of high significance in this ceremony.

The buckskin cape and skirt are adorned with fringes that represent fertility in the Apache tradition, and designs on the girl's clothing are symbolic. Circles are typically representative of the sun, and crescent moons are reminders of natural cycles, such as the phases of the moon. Crosses and four-pointed stars represent the four directions, and rainbows also may be shown. In Apache culture, these natural phenomena are all powers to be acquired by the girl during her puberty rites and for her life (Opler, 1941). Specifically, because tradition specified that White Painted Woman was impregnated by the beams of the sun, fringes are representative of the sunbeams. Dozens of tin pendants that jingle also are affixed to the buckskin, and when the initiate is walking they make a sound that symbolizes her walk down the pollen path or spiritual path of life (L. H. Clark, 1976). A small, downy eagle feather is attached to each of the shoulders of the initiate so that she may walk and run as lightly as a feather on air (Basso, 1966, 1970). The girl also wears the traditional Apache moccasins with the upturned toe. The cape, the skirt that is worn underneath it, and other ritual clothing and adornments are modeled after that worn by White Painted Woman, according to Apache legend (Opler, 1941). Indeed, in P. E. Goddard's (1919a) account of the White Mountain Apaches' adolescent ceremony, the girl, called Ests'unnadlehi, wears a fringed buckskin skirt and shirt.

The initiate's hair is worn long and flowing during the ceremony, and an eagle feather is fastened to her hair to symbolize longevity. The white or gray color of the feather will ensure she lives long enough to have hair of this color (Basso, 1966). It also has been stated to serve as the girl's guide for the remainder of her life, even though it will be removed at the end of the ceremony (Mails, 1988). An abalone shell is affixed to her hair and hangs on her forehead. Abalone is associated with the west and the color of the yellow sunset—the stated location of White Painted Woman's home (L. H. Clark, 1976). One informant thought that the abalone shell tied on the initiate's forehead was reminiscent of a seashell that White Painted Woman hid in during a flood, stating, "and she hid in that thing, and she was the only survivor of this." Basso (1966) spoke of the abalone shell as linking the girl to White Shell Woman or Changing Woman, whose power would be critical during the puberty ceremony.[20]

In Apache tradition, as in many other Native American cultures, it is believed that power can be derived from physical objects. Fetishes and sacred objects are constructed from various sources, including natural substances such as shells and cattail pollen. These substances are imbued with power that becomes transferred to the participant through her association with them (Lamphere, 1983). For example, the power of the abalone shell on the initiate's forehead will be transferred to her by virtue of its contact to her skin. The beaded Apache T-necklace that is placed on the initiate is a further example of transference of power. The necklace displays the power of the Mountain Spirits (Ga'an), who will dance at her ceremony, and are regarded as the spiritual guardians of the Apache people. It is also said that the necklace stands for a lifetime of wealth for the girl (L. H. Clark, 1976). Opler (1941) recounts the song surrounding the T-necklace according to Chiricahua tradition:

The words of Killer of Enemies, good through long life,
Have entered you;
They have entered you by means of your necklace;
Your necklace has gone into your body,
For its power is good. (p. 127)

Similar to puberty customs of numerous other North American Indian cultures, the initiate is required to use a drinking tube, constructed from a cattail plant, to take her beverages. She also must use a scratching stick to scratch herself. During the dressing ritual, her godmother attaches these objects, which were earlier tied to a long strip of rawhide cord, and places them around the initiate's neck. The existence of these objects extends back in Apache history; they were reportedly found at Geronimo's Mexican encampment (Bourke, 1892). In the Jicarilla puberty rites, both the initiate and her male partner are required to use these implements to prevent undesirable physical impacts (Opler, 1946). Informants in this study said the drinking tube must be used to prevent rain, which would ruin her ceremony, an observation also noted by L. H. Clark (1976). Consistent with Basso (1970), it was also explained to me that she could develop facial hair if she did not use her drinking tube. There is high agreement that use of the scratching stick is protective so that she will not permanently scar herself if she happens to use her fingernails during this time when her power could cause undesirable effects (e.g., Basso, 1970). Additionally, her fingernails could grow long and bend back if she does not use the scratching stick (Mails, 1988). According to L. H. Clark (1976), the scratching stick is made from the wood of a fruit-or nut-bearing tree and therefore will transfer its fertility properties to the girl when she uses it.

An important ritual item that the initiate must have in her possession for the 4-day dance is the wooden staff or cane (*gish ih zha ha*). This item is prepared and blessed early in the first day at the sweat bath ceremony (*gish ih zha ha aldeh*) of the medicine man and his helpers. This object represents longevity—the most important goal of the Sunrise Dance. The girl will dance with it and have it with her throughout the ceremony, and she is instructed to use the cane when she is older (Basso, 1966; L. H. Clark, 1976). It is stated that the cane is the girl's partner when she dances (Reagan, 1931), while P. E. Goddard (1919a) explained that it was the Sun's cane and the chief's cane. During the Sunrise Dance other people may link arms to dance with one another, but the cane always accompanies the initiate as if it were her dance partner. Symbolic of fertility, the cane is made from a hardwood tree to give it strength to last the girl's life (Basso, 1966). The cane has eagle feathers (representative of protection) and oriole feathers (symbolic of a good, happy disposition) attached to it; these are also reflective of the hope for long life (see Basso, 1966, for a more complete description of the cane and its symbolism). White feathers, especially, signify that she will grow old enough to have white hair. The feathers also are used to enable the initiate to run as lightly as on air during her dance. A white stone bead and a turquoise stone bead are attached to the eagle feathers, and the feathers and stones protect her from any "power-caused" illnesses (Mails, 1988). Jingles or bells attached to the cane enable others to always hear the initiate when she is approaching. As one mother explained, the noise from the cane is to remind people that the girl is approaching, and they are to exhibit respect toward her and keep a check on their thoughts and words. Still another purpose from one of Whitaker's (1971) informants is that the bells help the girl keep time with music. Four ribbons are attached to the cane, each of a different color to represent the four cardinal directions: black is the color of the east, blue or green is the color of the south, yellow is the color of the west, and white is associated with the north.

After the dressing, four cradleboard songs are sung in Apache that signify the changes occurring in the girl (Mails, 1988).[21] Upon conclusion of the singing, the medicine man switches to speaking in English and gives the girl additional private verbal admonishments and instructions related to her expected behavior at the present time and in the future. The evening of the first day culminates with singing by the medicine man and his singers (*bi til tih*, translated as "night before dance"). The initiate is clad in her ceremonial garb and, as in all evening dances, faces west toward the sunset and the singers. The cradleboard songs are again sung along with other songs that tell of good things to come (e.g., harvest, deer, horse, and antelope) to the girl (Mails, 1988). Guests in attendance will dance to the music in groups of two or more by hooking their elbows and moving forward and backward as they move clockwise around the singers. The purpose of the singing and dancing this first night is primarily social; as one informant stated, "It is get-acquainted night."

While ritual prescribes the number of songs that are sung, there appears to be some variation in practice. At the time of his research, Basso (1966) indicated that only 12 or 24 songs were sung during the first evening's events. However, my research concurs with Goseyun (1991), who stated that 32 songs are sung the first evening. Murphy (1993) explained that songs are timed to occur with the rising and settings suns, depending on whether it is the evening or morning segment of the ceremony. Hence, apparently the number of songs may vary depending on the natural cycles of the rising and setting sun. While the number of songs appears to vary, of most importance is that they always occur in groups of four. The language of the songs is in the classical Apache language, and initiates may need to have words interpreted, even if they should happen to speak Apache (Murphy, 1993).

In summary, separation is observed in multiple forms during the Sunrise Dance. Overall, the fact that the pubescent is singled out for this major event signifies her special, separated status. There are other manners in which separation is observed, such as her living in a separate wickiup that is only shared by a peer who has recently experienced her own Sunrise Dance. Her special clothing and her adornment with sacred objects further demonstrate her separated status. The requirements to use the drinking tube and scratching stick and adherence to other taboos also signify separation that endures through all days of the Sunrise Dance.

Separation to Transition

Numerous other events of the first day of the 4-day ceremony serve to intensify the initiate's separation due to the placement of new environmental demands. These demands also signify transition, particularly in respect to accommodation as she engages in role performance. For instance, the initiate rises early on the first day and is required to make four different kinds of bread, as previously described. Later in the morning, these breads, along with other prepared stews and dishes, will be given to the co-sponsors during a food exchange between the two camps. The industriousness she is expected to exhibit around the camp also reflects accommodation.

The initiate's liminal status, along with activation and agony, are quite apparent through several of the phases of the second day of the 4-day Sunrise Dance that begins just prior to sunrise. The medicine man and his helpers assemble and commence the singing and drumming with the initiate and her partner dancing in front of them. Initially, there may just be a few helpers with the medicine man, but more men join the ensemble as the morning progresses. The men who join in the singing may know the songs or are in the process of learning them. Two men stand on either side of the singers and drummers and hold Apache baskets that are filled with chewing gum, cigarettes, candy, and other items, gifts of which people are permitted to avail themselves during the ceremony.

Members of the initiate's extended family all stand to the right of the medicine man, and the co-sponsor's family stands to the left. A circle is more or less formed around the center of the ceremonial grounds, with the medicine man and his helpers and the initiate and her partner all facing the east. In front of the initiate and her partner are several blankets that belong to various individuals, with the buckskin piece on the top. This buckskin is used in various rituals, and it had been blessed in the sweat bath ceremony on the first day. In a perpendicular direction from the initiate are rows of boxes lined up that contain fruit, candy, soda, and other gifts that will be distributed to the crowd. In the early morning the crowd is initially small, with just a handful of family members looking on, but over the course of the morning numbers increase gradually and there may ultimately be a few hundred onlookers. The role of these guests is to support and pray for the girl.

There are eight identified phases to the activities of the second morning (see Basso, 1966; also see Table 3), and I observed these phases to last anywhere from 4 to 5 hours for a total of 64 songs in its entirety. During phase 1, *bihl de nił ke* ("All alone, she dances"), the initiate and her partner dance in front of the medicine man and other singers while all face east toward the sunrise. The singers hold drums, made with large pots or kettles and filled with a small amount of water, with hide stretched tightly across the top. A drum is played with a stick in accompaniment to the music. It is important that this phase begin prior to sunrise because the power of White Painted Woman particularly intensifies at the moment the first rays of sun strike the abalone shell on the initiate's forehead. This event might be conceived of as a sparking of the power that began the previous day when the initiate was dressed. While few people are present at this early hour, I am always keen to observe the first rays of the sun enlighten the initiate's face. The songs during this phase tell of the creation of the Western Apaches and detail the contributions of White Painted Woman (Basso, 1966). The medicine man calls on the power of White Painted Woman (or Changing Woman as stated by Basso) and directs the power to the initiate. It is believed that the girl has received this important supernatural being's power by the end of phase 1 (Basso, 1966).

During this initial phase of dancing, the initiate is instructed to keep her face expressionless as she looks off into the distance or looks down. One informant stated that she was told to watch for something and reported that she observed five eagles. Her father confirmed this observation, and both felt this observance was significant. The initiate bounces back and forth from one foot to the other in keeping with the music, and her ever-present cane is in her right hand keeping time with the music.

After a certain set of songs, the godfather dances and escorts the godmother around the ceremonial ground, moving clockwise, and she steps in and takes the partner's place. One of the medicine man's helpers dances with the partner around the ceremonial ground and leaves her to the right of the medicine man and his singers, where she continues to dance. Phase 2, *niztah* ("Sitting or kneeling"), then begins, during which time the initiate sways to the music while dancing on her knees. During this phase, she is kneeling on the stack of blankets that are topped by the buckskin. Consistent with my own observations, Basso (1966) described the girl's posture, stating: "she raises her hands to the level of her shoulder, and then, looking into the rising sun, begins to sway from side to side" (p. 155). Her posture is to represent White Painted Woman's first menstruation, as specified in oral tradition (Basso, 1966). These activities appear to be what P. E. Goddard (1919a) described relative to an event in the adolescent ceremony that was reminiscent of the woman sitting on her knees with the red light from the sun shining into her. A common belief is that this phase also signifies White Painted Woman's conception and pregnancy. However, this point was disputed by an informant of

Mails (1988), who emphasized the girl is a virgin and she was praying during this phase and that her swaying back and forth was in keeping with the music and not signifying impregnation. As previously noted, the special buckskin that she kneels on had been blessed by the medicine man during the sweat bath on the previous day.

This phase leads to phase 3, *nizti* ("Lying"), in which the godmother now massages the girl, who must lay face down on the buckskin with her chin held up and not touching the buckskin. The medicine man gives numerous instructions to the godmother as he guides her through this phase. She essentially massages the initiate from head to foot and even uses her feet at certain points as she touches the girl. The godmother begins by circling the girl four times, and then begins the massage. She walks in a circle around the girl several times during the massage before beginning a new segment, always moving in the clockwise direction. Movement in a clockwise direction or following the movements of the sun from east to west is a ritual practice incorporated into numerous actions of the Sunrise Dance.[22] Several initiates reported that the massage was a relief after prior segments of dancing, including dancing on their knees. This adult woman is a role model to the girl, and it can be conceived that by massaging the initiate she is shaping her according to desirable traits. It is believed that both physical and psychological characteristics of the initiate are affected through the actions of this phase. Of course, this ritual is only meaningful because of the belief that the pubescent is particularly impressionable at this point in the life span. Basso (1966) stated that the power of Changing Woman makes the girl's body especially malleable so that it can be molded. A similar ritual is performed with parallel purposes in the Navajo Kinaaldá in which the initiate's mentor, the Ideal Woman, molds her.

The "Lying" phase represents the step of numinosity in the transition phase of the RPP. It is a visible image of the initiate's receptivity toward influence from her adult mentor. The purpose of the massage is essentially the same as her massage during the initiate's first menses. She is being shaped into the image of White Painted Woman—both in her character and her physical demeanor. Turner (1967) speaks of initiates' willingness to be guided by their mentors in the broader scheme of coming-of-age ceremonies: "The passivity of neophytes to their instructors, their malleability, which is increased by submission to ordeal, their reduction to a uniform condition, are signs of the process whereby they are ground down to be fashioned anew and endowed with additional powers to cope with their new station in life" (p. 101). Indeed, initiates at the Sunrise Dance have many mentors—medicine men who continually instruct them, adult relatives, their partners, and their godmothers. The Mountain Spirit dancers, who become part of the ceremony on the evening of the second day and morning of the third day, also serve roles of guidance and mentorship to initiates. In all cases, initiates' numinosity represents their openness to be guided by these other individuals who possess varying experiences and forms of knowledge.

When the massage is completed, the male and female co-sponsor, as a couple, quickly lift the girl to a standing position. This action signifies their acceptance of her as their daughter. Events quickly lead to phases 4 and 5, which require the initiate to perform several rituals. At phase 4, *gish ih zha ha yinda sle dił ihłye* ("Cane set out for her, she runs around it"), the initiate's cane is placed at minor distances to the east on four subsequent occasions. Each time the cane is set further away, and after receiving a slight push from her godmother, the initiate runs around it. Her godmother, her partner, and others who choose to run follow her. The godmother retrieves the cane as she runs around it and returns it to the girl. Each subsequent run represents her passage through four life stages: infancy, childhood/adolescence, womanhood, and old age. With each circling of the cane, the initiate "'owns' the stage of life it stands for" (Basso, 1966, p. 157). As well, the running is to make the initiate physically strong (Mails, 1988). Upon conclusion of this phase, the girl is assured of long life. The following two songs from the Chiricahua tradition from Opler (1941) reflect two different stages of the life span; the first speaks of middle age:

> *White Painted Woman has reached middle age by means of it,*
> *She has reached middle age by means of it,*
> *By means of it she has entered long life,*
> *She has reached middle age by means of it. (p. 128)*

This second song speaks of the cane or staff of old age:

He made the black staff of old age for me,
He made the road of the sun for me;
These holy things he has made for me, saying,
"With these you will grow old."
Now when I have become old,
You will remember me by means of them. (p. 128)

Phase 5, *nistan* ("Running"), is similar to phase 4, but in this phase the initiate runs on subsequent occasions in the four cardinal directions—east, south, west, and north. *Nistan* enables the initiate to run fast without fatigue (Basso, 1970). Additionally, one informant in my research stated that it is "calling on the blessings of the four directions today." These two phases are consistent with P. E. Goddard's (1919a) account of the girl running around the cane four times as it is placed at further distances each time. According to Basso (1966), the first five benefit only the pubescent girl, while the next two phases offer blessings to those in attendance.

During phase 6, *sha nał dihl* ("Candy, it is poured"), the medicine man sprinkles the girl with cattail pollen and then a burden basket filled with candy is poured over her head as she and her godmother stand on the buckskin. Children surround the initiate at this phase and dash forward to gather all of the contents. The candy poured over the initiate's head is said to become holy, because the pieces have touched her while she is in a sacred state. Hence, the recipients of the candy will be blessed with having plenty of what is required in the future (Mails, 1988). On various occasions, people handed me candy acquired during this phase with the admonition that it was a good thing to receive these gifts. At the time of P. E. Goddard (1919a), the basket contained kernels of corn that people would take home to plant, with the expectation that these plants would grow large and yield a fruitful crop. The action of pouring a wealth of goods over the girl's head represents step 11 of the RPP model, transcendence, because the community recognizes that the initiate is empowered and that anything she touches can bring blessings to the recipients. After the candy is poured, the girl's relatives distribute the boxes of fruit, drinks, and other goods that were set before the initiate throughout the previous phases.

Like the previous phase, phase 7, *ba na ihl dih* ("Blessing her"), also represents transcendence. The medicine man and most of those present—first the men from the sponsor's side and then the men from the co-sponsor's side—bless the girl with cattail pollen. The women follow, with the women from the sponsor's side first and then the women from the co-sponsor's side. The initiate stands on the buckskin with her partner to her right and her godmother to her left. The ensemble is accordingly sprinkled with pollen. The pollen is applied first to the head, then to the chest, then to the shoulders, and sometimes to the feet. The individual placing the pollen may then dab it on his or her own cheeks. At the end of this ritual, the initiate, her partner, and her godmother are visibly covered with the yellow pollen.

During this phase it is common for individuals to request personal prayer and blessings from the initiate. At more than one ceremony I observed infants being brought to the initiate for prayer. The medicine man guided the initiate through the process, and the initiate held the infant over her head and toward each of the four directions. In another illustration of the significance of this phase, an initiate and her family described how a man came to her to receive help for his vision, and he found that it did improve after he received her prayers and blessings. The family believed that the girl had been prepared for this moment because a hummingbird had been attracted to her during an earlier time of prayer and she had felt her own vision affected. Hummingbirds, in Apache beliefs, bring blessings to people.

When interviewed, several initiates expressed the sense of empowerment that *ba na ihl dih* gave them. One initiate explained why this was one of her favorite phases: "Well, just the feeling of blessing other people and having them think that you could help them . . . and people really believing in you." In addition to transcendence, this blessing phase represents accommodation from the RPP model because the initiate is engaged in role performance as expected for her current status in life.

Phase 8, *gíhx ił ke* ("Blankets, she throws them off"), concludes the morning of the second day. The initiate and her female co-sponsor are instructed by the medicine man to shake the buckskin to the east and the blankets that they have been dancing on to the other directions. This ritual represents several things, including the anticipation that she will always have plenty of blankets and that her camp will always be clean. As well, shaking the buckskin is symbolic of always having deer meat in the camp (Basso, 1966). This role performance is indicative of accommodation and new identity in the RPP model. After the events of the second morning, the initiate and her partner are instructed to run the short distance (about an eighth of a mile) back to the camp. Her family and the co-sponsors and their family return to their respective camps to eat and rest. With the exception of some guests who return to the camps with the families, most visitors, who can number in the hundreds, leave the ceremonial grounds until the evening's events.

In their interviews, initiates stated that they were nervous as they anticipated the grueling events of the second morning, including the segment of dancing on their knees. This is where RPP stages of activation and agony come into play, both in the anticipation of these actions and in their actual performance. Girls appeared quite exhausted from the events of the second day. Indeed, I have observed initiates and their mothers and other female relatives sob with relief after the second morning was completed. Several informants reported how they had observed initiates breaking down and crying during their Sunrise Dances, as well as collapsing with fatigue. I was told that dances continue on in spite of such occurrences.

Separation and transition are apparent through many of the rituals of the eight phases of the second morning. The initiate's liminal status is magnified through rituals related to physical actions of dancing and running that are thought to build endurance and strength for the yielding of a long life. The godmother's massaging of the initiate serves to physically reshape her into someone who bears the physical and psychological attributes of an Apache woman. Implicit in these rituals is the belief, common to many other Native American Indian cultures, that at pubescence, as in infancy, the girl is especially impressionable and malleable. The opportunity must be maximized to steer her into the desirable path for life (Lincoln, 1991; Schwarz, 1997). Hence, there are many rituals indicative of physical shaping of the girl's physique and personality as well as to set her life course. Perhaps the ultimate physically transforming action is the painting of the initiate on the third morning that will complete her transformation into White Painted Woman and also ensure her a long life. This action is described more fully in the next section.

Transition to Reincorporation

The events of the second evening and the third morning best demonstrate aspects of transition and ultimately reincorporation. Because the new status or identity has not yet been incorporated, liminality must still be present during transition, but some of the emotional discomforts of earlier rituals have diminished. Transition replaces uncertainty with attitudes of respect and awe as well as a willingness on the part of the initiate to be guided. This step is called numinosity, and by this time the initiate is well into her rite of passage. Accommodation includes cognitive alterations that represent the initiate's incorporation of elements of her new roles. Ecstasy emerges with relief and joy because a transformation is well under way and the uncertainty and insecurity of liminality is rapidly diminishing.

Reincorporation is the final phase of the RPP, but some elements of this phase were evident in previously described rituals, such as the initiate's blessing of others on the second day. In general, reincorporation occurs as previously demanding rituals are successfully negotiated and the liminal state diminishes. During transcendence, the initiate and her community recognize that the former childhood identity has been abandoned and a new identity is emerging. Indeed, transcendence is shown through dressing rituals on the first day and culminates with painting the initiate on the third day. A new identity is being impressed on the initiate throughout the rite of passage—an identity that is composed of more mature roles, commitments, and responsibilities to be adopted by the initiate and demanded by her community. In the absence of experience and role mastery, the anticipation of performing these new roles and responsibilities can produce anxiety in the initiate. Members of her new support group can bring her comfort through their contributions as role models and mentors. Identity reinforcement, the last step of the RPP, consists of social reinforcements, such as support, encouragement, and assistance, from the new support group. The initiate's own intrinsic reinforcers can facilitate inclusion of the new identity into her self-concept. The following descriptions of ritual events serve to illustrate these and related points.

The evening of the second day of the Sunrise Dance is a public event that draws large crowds. A bonfire is prepared in the ceremonial grounds, and the medicine man and his singers assemble for an evening of 32 special songs and dancing by the Mountain Spirit dancers. The impressive events of this second evening are about 3 hours in length and have never ceased to amaze me. (In the past, girls danced all night, and this is still the practice at the Mescalero girls' puberty ceremony.) The ceremonial grounds are prepared by the medicine man and his associates late in the afternoon of the second day according to the placement of four poles made from two cottonwood trees and two willow trees that come together to form a large wickiup (see Mails, 1988, for details on the construction of the wickiup). The four poles are stripped except for foliage at the top, and each pole has a different color painted on it associated with one of the four cardinal directions. A rope is strung between two of the poles, and eagle feathers are attached to the rope. G. Goodwin (1939) stated that the wickiup of the girls' puberty ceremony is a replication of that of Changing Woman and described it in the following manner: "On each of the four poles was a long zigzag line, the same as they make in the girl's puberty ceremony now. On the east pole black lightning struck down in zigzag line, on the south pole blue lightening struck down in zigzag line, on the west pole yellow lightening struck down in zigzag line, and on the north pole white lightning struck down in zigzag line" (p. 17).

In addition to the large wickiup, four spruce trees are placed around the perimeter of the ceremonial grounds that more or less define the boundary of the dancing and other ceremonial activities for the evening and the next morning. Vehicles cannot intrude within this perimeter (Mails, 1988). For the events of the second evening, which consist of singing and dancing, three young women who have previously experienced their own Sunrise Dances join the initiate and her partner. Impressively arrayed in their buckskin costumes, the five young women dance together throughout the evening. I observed the festivities of this evening on several occasions and always perceived the high level of anticipation, excitement, and energy of the crowd. The spectators park their vehicles in a circle around the ceremonial grounds with the large bonfire in the center of the gathering. Some visitors sit on chairs they have brought with them, while others sit on the tailgates of pickup trucks. Most stand and observe, while others join the dancing. Car horns are blasted at various times, such as when the Mountain Spirit dancers initially appear or when the girls dance with the Mountain Spirit dancers. The initiate and her four peers dance in unison with the Mountain Spirit dancers; the on-lookers, consisting of the initiate's family members and numerous other guests, dance at other times. As a participant observer, I was always asked to link arms with others and join in the social and celebratory dancing of this second evening. While the evening segments of the Sunrise Dance appear to be primarily social on the surface, the pervasive spiritual underpinnings are significant.

Hoijer (1938) stated: "An Apache social occasion is not complete without its dance, and the most spectacular and vigorous dances of the Apache are those performed by their masked dancers" (p. 148). With a large bonfire within the ceremonial grounds along with singing by the medicine man and his helpers, the second evening's events commence with the five long-haired girls, impressively clad in their decorated buck-skin costumes, standing side by side and dancing. The Mountain Spirit or *gan* dancers (Basso, 1966) are heard, their jingles first from a distance, and then they are viewed entering the dance grounds with loud noises.[23] The general function of these dancers is protector of the Apache people and, for a particular Sunrise Dance, to chase away evil spirits and bring the presence of good spirits to the gathering.[24] These dancers are impor-tant personages in both Western and Mescalero girls' puberty rites. While Hoijer (1938) and Opler (1941) attributed an entertainment function to their involvement in the puberty ceremony, the spiritual component is significant. Nonetheless, my observation is that some in the large crowds attracted to the second evening's events are seeking entertainment and amusement. The Mountain Spirit dancers are believed to be people who lived on Earth in an earlier era but who left in search of eternal life and now reside in specific mountains, in certain places below the ground, living and traveling in clouds and water (G. Goodwin, 1938), and the physical representation of the Mountain Spirits signifies their spiritual presence at the Sunrise Dance (Lamphere, 1983). At Apache ceremonials other than the Sunrise Dance, the dancers serve more somber purposes, such as to "ward off epidemic and evil or to cure illness" (Opler, 1941, p. 87). The Mountain Spirit dancers are composed of five dancers, one of whom is the clown (*libaiyé*), who, as explained by Nichols (2002), is a "servant and messenger for the four main dancers, also painted white, the symbol of purity, with black markings" (p. B4). The bodies of the Mountain Spirit dancers are painted with black lightning-like symbols on top of the white paint that covers all exposed areas. They wear buckskin cloths painted yellow that hang from their waists to about their knees. Tin jingles are attached to the kilts, and bells around their waists and knees can be heard from a distance and are reminiscent of rain, which is so valuable to the Apaches. Each dancer other than the clown carries a wooden wand painted with a zigzag pattern representative of lightning, another reminder of rain. The clown wears a white hood over his head with a cross-shaped crown (representative of the four directions) affixed to the top of his head. The other four dancers wear black hoods with large crowns attached. The crowns are previously fashioned by the dancers and their leader at a sweat bath ceremony. Paintings on the crowns are representative of visions received by the dancer's leader or medicine man during the sweat bath (Nichols, 2002)—a finding confirmed in my interviews.[25] The crowns are impressive and rich in symbolism (see Mails, 1974/1993). The girl's family will be given the crowns upon conclusion of the Sunrise Dance on the fourth day; they are to be put in a secret place in the mountains because, according to oral tradition, that is where the Mountain Spirits live. An additional explanation is provided by Nichols (2002) that the crowns absorb all illnesses and bad spirits, and therefore can only be used one time.

At the onset of the second evening, the clown initially enters the ceremonial grounds and blesses the four cardinal directions. Indeed, the clown is regarded as the leader of the dancers and is always the first one to enter the ceremonial grounds from the east (Ganteaume, 1992). One informant stated that the clown is present on behalf of the girl and is actually dancing for her. The clown appears to be the figure that actually establishes the tone or mood for most of the evening's events and ensures proper behavior of the crowd. For instance, at one dance the clown targeted a rather boisterous and noisy woman and chased her from the scene. This particular woman was clearly subdued when she regained her courage to reappear at the event. In impressive displays, the clown dramatically whirls his bullroarer or rhombus (a piece of wood attached to a string), which sounds like the wind. Bourke (1892) explained that the purpose of the bullroarer is to compel the wind and the rain to come to the aid of the crops. The wind is believed to manifest the power of the Mountain Spirit dancers (Ganteaume, 1992); relative to the girls' puberty ceremony, the action and noise are believed to drive the evil spirits away. In contrast to the orchestrated and deliberate movements of the four dancers, the clown is unpredictable and spontaneous, reminding people of the uncertainty of life. He sometimes engages in humorous acts that perhaps remind people to not always take life or themselves so seriously. In contrast, the four dancers represent the four cardinal directions and, according to Apache beliefs, hold the world steady and in balance (Nichols, 2002). The importance of the Mountain Spirit dancers and the clown is exhibited in a ritual on the third morning in which they are individually blessed with cattail pollen and prayed for by those in attendance who choose to take part in this ritual.

The following observations of the dancing of the second evening are compiled from my attendance at several of these events. The medicine man and his helpers sing and drum while the Mountain Spirit dancers dance in time with the music. Initially, the clown and dancers form more or less a line with the clown leading, and the troupe dances with high energy around the ceremonial grounds. Then, the five young women join the Mountain Spirit dancers in what appears to be a choreographed sequence of dances. The initiate dances with the clown, the only one of the dancers who is allowed to be near her. Each young woman is intent on following the movements of her assigned dancer according to what must have been prior assignment of each young woman to a Mountain Spirit dancer. At times the troupe may dance in a vertical line and move in unison to the left and to the right. Such actions always delight the crowd and yield hoots and hollers and horns of vehicles blaring. I asked an informant if the initiate and her four peers rehearse the dancing segment with the Mountain Spirit dancers and was told they do not. That disclosure was amazing to me, because they appear as a unified troupe. Through these apparent movements the young women themselves appear to be transformed as they surrender themselves to the dance and abandon all self-consciousness. Relative to the RPP, the numinosity of the transition phase was apparent as the Mountain Spirit dancers guided the initiate and her four peers.

Later in the Saturday-evening segment, the medicine man and sing-ers move under the wickiup that was prepared in the afternoon. Ac-cording to the style of some medicine men, boys who are still virgins dance with the girls. This is not a uniform ritual, and I was told that it was the Whiteriver style and would not be used by medicine men from other locations. Individuals, linked by their arms in groups of three, four, or five, also danced during this phase, swaying back and forth and clockwise in synchrony with the music. The evening of the second day concludes with the initiate and her partner being instructed to run back to the camp.

The third morning's activities usually begin a bit later than the second morning's. The medicine man and his helpers commence the singing and drumming, with the initiate and her partner dancing in front of them under the large wickiup, which is said to be the home of White Painted Woman. In a sequence of events, a man comes to the partner and she joins him on a dance around the grounds. Shortly thereafter, the male co-sponsor or godfather steps in and dances next to the initiate. His primary responsibility in this rite of passage will soon commence.

The Mountain Spirit dancers appear and dance for a time. The medi-cine man then mixes a solution that will be used to paint the initiate. This solution is composed of colors of the four directions—blue and black stones previously ground by the initiate, white clay, and yellow cat-tail pollen. A brush has been fashioned for this ritual that, as described by Mails (1988), is an eagle tail feather tied to a dry, stiff shaft of field grass. Then, in a demonstration of transcendence, the Mountain Spirit dancers take the brush and begin painting the initiate. After she is almost fully covered with the white paint, the male co-sponsor or godfather paints her. The initiate, her godfather, and the Mountain Spirit dancers work their way around the circle of observers (clockwise) and use the brush to spray the crowd with the white paint. One is not to wash off this paint, or one runs the risk of graying prematurely. The painting of the initiate is a ritual of long historical endurance and is described in a similar manner in P. E. Goddard's (1919a) account of the White Moun-tain Apaches' adolescent ceremony.

The painting of the initiate is a peak moment in the Sunrise Dance, and the visual imagery of the initiate's transformation into White Painted

Woman is quite impressive. The symbolism is multifaceted, as explained by one informant: "She is the White Painted Woman and she is blessed on that day and painted by the Mountain Spirit dancers and her godfather. And with that, it's just to bless her overall, for more strength and more wisdom and she can withstand anything that might be in her way."

At my first Sunrise Dance, after the initiate was literally covered from head to toe with the white clay solution, I happened to glance away for a moment. When I looked at her again, I gasped out loud and said, "She is an old woman." With her gray hair, stooped posture (perhaps from the weight of the paint), and cane, she looked like an elderly woman. Her transformation into White Painted Woman—a transformation that had begun two days earlier when her godmother dressed her in regalia that facilitated absorption of traits of White Painted Woman—was complete. The symbolic hope of old age for this young woman was apparent; that is, by becoming White Painted Woman she would live long enough to have gray hair.

The visual transformation of the initiate through the painting is a climactic and significant point in the Sunrise Dance. One mother remarked on the maturity of her daughter after the Sunrise Dance and linked the change from the time she was painted, stating: "It's just like, after they painted her, it seemed like she just changed . . . she was different." Clearly, the initiate has moved to ecstasy relative to the RPP, an emotion noted in an initiate described by Mails (1988). A medicine man in Mails's research explained that the painting was like a baptism: "she is accepting the new life that she has been given during the ceremony, a new life in which she has all of the powers of Changing Woman that can be given to a human being" (p. 169). Indeed, as described in the preface, at one Sunrise Dance I was standing next to the grandmother of the initiate, and as we observed the girl being painted, the grandmother was overcome with emotion and began crying and exclaimed, "She is new again—born again!"

After the painting, the young woman, the medicine man and his singers, and, indeed, most of those in attendance, dance through the wickiup four times for each of the four directions. Upon entering the wickiup, one is to touch one of the four posts, remove one's hat, and pray each time it is entered, as a participant commented to me: "The wickiup is like a church and we are to pray when we enter it." Goseyun (1991) explained that this structure is symbolic of an altar and that prayers are said under it. Another interpretation of the symbolism of praying in the wickiup was that the initiate would always have a home (Quintero, 1980).

The third morning ends with further dancing by the Mountain Spirit dancers, around whom the crowd, including the initiate, form more or less a circle. The Mountain Spirit dancers engage in a ritual called "worshiping the fire," which consists of their moving single file in a clockwise direction around the fire in the ceremonial grounds. They approach the fire in a shuffling manner beginning in the direction of the east and then back up from the fire. They then approach the fire from the south, the west, and finally the north. The purpose of this ritual is to purify the setting and drive away any disease or evil (Hoijer, 1938). After this ritual, mature and respected persons may make speeches to the crowd. The content of these speeches, among other things, encourages listeners to respect their culture and adhere to the traditional ways. Frequently these speeches are given in the Apache language or in a combination of Apache and English. Bilingual Apaches have translated the essence of these speeches for me when they occurred. After that point, the wickiup or large tepee with four poles is disassembled and taken quickly away.

> *You have started out on the good earth;*
> *You have started out with good moccasins;*
> *With moccasin strings of the rainbow, you have started out;*
> *With moccasin strings of the sun's rays, you have started out;*
> *In the midst of plenty you have started out. (Opler, 1941, p. 130)*

After the events of the third morning, I always observed visible relief on the faces of the initiates. They had completed the two most difficult days of the Sunrise Dance. This point in the ceremony corresponds to ecstasy in the RPP model—the liminal status of the initiate has diminished, and she has successfully completed some very challenging rituals. At this point, much of the crowd disperses and family and friends gather at the camp for a meal. A gift exchange occurs between the sponsors and co-sponsors in the afternoon. The gift exchange alone is a very costly event and requires families to prepare months in advance. Extended family members assist by providing monetary assistance or purchasing and donating gifts.

At the gift exchanges, I have observed half a dozen or more pickup trucks loaded with household utensils, dishware, scores of 25-pound sacks of potatoes and flour, cases of soda, quilts and blankets, and various other assorted household and food items. Dozens of family members and guests in attendance carry some items in a procession that is led by the initiate and singers and drummers to the co-sponsors' camp. In the approach to the camp, one can hear the co-sponsor's singers and drummers. Ultimately, the two sets of musicians join together. The items are unloaded and the two families join one another in dancing as four songs are sung. This action is reciprocated on the part of the co-sponsors. Strong feelings of unity and connectedness emerge from these rituals that serve to bind the two previously unrelated families together.

Early on the fourth morning, the initiate is undressed in reverse manner from which she was dressed on the first day. The godmother is instructed by the medicine man to walk around the initiate in a clockwise direction as each item is carefully removed from the girl. In the order they are taken off, the items are laid on a cloth placed on the ground. After final blessings and prayers, the ceremony is considered basically over. One initiate reported a feeling of being let down at this point, stating: "and Monday, when they took it [her cane] away, it was really sad because it just felt normal again. It didn't feel like nothing was protecting me."

Although the ceremony concludes and the initiate may return to her home at this point, she is considered in a sacred state for 4 more days, since the power of White Painted Woman is believed to reside within her (Basso, 1966). She is no longer White Painted Woman, but she certainly was changed from that encounter and will never be the same. The transition back to her usual life is illustrative of step 12, new identity, of the reincorporation phase of the RPP. A consistent theme of Apache puberty ceremonies of the past is that the girl is to rest and reflect for 4 days after the ceremony. Indeed, a similar transition is found in the Navajo Kinaaldá whereby girls are encouraged to think about what they have just experienced and what it means for their lives for 4 days after the ceremony concludes (Markstrom & Iborra, 2003). However, these standards appear to be relaxed in contemporary times among the Apaches. Nonetheless, an Apache adult informant stated that if the ceremony is going to help the girl in the long run, she must continue with the activities she engaged in during her dance, such as praying and working hard.

In the weeks and months after the Sunrise Dance, the initiate is affirmed by her new support group, which is composed of her biological family as well as her co-sponsors and their family. Also, other members of her community will look upon her differently as one who has attained a new level of maturity. The gaining of a second family is of high significance, and virtually all of the initiates discussed how they had been incorporated into the lives of their godparents. The relationship between the sponsors and the co-sponsor's family is further solidified 1 or 2 years after the Sunrise Dance when another gift exchange occurs. The giveaway begins at the home of the initiate's parents, who hire a medicine man and singers to officiate the event. Family members and friends dance around the singers, and the girl dances between her godparents. One mother of an initiate had this to say about the gift exchange they held: "This final gift exchange would be our final 'thank you' and appreciation that everything was completed . . . that we've become family."

The Mescalero Girls' Puberty Ceremony

Mescalero Apaches' oral traditions relative to the adolescent girls' puberty ceremony and the contemporary practice of this ceremony have many commonalities with the San Carlos version. For example, in asking a Mescalero medicine person about the purposes of the ceremony, she related this story from oral tradition:

> You have to go back to the creation of time, the creation of the Earth, and how man was created. And how from the waters came the woman, from a shell. They landed on a beach. The shell landed and it opened and there came the woman, she came out. She was a supernatural person. She could not move her arms or legs or anything. So, the first people on the beach they took her. They

took her into their camp and rubbed her arms and her legs every day, and one day she got up and she walked and then started running. That is the main purpose for the girl's running to the east. It was to the east that she ran and the whole tribe, the group of people, just followed along. They were yelling with her and yelling for her. You know, just pushing her on. She was a supernatural person that kind of reigned at that time period. Then she had two boys—twins—one was named Child of Water and the other one's name was Killer of Enemies. So, from that period on the ceremony started and it has continued up to now.

Clearly, this account of oral tradition is consistent with that discussed previously in this chapter. However, in the contemporary practice of girls' puberty rites at Mescalero, sufficient numbers of differences from the San Carlos version are apparent to warrant a separate description of the ceremony.

As with the population of the San Carlos Apaches, the number of Mescalero Apaches has steadily risen over the years; according to Farrer (1980), the unequivocal reasons given are "the feast" and "tribal leadership." "The feast" refers to the girls' puberty ceremony. As described by Farrer (1980), it is "a re-enactment of events from the beginning of cosmological time and a recitation of ethnohistory," and it serves as "a ritual drama, a reenactment of creation" (pp. 126, 127). Certainly, these descriptors are consistent with those of the San Carlos Apache Sunrise Dance relative to the fundamental origins of this ceremony and reinforcement of Apache oral tradition as enacted in the puberty rituals.

The public, festive event at the Fourth of July celebration is more broadly known to outsiders. It is not common knowledge that Mescalero Apaches also hold ceremonies for girls individually during all seasons except for winter. What follows is a description of my observations at the annual Fourth of July festivities, of which the girls' puberty ceremony is the most notable component. Six girls-more commonly called maidens—were participants. Along with sources from the literature, my observations are supported by data from a formal interview with a Mescalero medicine woman and informal conversations with attendees at the dance.

At the time I observed the Mescalero girls' puberty ceremony, I had already attended several Sunrise Dances at San Carlos and had developed a sense of how the dance is conducted. I found it surprising, therefore, to observe a somewhat different event at Mescalero; for instance, there was the inclusion of cultural traits of Plains tribes not found in the dances of the Western Apaches. The tepee at Mescalero replaces the wickiup that is the central structure in San Carlos. Consistent with this and other observations, I discovered that Opler (1942) observed the use of a tepee in the Chiricahua girls' puberty ceremony; of course, the Chiricahuas and Mescaleros inhabit the same reservation and have integrated their puberty ceremonies. P. E. Goddard (1909) also observed parallels between Plains Indian cultures and the Mescalero puberty ceremony, noting a commonality with the Sun Dance of the Plains tribes relative to the erection of the lodge and the songs directed toward the sun.

There is a certain type of hierarchical structure according to each family's responsibility in the Fourth of July puberty ceremony. Girls and their families live in interconnected structures for the 12 days during which the ceremonial events occur, including the 4-day public event. As my informants related, a family makes an application to the tribe for the privilege of holding their daughter's dance in conjunction with the Fourth of July events. It is financially advantageous for families to do so, because the tribe underwrites some of the costs. A major consideration for inclusion is the girl's degree of Indian blood. It is highly desirable to have a full-blood Mescalero, Chiricahua, or Lipan girl to be in the first tepee, with mixed-blood girls more likely to be assigned to subsequent tepees. The actual order of initiates according to tepees is established at tribal meetings. The family that is assigned the first tepee or camp wields the most decision-making power, and also must be prepared to shoulder the greatest responsibility for the event. The members of the first tepee also must put forth the greatest effort and resources to ensure the success of the ceremony as a whole. After the first tepee, the power and responsibility of each tepee correspondingly diminishes.

Two individuals are of great importance to each maiden during her puberty rites: her godmother or attendant, and her medicine man (Hoijer, 1938). Together the medicine man and sponsor (as the godmother is called in Mescalero Apache tradition) share the critical responsibility of guiding the initiate through the experience.[26] One informant stated that they become something like parents to the girl, yielding a relationship that endures through life. The medicine man of the first tepee is the one who is most influential and makes decisions that affect all other tepees and their medicine men, such as those regarding any changes in the schedule of events or in determining whether certain rituals will be included or changed in some way. At the dance I attended, the maidens of the first and second tepees, who were related, experienced the loss of a family member, and the medicine man determined that their involvement in certain rituals should be curtailed as a result.

If one is facing the six camps or tepees located on the south side of the ceremonial grounds, the first camp is on the far right, followed by the second camp, all the way to the last camp, which, in this particular year, was the sixth camp. The maidens and their families reside in these camps, which are constructed as interconnected brush arbors with tepees attached. At the front of the arbors are more public, covered areas, each containing a small fire that burns nonstop for the duration of the 4-day ceremony. A groundskeeper is engaged to ensure that the fire burns at all times. After entering the public, open areas one can walk into the cooking and eating areas of a particular family, and a tepee is adjacent to the back of the family's quarters. Opposite the family compounds, to the north side of the ceremonial grounds, bleachers are situated for guests to observe the festivities. Surrounding the ceremonial grounds, hundreds of guests and visitors stay in tepees and tents for the duration of the Fourth of July festivities, which include rodeo events.

The Mescalero girls' puberty ceremony can be divided into four major components or categories of events. Two of these components constitute ceremonies in their own right and were described by Nicholas (1939). The first is a focal point of the larger ceremony, specifically, the putting up of the big tepee on the first day and then taking it down on the last day (the fifth morning). The big tepee is the site where the maidens will dance for four subsequent evenings. It is likened to the home of White Painted Woman and, hence, is the home of the maidens during their ceremony (Nicholas, 1939). Ritual and song accompany the construction and disassembly of the tepee, which is described in some detail by Farrer (1980), Nicholas (1939), and Opler (1941). The big tepee is a major focal point throughout the ceremony, and numerous rituals occur within and around it. The construction of the big tepee along with the previous construction of the arbors where the maidens stay along with their families is parallel to San Carlos rites relative to separation in the RPP. Opler (1941) related the following song about the big tepee in the Chiricahua tradition, but parallels to Western Apache tradition are apparent (e.g., the four significant colors and the name of the culture hero):

> *Killer of Enemies and White Painted Woman have made them so,*
> *They have made the poles of the dwelling so,*
> *For long life stands the blue stallion.*
> *Here Killer of Enemies and White Painted Woman have made them so,*
> *They have made the poles of the dwelling so,*
> *For long life stands the yellow stallion.*
> *Here Killer of Enemies and White Painted Woman have made them so,*
> *They have made the poles of the dwelling so,*
> *For long life stands the black stallion.*
> *Here Killer of Enemies and White Painted Woman have made them so,*
> *They have made the poles of the dwelling so,*
> *For long life stands the white stallion. (p. 95)*

The second major ceremonial event identified by Nicholas (1939) is called the Sun Greeting ceremony, which encompasses a number of rites. This event also occurs in the early morning of the first day and then again on the final morning. After construction of the big tepee, several rituals occur to heighten the liminal status of the maidens and to advance their transformations into White Painted Woman. Separation continues as the girls are dressed by what Mescalero Apaches call the sponsor or godmother (Naaikish). One informant explained to me that at Mescalero, because so many people are related to one another, it is permissible to have relatives serve as sponsors to adolescent girls. The dressing is a ritual that is under the control and observation of women, and men are absent from these early-morning events. Girls wash their hair with suds of the yucca plant prior to the dressing (Opler, 1941), and then their godmothers will take charge to guide the remaining rites. Maidens are dressed beginning on the left side of the body, the side of the heart. A scratching stick and drinking tube, pollen bag, and sometimes a medicine bundle will be placed on each initiate (Farrer, 1980). Then, sponsors ceremonially feed the maidens with traditional foods, such as fruits and pinon, to ensure that they will have good appetites in life (Hoijer, 1938). After the initiates are fed, the sponsors give their charges detailed instructions on the proper behavior that is expected of them during the puberty rites (Opler, 1941). It is evident that new environmental demands are being placed on the initiates at this stage as they advance into a liminal state that will endure through subsequent days.

After the maidens are dressed, each is led to the big tepee holding onto an eagle feather that is held by her medicine man (Opler, 1983b). Painting of the initiates follows; according to Nicholas (1939), this is indicative of the initiates' connection to White Painted Woman, who subsequently offers blessings to the maidens. In addition to heightening their separated status, the dressing and painting are indicative of the transcendence that initiates experience relative to their transformation into White Painted Woman. This transformation is broadly acknowledged to the degree that the maiden is not referred to by her own name but that of White Painted Woman (Hoijer, 1938). As is the case in San Carlos, the transformation of initiates into the holy person is believed to imbue them with power; hence, they may be approached for prayer.[27] In my observation of a pollen ritual at this time, maidens were sprinkled with pollen and offered prayers by those in attendance who chose to do so. An informant remarked to me that it was primarily family members of the maiden who approach her with this request. Similar to the tradition of Western Apaches, the maidens are massaged by their sponsors on unblemished buckskins that lie to the east of the tepee. Nicholas (1939) identified the purpose of this ritual as giving the maidens "graceful proportions." A ritual also occurs wherein the feet of the maidens, clad in moccasins, are traced with pollen and then the maidens are led through the footprints as songs are sung on their behalf (Nicholas, 1939; also see Hoijer, 1938).

As with the San Carlos Sunrise Dance, the maidens perform four runs to the east around a basket filled with ritual items (in the San Carlos version they run around the cane). The purpose is also the same as in San Carlos relative to its indication of successful progression through the four phases of life (Farrer, 1980). I observed all six of the maidens running in an established order that was consistent with the implicit hierarchy of their living quarters. Following the runs, each girl had a basket of candy and other small items poured over her head and, as in San Carlos, children ran to collect the contents. Families of the maidens drove pickup trucks into the gathering and tossed candy, apples, and other gifts to the crowd. One actually had to be quite attentive during this ritual so as to avoid being hit in the head with a flying apple or orange.

Following the morning rituals of dressing, blessing, running, and gift giving, the families of the girls prepared to feed the hundreds of onlookers in attendance. At midmorning guests were served stews, fry bread, and various traditional foods, including a pudding made from the mescal plant. Indeed, according to tradition, families of initiates must always be prepared to feed anyone or give cigarettes to anyone who requests these items. One informant explained that if generosity would not be exhibited in this and in other ways, the consequence would be that the girl would never have enough goods to share with others.

After the events of the first morning, the maidens may have some time to themselves until the evening. They also may be engaged in various tasks to acquire new skills, such as collecting yucca to be used as soap. It is under the discretion of the leaders of the dance to determine what tasks will be required of the maidens. For instance, one day I observed the maidens being instructed on how to start a fire in the traditional manner. Using a stick, and rolling it very quickly on a piece of board, the maidens were to work cooperatively by passing the responsibility from one to the next. They were not having great success with their efforts, and the men who were overseeing the activity intervened and provided assistance.

In addition to the two major ceremonies identified by Nicholas (1939) and previously discussed—the construction of the big tepee and the ceremony of greeting the Sun—two other major ceremonial activities are the nightly dancing of the girls in the big tepee and the dancing of the masked dancers (Hoijer, 1938) or Gahe (Opler, 1942) and other participants in the ceremonial grounds east of the big tepee. These two activities are major rituals and are described separately. The masked dancers (comparable to Mountain Spirit dancers of Western Apaches) perform around a large bonfire in the center of the ceremonial grounds. Relative to the teams of dancers, each maiden may have her own team that is hired by her family. However, I was told that it is permissible for related families to share teams. Each team consisted of six dancers, two of whom played the roles of clowns and appeared to be barely 10 years of age in several cases. The clown, also known as the "Gray One," entertains the crowd with his parodies of the movements of the other dancers (Nicholas, 1939). Hoijer (1938) identified the Gray One as the most powerful member of the troupe. Each team of dancers had different patterns painted on their bodies, which signified particular spiritual qualities of the team and set them apart from other teams. Indeed, Hoijer (1938) noted that one can tell by the symbols painted on dancers to whom the dancers "belong" according to the one who dressed and designed their costumes. The teams typically danced separately, but when all appeared on the dance ground at the same time an impressive and powerful sight was presented.

I found the music and dances quite distinct from San Carlos versions, because at Mescalero the music sounded like a blend of Apache and Plains musical traditions. The back-and-forth, arms-linked style dancing of the Western Apaches did not occur; rather, women danced in the style of Plains Indians with shawls around their shoulders and very slowly in a line around the perimeter of the ceremonial grounds. Neither was the camp dress of the Western Apaches (a calico full skirt with an untucked top) readily apparent among the women at Mescalero. The social dancing can continue well into the night, long after the non-Indian guests are required to adhere to their midnight curfew and leave the ceremonial grounds.

An additional major ritual activity of the evening components of the Mescalero girls' puberty ceremony is the dancing of the maidens in the big tepee for four evenings. This occurs at the same time that the masked dancers perform in the center of the ceremonial grounds. The dancing in the big tepee begins with the medicine man extending an eagle feather toward the initiate, which she grasps and then is led into the big tepee. The medicine man sings:

They move her by means of the finest eagle feather,
By means of it White Painted Woman walks into her home.
(Opler, 1941, p. 115)

Within the big tepee, which outsiders can peer into during the evening events, each maiden stands next to her attendant or sponsor. The medicine men sing on the east side of the tepee, opposite the maidens. The songs recount Apache creation stories and tell about the Earth, creation, and all of life. Between songs, a wooden poker is placed into the fire—the poker is used for the medicine man's support while he sings. Opler (1941) described this poker as the "age stick," symbolic of long life, and noted that it is the cane the maiden will use when she is older. Upon taking the sticks out of the fire, a new song begins and the girls immediately stand up and dance. Each maiden stands on her own piece of buckskin and dances in a motion of sliding back and forth with her arms, bent at the elbow, and held up in the air at shoulder height. After each dance, the girls sit down. The process repeats itself over and over again for the number of specified songs for the particular evening. During the fourth and final night, the maidens dance the entire night. Opler (1941) provides illustrations of the songs sung during this ritual, including the following:

> *I come to White Painted Woman,*
> *By means of long life I come to her.*
> *I come to her by means of her blessing,*
> *I come to her by means of her good fortune,*
> *I come to her by means of all her different fruits;*
> *By means of the long life she bestows, I come to her;*
> *By means of this holy truth she goes about. (p. 119)*

During their entire time in the big tepee, girls stare intently into the fire, having been instructed by their medicine men to look for something in the fire to acquire their spirit helper. So, this could be said to be their vision quest, because it is desired that maidens will acquire a spirit helper for their entire life. I was told that girls do report finding their spirit helper (such as a turtle or eagle), who will always appear to them in life before something significant is going to happen to them. In short, the evenings in the tepee are spiritual events, and all of those involved are to be engaged in prayer. An informant explained how the weight of the world is on the shoulders of the girls during these nights of dancing in the tepee, and that it is the heaviest the last night, "but she overcomes that and that's the way White Painted Woman did even when she was on Earth. She overcame things."

During consecutive mornings of the dance, up through the fifth morning when the ceremony closes, girls are blessed. The fifth morning is still considered part of the fourth day. The second, third, and fourth mornings are relatively low-key, but public attendance is once again large on the fifth, final morning. Various rituals are performed, including painting of the maiden by the medicine man (see Hoijer, 1938; Opler, 1941). On the fifth morning the maidens again run four times, as they did on the first morning, and each girl runs as far as she is able at the final run. The length of the run is indicative of her longevity and quality of life. Subsequent to the run, a naming ritual occurs in which corn pollen is placed into the girl's mouth and then her name is repeated four times. The name is sacred, and it was explained to me that the animals, the plants, the trees, and the Creator would know her by that name. In inquiring how broadly the name will be shared with others, I was told that the girl's family will know the name as well as others to whom she chooses to disclose this information. The medicine man determines what name will be bestowed, and the name is indicative of a significant event that occurred over the course of her ceremony. For instance, if it happened to be raining lightly during a girl's ceremony, she might be given the name "Misty."

After the naming, the girl is undressed in the opposite way that she was dressed on the first day. Her sponsor undresses her and then bathes or washes her. The maidens are considered to be in a sacred state during and shortly after their puberty rites, in particular, for 4 days as they gradually transition back to their everyday world. In the past, girls were expected to remain near the tepee for 4 days and nights after the main ceremony, to wear their ceremonial garb, to continue to observe taboos against washing themselves, and to use the scratching stick and drinking tube (Hoijer, 1938; Nicholas, 1939).

Summary

The purpose of this chapter was to provide descriptions of Apache girls' puberty rites according to historical and anthropological accounts and field research that included interviews and observations among the San Carlos Apaches and the Mescalero Apaches. The centrality of these rites to Apache culture was associated with their practice in the past and their enduring to the present (Mails, 1974/1993). Clearly, the puberty ceremony of Apaches is of strong spiritual significance, as summarized by Lamphere (1983): "The use of color, directional, and number symbolism, alluding to the cosmos, structures ritual actions and reinforces the connection between the ceremonial setting and the supernatural world" (p. 749). The proper conduct of puberty ceremonies—including the songs, paraphernalia, and rituals—creates a spiritual transformation and contributes to the ceremony's success (Lamphere, 1983). In addition to its spiritual significance, the Apache girls' puberty ceremony is a social occasion that requires the active participation and goodwill of the initiate's parents, her extended kin network, her co-sponsors or godparents and their extended kin network, the medicine man and his helpers, and the broader community.

Western Apaches believe that they and their culture will only continue with the ongoing practice of the Sunrise Dance. In other words, the future of the Apaches rests in the hands of a girl who is about 12 years old. True, many girls of various ages undergo the Sunrise Dance, but it is the occasion of any one of these dances on which the future rests. From a certain perspective, I would have to concur with Apaches that their future rests on the continual practice of the Sunrise Dance. This ceremony embodies all that is important to Apache people and contains the fundamental components of the culture, and the oral traditions, including the creation story, are expressed in the songs that are sung. As well, the songs and rituals encompass Apaches' beliefs and hopes for all good things in the future. The Sunrise Dance of the Western Apaches and similar rituals of Mescalero Apaches serve multiple purposes for the initiate, her family, the guests, the tribe, and, in Apache beliefs, the entire world. These purposes as well as other themes of the Sunrise Dance are elucidated in the next chapter.

Interpretation of the Apache Sunrise Dance

□   □   □

In the previous chapter, descriptions of Apache cultural beliefs and rituals and their associated meanings were presented for the San Carlos and Mescalero Apache versions of the Sunrise Dance. A multiple-method approach was utilized, and sources of data encompassed participant observation and corresponding field notes; semistructured, audiotaped interviews; numerous informal conversations with San Carlos and Mescalero cultural experts and participants; review of existing historical and anthropological sources of literature; examination of physical artifacts; photographs; and existing videotapes. At the onset, the findings were organized according to chronology of events for the Sunrise Dance and the steps of the Ritual Process Paradigm. It was noted in the previous chapter that triangulation and member checking were two tools utilized to heighten the validity of the descriptive findings. Relative to triangulation, my field observations of the Sunrise Dance were subjected to scrutiny according to published literature on the topic, and vice versa. Additionally, the hundreds of photographs I had taken at various Sunrise Dances were of immeasurable use in clarifying data that had been captured on film, such as artifacts of material culture, arrangements and actions of key individuals in the ceremonies, other participants, and onlookers, and the sequence of events over the course of the 4 days. For example, it was necessary to study photographs of the Mountain Spirit dancers to ensure that their costumes and adornments were accurately described. Most importantly, an ongoing process of member checking occurred as I queried trusted Apache informants on the performance and meaning of rituals.

Ethnographic and case-study forms of qualitative research were useful in the initial phases of data collection as well as the organization of content in the previous chapter, and continue to provide direction in the interpretation of the descriptive content. While it was stated in the previous chapter that an emic or insider's perspective was taken in this study, the etic perspective is also applicable to the researcher's attempts to interpret meanings and identify themes. To this end, the multiple sources of data were subjected to a more general form of content analysis as defined by Patton (2002): "any qualitative data reduction and sense-making effort that takes a volume of qualitative material and attempts to identify core consistencies and meanings" (p. 453). This analytic strategy is complex because it extends data from description and compels it to deeper probes to ascertain overarching themes that bring further enlightenment to the topic.

Rather than following a theory-driven research process as associated with deductive analysis, this study was consistent with most qualitative research in that it was data-driven. A primary goal of data collection and analysis was to create a context for the expressions of multiple "voices" of Apache informants according to their experiences and perceptions pertaining to the Sunrise Dance. The data sources were subjected to inductive analysis in order to determine relevant and useful categories for organization or themes (Patton, 2002). Inductive analysis encompasses the researcher's relationship with the data according to how it is understood, organized, and treated. In this study, the multiple data sources were analyzed with the aim of devising categories that seemed to best encapsulate themes of the Sunrise Dance according to their rootedness within Apache culture, past and present. The identification of meaningful themes extends data from its descriptive form in order to bring to light the most apparent and informative conclusions from the study.

The particular categories or themes derived were influenced by the initial research interests of this study, which were framed as questions in the semistructured interviews: the perceived purposes or functions of the Sunrise Dance for the initiates, the Apache people, and the world;

the activities families engaged in to prepare for their daughters' Sunrise Dances; the significance of the Sunrise Dance for contemporary Apache young women, including the perceived positive outcomes and contributions to identity formation; and initiates' understanding of the meanings and symbolism behind the rituals. Additional categories of knowledge were unanticipated, and thought-provoking insights and conclusions emerged simultaneous to data collection. That is, processes of analysis were ongoing throughout interviews, field observations, and review of the literature. For example, as the interview phase of data collection progressed, it became readily apparent that all interviewees, regardless of age or sex, identified building strength as a major purpose of the Sunrise Dance. In deeper probing of this theme, particularly in consideration of the oral tradition of White Painted Woman and the overwhelming symbolism of longevity in relation to ritual objects such as the cane, the implicit correspondence between longevity and strength became apparent. In short, statements from informants frequently cued me to what was of utmost significance in their thoughts about the Sunrise Dance, such as the financial costs or how it has changed from decades past. The following organizational categories or themes were ultimately determined and are accordingly discussed:

- Purposes of the Sunrise Dance for girls
- Purposes of the Sunrise Dance for the community
- Strengthening bonds of kin and fictive kin
- Influences from colonization, including Christianity
- The Sunrise Dance past and present
- The monetary costs of the Sunrise Dance
- Comparisons across Apache groups and with other Native cultures
- Girls' perceptions of the Sunrise Dance
- Impacts of the Sunrise Dance on the development of contemporary Apache girls

Purposes of the Sunrise Dance for Girls

According to Talamantez (2000), "Nature's seasonal renewal is studied by Apache religious specialists as the most consistent visible pattern which people can associate with the life cycle of the initiate. In other words, people's beliefs regarding the transformations that occur in nature are associated with the ritual transformations that a young girl experiences in her rite of passage from girlhood to female deity to womanhood" (p. 143). The Sunrise Dance has numerous purposes for the initiate, but the one that facilitates all others is the transformation of the initiate into White Painted Woman or Changing Woman (Basso, 1966; Mails, 1988). Along with the attainment of this status, the impacts of the proper performance of rituals extend to positive outcomes for the girl, her community, and ultimately the world. In the discipline of developmental psychology, optimal development is spoken of according to preexisting factors that may be described as necessary but not sufficient alone to produce an outcome. Menarche serves as a preexisting factor relative to the outcome of transformation into White Painted Woman and all the anticipated blessings this connection signifies for the girl's future. In other words, it is prerequisite that the initiate recently has experienced menarche, because this once-in-a-lifetime experience permits her to be a recipient of the blessings that can follow.

With menarche serving as the necessary but not sufficient condition, rituals are required to complete the desired outcomes of this rite of passage. The belief in the pubescent's malleable quality at this time of the life span compels that she be shaped and influenced in ways that will determine the course of the remainder of her life. The transformation of the initiate is an implicit aim interwoven throughout the phases of the Sunrise Dance, such as the dressing ritual that occurs on the first day of the 4-day sequence. Physically dressing the initiate according to the culturally derived image of White Painted Woman reflects the important internal changes that have set in motion the rites that will follow, which are expected to ultimately set her life course.

The initiate's connection to White Painted Woman is believed to be crucial on several accounts, most notably her longevity, which is the central and basic theme of the Sunrise Dance (Basso, 1966). In summarizing Apache ceremonialism, Lamphere (1983) explained: "identifying the patient with the sacred is to assure longevity . . . in a puberty ceremony, long life for the young girl and blessings for the entire community" (p. 749). Longevity encompasses not only the hope for a long life, but for a healthy one as well. As described in the previous chapter, the proper performance of rituals and the proper handling of sacred objects relevant to the Sunrise Dance serve to foster this goal. For example, the massage of the initiate by her godmother is believed to strengthen her for the life span and to impart desirable qualities of womanhood onto her. The ritual of running around the cane four times (phase 4) on the second day prepares the initiate to successfully pass through four stages of life (i.e., infancy, childhood/adolescence, womanhood, and old age) that will permit her to live a full life. The painting of the initiate on the morning of the third day reinforces this purpose, as stated by an informant: "That is the future. We see for her already becoming old, walking with a cane." Indeed, the cane is a continual reminder of the long life that is becoming possible for the girl. Opler (1941) explained that if a girl did not experience the puberty ceremony, it was thought that she would be unhealthy and face a short life. Mails's (1988) informant stated this same sentiment: that in Apache society it was the older women who had experienced the ceremony at puberty.

Relative to the interviews conducted in this study, nearly all of the informants stated that a major purpose of the Sunrise Dance is to build strength in girls. This assertion is clearly linked to longevity, because strong women will presumably experience long lives. Talamantez (2000) stated that the Sunrise Dance is both preventive and curative. Relative to the former, the dance serves a protection function, making girls strong for difficulties that are implicit to life. In particular, the prayers given during the Sunrise Dance and the performance of challenging rituals are key processes of building strength. Mothers of the initiates, especially, mentioned that the Sunrise Dance is imperative because life is difficult for women and they need to be strong. The initiates, as well, were unanimous in their assertions that the ceremony was needed to make them strong. Rather than assuming what it is about life that is difficult, I asked several informants to discuss this issue. A medicine person explained that it is expected that girls will face many challenges as teenagers and that they must be painted for these battles, just as the faces of warriors were painted in the past. The painting is thought to impart strength to girls so that they will not be afraid, so that they will ultimately be fighters and not losers. In today's context, being a fighter was explained as having the strength to say "no" to drugs and alcohol. Another informant explained: "you have to realize that there's so much in this world that's so evil. And I think that's why these dances are good, too."

Corresponding with the notion that the Sunrise Dance builds strength in initiates, it was observed that the challenging rituals also serve as tests. It is not without basis that the dance is physically and psychologically demanding. In a sense, a girl who successfully accomplishes the Sunrise Dance has demonstrated that she can overcome other difficult events in life as well. As one initiate asserted, "The Sunrise Dance was hard. Now life is hard, but I overcame that and I can overcome this." Others expect initiates to endure the challenges during their Sunrise Dances without complaint. Consistent with this belief, which was expressed at San Carlos, a Mescalero Apache informant stated that by enduring the demands of the puberty ceremony, the initiate acquires strength and maturity for a lifetime. The positive benefits will extend to children as well, who "will be stronger, withstand sickness, and withstand all kinds of mental problems."

A further purpose of the Sunrise Dance is to shape the physical and psychological qualities of the girl. This was articulated in the quote in the previous chapter from the godmother who described the significance of the specific actions of the massage. Shaping of initiates through massage is a theme common to other pubertal coming-of-age ceremonies, such as the Navajo Kinaaldá (Markstrom & Iborra, 2003). The massage during *nizti*, the "lying" phase, is believed to transfer desired physical and psychological qualities onto initiates. Their proper observance of restrictions and taboos, as well, is believed to have positive impacts on their physical appearance. For instance, the drinking tube and scratching stick are required to prevent physical imperfections (facial hair and permanent scarring, respectively). It was observed that girls are instructed not to smile during the Sunrise Dance or risk having wrinkles, a point made by Hoijer (1938) relative to excessive laughter by initiates. One informant in this study explained that if girls drank too much water during the Sunrise Dance, they ran the risk of growing a mustache. Apaches' observance of taboos is consistent with a theme found in many North American Indian cultures that require taboo adherence in order to affect physical and psychological qualities of pubescent girls (see chapter

5). Indeed, cross-cultural literature is indicative of the universal value of physical attractiveness, particularly among girls and women who are socialized to reflect a certain ideal (Striegel-Moore & Cachelin, 1999). Cross-cultural data indicate that rituals in girls' puberty ceremonies promote culturally specific criteria of physical beauty (Lutkehaus, 1995). Nonetheless, in puberty ceremonies of the Apaches, Navajos, and many other North American Indian cultures, beauty is regarded as more than skin deep. It is essential that the girl also be affected in her physical wellness (to be strong and healthy) and in her character (to be generous and kind). Indeed, it is believed that the character traits exhibited by initiates during the Sunrise Dance are indicative of their personality in adulthood. Hence, girls are cautioned to demonstrate restraint and not exhibit excesses of behavior, but rather to be helpful, respectful, and contain excessive behaviors.

Motivations of parents for having their daughters undergo the Sunrise Dance are the many hopes for their daughters' possession of the good things in life. As one mother explained: "Well, I hope the blessings and prayers will stay with her, but I hope it also makes her a stronger person. Life is hard, and it's kind of a journey through life, the dance . . . knowing that she can get through something difficult . . . having a four-day ceremony and life is difficult. I'm sure hoping that she can realize that she can overcome anything in life, and it'll be hard. Life is hard and she'll be able to just continue on, no matter how hard life might be." It was evident in this research that parents valued the Sunrise Dance for many reasons, such as its perpetuation of the values of Apache culture. Perhaps of equal importance, however, it was to provide their daughters the advantages that could be derived from this ceremony, as indicated in the previous quote.

Purposes of the Sunrise Dance for the Community

Cultural practices that endure over time serve functions of value to societies. Clearly, the Sunrise Dance serves multiple purposes for initiates, but it is equally important to acknowledge its impact on the Apache people and, according to Apache beliefs, the entire world, as explained by P. E. Goddard (1909) concerning Mescalero Apaches: "It would appear at first glance that the ceremony is only one of those most common and most widely distributed ceremonies for adolescent girls. Perhaps it is chiefly that, but a study of the songs indicates that it is also a dramatic representation of the creation and of the annual and diurnal re-creations which come to the world. Its celebration is expected to result not only in a fortunate life for the maiden about whom it happens to center, but in the general welfare of the community" (p. 386). The elaborate preparations and the multiple sacrifices of time, energy, and resources by family and non-family members alike attest to the value and relevance of this ceremony. Not only are material gifts shared to create a successful ceremony, but guests also are to be engaged in prayer. It would not be an exaggeration to say that the Apaches believe the benefits of the Sunrise Dance extend to the entire Earth. As stated by a Mescalero Apache informant, "that four day period, she [the initiate] is putting the whole world on her shoulders"; more specific to current world issues, this informant went on to explain, "if I go bless the girl, I'm going to ask that the Al Qaeda be overcome . . . the people that like to make trouble over in the other side of the earth."

Therefore, the common understanding is that the blessings stemming from an individual's ceremony will extend to all those in attendance and beyond. G. Goodwin (1938) likened the Apache puberty ceremony to agricultural ceremonies in that, in the latter, prayers said for one field are expected to have impacts that extend to all other farms in the region. The analogy is that the positive benefits of prayers said at a girl's Sunrise Dance will permeate the broader community. Indeed, the theme of community benefits from the Sunrise Dance is found repeatedly in the literature (e.g., P. E. Goddard, 1909; G. Goodwin, 1942).

Perhaps the most important category of benefits from the Sunrise Dance are the perceived blessings derived from the connection with White Painted Woman—blessings that are not exclusive to initiates, but become accessible to all peoples. As confirmed in the comments of a medicine person, the transformation of the initiate into White Painted Woman is thought to bring her presence to the Apache people each time one of the puberty ceremonies is conducted. However, in order to perpetuate the qualities of White Painted Woman in Apache culture, the specified rituals must be performed on pubescent girls. The coming together of the initiate and White Painted Woman is implicit in this often-cited legend: "Changing Woman never gets too old. When she gets to be a certain age, she goes walking toward the east. After a while she sees herself in the distance walking toward her. They both walk until they come together and after that there is only one, the young one. Then she is like a young girl all over again" (Basso, 1970, p. 65). Clearly, the young girl that White Painted Woman meets is the initiate, who refurbishes White Painted Woman with youth, representative of the broader scheme of renewal of life—a necessity for continuation of life on Earth. The continued re-creation of the Earth in its cycles connects to more expansive conceptions of newness, renewal, and hope within the human sphere. All that is dying, decaying, and damaged becomes reenergized and renewed through these encounters with the perpetual youth of oral tradition. Additional illumination of the mysterious connection between White Painted Woman and the initiate is expressed in this statement by Lincoln (1991): "When she takes on the role of the goddess, the initiate must abandon the historical moment in which she lives and enter the primordial, atemporal mode of existence characteristic of myth. . . . In becoming the goddess or cultural heroine, the girl shatters the temporal restrictions of her own existence and becomes a being who is beyond death, beyond aging, beyond time. Furthermore, all those who participate in her initiation accompany her into the mythic atemporality" (p. 96).

Basso (1966) suggested additional functions of the Sunrise Dance for the Apache people, specifically, that it serves as a major source for the reduction of anxiety and the enhancement of feelings of well-being. As noted by Basso: "In general, ritual may be thought of as a response to the anxieties of existence, a response which satisfies the individual's demands for a stable, coercible, and comprehensible world and which thereby enables him to maintain inner security against the threat of disaster" (p. 169). All cultures engage in rituals designed to meet a basic universal human need, namely, to feel a sense of security and safety. The investment of power in the initiate serves a protective function for the entire community by warding off potential disaster and catastrophe. People can feel reassured, sensing that forces greater than themselves are looking out for their best interests. The benevolence of White Painted Woman is brought into their day-to-day lives, and people can feel reassured that the good things of life (e.g., health, rain, abundance of food and material resources) will remain in their realm of existence in the present and the future (Basso, 1966). The initiate, while in this sacred state, may be approached for prayer by any who request it, because it is believed she has the power to share blessings and healing. The tangible gifts distributed during phase 6 ("Candy, it is poured") and the distribution of beverages, fruits, and other items to the crowd serve to disseminate the blessings of White Painted Woman via the initiate.

It should not be forgotten that one of the primary functions of the Sunrise Dance is to provide an opportunity to socialize (Hoijer, 1938). In general, the Sunrise Dance serves to foster good feelings and a sense of togetherness in the community—between relatives and non-relatives alike. Having served in the role of participant observer and as a non-Apache, I would say these feelings extend to others in attendance. Another function of the Sunrise Dance for the community is its encouragement of expressions of moral and proper behavior (Basso, 1966). Four life objectives (physical strength, a good disposition, prosperity, and old age) identified in Basso (1966, 1970) are continually reinforced through the rituals and verbal exhortations given by elders and other adults throughout the Sunrise Dance. The attendance of children at the Sunrise Dance is encouraged, and they are accordingly socialized. Basso (1970) sums up the social functions: "Taken as a whole, the girl's puberty ceremony symbolizes an era of happiness and plenty which, Apaches believe, actually existed in mythological times. 'In those days,' the people say, 'everything was good'" (p. 72).

It is apparent that the Sunrise Dance affirms values of the Apache people and all that is important to them. The dance incorporates all major components of Apache culture—the origin story, the beliefs, the music, the food, the clothing, the language, and important values such as kinship. Informants of Talamantez (2000) noted that Apache culture will survive as long as the girls' puberty ceremony is practiced, as summarized by the author: "the ceremony continues to emphasize Apache values and to instruct the people that it is also possible to continue to apply Apache concepts to the inevitability of having to live in a changing world" (p. 155).

Strengthening Bonds of Kin and Fictive Kin

Traditionally, kinship fostered survival in North American Indian societies. The maintenance of life was filled with the constant threat of danger, and individuals simply could not negotiate the complexities of survival on their own. Kin are those whom one can trust and depend on to perform roles and responsibilities that lead to survival of the group without imposing harm on others. The Sunrise Dance strengthens kinship in two major ways: first, within the sponsor's clan and extended family, and second, through the creation of fictive kin between the sponsor's and co-sponsor's families. Relative to the former, the Sunrise Dance strengthens kinship obligations; without family support it would be impossible for girls to have this experience. Indeed, Opler (1941) stated that girls who did not have the puberty rites were described as "poor in relatives." The Western Apaches do not operate according to a localized kin group structure, and clan members may live some distance from one another (Basso, 1966), and, as explained in the previous chapter, not all San Carlos Apaches know their clan membership. Hence, the Sunrise Dance serves to reunite clan and extended family members—both during the preparation phase and particularly during the dance itself, as noted by Basso (1983): "Nowhere, however, is the unity of the clan 'branch' so evident as in the long and costly preparation that precedes major ceremonials, most notably the girls puberty rite" (p. 485). An occasion is presented to socialize, and a holiday sense of excitement and anticipation is evident. At dances I attended in San Carlos, I met initiates' relatives who had traveled from Phoenix and Tucson and from as far away as California and Texas. Many of these individuals planned their vacations from work to correspond to a relative's Sunrise Dance.

The Sunrise Dance not only provides a "holiday" to bring clan and extended family members together but also strengthens family relationships due to the extensive cooperation that occurs to make this event a reality. It is an impossibility to orchestrate the dance without the labor and gifts of the clan and broad extended-family network. In short, the Sunrise Dance strengthens kinship obligations (Basso, 1966) and places high demands on close and extended kin. Through the observance of these obligations, kinship relationships are reaffirmed, and cooperative relations between kin are maintained and sometimes reestablished. Clan and extended family members donate gifts to be used in the gift exchange and provide food and other provisions to sustain the family and guests for the duration of the ceremony. Unity and interdependence is promoted through the exchange of gifts and favors within the entire complex of Sunrise Dances. That is, assistance that one receives at one's own daughter's dance is reciprocated at the dances of the daughters of one's relatives.

It is apparent that the parents of initiates rely heavily on their own parents, other elders, and their medicine men to guide them through the process of arranging and conducting a Sunrise Dance. A great deal of information sharing occurs as families work diligently to conduct this very complex event. The parents who were interviewed were clearly moved and touched by their daughters' Sunrise Dances. One father described his experience: "It has given me a better sense of who I am. It made me more proud of who I am because I had lost that." Virtually all families in this study had stories to tell of the overwhelming show of support from their relatives—in their words, without their kin, the dances simply could not be conducted. One mother explained: "You know, it was scary at first, like he [her husband] said, 'cause we weren't sure what to prepare ourselves for as far as the initial costs . . . a lot of our family took a lot of the stress away." This family also attributed the smooth operation of their daughter's Sunrise Dance to the fact that they followed the advice of more informed family members.

In addition to the strengthening of clan and extended family relationships and reinforcement of kinship obligations, fictive kin are created from the Sunrise Dance through the joining of two previously unrelated families (*shi ti ke*). In contrast, in European American society, the marriage ceremony is the predominant event that joins unrelated families. There are numerous examples throughout North American Indian history of the formation of fictive kin, particularly when kinship networks were sparse due to wars or disease and tribes would adopt captives in order to fill roles of deceased family members. These new fictive kin subsequently assumed the roles and responsibilities of the ones they had replaced. For contemporary Apaches, permanent unions are created through the joining of two family groups at the Sunrise Dance. Certainly one has a sense of the good feelings surrounding the union of two families, much like what is experienced at weddings.

When a woman accepts the blue stone and feather at the initial request to serve in the godmother's role for a pubescent girl, she and her family are committing themselves as kin to the initiate and her family for a lifetime. Generosity and sharing are values inherent in North American Indian cultures, and the exchange of gifts between the two families formalizes their new relationship. Other actions that signify the joining of two families are the singing and dancing that occur at various opportunities during the 4 days of the ceremony. In particular, specific efforts are made to dance with those of the other family. Dancing is a significant social act that fosters good feelings and connection, as explained by Ganteaume (1992): "Dance is one of the earliest and most enduring forms of communal expression. It allows people to come together and express feelings that lie deep within themselves" (p. 65). Hence, in the context of the Sunrise Dance, dancing expresses celebration and unity between the families central to this event.

Through the system of acquiring godparents, the Apache Sunrise Dance firmly embeds girls within their existing kin networks and provides them with an expanded kin network. Through this act, the girl's two sets of family are now related. Nonetheless, it is unknown exactly how deep the new sense of relatedness extends. That it, is it just the immediate families that form these new bonds, or do cousins, aunts, uncles, and others also now regard the girl's godparents and their kin as their own kin? At the Sunrise Dance itself, certainly the broadly extended family networks of the sponsor's and co-sponsor's families are deeply invested in the success of the event. In the longer term, however, my impression is that the connections weaken among the more distant members of the extended family. Over time, the permanent relationship seems to center on the girl and her godparents and their children, with frequent inclusion of the girl's siblings.

The category of fictive kin can be extended to those who are not related to the girl and her co-sponsor but who nonetheless demonstrate support for the dances that are held in the community. The Sunrise Dance is a social event, and both kin and non-kin participate and commit themselves to a successful event. As clarified in the previous section, the impacts of the Sunrise Dance extend to the broader community, and, likewise, community members are keenly interested and contribute in various ways. Informants explained that by contributing to the success of any Sunrise Dance, blessings would be experienced by the donor of money, material objects, and physical labor. One opportunity for donation available to everyone is to bring groceries and household items to the sponsor's and co-sponsor's camps in order that these items be used in meal preparation during the encampment or in the gift exchange between families. One signs his or her name in a ledger upon delivery of groceries and gifts to the camp. It is my practice as participant observer to participate by providing material donations of various types as well as physical labor in food preparation, such as cutting vegetables for stews and salads, cooking tortillas over hot coals, serving elderly guests, and so forth. Generosity, another theme of the Sunrise Dance, is reciprocated as families serve food to guests, provide beverages, cigarettes, chewing gum, and other items to guests during the dance, and generally exhibit hospitality. In addition to these immediate, tangible gifts, informants stated that those who contribute in any way to the success of a Sunrise Dance have promises of wealth and good things in the future.

I also observed at each Sunrise Dance a contingent of people who appeared impoverished but were actively involved in roles critical to smooth operation of the ceremony. One father explained the relationships he formed with these individuals who assisted at his daughter's Sunrise Dance: "we're talking about the guys that come to help out, people that have had it hard in their lives, are like homeless people. . . . They came over to help out and they know what's going on because they go to so many dances and help out. . . . You know, a lot of people think, '. . . they just drink' . . . but they were the ones telling me, 'This is what you need to do.'" The informant went on to say that permanent bonds were created with these same people, who now greet him at all subsequent Sunrise Dances he attends.

In summary, kinship is a fundamental value of North American Indian cultures of the past and the present. Ceremonials and rituals of Apaches and of other North American Indian cultures serve to strengthen existing kinship bonds and create new ones. The Sunrise Dance imparts positive feelings of kinship and connection at many levels. Existing kin relationships are confirmed through the performance of obligations and sacrifices that enable a successful event for the daughter of a relative. Even non-kin individuals are committed to a successful event, and a broad range of Apaches attends the weekend Sunrise Dances—if not for the spiritual benefits, at least for the opportunity to socialize. Rituals throughout the ceremony perpetuate important Apache values, and my impression was that positive feelings of affirmation and connection were generated between Apaches who were both kin and non-kin.

Influences from Colonization, Including Christianity

According to Basso (1970), "few Apaches became familiar with the intricate ideological underpinnings of Christianity; instead, they seized upon a limited number of key concepts—God, Jesus, prayer, and so forth. . . . The Virgin Mary was equated with Changing Woman, and Jesus with Changing Woman's son, nay en ez gane ('Slayer of Monsters')" (p. 95). The beliefs and practices of numerous North American Indian cultures have been affected by the encounter with Christianity. The Apaches, like other Native cultures, tend toward inclusiveness when exposed to other belief systems; that is, they attempt to determine how other beliefs might fit within the context of their own system of meaning and understanding. Such attempts were quite apparent in the thinking of many informants relative to the Sunrise Dance vis-à-vis Christian teachings to which they had been exposed. Perhaps the most frequently stated comparison by the adult cultural experts was that White Painted Woman and the Virgin Mary are the same person and that initiates become transformed into both figures during their Sunrise Dances. Initiates are thought to acquire the powers of these two parallel figures and, through the altruistic nature of their personalities, acquire the capacity to offer benevolence to others. Indeed, Goseyun (1991) dedicated her daughter Carla's Sunrise Dance to the Virgin Mary, explaining: "After all, she is Usen's mother, and is the symbol of motherhood for all women in our times" (p. 8).

The linkage between White Painted Woman and the Virgin Mary extends to Apache oral tradition of White Painted Woman's impregnation by the Sun. An obvious connection is made to the Immaculate Conception. The result of this impregnation was offspring that would confront the evil in the world (Jesus' coming to save the people, or Born from Water and Slayer of Monsters from White Painted Woman to rid the world of evil). This comparison is certainly a theme raised by other authors on the subject (e.g., Basso, 1966, 1970; P. E. Goddard, 1909). Informants in this study also compared the wickiup to the stable in which Jesus was born.

Many other Bible stories were mixed with Apache tradition in the reports of various informants. The creation of White Painted Woman is attributed to the Giver of Life (Mails, 1988). The great flood recounted in the Bible is applied to the hiding of White Painted Woman in an abalone shell that ensured her survival. It is stated in oral tradition that after the flood receded, her sons were born. In another linkage to the Judeo-Christian tradition, cattail pollen is sacred to the Apaches, and one Apache informant explained that cattails were used to hide Moses from the Egyptians. In a further parallel, cattail pollen is likened to holy water and one woman described how she rises every morning and faces the east as she makes the sign of the cross with it. The symbol of a cross, either drawn on some substance or on a human, such as the application of cattail pollen to the initiate, is a familiar representation of the four cardinal directions to Apaches. However, for some Apaches, the meaning also encompasses their Christian beliefs, such as the motions of making the sign of the cross. The rite of Christian baptism was linked to the painting of initiates on the third morning; they were said to be symbolically accepting the powers of the female holy person (Mails, 1988).

Ironically, while Apaches incorporated Christian stories and beliefs in their conceptions of the Sunrise Dance and other traditional ceremonies, Christianity suppressed the practice of these traditions for many years. Indeed, numerous Native ceremonials were banned by the government, as were the Mountain Spirit dancers (Nichols, 2002). For instance, in 1855 Dr. Michael Steck was appointed as agent to all of the southern tribes, and one of his major aims was the curtailment of the Apaches' celebrations, especially the girls' puberty ceremony (Debo, 1976). An informant in the present study attributed the drastic reduction of the Sunrise Dance prior to the 1970s to boarding school practices and the prohibitions of churches against their members' participation in the ceremony. This observation is consistent with Basso (1966), who stated that declines in the Sunrise Dance resulted from the discouraging influences of missionaries and the prohibitive nature of the costs of the Sunrise Dance (the latter are not to be taken lightly, as is discussed in a later section). With respect to the former, the widespread practice of forced assimilation served the agenda of both the U.S. government and formal religious institutions (see chapter 2). The government, and the white settlers they represented, sought domination of American Indians as a means to land acquisition, and the agenda of religious organizations was conversion. The linking of these two major societal institutions—which shared a similar goal but for different reasons—began early in the colonization process in the Americas and continued in not-so-subtle forms throughout much of the 20th century.

The boarding school system of educating North American Indian children was established through both governmental and religious efforts, and several generations of children were raised in a cultural and familial void according to the dictates and rules of educational institutions that were all-encompassing in their influence (see chapter 2). A strategy of these schools was to remove children from their homes, even prior to age 5, and immerse them within the totality of the white North American experience. Because of the boarding schools, several generations of children were disconnected from their culture, language, and traditions. Parents, grandparents, and elders did not have opportunities to pass down to the young the oral traditions and ritual practices. One elder Apache informant described the pattern in this way: "the white people must have pushed us into government school, boarding school, and people had said that they furnish everything, boots and clothes. . . . But, they were told not to speak their Apache language and sing their Apache songs during the ceremonial." For pubescent girls there would have been months and sometimes years between menarche and visits back to their communities where proper observances of puberty ceremonies would occur. This barrier and the general discouragement of and frequent prohibitions against the practice of traditions served to undermine performance of the Sunrise Dance and other ceremonials.

When exactly did the Sunrise Dance or girls' puberty ceremonies diminish in practice, and when did the current resurgence begin? Opler (1941) noted that, 50 years earlier, the puberty rites were performed for nearly every Western Apache girl (i.e., prior to Opler's time), and Basso (1966) stated that "not more than 70 years ago, almost every Western Apache girl had a puberty ceremony" (p. 124). Consistent with this assessment, Whitaker (1971) reported that one of her San Carlos Apache informants told her that probably 70 to 100 years earlier nearly all girls experienced the puberty ceremony. So, taking the dates of these articles into account, approximately 100 years ago or longer girls' puberty ceremonies were an institution of Apache culture. Certainly, historical evidence demonstrates observance of puberty rites in the 19th century. However, between this earlier time and the 1960s and 1970s, or perhaps earlier, its practice was drastically diminished. Basso (1966) reported that girls' puberty ceremonies were being performed perhaps only two or three times a year among the Cibecue Apaches and in some Fort Apache communities not at all. Apparently, this was the pattern at San Carlos as well (Mails, 1974/1993). One informant in the present study recalled that in 1962, the year he was married, only two or three Sunrise Dances were held in San Carlos. Another San Carlos informant stated that he remembers one summer in the late 1960s in which there were no dances.

The adult informants in this study were in agreement that the practice of the Sunrise Dance had increased in recent years. One San Carlos informant estimated that there had been a sharp increase in practice for the past 10 years and in other locations as well, such as Whiteriver, Camp Verde, and Fort McDowell. The absence of practice of the Sunrise Dance until recently fits a curious finding relative to this data. Specifically, the mothers of the initiates were all very keen that their daughters experience the ceremony, but they had not experienced it themselves at puberty. One grandmother explained this pattern, noting that at the time her daughters experienced menarche, the Sunrise Dance was not occurring.

The resurgence of the Sunrise Dance in recent years can be attributed to various factors. Activism of the 1970s certainly served to empower Native communities across North American as they reclaimed their heritage and the right to practice their traditional ceremonies unencumbered. Several federal acts were passed in the United States during this era that have particular relevance. The American Indian Religious Freedom Act of 1978 affirmed Native people's rights to believe in, express, and practice their traditional religions. The Indian Child Welfare Act of 1978 was designed to reestablish familial and tribal rights for Native peoples to rear their children according to their own traditions and culture. Of related significance to these previous two acts was the Native American Languages Act of 1990, which recognized that Indigenous languages are essential for tribal survival and self-determination.

Another factor that is likely related to the resurgence in the practice of the Sunrise Dance is that churches have become more permissive regarding their members' practice of it, according to several informants in the study. Most of the initiates and their parents did participate in organized Christian religions and felt that their traditional beliefs enhanced their church experiences, and vice versa. A few specific religious denominations were named that did not approve of the practice of the Sunrise Dance and discouraged their members from attending any of the ceremonies. A father of one of the informants explained how he felt caught between his family of origin, which is Christian, and his wife, who wanted the Sunrise Dance for their daughter: "I was stuck in between my dad and my wife. So when it actually came to making that decision, it was a tough one. . . . I told my dad, 'You know, I'm not being disrespectful to our religion. I'm being more respectful to our culture. . . . I see these kids day in and day out losing their culture, losing something that not everybody has.'" The linkage between traditional practices and formal religion is a theme Goseyun echoed (1991) as she explained how she tried to impart to her daughters a respect for both traditions: "I wanted them to understand that it is okay to practice our Apache beliefs and try to live by the principles taught by our Catholic faith. We are fortunate that our parish priest is very supportive of our native traditions and has encouraged us to keep alive the gifts passed to us from our Creator, Usen" (p. 8).

Nearly all of the adult informants were quick to point out in their interviews that their traditional practices were not "devil worship," as had so often been claimed. A medicine man informant explained: "Not one song is bad in the Sunrise Dance . . . it is always about the good life . . . walk in beauty . . . blessing . . . we are praying to one true God, but we do it the Indian way." A mother explained how she raised her children in both the church and according to the traditional ways: "I feel that as a parent it is my responsibility to teach my girls to learn about Christianity, about God, and to also learn our traditional ways and culture . . . we pray to God . . . we don't pray to any other God."

At one ceremony I attended, a woman pointed to the missionary church on the hill above the ceremonial grounds and explained that she had attended that church as a child. At menarche, she wanted a puberty ceremony but was told that she would be excommunicated from the church if she engaged in it. She acquiesced to the mandate of her church. After some years, she reconnected to her traditional culture and now attends the Sunrise Dances. In summing up this series of events, she stated: "Isn't it ironic that here I am at the Sunrise Dance and, when I glance up the hill, I see the church that told me I couldn't have my own."

The Sunrise Dance Past and Present

One lazy Saturday afternoon while at home in West Virginia, I happened to turn on the television and, much to my surprise, saw Mountain Spirit dancers being observed by James Stewart in an old Western called *Broken Arrow*. The story was based on the life of Thomas J. Jeffords, friend of the Apache leader Cochise. As the plot of the movie progressed, the Jeffords character was brought into a wickiup and introduced to an initiate undergoing her Sunrise Dance. In this film version of Jeffords's life, it was explained to him that the young woman was presently in a sacred state as she was transformed into White Painted Woman. In the film, Jeffords became enamored with the young woman as she prayed for him. It was conveniently explained in the movie that this young woman was older than usual to have the ceremony—an important point, because later, in this fictionalized account, Jeffords would marry her.

Aside from this Hollywood adaptation of the Apache girls' puberty ceremony, the ceremony has been transformed in various ways from earlier times. As discussed in the previous section, the practice of the Sunrise Dance diminished for a time, but the importance of the ceremony to Apache society has not changed. It is somewhat difficult to determine the exact nature of the practice of the Sunrise Dance in earlier times because of limited written historical accounts prior to the mid-to late 19th century (indeed, it is not until recent times that the label "Sunrise

Dance" was applied). Further, in reviewing written sources, one has to read through the lens of a particular historical era and of the individual writing the account. Nonetheless, it is apparent that the girls' puberty ceremony was highly regarded in earlier times. In 1882 Geronimo and his band had abducted Loco and his band from the San Carlos Agency and were attempting a fast escape to Mexico. In transit, a girl experienced menarche and the entire group had to stop long enough to perform the required puberty rites (Debo, 1976). A San Carlos informant marveled in conversation with me that these events were of such value to Apaches of the past that they were willing to risk their lives in such a manner: "Why did they do that, I wonder? Somebody's chasing us, we're about to get killed. Why do this sacrifice?" In my request for an answer to his own rhetorical question, he responded that women are the key of life and it is necessary to bless girls at this time of life.

It is told how, as prisoners of war in Florida, Geronimo, Naiche, and others were involved in the puberty ceremony of a girl called "Katie." It developed into something of a local attraction, but the tourists were unaware of the real purpose of the event, with the dancing by the Mountain Spirit dancers making the greatest impression on them. Nonetheless, this was a significant event for the Apaches, as Debo explained (1976): "To the spectators it had been an entertaining exhibition of savage customs. In actuality, it can be seen as a moving revelation of the Apache spirit. Circumscribed as they were, these prisoners, far from their mountains and facing an unknown future, living in a grim old fortress on a narrow strip of sand with the sea closing them in, were still true to their ancient faith" (p. 331). Another account of the puberty ceremony was told by Geronimo in his autobiography (as recorded by Barrett, 1906) concerning the coming-of-age of his 16-year-old daughter, Eva, in Fort Sill, Oklahoma, where he spent his last days.[1] He invited the Apaches, Comanches, and Kiowas in the area to attend, and Naiche led the singing while Geronimo and a medicine man directed the dance. The ceremony was reported to last 2 days and nights. Based on Geronimo's description, there appear to be parallels with contemporary practice of Mescalero and San Carlos puberty rites, such as the initiate's dancing with other girls, social dancing among the crowd, dancing by sacred dancers who were stripped to the waist and painted, and entertainment by clown dancers.

It appears that the dances of earlier years were shorter than those of the present day, as reported by one informant at San Carlos who explained to me that, in some cases, it was a much briefer ceremony perhaps with just four songs and lasting 2 to 3 hours.

As further evidence of 19th-century practice of puberty rituals, Bourke (1892), a member of General Crook's expedition into Geronimo's hideout in the Sierre Madre, Mexico, in 1883, reported that drinking reeds and scratching sticks were found at the site. Perhaps these were suggestive of girls' puberty rites, but Bourke linked the scratching stick to coming-of-age rituals for young men that were to be used at their first four battles. Indeed, as discussed in chapter 5, these implements were required of Apache boys during their coming-of-age initiation. The absence of present-day use of these implements and other rites for boys' coming-of-age are due to, in part, the U.S. government's ban on such practices to suppress the warrior culture (Norelli, 1994).

Bourke (1892) wrote extensively about the sacred pollen, called *hoddentin*, and discussed its use at the girls' puberty ceremony, wherein it was explained the girl would throw it to the Sun. Other accounts tell of critical elements that we find in the Sunrise Dance today (e.g., the eagle feathers in the girl's hair, the scratching stick, the drinking tube) that were included in the 19th-century version of the rites (G. Goodwin, 1942). Informants of Goodwin also discussed a period from the late 19th century to the early 20th century and explained that masks and other paraphernalia used by the Ga'an dancers at the puberty ceremony and other dances were stored in a particular cave.

In another account of 19th-century practices, G. Goodwin (1942) presented recollections of informants concerning how childhood play behaviors at earlier times reflected actions of the girls' puberty: "The boys always pretended to butcher the steers to feast the people at the ceremony. The girl for whom the ceremony was given tied any kind of a feather she could find in her hair to represent the downy eagle feather. From old sticks we made a cane for her and a drinking-tube and scratcher to hang around her neck. She had everything" (p. 484). In the 1930s, Goodwin observed girls playing the role of initiate at the puberty ceremony, and it was explained that boys enacted the roles of singers and dancers. A mock molding ceremony would be included, and the children would sing the Ga'an songs and dance. An account from Goodwin in the previous chapter tells of the young girl who was so inspired by these ceremonial activities that she attended that she play-acted the important elements of it, such as dancing, molding, and swaying on her knees, to the amusement of her parents.

Other sources based on observations in the early 20th century provide additional insights into Apache puberty rites. Reagan's (1931) field notes from 1901-1902 on the Fort Apache Reservation indicated the girls' ceremony as more elaborate and public than the boys'. He observed a ritual during which the girl, at the threshold of womanhood, ran through the vicinity while being chased by others. When caught, she was then heated in some manner while being examined. While I have no knowledge of these rites today, various other rituals described by Reagan can be observed in contemporary times, such as the dancing of initiates on blankets that cover the ground while they are being accompanied by the beating of the pot drum, as well as feasting, running in the four directions, and being sprinkled with the sacred pollen. The Mountain Spirit dancers also were presumably observed, although Reagan's term for these dancers was "devil dancers." Some form of a dressing ritual also occurred, but there was no mention of the involvement of the female co-sponsor. Reagan also wrote of the evening dance of the initiate and other girls (with no mention of the Mountain Spirit dancers), where women danced in the roles of clowns. The ceremony was concluded on the next day with men giving presents to the initiate, including a horse at one dance.

Additional reports of the adolescent ceremony of the White Mountain Apaches are found in P. E. Goddard (1919). Striking similarities exist between his descriptions and my observations of the present-day dance, most notably the following: the girl sits in the kneeling position to allow the sun's rays to enter her; the girl is straightened; the girl runs around the cane; the basket of items are poured over the girl's head (it contained corn kernels in Goddard's day); the girl throws the blankets in all directions; and the girl is painted with white clay for the purpose of longevity. Additionally, the White Mountain Apache girl would dance all night for 4 nights while following the Ga'an dancers. The reports of Goddard and of Reagan (1931) are inconsistent concerning the dancing of initiates with the Mountain Spirit dancers.

P. E. Goddard (1909) also addressed the Mescalero Apaches' puberty ceremony for girls. Striking similarities between his reports and my observations at Mescalero include singing and praying for 4 nights, the performance of various responsibilities by the medicine man, and extensive dancing and running on the part of initiates. Further, it was stated that during the 4 nights when the initiate danced inside the lodge, a separate ceremony was described as occurring outside the lodge around a fire with the appearance of Ga'an dancers. These rituals, in the broad sense, also were observed in my fieldwork. However, obvious differences were that, in the past, for 4 days after the ceremony, initiates were to continue to wear their ceremonial garb, use the drinking tube and scratching stick, and not wash themselves (Hoijer, 1938). Today, girls are undressed on the last morning, resume the wearing of contemporary clothing, are no longer required to use the scratching stick and drinking tube, and move back to their permanent homes.

The nature of the woman who plays the role of co-sponsor may have changed from earlier times. In some accounts she is not mentioned (e.g., Reagan, 1931). Opler (1941), however, identified the female co-sponsor as typically elderly and one who had acquired some kind of ceremonial expertise or had a supernatural experience with White Painted Woman. In Opler's account the female attendant was somewhat of a cultural expert who was responsible for giving the initiate numerous instructions at the dressing on the first day, including a mandate that the girl stay in her dwelling most of the time for the 4 days and the subsequent 4 days after the ceremony. Today, the co-sponsor or godmother is typically the young side of middle-aged and may not have experienced the Sunrise Dance herself. It was my distinct impression that serving as a co-sponsor is a form of an initiation for adult women, particularly the first time a woman serves in this role, because she is acquiring cultural knowledge along with the initiate. Since many women have not had the benefit of their own Sunrise Dance, serving as a co-sponsor is perhaps their own rite of passage into the ceremonial aspects of their culture.

On matters of sexuality and marriage, there are both similarities and differences between the past and the present. It was emphasized among Chiricahua Apaches of the past that the initiate was expected to be a virgin or there could be dangerous consequences for the singer or medicine man (Opler, 1941). This observation is consistent with comments made to me by informants who stated that there is still an expectation that the girl has not engaged in sexual activity—if she has, she should not have a Sunrise Dance.

The Sunrise Dance has changed from earlier times in regard to its function as an announcement of availability for marriage (Opler, 1941). Such a proclamation has been a common function of coming-of-age ceremonies cross-culturally, but this no longer applies to Apaches. For instance, Tiller (1983) observed that, among the Jicarilla Apaches, by the 1940s the girls' puberty ceremony was no longer an announcement of eligibility for marriage. Two major reasons can be suggested for this particular change in function: the stage of adolescence has lengthened, and the age of menarche is earlier. Relative to the former, adolescence is now a longer phase of the life span in both Western and non-Western societies, and courtship and marriage are delayed well beyond pubescence. In the technological society in which all adolescents are socialized, it takes many more years to acquire the necessary education to become a fully contributing member of adult society. Marriage is viewed as an event that follows educational completion and career stability. Numerous comments from adult informants and verbal directives given to initiates at their Sunrise Dances confirmed the Apaches' value for education and career paths for these pubescent girls, along with implicit and explicit recognition that they would ultimately assume the role of wife and mother as well. This finding is consistent with my research on the Navajo Kinaaldá, in which I observed a particular medicine men explicitly directing an initiate to acquire all of her needed education prior to pursuing marriage and children (Markstrom & Iborra, 2003).

A second reason for the negation of the earlier function of the Sunrise Dance as an announcement of eligibility for marriage is the secular trend. Specifically, menarche now occurs at a much younger age than in the past. In the earlier part of the 20th century and prior to that time, and in more traditional societies, it was considered appropriate and reasonable that a girl's marriage availability would be associated with her coming-of-age event at menarche (around age 15, 16, or 17). In today's society, with the average age of menarche being 12.5 years of age, it is unthinkable that a girl would be viewed as ready for marriage upon

Table 4. Past Characteristics of the Sunrise Dance

- Pubescent girls were required to stay away from crops and meat sources that could become contaminated.
- Pubescent girls lived in separate shelters away from their families and were attended to by older persons or their co-sponsors.
- Puberty rituals were incorporated into everyday life and not necessarily set aside in separate rituals (e.g., mothers would massage their daughters, daughters would be required to work very hard for 4 days and to work outside, and girls were taught useful skills such as sewing).
- Initiates danced all night (which still occurs at Mescalero but not at San Carlos).
- People ate more simply, and food was taken from the land. Today there is inclusion of non-Apache food items (e.g., jello and doughnuts) that are Western and commercial. The traditional Apache foods are still prepared and served at the puberty ceremony, but Western foods are included.
- Girls had to work harder at their Sunrise Dances. For example, they were required to grind their own corn and make the charcoal for the Mountain Spirit dancers.
- Children did not attend Sunrise Dances in the past because their spirits were not strong enough.
- The proper procedure was for family members, particularly the elders, to decide whether the Sunrise Dance would be held. Parents would be informed, and then they would talk to their daughter. In contrast, in current times, most girls are permitted to make the decision.
- The emphasis was on the sacrifices the godmother was making for the girl and her family. Girls were not to expect anything from their godmothers. Nowadays, it is said, girls want the dance so they can obtain a godmother because she is someone who will provide them with material benefits.
- Girls wore camp dresses all week while staying at the camp. Today they sometimes wear shorts and T-shirts up until the day they are ceremonially dressed. (An adult informant and her daughter clashed on this point at a contemporary Sunrise Dance, and the daughter retorted, "That is not how it's done anymore.")

completion of her Sunrise Dance. The function of preparing the girl for assumption of adult female roles and responsibilities is still relevant, but it is recognized (and desired) that it will be some time before she fully adopts roles of a spouse and mother.

Several of the informants in this study discussed changes in the Sunrise Dance from the past to the present. These points were based on informants' own realm of experience or recollection and frequently reflected what they perceived as the ideal way the dance should be conducted. There is wide variability in the statements made concerning characteristics of the Sunrise Dance in the past as compared to the present, as shown in Table 4. In spite of these changes, the basic components of the ceremony remain intact. An informant at Mescalero noted that it is still the same dance relative to the songs, prayers, and rituals, but modern conveniences that are less central to the meaning of the dance are used. For instance, electrical appliances may be of assistance in food preparation, and tables may be brought in to facilitate meal preparation. In the past, all of the wood was to be cut and not sawed, but today it is permitted to saw the cooking wood.

An important activity of the Sunrise Dance is the instruction of initiates on roles and tasks of adult women. It appears that the instruction of girls in this manner coincided with pubescence among Apaches of the past (G. Goodwin, 1942). While not necessarily associated with menarche and the formal puberty rites, in the past, either slightly before or during the pubertal years, girls were taught how to sew their own clothes, build wickiups, and construct baskets. As well, it was expected that they would begin assisting their mothers with tasks around the camp, such as cooking (G. Goodwin, 1942). Role modeling was a tool employed as girls were instructed to first observe their mothers perform complex tasks of food preparation and then begin to attempt these tasks themselves. However, by Goodwin's time it was noted that these traditional female activities were changing due to the purchase of store-bought items and that school attendance curtailed the involvement of youth in household activities.

In the present day, instruction is still an integral component of the Sunrise Dance, but some of the content of instruction has changed. Certainly role performance is still expected, as shown in the rituals performed by the initiate relative to building her own wickiup, preparing four kinds of bread on the first morning, shaking the blankets at the end of the second morning, and various other rituals. Mescalero girls also are instructed in traditional tasks such as starting a fire. However, these are more or less symbolic enactments that serve to perpetuate knowledge and history according to the traditions of their culture, and they may have less to do with specific role performance in the present day or the future.

Instruction of initiates in the present study extend to certain verbal admonitions and directives. Girls are warned to be cautious in their behavior with the opposite sex—a theme also evident in instruction of initiates in the past. They also are instructed to listen to their elders and to not talk back to them. The main piece of advice one Apache initiate retained from her Sunrise Dance was to respect herself and others, including her parents. Broader societal changes that have affected Apaches have yielded additional components of instruction. Girls are warned of contemporary problems, such as the dangers of alcohol and drugs. Further, as previously reported, at Apache Sunrise Dances and Navajo Kinaaldá ceremonies girls are encouraged to obtain their education and establish themselves in careers prior to marrying and raising children. In this respect, one informant related the words of her medicine man: "after my Sunrise Dance he said he wants me to go to college and finish school, and don't go on the wrong path. And don't drink and stuff like that." It was reported that initiates were informed on what they might expect in future years relative to forming a permanent relationship with a partner and having children. Consistent with these observations, Talamantez (2000) noted that Mescalero Apaches initiates are instructed to use the teachings of the ceremony for their careers, families, and their lives: "The ceremony is a symbolic representation of transformation and a behavioral model for how to handle change, whether it be personal, familial, or social" (p. 155).

The Sunrise Dance, as it is called today, is a ceremony of historical endurance as evident through oral tradition and earlier written accounts. There appears to be continuity in the practice of major rituals of the Sunrise Dance, but more peripheral components have evolved and changed with the times. In the past, a stronger emphasis was placed on girls' acquisition of skills indicative of the female role that would ultimately contribute to the well-being of family and camp. It continues to be of value that girls acquire important household management skills, and they certainly are verbally directed to assume expected responsibilities, but actual ritual enactments are typically reflective of earlier traditions and lifestyles. Contemporary additions to the Sunrise Dance include admonitions to avoid deviant behaviors and to stay academically focused in order to acquire occupational success. An additional change in the Sunrise Dance that is addressed in the next section is the escalation of costs relative to its practice.

Monetary Costs of the Sunrise Dance

In recent years the production cost of the Sunrise Dance has escalated to an excessive degree—a common complaint of informants. Several informants asserted that it could cost as much as $10,000 to conduct a Sunrise Dance today, and that it had become something equivalent to a coming-out ball for a debutante. In spite of these criticisms, it appears that the Sunrise Dance has always been costly and exacted great sacrifices of families. Whitaker (1971) reported that it cost in excess of $500 at that time, and Opler (1941) stated that families' resources were drained to sponsor the puberty ceremony. Granville Goodwin reported a dance in Bylas on the San Carlos Reservation that cost $200 to $300, a small fortune at the time he conducted his observations (1928-1939, as cited in N. Goodwin, 2001).

As an outsider, I found the great financial expense and other elaborate preparations of the Sunrise Dance quite staggering. The families in this study were of low to modest incomes, and hosting an event that could cost up to $10,000 was a major sacrifice. Many of the parents were concerned about the cost of the ceremony, but in the final analysis they stated that all of the needs and requirements for the ceremony were met. Prayer was cited as a critical component to making the Sunrise Dance a success. Nearly all of the families had stories to tell of how certain needs were met by family and non-family members alike who contributed money, ritual objects, and various other items. The following quotes illustrate these stories:

If you pray and have the belief in the culture and the medicine man, if you really have faith in it, it really does happen. . . . People start coming saying, "You need help with this? I'll pay for this. I'll help you buy this. I'll pay for Crown Dancers."

I needed about $400 to pay the other half of the payment to the medicine man. And here this lady comes and said, "I need six camp dresses." So, there, my money came on its own, came, and I had $250. Then another lady came, said, "I need four camp dresses." So, I made another $100. . . . Some people say, "It's hard, it's hard. You have to be rich. You have to have a lot of money." But, it's not that. It's the faith and the belief that you have in God that can pull you through all the things like that.

They say in Christianity if you believe in God and have faith in

God . . . if you ask for something believing that you have it, that you'll receive it. I guess that's the same way when you're going through this traditional dance. If you have prayer, you have faith, and you believe, help will come unexpected.

The puberty ceremony is the central ceremony of the San Carlos Apaches as a people, but in all likelihood it is the central ceremony of the initiate's life. It would not be inaccurate to say that it is more important than a marriage ceremony. In the historical perspective, Bourke (1892) stated that the marriage rite of Apaches in the 19th century was an event with little or no ceremony. He went on to accentuate the importance of the girl's puberty ceremony to her own life and that of her people. The preparation and expense required for the Sunrise Dance are comparable to that of a wedding (including the elaborate dress). The comment of one mother in this study illustrates this point: "I see this stuff hanging on the wall . . . it brings back so many memories. It's almost like a wedding dress, you know. Some people get a wedding dress and they hang on to it for forever. This is like it. I helped make that thing." The father of the initiate added: "The basket here. It means something to me. The feathers, the cane, the moccasins, you know, it means something to me."

The comparison in white society is apparent—a woman's wedding is the most expensive, elaborate, and anticipated ceremonial event in her life. Is it the meaning behind the event, the social implications, the pageantry, and related factors that elevate the wedding ceremony to such a status? A combination of reasons accounts for its importance, just as a variety of reasons can be given for the commitment of the Apaches to their girls' puberty ceremony. Cultural differences relative to values and beliefs explain why and how certain ceremonies are elevated in each culture. The purposes of the Sunrise Dance, as previously articulated, give important clues to the values of Apache people: family, women, young people, tradition, goodness, well-being, blessings, and long life. A medicine man's remarks on prayer accentuate values of Apache society: "we ask Usen to give this girl knowledge, wisdom, and love in her heart. And, it is not just a word, but it comes with spirit and power. She will get what the medicine man told her in the dance . . . good life . . . happy family."

Comparisons across Apache Groups and with Other Native Cultures

Rituals common to all Apache groups (i.e., Western, Chiricahua, Mescalero, and Jicarilla) continue to be observed in girls' puberty rites. As discussed in the previous chapter, the essence of the creation stories includes the central figures of a Creator (Usen), White Painted Woman, Born from Water, and Slayer of Monsters. A giant enters the picture and seeks to take the life of the sons of White Painted Woman. In addition to the creation story, numerous other components of the girls' puberty ceremony are shared across Apache cultures, such as the physically exerting tasks of running and dancing, assigning a female mentor or attendant, using the scratching stick and drinking tube, molding the initiate, wearing of special clothing, painting, singing, giving of foods and other gifts, and blessing with some kind of pollen (Murphy, 1993). The belief in the empowered state of the initiate due to her transformation into White Painted Woman is apparent across Apache groups. Corresponding to this belief is the inclusion of rituals that permit guests to approach the initiate for prayer and blessing. All Apache groups believe that continual practice of their girls' puberty rites is essential for their own welfare and for that of all people. All Apache groups agree on the significance of the number 4 in its numerous iterations relative to this ceremony and others. The timing and expression of the rituals vary somewhat, as do the players or participants, but the fundamental meanings and expected impacts of their puberty ceremonies are predominantly congruent.

Nonetheless, the Sunrise Dance is fluid, not static, and there are numerous individual differences in how it is conducted. The result is that no two ceremonies are alike. Murphy (1993) wrote of the incorporation of new rituals in girls' puberty rites stemming from visions received by Apache leaders, a finding confirmed in my interview of an Apache medicine man. Such lack of uniformity in practices is not problematic for the Apaches. For instance, a ritual that occurs across Apache groups requires the girl to run in the eastwardly direction four times to represent success in accomplishing four stages of the life span. However, the object she runs around is varied: it is either a basket (Mescalero Apache) or a cane (Western Apache). Jicarilla girls also run to the east four times, but

they are followed by an adolescent boy (Murphy, 1993). More specifically, in the Jicarilla tradition a boy is selected to play an important role
in the puberty ceremony in the impersonation of Child of the Water; the
boy essentially assumes the role of the girl's partner (Opler, 1936, 1946).
Elements of Plains Indian culture are found among contemporary Mescalero and Chiricahua versions of the girls' puberty ceremony, and some
of the practices of the Jicarillas are similar to those of Navajos.

There are many other meaningful points of correspondence between
the rituals embedded in Apache girls' puberty rites and those of numerous North American Indian cultures as reviewed in chapter 5. The usage
of a scratching stick is one of the most widespread practices and, according to Driver (1941), is a very ancient practice. It was theorized that the
oldest practices are those that have disseminated the furthest across cultures and are most difficult to trace according to their origins and routes
of dispersion. In addition to use of the scratching stick, several other
widespread traits are identified, including seclusion and a separate dwelling for the initiate at the first menstrual cycles, the role of the attendant,
food and drink taboos, a scratching taboo, the value of work at puberty,
bathing and changing clothes at the end of seclusion (or, in the case of
Apaches, at the end of the ceremony), the significance of the number 4,
and instruction by adult mentors.

In my research I observed commonalities between the Sunrise Dance
and the Navajo Kinaaldá (the latter ceremony is described in the next
chapter), including the various iterations of the sacred number 4, dressing of the initiate in the image of Changing Woman or White Painted
Woman, the belief in the initiate's transformation into Changing Woman
or White Painted Woman and her resultant power to bring blessings to
others, the incorporation of running rituals to bring strength and long life
to the girl, mentorship by an adult female role model, the molding of the
initiate, the preparation and serving of traditional foods, and singing by
a medicine man. Driver (1941) observed that Apache puberty rituals were
most similar to those of the Maricopa and Papago cultures, followed by
the rituals of Indigenous cultures of northern California. The most pro-
nounced similarity was stated to be the belief in the girl's curing powers—a
belief also observed among Pacific Northwest Coast cultures.

The rituals of the Apache puberty ceremony have also been compared to those of cultures in the Great Basin cultural area. For instance, Jorgensen (1986) equated the Ute Bear Dance with the Apache puberty ceremony. Northern Paiute pubescent girls were required to run every morning for 5 to 10 days and to carry a staff that was painted white and decorated with sagebrush and beads (Fowler & Liljeblad, 1986). Numerous puberty rituals were practiced by the cultures of the California region, and many of these have certain expressions in common with Apache puberty rites, such as the use of the scratching stick, singing, dancing, feasting, running to the east, having a peer companion, and being instructed by adult women (see chapter 5). Relative to several northern Athabascan cultures, the use of a scratching stick and drinking tube were of widespread use (Libby, 1952). It was thought that the power attached to the girl placed her at risk for harming herself or others during this special time. For instance, Teslin pubescent girls of the southern Yukon Territory were not permitted to use sharp cutting implements such as axes and were required to twist and pull bark off trees to be used for firewood. The reason for this taboo was so the pubescent girl would not break the "web of life" or the connection to heaven of her brother or uncles (Libby, 1952). The taboo on cutting instruments certainly has its parallel practice in the requirement that Apache girls not use any cutting implements in building their wickiups.

It is beyond the scope of this book to attempt the task of Driver (1941), that is, to trace the dissemination of puberty rituals across cultural areas. The major point to obtain from this present discussion is that while Apache girls' puberty rites are unique in their inclusion and expression of particular rituals, similar puberty rituals are found in numerous other North American Indian cultures. Certainly this was a point emphasized in discussion of the widespread practice of puberty observances across cultural areas as illustrated in chapter 5. The significance of this point is reflected in a reoccurring theme of this book: pubescence is a meaningful phase of the life span according to North American Indian beliefs.

Girls' Perceptions of the Sunrise Dance

Of interest in this study were the perceptions, including comprehension, of initiates relative to the multitude of ritual activities of the Sunrise

Dance. In particular, in addressing understanding and comprehension, it is concluded that initiates (at least those interviewed) did not understand the words to the songs that are sung at their ceremonies. Further, it was apparent through both the interviews of the initiates and the opinion of the adult cultural experts that girls were not very well informed on the meaning and purposes of the Sunrise Dance and its rituals. Apache informants lamented this fact, and all agreed that girls would benefit further by knowing the words of the songs. Nonetheless, it was implied that the songs still have their spiritual impacts by virtue of one's being exposed to them, even in the absence of cognitive understanding and comprehension.

Initiates' most common sources of knowledge for the underlying meaning and significance of the Sunrise Dance appeared to be their medicine men, their godmothers, and other elders. For example, one informant stated that grandmothers frequently instruct initiates on the meaning of the ceremony and that this instruction continues long after the ceremony's conclusion. The medicine man bears a major responsibility in attempting to bring some translation to the meanings behind the rituals and the songs that initiates do not understand. A San Carlos medicine man explained how he provides girls with reasons for the dance and its purposes, such as to make them into strong women.

Initiates' lack of understanding of their oral history that is told in the songs at their ceremonies led me to question informants on whether there should be formal instruction through the school system about the Sunrise Dance. A San Carlos medicine man stated that while it is acceptable to teach the Apache language in school, it is not permissible to impart culture in this manner, because "we are not the ones who do the teaching, it is the spirit." This statement at first surprised me, but then I realized that according to a certain kind of logic his statements were understandable and meaningful. In many North American Indian belief systems, it is asserted that the spiritual beings determine who will be the recipient of certain spiritual power and knowledge. Further, this medicine man was essentially saying that matters of the spirit cannot be taught through formal education. Traditionally, instruction and learning occur both socially and through solitary activities, such as vision quests. It is not always necessary to possess understanding prior to engagement in a new task or spiritual venture, because comprehension that will emerge through experience and participation is regarded as the primary tool for learning. In contrast, in the Western orientation of learning, the strategy is to become intellectually immersed in a discipline prior to participation in it. For instance, formal instruction and study occur prior to the Jewish bar mitzvah or bat mitzvah and Protestant and Catholic confirmation—ceremonies that typically coincide with the pubertal years. But that is not the pattern of Native pedagogy, in which the strategy for acquisition of knowledge is through some instruction and mentorship, which coincides with engagement and participation.

A godmother who served as an informant in this study echoed this sentiment by stating that it is actually from the Sunrise Dance itself that girls learn its purposes and meanings. The cognitive reflection and reinforcement of comprehension occur during the days, weeks, and months afterward. An important variable to include in this discussion is the range of the ages of initiates. In my interviews of initiates, it was clearly evident that older girls (e.g., age 13 or 14) had greater understanding of the abstract dimensions of the ceremony than younger girls did (e.g., age 10, 11, or 12). In terms of cognitive development, younger girls are less experienced in formal operational or logical and abstract thought processes; hence, they are not as well equipped to comprehend the complex rituals that are laden with abstract meanings. It could be years before the full impact of the ceremony acquires greater meaning for them.

Lending support to the hypothesis that understanding comes after the actual ceremony, interestingly, the mothers of the initiates have rich and complex understanding of the multiple meanings and purposes behind the Sunrise Dance and of their traditional culture in general. What is surprising is that they acquired this knowledge in spite of the fact that none of them experienced the Sunrise Dance for themselves at puberty. As clearly indicated in an earlier section, 20 to 30 years previous (the time of pubescence for these mothers), the practice of the Sunrise Dance was less frequent. Clearly, these women found other means to become informed on the ways and manners of their traditional culture. Frequently cited as sources of this knowledge were mothers and grandmothers as well as other adult women who took on the responsibility of mentoring younger women. Additionally, some of the mothers in this study had served as godmothers for other girls. As discussed previously, it appears that serving in the godmother role is a tremendous source of experiential learning for adult women. Older women socialize younger women according to the responsibilities of assuming a godmother's role, and the medicine men instruct them at the time of the ceremony as they progress through the numerous rituals along with the young initiates. It could be speculated that, more so than the initiates, it is actually the godmothers who are beneficiaries of understanding at the time of the Sunrise Dance because of their more developed cognitive skills in contrast to the immaturity of their young pubescent charges.

Of additional interest were the actual perceptions of the initiates according to the experience of the Sunrise Dance. Initiates in this study reported mixed feelings prior to their Sunrise Dances, but after the fact all were pleased that they had undergone the experience. They knew beforehand that it would be rigorous and demanding, and they had fears about their performance of certain rituals. For instance, the parents of one initiate described their daughter's ambivalence:

> She was not to cut her hair, we told her no makeup and stuff like that, and she kept saying, "Well, I don't know if I want a Sunrise Dance." And then we explained to her about how it starts off with the first menstrual cycle, and then she says, "You mean everybody wants to know? I mean everybody's going to know?" . . . That's like the white person in her saying that. . . . And that's where we had to push—we started then thinking, getting a little bit stronger and thought, "Okay, we're going to go ahead and do this. We think she needs to know her culture."

Additional reactions reported by initiates of their thoughts and feelings prior to the Sunrise Dance included fear and nervousness; anticipation that dancing on their knees would be difficult; having to run back from the site of the men's sweat on the first day; dancing with the Mountain Spirit dancers; having to keep one's head up while being massaged; and just generally thinking it would be difficult.

Once girls began their Sunrise Dances, the feelings of anxiety and worry dissipated, as one initiate explained: "On Friday, before she dressed me and everything . . . I was kind of afraid. 'Can't it just be Monday,

Table 5. Difficult Components of the Sunrise Dance

- Not being able to touch one's body or hair
- Having to use the scratching stick
- Having to use the drinking tube
- Dancing on one's knees
- Having to keep one's head and chin up during the massage on the second morning
- Running back from the site of the men's sweat on the first day
- Having to get up early each morning
- Having to dance for a long time on the second evening
- Following the Mountain Spirit dancers during the dancing on the second evening
- Having to dance in inclement weather (e.g., heat, rain, etc.)

when it's over with?' Then, when she put everything on me, I felt like, really safe being there because everyone was like, protecting me. . . . I felt really respected from everyone that was there . . . and now, after it, I feel even more respected because they don't see me as a little girl anymore." During the 4 days of extensive rituals, girls appear to be caught up "in the moment" and likely find it difficult to ruminate on anticipated activities, but, retrospectively, they did report several difficult aspects of the dance (see Table 5). Clearly, the physical demands of the dance are challenging, as would be expected. Additionally, use of the scratching stick and drinking tube was reported to be awkward and uncomfortable.

In the final analysis, however, initiates were unanimous in their positive feelings after the dance. Some reported not wanting it to end, and a few even expressed a desire to experience it again. Initiates had several comments to make relative to the gratifying impacts of the Sunrise Dance (see Table 6). The sense of being empowered to the degree that others would seek their spiritual assistance was a novel and rewarding experience for initiates. Indeed, as an observer I found this to be an impressive component of the ceremony, because one does not typically find pubescent girls elevated to a status where people of all ages and both sexes are seeking their assistance.

Impacts of the Sunrise Dance on the Development of Contemporary Apache Girls

An adult informant remarked on her observations of initiates, "The fourth day they mature. They're very mature. They're not boisterous.

Table 6. Gratifying Aspects of the Sunrise Dance

- Felt good to be painted on Sunday morning because it had a cooling effect
- Enjoyed dancing with the Mountain Spirit dancers
- The knowledge that the dance was for herself and that other people were there to see her
- The knowledge that prayers could be said for others and believing that the prayers would be answered
- Enjoyed offering blessing to others
- Felt the spiritual nature of the event
- Enjoyed having the candy poured over her head
- Enjoyed cooking
- Enjoyed dancing
- Felt relief when it was over

They're not goofing around. . . . And by the end of the 4-day period, they rub that white paint off, and it's done. Then they start to realize what people try to tell them. And if all girls went through that, I think, the whole world would be in peace." This section explores the deeper impacts of the Sunrise Dance on the development of adolescent girls. The first section of this chapter addressed the broader purposes of Apache girls' puberty rites. Here we examine those and other purposes relative to contemporary Apache adolescent girls. The oral tradition of the Apaches specifies that numerous positive outcomes emerge from the Sunrise Dance, especially strength and protection to endure the challenges of life as well as success in negotiating the stages of life (e.g., Ganteaume, 1992; Mails, 1988; Stockel, 1991; Talamantez, 2000). For contemporary adolescents these impacts should be reflected in psychosocial adjustment and optimal identity formation. Examination of these and other impacts of the Sunrise Dance and puberty ceremonies of other North American Indian cultures have remained largely unexamined. One exception is Keith's (1964) study of the Navajo Kinaaldá, which examined the meaning of that event for adolescent girls. Keith noted that there were changes in girls' conceptions of themselves, according to their attitudes toward the self, home, and the opposite sex; their status in the family and community; their potential for health, beauty, and prosperity; and their actual behavior. In short, Keith's findings indicated that the self-concept is altered through the experience of a puberty rite, and it is speculated that similar impacts occur from the Sunrise Dance.

Basso (1966, 1970) recognized the Sunrise Dance as emphasizing four critical life objectives for girls: physical strength; an even temperament or good disposition; prosperity; and a sound, healthy old age. These are consistent with purposes of the Sunrise Dance that were identified previously, but they warrant more specific examination relative to the development of adolescent girls. Physical strength and—I would add—psychological strength are broadly desired traits of Apache women. The comment "life is hard for women" was quoted by numerous sources in this study, and certainly it was recognized in Basso's work among the Cibecue Apaches. Engagement in physically demanding labor is an implicit characteristic of Apache life, but so are the psychological demands of contemporary life. Rituals performed in the Sunrise Dance, such as the physically exhausting segments of dancing for hours and the psychological strain of being at "center stage" for several days, both test and build the strength of the young person. By successfully accomplishing this ceremony, it is believed, one's prospects for a long, healthy life are greatly increased. The initiate has proven that she can endure and has acquired strengths that will serve her well in the future.

Values of a good disposition and an even temperament are reflected in the rituals of the Sunrise Dance, both in Basso's work and in this study. Basso (1966) explained that these traits have the greatest impact on kinship values and the belief in witchcraft: "A highly esteemed person is one who is friendly, generous, and adroit enough to avoid situations which might result in interpersonal conflict. Such a person goes out of his way to mask signs of aggression, and is always reluctant to pry into other people's affairs" (p. 165). The individual with a good disposition is a helpful, responsible relative. A protection against the ill effects of others (relative or non-relative) is offered by keeping her relationships with relatives intact and harmonious. Elements of the initiate's costume are included to influence her absorption of traits illustrative of a good temperament. The yellow and black in the girl's traditional dress and the oriole feathers attached to the eagle feathers on her cane and used during her Sunrise Dance represent the value of an even temperament that will facilitate proper relationships with others, especially kin, and safeguard her from the dangerous effects of the ill intentions of others or witchcraft. The oriole is understood to be a happy, humble bird, and it is hoped that the girl will absorb the qualities of the oriole's good disposition in being a kind, hospitable, and generous person. Certainly the notion that the oriole serves as a role model was explained by informants in this study and is consistent with reports from the literature.

Prosperity is a further life objective identified by Basso (1966, 1970). Prosperity does not mean that the girl will acquire wealth exceeding that of others but rather that she—and ultimately her family—will have sufficient resources to manage the needs of life. As described by Basso, for Apaches, prosperity means freedom from hunger and periods of deprivation. This value is shown in the Sunrise Dance through the ritual of pouring the burden basket of candy over the initiate's head in phase 6 to bring good things to others. It also is observed in phase 8 when she shakes the blankets in the four directions at the closing of the second morning, which, among other meanings, is symbolic of always having enough to eat.

The fourth life objective—a long, healthy life—is achieved through the girl's establishment of good relations with the powers that can cause this to happen. As noted earlier, White Painted Woman is believed to be the major source of power at the initiate's disposal, and her transformation into this important being facilitates longevity. The proper performance of rituals by key individuals, such as the medicine man and the initiate, contributes to the establishment of proper relations with the supernatural powers. By virtue of participation in the Sunrise Dance, the initiate is believed to have acquired protection that will endure throughout her life span. Physical objects imbued with power (e.g., the cane she walks with during her ceremony and in old age, the eagle feathers in her hair and on the cane, and her wearing of the T-necklace described in the previous chapter) as well as her proper observance of taboos and performance of rituals, such as running through the four life stages in phase 4, will help to ensure longevity. In short, "By instructing the pubescent girl how to live safely in a world of threatening supernatural forces—by giving her power, and by stressing the need for prayers and taboo observance—na ih es shows her how this reward may be attained" (Basso, 1966, p. 162).

In addition to the four life objectives specified by Basso (1966, 1970), there are other implications of the Sunrise Dance relative to the development of Apache girls. Several adult informants, including parents of the initiates, noted that girls were more mature after their Sunrise Dances. The ceremony appears to be an accelerated course in growing up, and parents perceived that their daughters behaved with greater maturity and responsibility after their ceremonies. For instance, daughters were reported to be more helpful around the house, more responsible in their behavior, and more willing to complete tasks upon request. A medicine man offered an explanation for these observations, stating that the discipline girls are required to exhibit during the Sunrise Dance extends into their everyday lives.

It also appears that the ethnic identity of initiates is affected by the Sunrise Dance. It is undoubtedly an identity-shaping event, as related by Talamantez (2000), who interviewed Apache women from 10 to 75 years of age who perceived 'Isánáklésh as important to their identity. In the present study, when informants were asked about the positive outcomes of the Sunrise Dance, responses relevant to ethnic identity included the following: "to learn about her culture," "to have respect for her culture," "to feel better about herself," "to be proud of herself," "to know who she is as an Apache." Further, it is thought that the positive identifications girls form to their culture and tribe will be reflected in their service to others as they mature. An informant from Mescalero stated that the girls who experience puberty ceremonies are the ones who ultimately contribute to the welfare of the people and the tribe when they are older, such as serving as an announcer at tribal events.

Are girls who undergo the Sunrise Dance different from those who do not? In posing this question to initiates the answer was in the affirmative, but one girl observed: "Some are, but the ones that really didn't try during their Sunrise Dance, you could tell like, the way they turn out and stuff." Nonetheless, this question cannot be answered in the present study except with the general perceptions of informants. If a study could be conducted and girls were retrospectively compared on the basis of having or not having the Sunrise Dance, it would be difficult to isolate the impacts of the ceremony from the general effects of being reared in a traditional home. That is, are the positive impacts on adolescent development due to the Sunrise Dance as a single event? In addition to the dance itself, as is quite likely, these girls are raised in families that value their traditions and have been socializing their daughters accordingly from early childhood. As explained in the previous chapter, in childhood long before these ceremonies occur, adults socialize girls to be attuned to their cultures; and the Sunrise Dance subsequently reinforces and builds on earlier learning and experiences. In addition, the fact that families are willing to extend themselves financially and physically to conduct the ceremony alludes to both the sense of importance of both their daughters and their culture. It is unknown whether families of higher income are more likely to sponsor these ceremonies but, if that were the case, then income would also need to be considered as a causal factor in girls' outcomes in addition to the Sunrise Dance. However, I have observed families of little income somehow locating the means to conduct the Sunrise Dance when it was deemed important to them. The point is that it would be difficult to isolate the Sunrise Dance as a single factor of impact due to a combination of intertwining sources of socialization and possibly demographic and income factors. In short, the Sunrise Dance is embedded in a social context that values traditional cultural beliefs, values, and practices, all of which are quite likely reinforced in girls throughout childhood, over the course of their Sunrise Dances, and for years to come.

Taking into account the scope of socialization of traditional Apache culture that occurs during the Sunrise Dance, this ritual represents a remarkable 4 days that really begins some months previous. The overwhelming show of support to initiates, the lavish attention that is paid to them, and the empowerment that must be felt through immersion in a sequence of culturally validated events—all these must have some remarkable consequences for initiates. In the figure of White Painted Woman, girls have a role model of endurance and strength. Their emulation of this figure signifies the belief that these components of her character will become part of their lives.

Summary

The purpose of this chapter was to bring meaning and understanding to the descriptions of the Apache Sunrise dance (both Western and Mescalero versions) given in the previous chapter. Clearly, puberty rites of

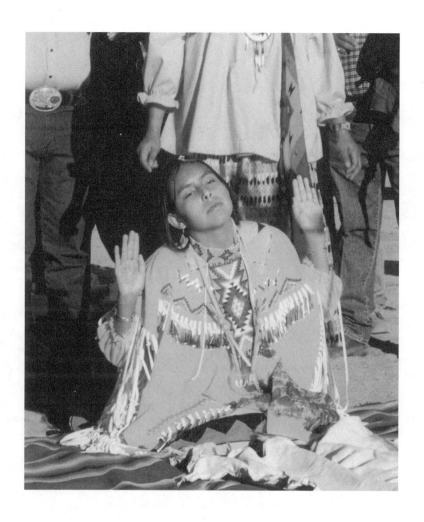

1. Apache initiate during sitting or kneeling (*niztah*) phase

2. *(left)* Apache initiate during lying (*nizti*) phase

3. *(above)* Candy being poured over the head of Apache initiate (*sha nał dihl*)

4. *(top left)* Apache initiate being painted on the third morning, with Mountain Spirit Dancer

5. *(bottom left)* Apache initiate having her face wiped by her godmother after being painted on the third morning

6. *(above)* Apache initiate with her partner after being painted on the third morning

7. *(left)* The author with friend Sadie Kniffin at Sunrise Dance at San Carlos

8. *(above)* Elizabeth Compton, research assistant, visiting with an initiate and other girls

9. *(above)* Corn batter placed in the ground in preparation for all-night baking of *'alkąąd* at a Navajo Kinaaldá

10. *(top right)* Navajo initiate having her hair combed in a ritual manner

11. *(bottom right)* Navajo initiate being massaged and shaped by her mentor, who is called the "Ideal Woman"

girls had great significance in the past and have amazingly endured to the present. Having experienced a resurgence (reported in San Carlos), the Sunrise Dance has emerged as the central ceremonial activity of the Western Apache people. The endurance of the Sunrise Dance over time can be explained by the fact that it serves multiple functions and purposes. It affirms and validates the importance of women in the matrilineal Apache culture and demonstrates the belief of Apaches that proper socialization of children, especially at pubescence, is critical for a beneficial life course. However, the purposes of the Sunrise Dance extend far beyond the initiate and her family: the ceremony is meaningful for the Apache people and the world in which they live. It appears to be as relevant today as it was in the past, and in all likelihood it will continue to serve important functions in the future. The Sunrise Dance encompasses traditions entrenched in oral traditions and origin stories and connects the Apache people to their culture's values, beliefs, and history. Yet, it is a fluid ceremony that has been adapted in its purpose and form to contemporary issues of concern for the development of young women. It is this expression of flexibility and creativity on the part of the Apache people that perhaps accounts for the fact that the Sunrise Dance has endured over time and will likely be a part of their future.

CHAPTER EIGHT

Contemporary Navajo, Lakota, and Ojibwa Puberty Customs

□   □   □

The two previous chapters contained detailed description and interpretation of historical and contemporary practices of the Apache Sunrise Dance. A depth of analysis was applied to carefully interpret the meaning and symbolism of the complex rituals that make up the Sunrise Dance. This ceremony of long historical duration was shown to be highly significant within Apache culture, with anticipated impacts extending far beyond the coming-of-age of an initiate. The present chapter continues in a similar manner with illustrations of contemporary puberty customs of Navajo, Lakota, and Ojibwa cultures. The customs of these cultures are embedded in ancient oral traditions and have shown continuance of practice, in some forms, to the present day. The Navajo coming-of-age ceremony, Kinaaldá, like the Apache Sunrise Dance, provides an illustration from the Southwest cultural area. The Lakota Ishna Ta Awi Cha Lowan is an illustration of coming-of-age in the Plains cultural area, and the Ojibwa coming-of-age ceremony, sometimes called the Womanhood Ceremony, represents an event from the Northeast Woodlands. Interestingly, the puberty customs of the bands of the Ojibwa informants in this study appeared to possess stronger similarity to those of the Subarctic cultural area than to other tribes of the Northeast, a factor that was most likely due to geographic proximity to the Subarctic (see chapter 5). While some additional North American Indian cultures continue to recognize and celebrate the coming-of-age of young women, the four cultures addressed in greater detail in this book were selected, in part, for pragmatic reasons.[1] Specifically, Indigenous and scholarly sources of literature were available to draw on relative to these practices, and, in the case of Apache, Navajo, and Ojibwa cultures, it was possible to conduct fieldwork that was facilitated by key individuals and leaders in these tribes and bands.

Navajo Kinaaldá

The Navajo Reservation is geographically the largest in the United States and encompasses lands in New Mexico, Arizona, and Utah in the Four Corners region. In 2000, 269,202 individuals identified solely as Navajo (U.S. Census Bureau, 2002), and approximately two-thirds of that number resided on the Navajo Nation (U.S. Census Bureau, 2000c). Navajos are currently the second-largest tribe in population (following combined numbers of Eastern and Western bands of Cherokee). Navajos are a Southern Athabascan culture, as are their relatives the Apaches. These Apachean groups migrated to the Southwest from the Subarctic somewhere around the middle of the 14th century or slightly later (Dutton, 1983). Distinct groups evolved that are known today as Navajos and the various groups of Apaches (i.e., Western, Mescalero, Jicarilla, Kiowa, and Lipan).

The following description and discussion of the Navajo Kinaaldá is adapted, in part, from Markstrom and Iborra (2003), an article that contained results of my fieldwork on the Navajo Nation. In addition, works of several authors on the topic are cited, including those of Navajo authors (i.e., Beck et al., 1996; Begay, 1983; Roessel, 1981; Woody et al., 1981). The field research is based on attendance at two Kinaaldá ceremonies in 1999 and 2001; however, I have attended many other Kinaaldá ceremonies since that time. The two initiates were second cousins on their maternal side, and their ceremonies occurred at the same rural compound of their grandparents, who lived on the Navajo Nation. The initiate of the 1999 Kinaaldá was 13 years old and had experienced menarche 1 month prior to the ceremony. The initiate at the 2001 Kinaaldá was 12 years old at the time, and the ceremony was planned to occur during her second menstrual cycle. Both girls and their families lived in towns apart from the rural setting of their grandparents (see Markstrom & Iborra, 2003, for further details on the participants). In addition to attending these Kinaaldá, I obtained information through numerous informal discussions with Navajo colleagues and friends, as well as attendance at various ceremonial and cultural activities that began during my 1999 research leave on the Navajo Nation and has continued with numerous follow-up visits.

The girls' puberty ceremony, or Kinaaldá, is clearly embedded in the Navajos' complex system of beliefs surrounding their origins and their relationships with a pantheon of supernatural figures, called the Diyin Dine'é (Holy People). The Diyin Dine'é play central roles in the broad range of Navajo ceremonials that center on curing, purifying, and blessing. The Blessing Way complex of ceremonies, of which the Kinaaldá is part, encompasses celebrations and demonstrations of appreciation for all forms of goodness and beauty. Within the Blessing Way the desired state of *hózhó* is perpetuated—a state of harmony, balance, well-being, and normality (Woody et al., 1981). It is significant that the Blessing Way, and particularly the Kinaaldá, occurs in the context of the hogan or home where all blessings associated with events of family life are represented (Woody et al., 1981). The Kinaaldá is said to be the original of the foundational Blessing Way complex of ceremonies (Frisbie, 1993; Roessel, 1981; Woody et al., 1981), as well as the most important (Lincoln, 1991).

In speaking of the Diyin Dine'é, Changing Woman (Asdzáá Nádleehé) is one of the most important figures and is significant in a variety of ceremonies, but especially the Kinaaldá. According to Navajo oral tradition, Changing Woman was found by First Man and First Woman on Gobernador Knob—a geographical site just to the east of the present-day location of the Navajo Nation. It is stated that the first Kinaaldá was formulated by the Diyin Dine'é especially for Changing Woman on the twelfth day of her life when she reached womanhood (Roessel, 1981). This rite (as well as the character of Changing Woman) serves as an example for all Navajo women to follow. The significance of Changing Woman's Kinaaldá cannot be understated. It was found to be the most common theme in Dickinson's (2000) statistical dissection of Frisbie's (1993) summary of 19 anthropological reports on Kinaaldá. In this light, meticulous efforts are taken to follow teachings of the Diyin Dine'é to replicate the highly symbolic rituals of the first Kinaaldá.

Changing Woman is a complex, multifaceted figure and encompasses multiple purposes, including her role as mother of the Hero Twins, who ultimately rid the world of monsters or evil (observe commonalities with the Apaches' creation story related in chapter 6). She is said to have created the Navajos from peelings off the skin of her body, and gave them the original Blessing Way rite. Changing Woman possesses the persona of a Mother Earth–type figure as one who creates and regulates all forms of life, such as fertility in humans and the annual rejuvenation of the Earth as shown through the change of seasons. As a metaphor of her Mother Earth persona, rivers and streams are said to be her veins, and her sensibilities can be offended when people engage in destructive practices toward the Earth. Perhaps most importantly, Changing Woman is regarded as the ultimate mother and demonstrates traits of unwavering goodness, kindness, and nurturance (see Beck et al., 1996; Frisbie, 1993; Hirschfelder & Molin, 2001; Lincoln, 1991; Moon, 1984; Reichard, 1977; Schwarz, 1997). Gill (1987) identified Changing Woman as inseparable from Navajo creation but clarified that she is not regarded as the cosmic creator. As well, he noted her benevolent nature, in contrast to the mixed intentions of other Navajo supernatural beings. Certainly the name of Changing Woman is indicative of the cycles of change that she undergoes—"She is time, the force of the temporal process. She is life and the power of life" (Gill, 1987, p. 4).

Oral tradition states that Changing Woman instructed the Navajo people that Kinaaldá should coincide with girls' first and second menstrual cycles (Begay, 1983). Consistent with this belief, some traditional Navajos have told me that it is desirable for girls to experience the Kinaaldá at both the first and second menstrual cycles, because this is the time of their greatest empowerment. In its ideal form, Kinaaldá should be 4 days in length, but I have been told of 2-day versions that occur over weekends.[2] This abbreviated version certainly represents a change in Kinaaldá to adapt to modern-day requirements of school attendance. Some families also opt to sponsor their daughter's Kinaaldá not at the first or second menses but at a time when school schedules permit 4 continuous days of recess, such as on holidays and during the summer.

The purposes of Kinaaldá are parallel in many respects to those of other North American Indian cultures as delineated in chapter 3. As with other puberty ceremonies, Kinaaldá is a celebration of an important life transition from childhood to adolescence or adulthood. Kinaaldá serves to firmly embed the initiate into the context of kin and culture, and numerous rituals reinforce values of connection and social responsibility. As with Apache culture, shaping the girl's physical and psychological traits is of particular importance in rituals requiring physical actions or manipulations (i.e., molding, hair washing, painting, running, and corn grinding in the case of Navajos). Another parallel with Apache culture is the goal of transcendence to Changing Woman (White Painted Woman) and the incorporation of an identity that is reflective of the qualities of this personage of oral tradition. Through such an impressive connection with this being, longevity, strength, and protection can be secured for the girl's future, and blessings become accessible to others.

It is of further significance that Navajos regard Kinaaldá as the most important personality-shaping event in a woman's life, and it is believed to set her life course (Frisbie, 1993; Keith, 1964). In particular, it is a ceremony that reinforces the feminine side of the personality, but it should be noted that both masculine and feminine aspects of the personality are equally valued in Navajo culture (Moon, 1984). Certainly, Kinaaldá, like other coming-of-age ceremonies, can be said to be an important identity-shaping event in the life of young Navajo women, particularly with respect to social and ethnic forms of identity.

Traditional families begin to think about their daughters' Kinaaldá from birth. Hence, the ceremony encompasses much more than a 4-day sequence of rituals at menarche. As described in Markstrom and Iborra (2003), one Navajo mother asserted that preparations for her daughters' Kinaaldá ceremonies began early in their lives. A girl who is raised in the traditional fashion will be exposed to the ceremonies of her older sisters and female cousins, as well as numerous other customs, beliefs, and ceremonies of her culture. When menarche occurs, as Keith (1964) explained, "Kinaaldá is a summary, or way of giving meaning to skills and values learned gradually in childhood" (p. 35). The performance of rituals throughout the 4 days reinforces tasks learned in childhood and educates the girl on the meaning and importance of these skills and tasks relative to adult roles (Keith, 1964).

Separation signals the onset of the ceremony, but Kinaaldá does not require complete seclusion or isolation of the initiate as in some cultures, at least not in present-day Navajo culture (e.g., see Leighton & Kluckhohn, 1947). Rather, separation is shown by the special clothing worn by the initiate, her physical proximity to the hogan (the traditional Navajo ceremonial structure representative of the home), and various rituals that situate her current state distinct from earlier states. Specialized dressing of the initiate resembles that of Changing Woman and was shown to be the second most frequently cited occurrence in Dickinson's (2000) analysis of Frisbie (1993). Donning of special clothing occurs on the first day when her hair is tied back with a strip of hide from a fawn and she dresses in a velveteen or satin skirt and blouse, deerskin leggings, moccasins, and turquoise and silver jewelry. A shawl also is worn at significant times during the ceremony. Interestingly, across three age groups, informants from Frisbie (1993) stated that the features they disliked most about Kinaaldá were the hot clothes, the heavy clothes, and the heavy jewelry.

In addition to her stylized appearance, the Navajo initiate is subjected to various rituals that heighten her separated status and induce transformation to occur. Consistent with the beliefs about pubescent girls presented in chapter 3, Navajos believe that the girl's body and psyche are especially malleable, similar to a newborn, and it is important to maximize such an opportunity to set her future life course (Lincoln, 1991; Schwarz, 1997). In Navajo tradition, the bodily manipulations indicate that the girl is affected in the four areas of her being—spiritual, emotional, intellectual, and physical. The ultimate event that transpires over the 4 days of rituals of molding and shaping is her transformation into Changing Woman (Beck et al., 1996; Schwarz, 1997).

Markstrom and Iborra (2003) identified five types of physical actions or manipulations—molding, hair washing, painting, running, and corn grinding—and placed them in the separation and transition phases of the Dunham et al. Ritual Process Paradigm RPP (see chapter 6). While these five are not the only physical actions, they appear to be the most prominent. As in other pubertal coming-of-age events, the initiate's family selects an adult female mentor who, in this case, is called the Ideal Woman (Begay, 1983; Schwarz, 1997). Her character, physical strength and health, physical beauty, and demonstration of accomplishments are all traits that are desired to be impressed on initiates. She may possess special talents, such as rug weaving or sheepherding. Above all, the Ideal Woman follows the traditions of Navajo culture and, presumably, has an established linkage with Changing Woman that permits her to be the liaison between the initiate and Changing Woman. As with the case of the Apache girl and her mentor, the Navajo girl identifies with the mentor, but this is best conceived as "identification by absorption" (Reichard, 1977). That is, the actions performed on the initiate by the Ideal Woman serve to reshape and remold her in the image of her mentor and ultimately Changing Woman.

During the molding or shaping ritual, the initiate passively lies on layered blankets and sheepskins, and the Ideal Woman massages every part of her body (Kinaaldá yik'ąąs). Both physical and psychological attributes are believed to be transferred in this ritual. As a purification rite, the Ideal Woman ceremonially washes the initiate's hair and jewelry with yucca plant in the highly symbolic Navajo basket (ts'aa).[3] The initiate's mother is given the rinse water to pour out near the doorway of their home so that her daughter will always be connected to home. The initiate is also painted on her face with white clay, which serves a purpose of minimizing signs of physical aging and increasing her height (Frisbie, 1993).

More physically challenging rituals of the Kinaaldá are running and corn grinding. Dickinson (2000) reported the racing or running ritual to be the third most frequently cited event concerning Kinaaldá. For the 4 days of their ceremony, the initiate must run two or three times a day, depending on local customs. The run is both an endurance test and an activity that will have a beneficial impact on her future. Each run is to be longer than all previous runs, and the length of the run is predictive of the quality and longevity of her life. Running at this time in her life span is thought to build strength and to prepare her for life's adversities. These actions are reflective of the belief noted in chapter 3 that actions at puberty affect the future of the initiate. Reichard (1977) linked the girl's running or racing to Changing Woman at her Kinaaldá and stated that it represents strength and fortitude. Others at her Kinaaldá run with the initiate, usually children and women, and they shout to capture the attention of the Diyin Dine'é on behalf of the initiate, who herself is to remain quiet. The running ritual is modeled after that of Changing Woman, who, according to oral tradition, ran in four directions at her Kinaaldá. It is most common for present-day initiates to run only to the east and then return. Those running with her cannot pass her, and those who can run no further are to stop and must wait for the initiate to pass them on her return before resuming the run back to the hogan.

Corn grinding serves as a physical action on the part of initiates that is a demonstration of role performance; more pragmatically, however, the ground corn will serve as an ingredient in the highly meaningful corn cake (*'alkąąd*). Informants have told me that, in the past, girls were required to grind all of the corn for the cake—a major task according to my observation that the amount of corn required, at least today, would fill a 30-gallon plastic bag. In current times, girls grind part of the corn, more for ceremonial purposes, and most of the corn is ground commercially.

The preparation and baking of the round corn cake is a focal point of the Kinaaldá and represents the most important aspects of the ceremony (Schwarz, 1997). The cake is a metaphor for Changing Woman, and the pubescent is to emulate the traits of this important personage. It is reflective of a solar image and is baked in the ground (womb of the Earth) as an offering to the Sun (Lincoln, 1991). Schwarz (1997) stated that the corn cake is the dominant symbol of this rite of passage and that it summarizes the most important aspects of the ceremony, namely, "physical fitness, endurance, education, reciprocity, and the maximizing of potential positive effects" (p. 203). Corn is highly symbolic of food, fertility, life, and altruistic sacrifice in a variety of North American Indian cultures (as discussed in chapter 4). At her Kinaaldá, the girl, in a highly symbolic sense, represents (and becomes) the corn and the cake that, according to Witherspoon (1977), is representative of her fertility. Furthermore, she is not allowed to eat the cake (because she is the cake), and she serves it to others to demonstrate her understanding and acceptance of the female role of sustenance provider (Schwarz, 1997). A parallel theme can be observed between the significance of corn in the Navajo Kinaaldá and buffalo in the Ishna Ta Awi Cha Lowan (see next section).

Preparation of the corn cake encompasses many rituals of great consequence that surround its baking and distribution to the gathering of people. It is ideally made from ground yellow corn, with ground white corn placed on top as a final seal or blessing. White corn is associated with male fertility and yellow with female fertility—items and concepts that are representative of matters of complementarity and balance that are so foundational to Navajo beliefs. It is very important that the cake emerge properly baked from its clay oven in the earth; therefore, all those who participate in the Kinaaldá must adhere to important rules. Men and women must be sexually abstinent during the 4 days of the ceremony and wives and husbands are to refrain from touching each other during that time frame—either at the site of the Kinaaldá or elsewhere. One is to be careful to not ridicule others and must show restraint in joking or laughter. The cake, as well, must be assembled in the prescribed manner, with the layered corn husks placed on the top and bottom of the batter following a sunwise (east to west) direction in their placement.

Relative to the RPP, Markstrom and Iborra (2003) described movement from the deliberate separation rituals of Kinaaldá to the transformative event of the third night (or fourth night depending on local custom) that consists of an all-night sing under the direction of a *hataali* (singer or medicine person).[4] This event taxes the girl's energy, because she is required to remain awake and alert the entire night. The sing is a culmination or a spiritual affirmation of previous events that have transpired, and is referred to as Kinaaldá Bik'i Doo Lighaasha Da, or "The Pubescent Girl's All-Night Ceremony" (Begay, 1983). It occurs in the hogan, where, according to Lincoln (1991), the girl's identification with Changing Woman becomes complete. The all-night sing is significant, as evidenced by its placement as fourth most frequently cited event mentioned in anthropological reports of the Kinaaldá (Dickinson, 2000).

In the early evening of the third day the girl usually rests, but later in the evening the *hataali* announces the beginning of the sing, and the girl, her family, and guests enter the hogan. The following sequence of events of the all-night sing is drawn primarily from Begay (1983). As the first act after guests gather, the hogan is blessed with corn pollen. The initiate is instructed to walk clockwise around the hogan, and she is then blessed with corn pollen while the *hataali* prays. At this point the pouch of corn pollen is passed around for everyone to partake in a blessing.

The singing begins with a set of 12 "Hogan Songs," or Hooghan Biyiin, which are considered the most sacred songs of the ceremony. After these are sung, a short break may be taken with snacks served and then singing resumes until shortly prior to sunrise. Between sets of songs during the all-night sing, it was heartening to listen to the practical advice given by the *hataali* to the initiate, such as to finish all of her education prior to marriage.

After the all-night sing, the final morning of Kinaaldá culminates in several rituals. The Ideal Woman prepares the yucca plant with water in the ceremonial basket (*ts'aa*) and then washes the girl's hair along with her jewelry. The jewelry is placed back on the initiate, and she sets out on her last run to the east, prior to sunrise, with wet hair. Upon her return, several other rituals ensue that are indicative of the reinforcement phase of the RPP and are suggestive of a shared belief in the power of the pubescence. She is massaged by her mentor while lying on top of the blankets and sheepskins of onlookers, and it is thought that the owners of these items will be blessed by virtue of their physical contact with the initiate. As well, on the stack of blankets on which she is shaped, people place various personal objects that are meaningful to them or are representative of something they wish to have blessed in their lives, such as wallets and purses (representative of material needs), keys to cars and homes (to be blessed), and musical instruments and games (presumably to become more proficient). These items also were placed in the hogan during the all-night sing. After she is molded, the initiate now performs a ritual on others called "stretching," whereby she runs both of her hands on the sides of their bodies in a fast upward motion. The children are stretched so they will have good lives and grow tall, and adults also may be stretched because it is believed that her touch will bring blessings into their lives. In a further demonstration that affects the initiate and others, ashes from the bark of an aspen tree are painted on her cheeks and forehead with the intent to make her skin stay smooth and free from wrinkles. She then paints the ashes on the faces of others to bring blessings to them.

One of the last public acts of the Kinaaldá ceremony is the cutting and distribution of the corn cake. During the all-night sing the corn cake bakes in a clay oven carved in a space in the ground that lies to the east of the opening of the hogan. In a demonstration of generosity and thanks, the initiate gives pieces of the cake to all in attendance, along with other gifts. The *hataali* typically receives the prime cut of cake out of the center (Begay, 1983). Puberty ceremonies are key opportunities to assign a new name, and I observed this to occur at one Kinaaldá. Certainly the transitional phase of development, the successful completion of challenging rituals, and the initiate's association with Changing Woman justify the assignment of a new name. The act signifies to the recipient as well as her social network that an important transformation has occurred (Alford, 1988). A name change can also bring about changes in identity and may serve as a culminating act of reincorporation at the end of a rite of passage. Indeed, it was explained in chapter 5 that boys might earn a new name after a successful vision quest. The name assigned after completion of a particularly meaningful ritual or ceremonial event is typically one that is secretive, known only by a few close associates, and used only for sacred purposes.

Several statements made in the previous chapter on the Apache Sunrise Dance are applicable to the Navajo Kinaaldá. The matrilineal and matrilocal qualities of both of these cultures perhaps contribute to the continuance of girls' puberty ceremonies into the present day. An interpretation is offered that in both the Kinaaldá and the Sunrise Dance, the matrilineage can be conceived as a line of continuity that extends from Changing Woman or White Painted Woman, respectively, to the female mentor, and ultimately to the initiate. Regarding Navajos, Witherspoon (1977) discussed the relevance of Kinaaldá according to critical concepts of mother and child. The Earth is called mother, corn is called mother, and sheep are called mother—entities all sharing characteristics of source, sustenance, and reproduction. The Kinaaldá, then, gains particular meaning as an event that ensures continuity of the Navajo people because the initiate is transformed into Changing Woman. Hence, Changing Woman, who has aged, is now once again young and is brought into the presence of the gathering, a very similar concept to that of White Painted Woman in Apache culture. All the blessings of life, including new and renewed life, are made possible through the perpetual return of Changing Woman. Hence, the youth, vitality, and fertility of the initiate represent potentials for the ongoing regeneration, continuation, and preservation of her group.

Lakota Ishna Ta Awi Cha Lowan

Oceti Šakowin, or the Seven Fireplaces, have been known as the Sioux since 1640.[5] Actually, the term *Sioux* is a linguistic alteration of the Algonquian term *nadowe-is-iw-ug*, which means "little adder" (W. K. Powers, 1977). The three major divisions of the Sioux are the easternmost Santee, the Yankton, and the westernmost Teton. The language dialects of these three divisions are Dakota, Nakota, and Lakota, respectively, but Nakota adopted the Dakota dialect in the mid-1800s. The seven fireplaces consist of the Santee divisions of Mdewakanton, Wahpeton, Sisseton, and Wahpekute, the Yankton divisions of Yankton and Yanktonais, and the Teton division of Oglala, Sicangu, Hunkpapa, Mnikowoju, Sihasapa, Oohenunpa, and Itazipco (the Teton division was one fireplace). Most of the authors cited in this section referred exclusively to Lakota culture, so this signifier is most commonly applied. However, similar customs have also occurred in Nakota and Dakota cultures, and these are presented.

Today the Sioux are one of the ten largest American Indian tribal groupings; 108,272 persons identified solely as Sioux in the 2000 census (U.S. Census Bureau, 2002). Sioux reservations are located in South Dakota, North Dakota, Minnesota, Nebraska, and Montana. In Canada, Dakota bands are located in the provinces of Manitoba and Saskatchewan. Indian and Northern Affairs Canada (2004) estimated that 10,570, or 2.4% of the registered Indian population, were Dakota (based on 1991 Statistics Canada data). Traditionally, there is evidence that, of the Sioux, at least the Lakotas were matrilineal (M. N. Powers, 1986) with residence patterns tending toward patrilocal, but the latter was not a fixed rule (DeMallie, 2001a, 2001b).

The oral history of the Sioux is fundamental to understanding any aspect of their ceremonial lives, including the girls' puberty ceremony (Ishna Ta Awi Cha Lowan or Išnati Ca Lowan or Išnati Awicalowanpi). *Išnati* literally means "to dwell alone," and it refers both to the act of menstruation and to the isolation of women during their menstrual cycles (M. N. Powers, 1986). To situate the cultural context of this ceremony, a brief synopsis of oral history according to various sources is provided in the following paragraphs.

In the 18th century the Sioux were displaced by the Ojibwas from the woodlands of the Great Lakes region and moved west to the prairies. To help them through this difficult time of transition, Lakota oral tradition tells of the coming of White Buffalo Calf Woman (St. Pierre & Long Soldier, 1995). She was a female spiritual figure who provided guidance to the Sioux for the future and brought them the sacred pipe. The Sioux are a profoundly spiritual people, and the story of White Buffalo Woman is particularly poignant. She is commonly viewed as a female messiah, but she also encompasses the ideals of womanhood and serves as a role model for women. Some have even viewed White Buffalo Calf Woman as the coming of the Virgin Mary to the Lakotas (St. Pierre & Long Soldier, 1995), a parallel indicated in the previous chapter relative to White Painted Woman of the Apaches. There are various versions of the story from which the following is derived (primarily from St. Pierre & Long Soldier, 1995, with contributions from J. E. Brown, 1953/1989; Neihardt, 1932/1959; M. N. Powers, 1986; and W. K. Powers, 1977):

The story begins at the camp of Standing Walking Buffalo of the Itazipco or Sans Arc band. The band was experiencing hard times because of a lack of buffalo near their village. The chief selected two young men to scout for the buffalo. After searching for some time, the young men saw something moving far off on the prairie. When they drew closer, they saw that it was a beautiful young woman who was naked and had long hair that covered her body (some versions say that she wore a white buckskin dress). She carried sage in her hands and a bundle on her back. One of the young men recognized the woman as sacred, or Wakan, and averted his gaze to not look upon her naked body.

The other man thought that he might have sex with this woman, and there was no one to protect her from him. The sacred woman could read his thoughts and invited him to come forward. The man went forward and she acted as if to lie with him, but then they were covered by a mist. The other young man was amazed and heard the sounds of locusts from the cloud. When the cloud lifted, all that was left of the bad man was his skeleton encompassed by snakes. The good man was frightened, but the sacred woman reassured him, knowing the kind of man he was. She told him to inform the village of her impending visit and to prepare a big tepee for her. She would bring a sacred relic to the village.

The good man ran back to his village and informed others of her coming and what had happened to the other young man. The leader, Standing Walking Buffalo, believed the young man's account and urged others to prepare the village for the sacred woman's visit. They watched the beautiful woman come across the prairie on the next day, and as she came she sang:

> *With visible breath I am walking*
> *A voice I am sending as I walk.*
> *In a sacred manner I am walking.*
> *With visible tracks I am walking.*
> *In a sacred manner I walk.*

The people demonstrated respect by dressing in their finest buckskins, and the men did not look on her nakedness. She communicated to the people that she had been sent by the Buffalo Nation and that she would give them instructions on how to live. She gave the chief a sacred pipe and told the people that their voices would be heard by Wakan-Tanka. She told the people that if they followed her advice and lived with respect for one another, they would always have plenty. She gave many specific instructions to the men, to the women, to the boy children, and to the girl children. She told the women that they were to remember her in the White Buffalo Calf (coming-of-age) Ceremony and the Throwing of the Ball Ceremony. She said that following these rituals would enable women to have good lives. She taught the people about all of the seven sacred rites or ceremonies to be practiced by the Lakotas.

White Buffalo Calf Woman stayed with the people for four more days and continued to teach them many things. On her last day, she lit the pipe and smoked it. She offered the pipe to the sky, then to the east, south, north, and west, and then to Mother Earth. She then gave the pipe to Standing Walking Buffalo.

As she walked away from the camp, she rolled on the ground

like a buffalo and turned into a red and brown buffalo calf. She
rolled again and turned into a white buffalo calf. This was followed by her rolling again and turning into a black buffalo calf.
The buffalo then bowed to each quarter of the universe and then
disappeared. That was the last people saw her, but the pipe still
remains with the Sans Arcs people on the Cheyenne River Reservation in South Dakota.

Perhaps St. Pierre and Long Soldier (1995) encapsulate the essence of
this story most poignantly: "This is the most powerful story in Lakota
religious life . . . the core is always the same, involving bravery and long-
suffering, generosity, humility, honesty, and respect for all things in creation. Each aspect of the story has meaning . . . the woman's age, beauty,
virginity, and apparent defenselessness, the death of the immoral hunter,
and the respect shown to her in the camp of Standing Walking Buffalo. Other values taught or reinforced by her, such as industry, humility, proper parenting, and vanity, are still influencing Lakota belief and
behavior" (p. 41).

White Buffalo Calf Woman and the seven sacred rites are most commonly discussed in connection with the Lakotas, who are said to hold
the sacred calf bundle to this day on the Cheyenne River Reservation in
South Dakota. The sacred rites brought by White Buffalo Calf Woman
include the Sweat Lodge, or Inipi; Crying for a Vision, or Hanbleceya;
Keeping of the Soul, or Wanagi Yuhapi; Ceremony of First Menses or
Ceremony of Isolation, or Ishna Ta Awi Cha Lowan; Making of Relatives, or Hunkapi; Sun Dance, or Wiwanyag Wachapi; and Throwing of
the Ball, or Tapa Wanka Yap. Along with the Ishna Ta Awi Cha Lowan,
the Hunkapi and Tapa Wanka Yap appear to have some connection to
the coming-of-age of girls.

The Making of Relatives (Hunkapi) ceremony serves as a mechanism
to create kin in the absence of biological or marriage ties. As explained by
Black Elk in J. E. Brown (1953/1989), this is a threefold rite that encompasses the first peace between humans and Wakan Tanka. It is this peace
that serves as the model for all other relationships. The second peace is
a relationship that is formed between two humans, and the third peace
is that which occurs between nations. The first peace, however, is fun-

damental to any other forms of peace or relationships that are created. Hunkapi has been described in the context of the present-day puberty ceremony for girls (St. Pierre & Long Soldier, 1995) or as a modern-day form of initiation for young people (W. K. Powers, 2000). This application will be discussed in greater detail in a later section.

The Throwing of the Ball (Tapa Wanka Yap) ceremony diminished in practice and was probably nonexistent for some time, but it was reinstated among the Lakotas in the 1990s (W. K. Powers, 2000). Black Elk described it in J. E. Brown (1953/1989) as a sacred game that young people played that represented the course of a man's life, but more importantly, reflected the integration and wholeness of Heaven and Earth. After explaining the rites associated with the game, Black Elk offered an interpretation: "First, it is a little girl, and not an older person, who stands at the center and who throws the ball. This is as it should be, for just as Wakan-Tanka is eternally youthful and pure, so is this little one who has just come from Wakan-Tanka, pure and without any darkness" (p. 137). It is said that an innocent child should throw the ball so that he or she would not favor anyone in throwing it in a particular direction (M. N. Powers, 1986). W. K. Powers (1977) indicated the close relationship between humans and buffalo in this game as it appeared in the initial vision with a buffalo calf growing into a human. Specifically, the girl tossed a ball made of buffalo hide stuffed with buffalo hair into a herd of buffalo that subsequently turned into humans. DeMallie (2001b) stated that Tapa Wanka Yap originated with the puberty ceremony, when girls would toss the ball in the four directions, but M. N. Powers (1986) asserted that the ball was to be thrown by a child prior to puberty. At any rate, an illustration is provided in a later section to show some version of this rite occurring during a girl's Ishna Ta Awi Cha Lowan.

Noted Dakota Sioux Charles Eastman (Ohiyesa) (1911) discussed another ceremony that announced the marriageability and chastity of young women, called Feast of Virgins. It is unclear from reading Eastman's work how Feast of Virgins might have been connected to the seven sacred rites, including the puberty rite, but it is mentioned here because it was a ceremony associated with youth. The event occurred in midsummer when several clans came together. Initially, a public announcement would be made on behalf of a particular girl who was indicating her intent to affirm her virtue. Other young women in the same status were invited to join her in the event. Apparently, this was not a trivial occurrence, as noted by Eastman, who stated that its importance was considered next to the Sun Dance and the Great Medicine Dance. Around a heart-shaped rock that had been marked with red paint, the maidens formed an inner circle and their grandmothers or chaperones formed an outer circle. Any man could challenge the virtue of any girl at this point, but false accusers were severely reprimanded. Each girl would touch the rock to signify her virginity and a promise to remain so until marriage. Maidens could repeat this ceremony on multiple occasions. A similar ceremony was held for young men, who were held to an even stronger code of conduct to have not even spoken of love to a woman. According to Eastman, a young man should not have spoken to any young woman beyond his sister until he gained distinction in battle and had been invited to sit on the council. M. N. Powers (1986) told of a related rite to declare virtue in which boys would bite an arrow and girls would bite a knife after both items had been inserted in the ground.

Black Elk called the girls' puberty ceremony in Lakota tradition Ishna Ta Awi Cha Lowan, which translates as "Her Alone They Sing Over." It is also spelled Išnati Awicalowanpi, which M. N. Powers (1986) translated as "they sing over her first menses" (p. 101). It has also been called the Buffalo Ceremony because of the summons to the buffalo spirit during the rites (M. N. Powers, 1986; W. K. Powers, 1977). In describing the girl's preparation for womanhood, Black Elk stated:

> These rites are performed after the first menstrual period of a woman. They are important because it is at this time that a young girl becomes a woman, and she must understand the meaning of this change and must be instructed in the duties which she is now to fulfill. She should realize that the change which has taken place in her is a sacred thing, for now she will be as Mother Earth and will be able to bear children, which should also be brought up in a sacred manner. She should know, further, that each month when her period arrives she bears an influence with which she must be careful, for the presence of a woman in this condition may take away the power of a holy man. (J. E. Brown, 1953/1989, p. 116)

The traditional practice of this ceremony was related by Black Elk and recorded by J. E. Brown (1953/1989). The key players in this account are a Lakota man called Slow Buffalo, who received the initial vision and conducted the first ceremony; White Buffalo Cow Woman Appears, who is the initiate at the first ceremony; and Feather on Head, who is the father of the young woman. It began with Slow Buffalo's vision of a buffalo calf being cleansed by its mother. He ascertained from this vision that the rite was to be given to young women of his nation. A few moons later, White Buffalo Cow Woman Appears experienced first menstruation, and her father, Feather on Head, remembered Slow Buffalo's vision and approached him with a request to purify and prepare his daughter for womanhood. Feather on Head was instructed to build a tepee outside the camp circle and to gather a number of sacred objects, including a buffalo skull, a wooden cup, some cherries, water, sweetgrass, sage, a pipe, some Ree tobacco, *kinnikinnik* (dried inner bark of the red alder or red dogwood), a knife, a stone hatchet, and some red and blue paint. Slow Buffalo was given a gift of horses and then departed to prepare for events that would commence the next day.

The ceremony began with Slow Buffalo burning sweetgrass while offering a prayer of purification. It was significant that the prayer was offered not only to purify and make sacred the girl but also to extend to the entire generation. Tobacco was offered to the four directions, to the Earth, and to Wakan-Tanka in the sky. This excerpt from the prayer to the north gives strong insights into the nature of this ceremony: "Help us especially today with your purifying influence, for we are about to make sacred a virgin, White Buffalo Cow Woman Appears, from whom will come the generations of our people" (p. 120). Slow Buffalo again purified his whole body with sweetgrass. To demonstrate that he had acquired the power of the buffalo, Slow Buffalo's imitated a buffalo by emitting a large bellow and then blowing red smoke onto the girl and throughout the tepee.

Slow Buffalo took a stone hatchet and hollowed out a space in the ground in the shape of a buffalo wallow. A cross was made in that place with tobacco, and blue lines were drawn on top of the tobacco. The blue symbolized Heaven, and tobacco symbolized the Earth; together the two had been united into one. Of additional significance was the placement of a buffalo skull on the mound of earth that had been set aside from the previous digging. Red paint was strategically drawn on the buffalo skull, and balls of sage were put in the eyes of the skull. A wooden bowl of water was set in front of the buffalo's mouth, and cherries were placed in the water (cherries represent the fruits that trees bear; they are red like the two-leggeds or humans).

As additional rituals ensued, at one point White Buffalo Cow Woman Appears stood and held a bundle of sacred items over her head that included sweetgrass, the bark of the cherry tree, and the hair of a live buffalo. At this climactic moment, Slow Buffalo stated: "This which is over your head is like Wankan-Tanka, for when you stand you reach from Earth to Heaven; thus, anything above your head is like the Great Spirit. You are the tree of life. You will now be pure and holy, and may your generations to come be fruitful! Wherever your feet touch will be a sacred place, for now you will always carry with you a very great influence" (pp. 123–124).

Slow Buffalo then mimicked the buffalo and pushed the girl to the bowl of water with cherries, which she drank taking four sips. While holding a piece of buffalo meat up to the girl, Slow Buffalo stated: "White Buffalo Cow Woman Appears, you have prayed to Wankan-Tanka; you will now go forth among your people in a holy manner, and you will be an example to them. You will cherish those things which are most sacred in the universe; you will be as Mother Earth—humble and fruitful. May your steps, and those of your children, be firm and sacred! As Wakan-Tanka has been merciful to you, so you, too, must be merciful to others, especially to those children who are without parents" (pp. 125–126).

As the ceremony neared completion, Slow Buffalo offered a prayer as he held the pipe upward. When White Buffalo Calf Woman Appears came out of the tepee, the people rushed forward to touch her because of her sacred state. A feast followed along with a giveaway. Black Elk concluded this telling of this first Ishna Ta Awi Cha Lowan: "It was in this manner that the rites for preparing a young girl for womanhood were first begun, and they have been the source of much holiness, not only for our women, but for the whole nation" (p. 126).

Lakotas believe themselves to be close relatives of the Buffalo Nation (St. Pierre & Long Soldier, 1995), who are said to have emerged from the same subterranean origins as humans (M. N. Powers, 1986). Historically, buffalo were an important source of food, clothing, shelter, and fuel; hence it is not surprising that they attained such a sacred status in the beliefs of Lakota culture. The linkage between buffalo (*tatanka*) and humans is profoundly apparent in Slow Buffalo's vision and the subsequent performance of Ishna Ta Awi Cha Lowan, as stated in the story: "It is true that all the four-leggeds and all the peoples who move on the universe have this rite of purification, and especially our relative the buffalo, for, as I have seen, they too purify their children and prepare them for bearing fruit" (p. 118). Further, women and buffalo are linked as entities that create and sustain life (M. N. Powers, 1986). The significance of White Buffalo Calf Woman to the girls' coming-of-age ceremony is equally apparent. Indeed, the name of the first recipient of this ceremony, White Buffalo Cow Woman Appears, is an obvious indication of what transpires, as this important female supernatural being comes again to the Lakotas within the girl who bears her name.

The Lakota term *Whope'* refers to the embodiment of feminine ideals and is the most descriptive term of White Buffalo Calf Woman according to St. Pierre and Long Soldier (1995). Indeed, these authors stated that the puberty ceremony is "so strongly related to Whope' that it is also known as the White Buffalo Calf Ceremony" (p. 47). In the Lakota creation story, Whope' was actually the daughter of the male Sun and the female Moon, and she is regarded as the precursor to White Buffalo Calf Woman.[6] Hence, the identification of the female pubescent with White Buffalo Calf Woman is consistent with the theme of the centrality of a female supernatural being in the puberty ceremony and the goal of transformation of the initiate into this personage. The symbolism is further indicated by W. K. Powers (1977), who explained that at one point in the puberty ceremony the girl is instructed to take off her dress and place it over the buffalo skull. This act signifies sacrifice and generosity as the dress is offered to the buffalo woman for any needy person, at which point in the rite a woman enters the tepee and takes the dress.

Dakota scholar Ella Deloria wrote of Dakota girls' coming-of-age (1944/1979), and her thoughts resonate with the previous comments. In telling of the Buffalo Ceremony or Dakota coming-of-age for girls, values of purity, chastity, wifehood, and motherhood were emphasized.

The following words given to the girl at this time are indicative of this theme: "A real woman is virtuous and soft spoken and modest and does not shame her husband and neglect her children. She is skillful in the womanly arts and hospitable to all who enter her dwelling. She remains at home ready to receive guests at all times. Her fire burns permanently cheery and smoke curls prettily upward from her tipi head" (p. 43). Clearly, these comments are consistent with the kind of instruction given to pubescent girls in a variety of cultures, as discussed in chapter 5. Deloria also discussed the pressure placed on girls to protect their reputation or risk shaming their brothers and cousins who generously gave gifts to them at their coming-of-age.

Relative to contemporary practice of the Ishna Ta Awi Cha Lowan, Young and Gooding (2001) stated that it was near extinction, and this may be the case in its most strict or traditional form. Such practices significantly diminished over the 20th century due to various factors, including the strong pressure for discontinuation by missionaries and the federal government and their agents located on reservations (Bol & Menard, 2000; St. Pierre & Long Soldier, 1995). There are two 20th-century accounts of Ishna Ta Awi Cha Lowan to relate that encompass several components found in puberty observances of other cultures. St. Pierre and Long Soldier (1995) described an experience related by Madonna Swan, and Bol and Menard (2000) includes the recollections of the second author's Ishna Ta Awi Cha Lowan in 1925. In both cases the element of seclusion occurred, as the initiates were isolated in a cabin or tent some distance from their homes. The doorway to the menstrual lodge always faced to the east. It was explained in Bol and Menard (2000) that the initiate was not to even go near boys or men—that menstruation was a threat to warriors and their implements of war. Indeed, it was believed that contact with men by any menstruating woman could be harmful to both the woman and the men she might encounter. Both menstruation and the odor of the flow were thought to render other forms of needed medicine ineffective.

At the time of coming-of-age, grandmothers were central figures as the primary guides and mentors to the young initiates. They engaged girls in industrious tasks as they acquired new skills in sewing, beadwork, and working with porcupine quills. Menard was required to use sinew as thread and sew porcupine quills on buckskin. She stated that her acquired knowledge of traditional handicrafts directly linked to her performance of these tasks at puberty. Swan reported that she was instructed by her grandmother to think good thoughts and have a pleasant disposition during this time (a prevalent theme in coming-of-age rites of other tribes, as well). Both women were required to use a special scratching implement to scratch themselves. Menard was required to sit on a small pit that had been dug out of the ground with sage placed in it. When the sage became soiled from her menstrual flow, it would be replaced with new sage. It is noteworthy that in Lakota tradition, sage serves various functions including protection. M. N. Powers (1986) told how the bundle from the first menstruation was to be placed in a plum tree, which symbolized fruitfulness. In both Menard's and Swan's experiences, they were bathed by their mothers or grandmothers in water with sage placed in it. Swan's grandmother prayed for her with bequests on behalf of her character formation and her future roles as wife and mother. According to Menard, after 4 days of menstruation she was bathed and then dressed in new clothes. The clothing worn during her time of menstruation was burned.

Instruction was an integral component of these coming-of-age events. Swan's grandmother taught her about the relationships of humans with the facets of creation, as well as teachings on the four great virtues—generosity, bravery, fortitude, and moral integrity (or chastity, fecundity, industry, and hospitality as reported in M. N. Powers, 1986). As well, Menard recalled being instructed by a man (after her 4 days of seclusion) who told her to "do right." Celebration and feasting followed 4 days of seclusion. Menard's celebration included the Throwing the Ball rite in which the ball was caught by another girl who subsequently was given gifts, including a horse. Black Elk in J. E. Brown (1953/1986) did not connect this rite to the girl's pubertal coming-of-age, but apparently some version of Throwing the Ball was performed in Menard's rite. The term *Buffalo Ceremony* also was applied in Bol and Menard (2000) to specifically indicate the girl's reintroduction into society as a woman.

In addition to the two previous accounts, St. Pierre and Long Soldier (1995) offered additional illustrations of contemporary puberty observances in Lakota culture. They explained that in the past 20 years the girls' puberty ceremony has been combined with the Hunkapi, or Making of Relatives. W. K. Powers (2000), as well, stated that Hunkapi is performed today as an initiation in which a relationship is formed between younger and older persons. The elder person ties a feather in the hair of the younger person as a symbol of the young person's new status. Names may be bestowed on the young adoptees, as well.

In the St. Pierre and Long Soldier (1995) account, the puberty ceremony may occur shortly before or after a girl has her first menstrual flow and may occur as part of a larger ceremonial gathering, such as a Sun Dance. Further, more than one girl may experience the event simultaneously. An older person serves as a sponsor and is selected by the girl's family. The man who conducts the ceremony provides strong reinforcement of the Lakota heritage of the girls. Other events include offerings of ritual foods (i.e., chokecherry juice and pemmican) to Mother Earth and the Grandfathers (spirit beings who are helpers [W. K. Powers, 1977]). Each girl is assigned a spirit name of a deceased ancestor who possessed admirable qualities. This spirit name is now permanently attached to the girl and is to be protected for ceremonial use only. Girls may adopt an older person as a relative at this time. Similar to the Apache Sunrise Dance, in which the initiate acquires a new family through her godparents, the Lakotas' form of adoption signifies a permanent relationship that also includes the kin network of the adopted person. The event closes with a large giveaway for each girl. The display of generosity at these events is impressive, with the obvious sacrifice of time and money committed to the gifts that are to be provided to every guest in attendance.

There are additional symbolic events of contemporary girls' puberty ceremonies. Red paint may be applied to the girl's head to signify her dedication to the truth and the Red Road, or the good way. Additionally, three marks may be painted on her chin to indicate her new status as a woman. Her virtue is shown through a white vent plume from an eagle feather that is tied to her hair. St. Pierre and Long Soldier (1995) stated that instruction of pubescent girls still occurs in their households, such as admonitions to be industrious, because their level of activity will affect their future roles as wives and mothers. As already shown in this book, such an admonition is prevalent in North American Indian beliefs regarding pubescence.

There are a few additional illustrations of contemporary Lakota puberty observances to examine. The American Friends Service Committee (1998) described a program they support among the Oglala on the Pine Ridge Reservation. Several young women were participants in the coming-of-age rite that occurred over the course of the summer and involved mentorship by elders. The young women worked with the selected elders to acquire spiritual knowledge, to learn about the responsibilities of adulthood and parenting, and to perform tasks such as needlework using porcupine quills. This preparation culminated in a special day of prayer, blessing, feasting, and gift giving. A similar illustration of a contemporary coming-of-age ceremony was reported by J. R. Lee (2001) as it occurred on the Yankton Reservation (Nakota). Six girls lived and even slept at a tepee that had been constructed for the rituals of their coming-of-age ceremony. Over a 4-day period the girls wore long skirts and spoke with elders, with one another, and with girls who had previously experienced the puberty ceremony. Traditional culture was reinforced as the girls sang songs, sewed, and learned words from their language. A total of 37 young women have completed this ceremony since it was reestablished 4 years previous on the Yankton Reservation. In both the Pine Ridge and Yankton illustrations, the motivation to perform these ceremonies for young women was apparently twofold: to promote the traditions of the culture and to foster and nurture the development of women in contemporary society.

No single fixed or static version of Ishna Ta Awi Cha Lowan was uniformly performed in the past or in the present. Bol and Menard (2000) commented on discrepancies across various historical accounts: "The differences in these versions make clear that the woman's puberty ceremony had a number of variables depending on the person, place, time, and interpreter" (p. 33). In spite of deviations in practices, several key components were observed across the accounts summarized: seclusion, special clothing and adornments, requirements of industry, instruction, and celebration. Certainly these components were observed in the practices of other cultures. Relative to separation, historically the custom at the initial and all subsequent menstrual cycles was for seclusion of Lakota, Nakota, and Dakota women, who would retire to a separate tepee, tent, or shelter away from the camp circle. While contemporary women are not entirely secluded for all menstrual cycles, they are required to remain apart from certain ceremonies. Pubescent girls may or may not be restricted to a separate tepee, but at the very least, separation may be designated in their special clothing and adornments and the specialized rituals they engage in, which serve to heighten the liminal nature of their transition.

Clearly, in both the past and the present, Lakota, Nakota, and Dakota girls were supervised and instructed by older women who taught them about their responsibilities to family and others and also taught them domestic skills such as sewing and working with beads and porcupine quills. Eastman (1911) emphasized the importance of both grandmothers and grandfathers in the maturation of girls and boys, explaining that around age 8 children would be turned over to the care of their grandparents: "Indeed, the distinctive work of both grandparents is that of acquainting the youth with the national traditions and beliefs. It is reserved for them to repeat the time-hallowed tales with dignity and authority, so as to lead him into his inheritance in the old stored-up wisdom and experience of the race" (p. 34). The female adult mentor also serves as a role model to the girl. She is regarded as a good and holy person, and these and other virtues will be passed on to the girl (J. E. Brown, 1953/1989). Lakota, Nakota, and Dakota coming-of-age observances are events of spiritual affirmation, as well. Near the end of the event, celebrations such as feasting and giveaways solidify the initiate's reincorporation into society as a young woman.

Ojibwa Coming-of-Age Customs

Historically, the Ojibwas lived primarily north of Lakes Superior and Huron, but during the Fur Trade Period (1670–1800) a major expansion occurred that ultimately led to a delineation of the Ojibwas according to four major areas (Ritzenthaler, 1978). The Southeastern and Southwestern Ojibwas are associated with the Northeast cultural area and are found around the Great Lakes region of Canada and the United States. The Northern Ojibwas are linked to the Subarctic cultural area, and the Plains Ojibwas are found in the Plains cultural area. The reports of puberty customs in this section are based primarily on Southwestern Ojibwas, who are located in the regions of present-day northern Minnesota and Wisconsin, as well as their Canadian relatives located to the north in Ontario. Perhaps due to the physical proximity of these bands to the Subarctic cultural area, their puberty customs bore stronger similarity to Subarctic cultures than to those of the Northeast Woodlands.

The Ojibwas are of the Algonquian language family and traditionally consisted of small, autonomous bands based in economies of hunting, fishing, and gathering. They became heavily involved in the fur trade when the French and English established trading posts in the 17th and 18th centuries. Traditionally, they were patrilineal according to clan membership of children but were matrilocal after marriage, particularly in the first year, when the husband would move his belongings into his wife's family's wigwam where the couple would reside (Ritzenthaler, 1978). In the United States, 105,907 people self-identified as solely Ojibwa in the 2000 decennial census (U.S. Census Bureau, 2002), and Ojibwa reservations are located in Michigan, Wisconsin, Minnesota, North Dakota, and Montana. Indian and Northern Affairs Canada (2004) estimated that 94,350, or 21.5% of the registered Indian population, was Ojibwa (based on 1991 Statistics Canada data). Ojibwa bands are found in Ontario, Manitoba, and Saskatchewan. Clearly, Ojibwas compose a group of large numbers on both sides of the border.

Ojibwa culture is included in this chapter because of the firsthand reports provided to the author about puberty practices and available literature on this group. Information on Ojibwa customs was related by four adults—all living in the United States, but with connections to Ojibwa bands in the United States and Canada. Three Ojibwa adults (two males and one female) were linked to bands that more or less hug the Minnesota-Ontario border. The female informant had experienced her pubertal coming-of-age rites some years previous in the traditional manner. An additional source of information was a male relative of an Ojibwa initiate who had recently experienced her puberty ceremony in Canada.

In my research on Ojibwa puberty customs, I did not find as clear a connection with stories of origin, cosmology, or other stories of significant supernatural personages of oral tradition as with Apache, Navajo, and Lakota cultures. Nonetheless, some linkage with stories of the cosmology is associated with a theme I repeatedly encountered in both the literature and interviews with Ojibwa informants, specifically the emphasis on dreams, fasts, and vision quests for both boys and girls as young as ages 4 and 5 and throughout childhood and pubescence (see chapter 5; Hilger, 1951/1992). A dream or vision secured through fasting, isolation, and meditation had as its object the acquisition of a guardian spirit or helper to protect and guide the individual for the life span (Densmore, 1929/1979). Hence, the guardian spirits are entities of the cosmology, intermediaries between the Supreme Being and the people (Hilger, 1951/1992). Densmore's informants spoke of returning to previous states of existence in their visions and dreams as well as having events in the future revealed that ultimately came to pass. There is some basis for these practices being embedded in origin stories about the first earth and its people as related to Densmore by an informant: "The Ockabewis [a messenger, the spirit of the creator] told them that they must fast and find out things by dreams and that if they paid attention to these dreams they would learn how to heal the sick. The people listened and fasted and found in dreams how to teach the children and do everything" (1929/1979, p. 98). In terms of girls' puberty rites that encompass separation and ritual behaviors described in the following sections, specific associations with origin stories were not encountered in my work. It is not to say such associations do not exist, because the shortcoming was perhaps my lack of diligence in exploration of the literature as well as my limited field research on this culture. Conceivably the identification of the Everlasting-Woman in the girls' puberty fast as related by Radin (1936) in a later section is suggestive of a connection to a supernatural figure of oral tradition. This and related connections certainly warrant further investigation.

Informants emphasized that, ideally, preparation for puberty customs should begin at birth. In the traditional fashion, the infant is kept close to her mother while strapped on the cradleboard for the first year of life. Until the child can run on her own, the norm is for physical proximity to the mother. As the child grows older, developmentally appropriate socialization occurs as she gradually acquires sacred teachings from her mother and grandmother. She also learns about proper behavior, such as not stepping over objects of her brothers and men (see chapter 4). By the time the coming-of-age rites occur, the child has been as prepared to the degree it is possible according to her developmental capabilities of understanding. These statements are consistent with those of the Navajo woman reported previously in this chapter who emphasized the necessity to socialize children from birth onward for their Kinaaldá ceremonies.

In comparing accounts of Ojibwa puberty customs we find variations according to distinctions by bands, but it is clear that seclusion of the girl in a separate wigwam or *bākā nēd'jē* (translated as "a tent made by herself") was the most common custom. She could be isolated for 4, 5, or even 10 days while receiving instruction on the responsibilities associated with being a woman (Densmore, 1929/1979; Fox, 1999; Hilger, 1951/1992; Torrance, 1994). Informants indicated that, among their band, the entire sequence of puberty events began with a seclusion of 21 days in the bush and continued for 1 year and 3 hours. At the first indication of the onset of menses, the girl was taken to the bush to live in a wigwam or tepee for 21 days of isolation and seclusion and was attended to by her mother or grandmother. Indeed, the monitoring and instruction by mothers or grandmothers was a consistent theme found in the literature. According to Hilger (1951/1992), the time of isolation was called *måkwå'* or *måkwa'wē* (translated as "turning into a bear" or "the bear lives alone all winter"). The wigwam was built by the girl or the girl and her mother or grandmother and was only large enough for her to stand or to lie down. Hilger gave further details on the wigwam regarding various distinctions for the summer or winter, including the addition of mosquito netting in one instance.

The female informant in this research told of wearing a cone-shaped hat that was constructed from birch bark. The hat was large and designed to greatly restrict her visual range, only allowing her to see where she was walking. It also was common for the cheeks and sometimes forehead of girls to be darkened with charcoal or soot (Hilger, 1951/1992). Ojibwa informants interviewed for this study told of spreading cedar ash around the eyes of the pubescent girl, giving her face an appearance of a raccoon. The purpose of the hat and the cedar ash was said to be the protection of all that she was seeing because of the effects her gaze might have on others during her empowered state. Certainly, this practice and similar practices were widely noted in the puberty customs of cultures in the Subarctic (see chapter 5).

Hilger (1951/1992) also explained that the girl's hair was tied back or completely covered with buckskin or cloth and that she could not touch her hair during the time of seclusion at risk of it falling out. Indeed, she could not touch herself and was required to use a scratching stick (also see Densmore, 1929/1979). The female informant in this study, as well, related that for the full year's time she was not to touch her hair or risk losing it. A cedar scratching stick was used for such purposes. She told how she had initially touched her head and hair and subsequently lost a great deal of her hair as well as its thickness. It took some time for the recovery of a full head of hair. She also explained that she was required to cut her own wood, but, due to her empowered state, was required to use cedar shavings as protection on her hands prior to touching her firewood.

This informant also explained that she was not required to use a drinking tube but did drink out of a birch-bark cup for the entire year. This practice is supported in the literature according to the customs of other Ojibwa bands. Hilger (1951/1992), as well, explained that during seclusion the girl was required to use her own dishes. In some instances she was required to use and take care of these dishes for 1 year following the initial seclusion. No food that was in season could be brought to the girl during the puberty observances, or the entire group's food procurement could be hampered. In further expansion of these ideas and related practices, Hilger explained: "If a girl at puberty touched plants, it withered them; if she went into lakes or rivers, 'she was liable to kill the fish, or at least all fish would go away from there.' By looking at a person, touching a child, or crossing the path of any person, she paralyzed that person. In fact during the entire year following first menses, she was not to touch babies, or clothes of her father, or brothers, or of any man, for it would cripple them" (1951/1992, p. 52).

During the time of seclusion the girl was to avoid contact with men or any implements that men might use. This custom is similar to that of many Subarctic cultures that secluded pubescent girls to manage their power, which might interfere with the necessity of success in hunting. Informants in this study stated that it was not required that women be secluded for subsequent menstrual cycles. Fox (1999) concurred relative to Ojibwas in general but indicated some restrictions on the activities of menstruating women due to their empowered states and potential impacts they could have on others.

As was found across Native cultures of North America, during their time of seclusion Ojibwa girls were kept occupied with tasks such as sewing and beadwork (Hilger, 1951/1992). They were also instructed on the responsibilities and roles expected of them now that they were women. According to the informants in this study who related past puberty practices, after 21 days in the bush the girl was permitted to return home, but she was required to adhere to several restrictions for 1 year. She used separate cooking utensils and dishes for eating and drinking and was basically restricted to her home, with perhaps school attendance the only exception. She was instructed to not engage in boisterous play with her brothers, but to display only reserved and modest behaviors. During this year of containment, her mother and grandmother continued to instruct the girl according to the kinds of knowledge necessary for women. This was an austere time in the girl's life, and she was to be vigilant in maintaining the rules during the year. Modesty was required during that time, and the girl was to wear a dress that covered a good deal of her body. To this day, the informant who related her experiences to me remarked that she feels uncomfortable wearing shorts or even sandals on her feet because of the lessons in modesty that she acquired at puberty.

A feast and celebration at her village, called the Womanhood Ceremony, sometimes followed the girl's time of seclusion. Hilger (1951/1992) stated that the girl bathed herself and washed her clothes after seclusion. Then, her mother prepared a meal of the products of her father's hunting expeditions. Older women were invited to this meal. An interesting ritual occurred that required the girl to walk from her separate wigwam to the family's wigwam on cedar boughs or the bark of some tree. This was done so the girl would not directly step on the ground, which would then make it impossible for a man to walk on the same path because it could result in paralysis for him (Hilger). In the public component of puberty ceremonies that included feasting, some restrictions were still placed on girls relative to what they could eat. In some cases, rituals had to be performed to reintroduce girls to certain foods. For instance, Densmore (1929/1979) explained how, in a lesson of patience and discipline, the girl was ceremonially fed fresh berries that would be brought to her lips four times and then taken away. The fifth time she could eat. This ritual was repeated with each introduction of another food to the Ojibwa girl.

The informants explained that after the full course of the puberty observances (i.e., 21 days, 1 year, and 3 hours), the girl would go to the lake and swim as a ritual of purification. A ceremony then ensued in which the girl was required to prepare dishes using every kind of berry. She had to pick the berries herself, with the cedar ash on her hands as a protective measure. She worked with her family to prepare the site for the celebration. At the time of celebration, her father or another man sang four songs, followed by singing by women.

This female informant's coming-of-age event occurred in the most stringent traditional fashion. She indicated that contemporary girls are unlikely to experience the same full range of experiences, but certain components continue. For instance, while it is rare for a girl to be sent to the bush, she may be secluded in her home for 21 days. As well, intense instruction and teaching may occur during seclusion when she is taught the responsibilities of womanhood. This woman and her husband (a spiritual adviser) stated that the lack of adherence to puberty customs in the present day has had undesirable consequences, such as lack of berries or infertility in women, lack of reproduction being the common theme.

Traditionally, the girl would be considered a young woman after puberty and was carefully monitored by her mother and grandmother. She was never allowed to be alone with a man prior to marriage (Fox, 1999). Hilger (1951/1992) was in agreement that postpubescent girls were always chaperoned by their mothers or another responsible woman, according to various reports. They also were now considered women with the expectation that play had ceased in their lives, to be replaced by activities that would help them gain knowledge to become wives.

Concomitant with their seclusion at first menses, it was sometimes expected that girls fast (e.g., Densmore, 1929/1979; Hilger, 1951/1992). In some cases of fasting girls sought visions, but according to Ritzenthaler (1978), a vision was not a necessity for girls as it was for boys. Radin (1936) related a description of a puberty fast and vision at first menses according to a report by H. R. Schoolcraft. The particular experience was believed to have occurred among Ojibwas of Michigan and began with a girl of about age 12 or 13 who, upon discovering her first menses, ran far from the lodge. Her mother found her, and the two constructed a small lodge of spruce tree branches. The girl was instructed to remain in that location and to stay busy by chopping wood and twisting basswood into twine. She was left alone initially for 2 days with the instruction to not taste anything, even snow. The girl was surprised when her mother did not bring her food after 2 days, but instead her mother brought these instructions: "Now, my daughter, listen to me and try to obey. Blacken your face and fast really [sic] that the Master of Life may have pity on you and me, and on us all. Do not, in the least, deviate from my counsels, and in two days more, I will come to you. He will help you if you are determined to do what is right. Tell me whether you are favored or not by the true Great Spirit; and if your visions are not good, reject them" (p. 243).

After her mother departed, the girl continued her wood-chopping and cord-twisting tasks and followed her mother's directives. After 4 days of fasting, her mother returned and gave her some snow to drink, but not a sufficient amount to satisfy the girl. Her quest was not yet completed, as she was instructed to seek a good vision that "might not only do us good, but also benefit mankind" (p. 243). After 2 more days of isolation and fasting, a vision was experienced that began with a voice reassuring her that pity had been taken upon her condition. Following the voice, she was led down a shining path forward and upward and ultimately perceived the face of Kaugegagbekwa, or Everlasting-Woman. This personage identified herself to the girl and then gave the girl her name, which the girl could also bestow upon another. The girl was promised everlasting life, long life on Earth, and the ability to save life in others. The girl's vision continued with encounters with additional beings that also promised longevity and assigned her names that she could give to others.

The girl's mother brought food on the sixth and seventh days, but the girl had lost her appetite by that time. She related her vision to her mother and was then instructed to continue to fast for 3 more days. After she had spent 10 days alone, her mother brought the girl home and a feast was held in her honor for a successful fast. Clearly, this type of experience involved several facets of puberty customs: isolation, fasting, instructions to be industrious, visions, and feasting. The vision quest is more common to boys' coming-of-age, but it may correspond to menarche among girls in some cultures, including Ojibwa. Certainly, the notion of timing is implicit in this case study, with the mother clearly directing events at this critical point of her daughter's life cycle and instructing and monitoring her progress during the 10-day ordeal.

An account of a more recent Ojibwa pubertal coming-of-age ceremony was related to me in a telephone conversation by a man who described the Moon Ceremony of his daughter's aunt from an Ojibwa band in Ontario. At the time of her first menses, the girl's family began planning a giveaway that occurred 1 year subsequent. At the actual first moon, however, the girl and her family engaged in various ritual activities that began with building a lodge in which she was isolated and fasted for 1 day. A fire was maintained, and the community gathered and sang and prayed throughout the night.

After this initial ceremony, the initiate was required to fast from berries for 1 year. Additionally, she was required to adhere to various behavioral prohibitions, including not picking up children, having no contact with boys, not wrestling or playing around with her brothers, and not stepping over pillows and other belongings of male members of her family. These sacrifices were meaningful because they represented those things that would be important to her for the remainder of her life, as explained to me by the informant.

The men and boys in the family were also required to assist the initiate in numerous ways throughout the year, such as providing transportation and generally being attentive to any of her needs that might arise. In essence, male relatives were to take responsibility for the girl during that year. This informant stated that men's roles had been lost through processes of colonization and now, as a group, they are learning their expected responsibilities. Therefore, over the course of the year-long coming-of-age event, male relatives were informed of their cultural traditions along with females. The acquisition of respect for and honor of women was a major goal of learning for boys during this year's time. According to this informant, honor equals respect. and men are to acquire value for the roles that women perform, such as taking care of their households and families. These sentiments hearken back to earlier discussions in this book on gender-typing and its meanings in North American Indian cultures (see chapter 4). The male relative of this initiate emphasized the notions that both men and women must learn of their equal standing in their culture and their separate but equal forms of responsibility. In essence, the Moon Ceremony is not exclusively about the coming-of-age of a girl but also, in this informant's experience, an immersion into cultural values and practices for her associates.

After the initiate's year of sacrifice, a lodge was built once again and she again was separated and required to fast for 1 day. She could only drink a special tea made with cedar that the women prepared and had prayed over. The community was present at her emergence from the lodge after the 1-day separation and fast. The initiate wore a shawl over her head, and others were to avert their gazes from her. Singing and prayers commenced. Then the initiate was offered foods that she should reject for the time being to demonstrate her humility. At the end, she accepted these items only after everyone else had eaten and was satisfied. The girl's demonstration of patience and denial of her needs was consistent with Densmore's (1929/1979) description of the offering of berries and other food items to the initiate four times, after which she could accept them. As the final act of this coming-of-age event, the girl's shawl was removed, and the 24-hour conclusion of a year-long event was completed.

This informant also noted that during the Moon Ceremony, medicine men offered the prayers but women controlled the event. An important lesson for the girl was that she was a mother of the Earth. But it was evident through the perspective of this male relative that the ceremony was also meaningful for men because it gave them purpose and understanding of their place in the social order of their culture. In cultures across Native North American, men's traditional roles as warrior, provider, and protector were demolished through colonization. Hence, validation of the contributions of men in the Moon Ceremony imparted a deep sense of worth. Even a seemingly insignificant task of fetching water with a small bucket several times a day as opposed to using one large bucket was a meaningful action that taught humility and purpose. A final point shared by this informant was that perhaps only 10% or fewer of the families of this band of Ojibwas were traditional and would practice this ceremony in contemporary times.

In summarizing this section on Objiwa coming-of-age practices, it is apparent that data were derived from various sources, including historical, anthropological, and firsthand accounts. Ojibwas constitute a major cultural group in the United States and Canada and encompass an immense geographic area. For scholarly purposes they have been divided into four groups, and the Southwestern Ojibwas were the subject for review in the present work. Between-band differences are to be expected even within the Southwestern Ojibwa subcultural area, and this was confirmed through various practices related in this section. Nonetheless, there were many parallel practices across bands, such as separation of initiates, fasting and self-denial, the use of separate eating and drinking vessels, instruction, taboos regarding contact with men or male objects, covering the head, and feasting. These customs were found, as well, in other cultural areas, with perhaps some conspicuous similarities with customs of the Subarctic, as reported in chapter 5.

Comparison of Contemporary Practices

Puberty customs of three North American Indian cultures—Navajo, Lakota/Nakota/Dakota, and Ojibwa—were reviewed in the present chapter, and the previous two chapters reviewed those of the Apaches. People of these cultures have either maintained or reestablished some form of puberty rites into the present day. There are certain similarities across cultures, with perhaps the most common practice being that of separating initiates at or around first menses by relocation to some kind of physical structure. The structure might not serve as a complete containment in which the initiate is isolated at all times, but the usage of a structure that is set apart from the mundane symbolizes the distinctive state of the initiate. Further, structures provide a physical context within which specialized rites can be performed. The types of structure built and utilized are consistent with the traditional housing of each culture—wickiups among Western Apaches (tepee among Mescalero Apaches), hogans among Navajos, tepees among Lakotas, and wigwams among Ojibwas. These traditional structures are regarded as sacred in their own right and are sometimes reused for other ceremonial activities, such as with the Navajo hogan.

The psychological salience of traditional physical structures relative to coming-of-age rites is of additional interest. As noted, separation of pubescent girls is facilitated through such structures, but they also are representative of the traditional home of the initiate's culture. In this sense, traditional structures are visual reminders of creation stories and oral traditions of which such structures were frequently implicit components and within which formative events occurred. Additionally, these structures served as homes for the ancestors of initiates—in some cases, they may continue to do so. For example, some contemporary Navajos choose to live in hogans, which, as stated by Woody et al. (1981), are structures in which all blessings associated with events of family life occur.

The centrality of the traditional home in puberty ceremonies is also consistent with the form of instruction directed toward initiates, such as the reinforcement of their connections to kin, clan, and tribe as well as their future roles as wives and mothers. This point leads to the next, namely, that instruction is a prominent feature of Apache, Navajo, Lakota, and Ojibwa contemporary puberty customs, as well as numerous historical practices of other cultures reviewed in chapter 5. Further, instruction is facilitated through the inclusion of an adult female to mentor and guide the initiate. The necessity of initiates' ultimate fulfillment of their expected roles and responsibilities is recognized and valued, and puberty is regarded as the ideal time for explicit socialization to occur in these respects.

It is believed by informants of the cultures reviewed, and also confirmed in the literature, that it is in the best interest of girls to undergo puberty rites for purposes of longevity, health, and well-being. These events are causes for celebration according to the life potential that is represented in the physical changes of pubescence. Life is a multidimensional concept in which reproductive viability is one facet of a broader understanding of women's responsibilities as sustainers of life. It is believed not only that initiates are blessed at their coming-of-age events but also that blessings are extended to their families and associates and potentially to the entire world or Earth. The initiate's connection to the supernatural realm makes all hoped-for outcomes possible. In Apache and Navajo traditions, rituals are included in which initiates are situated to offer specific blessings to those who approach them. For the Lakotas,

Black Elk states that puberty rites are for the entire generation. In the Ojibwa vision related by Radin (1936), the girl's mother instructed her daughter to seek a vision to benefit mankind.

A further parallel theme across cultures is the connection of the initiate to a primary female being of her culture's oral traditions. As discussed in the previous and current chapters, Apache and Navajo beliefs specify that the initiate is actually transformed into White Painted Woman or Changing Woman, respectively. Lakota coming-of-age rites offer the potential to bring White Buffalo Calf Woman into the gathering of the people. The inclusion of a female spiritual being was not as uniformly reported among Ojibwas, but a figure called the Everlasting-Woman emerged in the puberty fast related by Radin (1936). As demonstrated in one of the beliefs about pubescence delineated in chapter 3, the initiate's connection to the spiritual realm and her subsequent empowerment are believed to bring blessings to others. Specific rituals are incorporated into pubertal coming-of-age events to extend beneficial impacts to all participants. The next chapter addresses additional themes to provide a broader understanding of coming-of-age rites for North American Indians girls.

Broader Perspectives on Coming-of-Age

□   □   □

In the attempt to understand the historical and contemporary significance of girls' coming-of-age ceremonies among North American Indians, it was necessary to engage in detailed examination of these rituals
and their meanings. It is useful at this point to depart from this form
of inquiry and consider the broader meanings and implications of the
multitude of expressions of coming-of-age described in this book. Considering the prohibitive influences of colonization, it is remarkable that
these events still occur in some North American Indian cultures. Clearly,
many tribes continue to value these ritual-filled events and believe that
they are applicable for contemporary young women. A core argument in
this book is that coming-of-age ceremonies are positive identity-shaping
events that not only empower young women for the present and the
future but also contribute to the continuation of their cultures according
to a variety of expressions. In broader examination of the rituals associated with these events it is possible to ascertain clues on cultural values
relative to adolescents, women, and societal well-being in general. Before
addressing the implications of this work in these respects, there are a few
comments to be made relative to theory and methodology.

In addition to my own discipline of developmental psychology, this
work's multidisciplinary orientation also encompassed cultural anthropology, women's studies, North American Indian studies, and history.

Preeminent status was given to Indigenous sources of knowledge relative to theories of human development, including the stage of pubescence as well as interpretations of menstrual customs and the experiences of women. Consistent with the multidisciplinary approach, data were derived from multiple methods, including critical examination of documents from various disciplines, worldviews, and historical eras and field-based tools of data collection, including participant observation and interviews. Perceptions of informants were sought to understand both the individual psychological as well as societal-level impacts of contemporary coming-of-age practices that are embedded within ancient beliefs and traditions of cultures. Participant observation augmented the phenomenological reports of informants in order to bring further perspective to the topic.

As a psychologist, I found an illuminating outcome of this research to be a deeper realization that all people, in part, are products of the oral traditions and history of their cultures. However, this actuality is not always recognized, nor are the processes considered according to how historical foundations convey individuals within their social group to their present state of self-expression and self-understanding. It was shown that contemporary coming-of-age practices are embedded in oral traditions that can encompass origin stories and beliefs about cosmology. The Apache Sunrise Dance, Navajo Kinaaldá, and Lakota Ishna Ta Awi Cha Lowan were especially considered relative to the foundational roles of oral traditions in contemporary ritual practices that serve to shape the personalities of initiates as well as their roles in their cultures. Expressions of oral tradition in the practice of rituals reinforce the characteristics of connection and interdependence associated with North American Indian societies. As such, connection is not only horizontal to one's contemporaries but is also vertical in the sense that history is spanned and linkages are pursued with significant figures of oral tradition who played creative and instructive roles relative to humans. For example, Changing Woman of the Navajos and White Painted Woman of the Apaches are regarded as beings that played fundamental roles in the formation of humans and other facets of life, including ongoing maintenance of life. White Buffalo Calf Woman was pivotal in bringing sacred rites to the Lakota people—including the coming-of-age rite for girls. Contemporary young women are called on to emulate these role models and, in some cases, to become transformed into these personages. Hence, earlier eras are brought into the present as ancient stories are retold, and sometimes reenacted, according to oral histories that tell of formative relationships between the supernatural beings and humans at times when spiritual transcendence was perhaps most apparent. That a pubescent girl serves as the catalyst for the animation of oral traditions is suggestive of values affixed to both the time of coming-of-age as well as women. These notions were explored more carefully in chapters 3 and 4, but they merit additional interpretation according to the cultural values that are indicated in female coming-of-age ceremonies.

Rituals and Values

It can be generally stated that rituals performed in association with the transition from childhood to adulthood reflect values of greatest importance to a group. This conclusion is based on the fact that coming-of-age rites occur at considerable personal sacrifice and expense, including the commitments required of the initiate and her associates. For instance, it was explained in chapter 4 that taboos and restrictions required by pubescent girls were extended to her social group, as occurred among Subarctic and other hunting cultures that required all members to adhere to rigorous behaviors relative to the separation of menstruating women and menstrual fluids from anything related to hunting. It was further demonstrated that, in the past and present, restrictions at puberty were and are frequently demanding, arduous, and certainly pose impositions in contrast to the relatively carefree nature of childhood. In contemporary times, pubertal rites of passage can continue to place rigorous demands of separation on girls, requiring personal commitment and sacrifice. Further, great expenses of time, money, and energy on the part of the initiate's family are evident, such as with the Apache Sunrise Dance. The question becomes, then, what is of such high value to people that compels them to suspend concerns and matters of everyday life for the welfare of both pubescent girls and themselves?

To answer this question, it is useful to recall the purposes of puberty observances as delineated in chapter 3 and reiterated throughout this

Table 1. Beliefs about Pubescent Girls Held by North American Indians

1. Menstruation and menstrual fluids are powerful in general, and the first menstrual cycles are particularly powerful.
2. Feminine representations in cosmological constructions including origin stories are instructive to the pubescent girl, as well as for all women.
3. The special quality of menarche is a necessary (but not sufficient) event for connection of the initiate to the spiritual realm (rituals complete the process).
4. The proper performance of rituals ensures the initiate's successful transition into adulthood and influences her life course.
5. The initiate's performance of tests of endurance will subsequently affect her life course.
6. The malleable state of the initiate at puberty necessitates her subjugation to the instruction and influence of adults, particularly an adult female mentor.
7. Due to her empowered state, the initiate's behavior at puberty will have an impact on her future; hence, taboos and behavioral restrictions must be followed.
8. Due to her empowered state, the initiate can influence the welfare of others.
9. The coming-of-age event is not only a transition from childhood to adulthood but also a transition into the world of the spiritual.

book. These purposes are the reasons why these ceremonies and customs occur, and they may also be considered according to the functions that are served through the performance of puberty rituals. Two sets of purposes were delineated according to outcomes for initiates as well as others. Relative to the former, the nine North American Indian beliefs about pubescence are shown once again in Table 1 (above). These beliefs, which were derived from careful examination of the literature on North American Indian pubertal customs and the field research conducted for this book, provide critical philosophical underpinnings to the multitude of expressions of puberty rituals. In essence, the beliefs about pubescence provide insights on the functions of specific rituals and have led to the conclusion that rituals are not random or without purpose.

Rituals are fluid, however, and can change in form over time and their meanings may change across generations. Earlier meanings may be forgotten or lose their relevance for a group, at which point new meanings may emerge that offer contemporary application. For example, the strength that Apache women are to derive from the rituals of the Sunrise Dance is to buffer against modern-day enemies of drugs and alcohol, as explained by one medicine man. On the other hand, in contrast to explanations that change or expand earlier meanings, it is interesting to note the rather stable function of other rituals, such as the scratching stick required by pubescent girls, who are not to touch themselves. This is an ancient custom that is still applied in some cultures, and its beautification function (to protect the complexion of the girl) has been maintained over time. Of course, this ritual connects to the belief that pubescent girls are in empowered states during which time their own touch can cause permanent scarring of their skin. In short, rituals are cultural constructions designed to serve the perceived needs of the developing adolescent and her society and reflect current values and needs of the group.

This book has maintained that fertility is not the central purpose of pubertal coming-of-age ceremonies practiced among North American Indian cultures. Nonetheless, beliefs and their associated rituals require the involvement of a girl at the critical life phase at and around menarche. At a superficial level, therefore, it could be concluded that this does indeed suggest a fertility function of female coming-of-age rites. The connection cannot be ignored, but in departing from the obvious it is necessary to consider the broader meaning of fertility and menstruation in North American Indian cultures. The first belief shown in Table 1 is foundational to all others—menstruation is the critical factor that propels all beliefs. The next two beliefs are corollaries of the first, and together these three make the enactment of all remaining beliefs possible. However, menstruation is an indicator of something more than the ability to procreate. It represents a life-giving power that is intimately linked to powers of the universe that are believed to have been active in the initial creation of humans and involved in the ongoing maintenance of the universal life cycle. Hence, powerful and creative life processes, in all of their forms, are recognized and celebrated in girls' pubertal coming-of-age ceremonies. Even when coming-of-age events are not necessarily celebrations per se but require adherence to rigorous menstrual taboos, the underlying themes are respect for and containment of a form of power that could counteract other forms of power necessary for survival of the group, such as the powers active in hunting or curing (see chapter 4). In short, the value of life is a central theme of coming-of-age events—not only life as an ongoing state of existence, but the quality of life as well.

Following the foundational first three beliefs, additional beliefs in Table 1 are indicative of the desire to influence the future well-being and life course of initiates. In particular, beliefs 4, 5, 6, 7, and 9 mandate the performance of rituals to shape desired qualities (e.g., character, discipline, skills, beauty, and strength) as well as valued life outcomes (e.g., health, happiness, wealth, and long life). Of additional importance is the spiritual transcendence that is offered to initiates as the rite of passage serves, in a sense, as an introduction to the spiritual realm. The efforts taken and the sacrifices required to perform rituals to produce these outcomes clearly indicate what is valued for the life course of women. Perhaps all of these outcomes are subsumed under the construction of a healthy, well-functioning adult female who will assume responsibility in maintenance of the social order. As explained earlier in this book, the female role of sustenance and care provider was traditionally highly valued in Native cultures, and facets of these expectations continue to the present day. To successfully perform the tasks of adult women, it is necessary to possess all of the other outcomes of interest (e.g., character, discipline, health, strength, etc.). In essence, this interpretation is congruent with the discussion in chapter 3 according to the coexistence of properties of interdependence and cooperation with personal autonomy and individualism. Specifically, a pubertal rite of passage is typically about the optimal development of a particular girl who has experienced menarche (an individual experience); however, the acquisition of healthy biological and psychosocial outcomes brings long-term benefits to her kin, clan, and larger group (reflective of interdependence).

The indication is, therefore, that puberty rituals occur in the context of connectional and relational social systems and that the desired outcomes extend to others beyond the initiate. Perhaps the performance of these rituals has the potential to address universal human needs for feelings of stability, security, well-being, comfort, and predictability. Indeed, it is frequently deemed a necessity to perform the rituals to head off potential disaster and to secure successful, prosperous, and harmonious futures for all people. This theme was certainly explicated in chapter 7 relative to the functions of the Apache Sunrise Dance. Coming-of-age practices offer respites from day-to-day stresses and struggles and, through ritual activities, bring reminders of a broader spiritual context of existence. Uncertainty and worries are temporarily forgotten and are replaced by psychological comfort and assurance—states that are reexperienced with each occurrence of this type of an event. Additionally, perhaps participants depart from the event with some sense of comfort that life will now be different and somehow less harsh than previously.

Feelings of comfort and security are facilitated through the proper performances of rituals that are embedded in the belief of the pubescent girl's empowered state. The initiate is perceived to now possess the capability to extend blessings to the very real needs of participants (belief 8). Indeed, it was observed in chapter 7 that the Apache initiate can be likened to a medicine man and that her power becomes a form of public property (Basso, 1966). Apart from overall perceived direct impacts of these events, it should not be forgotten that, in the larger scheme of understanding, coming-of-age rites ensure continuation of cultures. That is, customs, beliefs and oral traditions, languages, dances, foods, and prayers are implicit components of these rites and therefore are reinforced and perpetuated among the gathering. For example, these and related factors are evident during an Apache Sunrise Dance, which has emerged as the most important ceremonial of the San Carlos Apaches and perhaps is the primary source for socialization of Apache culture.

Perhaps more importantly, younger generations are accordingly socialized to serve as the carriers of these traditions into the future. Indeed, customs would quite obviously wane if not inculcated by the young, who are likewise expected to take responsibility for the perpetuation of their culture. In short, coming-of-age events serve multiple purposes that reflect states of existence that are of value to social groups. For the initiate, of prime importance is her future welfare and the necessity of incorporating her into the social sphere of the group. For others, it is to once again bring all of the good things in life—prosperity, health, safety, and security—into the day-to-day realm. In addition to the purposes of coming-of-age ceremonies, it is of value to consider the implications of these rites relative to the position of women in Native societies.

The Status and Value of Women

Chapter 4 was written, in part, to consider female coming-of-age experiences according to current feminist thinking—Western and Indigenous. It was asserted that it is not generally appropriate to interpret the experiences of North American Indian girls and women according to those of white women or to impose models of white feminism on the interpretations of the experiences of North American Indian women. Unlike their white counterparts, North American Indian women must contend with issues of white supremacy and white privilege and the ongoing effects of colonialism that began more than 500 years ago. Indeed, both Indigenous men and women have been affected by such experiences, as detailed in chapters 2 and 4. For Native women, the intersection of gender, race, and class set their experiences apart from those of white women, particularly middle-or upper-class white women, and their gender brings some distinctiveness to their circumstances relative to North American Indian men.

One focus of pubertal rites of passage is the socialization of initiates according to valued traits of a culture, and these traits encompass traditionally female-linked roles as well as masculine and gender-neutral traits. The aim to empower female initiates is indicative of a stereotypically masculine trait in gender-role theory; nonetheless, it is regarded in North American Indian cultures to be a necessity for the life span of women. Relative to the socialization of female-linked roles, it should not be automatically assumed that this process serves to delegate women to a subservient status, a more applicable interpretation in European American society. It was argued in chapter 4 that the emphasis on role compliance at North American Indian puberty rituals does not serve as a source of male control of women, nor does it diminish the status of women. Historically, gender-linked roles of both men and women were regarded as necessities for the survival of the group. Women were valued for their life-giving properties, which included being the sustainers of life through their contributions to sustenance patterns. These qualities were regarded as sacred, as was life, and an implicit connection existed to the feminine in belief systems and cosmological constructions. Further, women were clearly valued for their roles as carriers and conveyors of the culture. Unfortunately, practices of colonization served to undermine traditional values, including the affirmation of women. North American Indian peoples of today are working to reestablish the status of women in various forms. Such efforts must address their male counterparts, who, in some cases, have also become their oppressors, such as what occurs with intimate partner violence and other forms of domination and control. Clearly, processes of colonization have undermined the traditional roles and statuses of women and men and have destabilized the inherent balance operative in their traditional relationships and lifestyles.

These comments aside, it is important to recognize the temptation to romanticize the past by diminishing the problems of earlier times and constructing a reality that represents the desired projection of the writer. It is reasonable to assert that no society is or was perfect, and the status of North American Indian women most certainly varied from one group to the next. However, there are several sociocultural indicators of the respect toward and status of women in many of these cultures of the past (see chapter 4), including the practice of matrilocal and matrilineal customs associated with numerous cultures; the absence of patriarchal control (or not to the extent associated with the cultures of the European colonizers); the influence of women in governance of the group; the value for the roles and contributions of both women and men to the survival of the individual, kin, clan, and group; and the incorporation and high regard for feminine elements in cosmologies and belief systems. These characteristics are being spoken of in the historical sense, and it is beyond the scope of this book to state with any certainty the degree to which they are represented in the present day. Nonetheless, the contributions of women to the good of the social order have historically been valued in North American Indian societies; and, in spite of the undermining influences of colonization, there are remarkable illustrations of strong and influential Native women in contemporary times.[1]

In theory, therefore, puberty ceremonies should bring status and recognition to women by reaffirming their important traditional roles in societies that encompass feminine, masculine, and gender-neutral traits. Hence, it might be suggested that contemporary practices of coming-of-age rites are acts of decolonization that serve to reestablish the integrity of cultures as well as that of individuals. When the initiate is connected to the feminine elements in cosmological structures, such as White Painted Woman, Changing Woman, or White Buffalo Calf Woman, her status and the status of all women is raised. There is implicit recognition that all of life is sacred and that women, through their contributions to the maintenance of life, broadly defined, serve sacred purposes. One of the most important values that is reinforced at coming-of-age rites is women's connection to others and their associated performance of behaviors that contribute to the well-being of kin and tribe. The same expectations are placed on men, but they are emphasized in rituals of other forms. For instance, the case study in chapter 8 provided by the Ojibwa man stressed the responsibility that men were to acquire at girls' coming-of-age ceremonies through their performance of tasks of service. This illustration demonstrates how a present-day North American Indian band is seeking to recapture something of traditional roles that accentuated the value of all persons.

The work of Schlegel and Barry (1980) also contributes to the discussion on the status of women in North American Indian societies according to the purposes of adolescent initiation ceremonies. As summarized in earlier chapters, these authors concluded, relative to female adolescent initiations in food-collecting societies (the type of society commonly found in Native North America), that "the focus of the ceremony is the protection of the girl, and the ceremony is conducted for her future physical and spiritual well-being. The picture conveyed by initiation ceremonies in simple societies is one of high evaluation of females, who are given social recognition and possibly magical protection as well" (p. 711). Hence, the promotion of future physical and spiritual well-being of initiates is one of the primary interests of these rites. An additional finding of interest from these authors was that responsibility and the associated assumption of adult roles (and not reproductive viability) was the major focus of adolescent initiations of girls in North American Indian societies. These findings are consistent with the literature reviewed in chapter 5 on puberty rituals from 10 cultural areas, as well as the present-day field research reported in later chapters. Reproductive viability of initiates was not shown to be the central interest; rather, it was the incorporation of girls as responsible members of societies in which cooperation and connection were of principal importance. Further, the necessity of acquisition of spiritual power and strength was deemed critical for the life journey, and puberty was the prime time for such spiritual encounters to occur. In summary, the research presented in this book and in related writings on the topic is highly indicative of the multifaceted purposes of girls' coming-of-age rites, including those that affirm and advance their development.

Implications for Identity Formation

In consideration of the implications of coming-of-age ceremonies for the development of contemporary North American Indian girls, it is useful to be reminded of E. H. Erikson's (1968, 1987) four indices of optimal identity formation: becoming and feeling most like oneself and experiencing a subjective sense of comfort with the self; having a sense of direction in life; perceiving sameness and continuity of the self from the past, at the present, and to the anticipated future; and expressing an identity that is affirmed by a community of important others. It was asserted in chapter 1 that the rich array of rituals implicit in coming-of-age ceremonies yield these outcomes (see Markstrom & Iborra, 2003). While it is the psychosocial components of maturation that are of interest in the present discussion, the rite of passage at puberty makes use of an event that signals biological maturation (i.e., menarche) and compels maturation in other domains of the girl's development. It is the arena of social identity, which includes social roles and ethnic identity, that appears to be the primary target of identity transformations at pubertal rites of passage, but there are additional applications that are addressed in the following discussion.

All four indices of optimal identity are intricately linked, and they encompass especially interesting parallels to the Ritual Process Paradigm (RPP, Dunham et al., 1986) as applied to the Apache Sunrise Dance in chapter 6. It was shown that earlier stages of this rite-of-passage model are associated with personal discomfort; specifically, the separation phase, which comprises new environmental demands, liminality, activation, and agony. The new environmental demands placed on initiates intensify the sense of their separated states and present a temporary state of psychosocial confusion. For instance, in a study of the Navajo Kinaaldá by Keith (1964), initiates reported that they were not treated as women, nor were they allowed to play with children, and felt "awkward, tired, and almost unhappy" (p. 29). In short, interpretations of rites of passage from both anthropological and psychosocial perspectives recognize the personal discomforts and identity confusion of the liminal state (Markstrom & Iborra, 2003). More specific to the anthropological view, Turner (1967) observed that "undoing, dissolution, decomposition are accompanied by processes of growth, transformation, and the reformulation of old elements in new patterns" (p. 99). Similarly, E. H. Erikson (1968) observed that "the adolescent, during the final stage of his identity formation, is apt to suffer more deeply than he ever did before or ever will again from a confusion of roles" (p. 163). The initiate is separated from an earlier, secure state without the comfort and security of the next stage of development, which offers greater solidification of social roles and heightened social status. The *huskanaw* ceremony practiced by eastern Virginia and North Carolina Iroquoians and Algonquians, as described in chapter 5, offers an illustration of one of the most extreme and demanding forms of ritual separation at puberty. Children were separated from their families and subjected to physically demanding and painful rituals for several months in the wilderness and were subsequently returned to their families as young people who were reborn without connection to their earlier dependent stages.

In contrast to the insecurity of separation, later RPP phases of transition and reincorporation are associated with greater subjective comfort and yield processes of growth and transformation; hence the first point of optimal identity is experienced. Self-confidence is fostered through the initiate's success in performance of the complex rituals of her rite of passage. Further, her significant social community shares the celebration and provides social reinforcement, affirmation, and acknowledgment. The shared value of a successful rite of passage likely compels the initiate to a deeper level of personal value and self-understanding. All the rituals performed are meaningful, and many connect in some way to her expected future roles as a woman of her culture. In this respect, ethnic identity is reinforced, as is another aspect of optimal identity formation, namely, the acquisition of a greater sense of direction in life. At pubertal coming-of-age events, the forms of the rituals and the content of instruction reinforce social and ethnic components of identity that are familiar to the young person. That is, throughout childhood she observed the behaviors of her adult role models and, in a more limited sense, engaged in role play and role performance that mimicked the behaviors of adults. In this respect, the third point of optimal identity formation is significant. Continuity of identity is experienced, and the coming-of-age event serves as a culmination of earlier experiences that are embellished in the present context with an expectation that targeted behaviors will continue into the future.

This discussion has centered on the ascription and reinforcement of social and ethnic forms of identity during the coming-of-age event, but rites of passage serve as springboards for achieved components of identity as well. Chapter 3 dissected the false dichotomy between patterns of interdependence and communalism on the one hand and patterns of individualism and personal autonomy on the other, and both sets of orientations were shown to be applicable in North American Indian cultures. In essence, because both ascribed and achieved forms of identity are influenced by the young person's social context, it is difficult to separate them. For instance, contemporary North American Indian adolescent girls are like their counterparts throughout the broader society in their possession of personal aspirations relative to education and occupation—domains of identity that are typically considered to be achieved. But, assuming they value the social approval of their group in their formation of an optimal identity, adolescents will choose occupations that are socially validated. In North American Indian societies of the past, adult pursuits were somewhat straightforward according to gender-role distinctions, and women's roles centered on child rearing, management of the home or camp, and fulfilling responsibilities toward others. As well, women served important roles in procuring, processing, and preparing food. During their coming-of-age events, girls continue to be instructed according to the value of interpersonal connection and their responsibilities toward others. However, it is clearly evident from the numerous pubertal coming-of-age ceremonies that I have attended that initiates are also encouraged to pursue individualistic pursuits, especially in respect to education and occupation. An example was given in chapter 3 of the social reinforcement provided to the Navajo initiate who desired to become a veterinarian. At one Apache Sunrise Dance it was clearly communicated to me on several occasions that the particular female co-sponsor or godmother was selected because she was educated and held a high-status professional position. It was the desire of the initiate's parents that their daughter ultimately emulate these traits.

These illustrations from Navajo and Apache cultures are significant in several respects, beginning with the fact that recognition was shown to the desire of many contemporary young women for accommodation of both career and family (Markstrom & Iborra, 2003). It was acknowledged by the adult community that such pursuits are permissible and desirable. The pursuit of both education and career is not regarded as contradictory to traditional teachings or the examples of the ultimate female roles models of these cultures (i.e., Changing Woman or White Painted Woman), who, among other traits, demonstrate strength, power, and purpose. Rather, initiates are encouraged to consider timing through first pursuing their needed education, then establishing a career, and finally beginning their family of procreation. Again, this is the same kind of socialization received by young people across the broader society. What may be distinct in North American Indian societies is the kind of occupations that young women are encouraged to pursue. Specifically, the Navajo girl who desired to become a veterinarian had made an occupational selection that was of value to the Navajo people; that is, working with animals is a useful and familiar occupation among the rural members of this tribe (see Markstrom & Iborra, 2003). Relative to the Apache initiate whose parents selected a godmother they hoped their daughter would emulate, this female mentor was an administrator of Indian Health Service. Again, this occupation reflected a valued and useful source of health and well-being for contemporary American Indians. (Additionally, I have observed on multiple occasions familial and community pride in young people who join the military service. While I was first perplexed by the irony of serving the U.S. military system, it occurred to me that these are the modern-day warriors, and opportunities are provided for display of traditional traits of bravery, sacrifice, protection, and strength.)[2] The fourth component of Erikson's comments on optimal identity, affirmation by the adolescent's significant social group, is certainly reflected in these examples of components of identity that are achieved, but they are nonetheless choices influenced by the significant social groups of the initiates. Certainly for North American Indian adolescents as well as other ethnic adolescents, ethnicity is a pervasive force in all identity commitments—ascribed or achieved.

A further observation on ascribed and achieved aspects of identity formation returns this discussion to specific coming-of-age rituals and their associated meanings. The desired positive outcomes of rituals are believed to situate the girl for her future. But, she is a participant in these rituals; and the outcomes, in part, depend on her performance (Markstrom & Iborra, 2003). The physical endurance she displays and her attitude toward the rituals are thought to influence the degree to which she might absorb hoped for positive outcomes. It is contended, therefore, that ascription of identity occurs through the rituals and instruction of the initiate at the coming-of-age event, but critical components for success are her engagement in these processes and her willingness to be influenced.

A related consideration previously not addressed is that of timing; specifically, optimal identity formation is a process that occurs over a period of years, and coming-of-age ceremonies occur in early adolescence when it is premature to expect lifetime identity commitments among adolescents, outcomes normative to the later adolescent years and early adulthood. As asked by Markstrom and Iborra (2003): "So, how can only four days of rituals make a significant impact?" (p. 419). These authors go on to explain relative to the Navajo Kinaaldá: "Keith (1964) argued that these are not just any four days. They are highly dramatic and encompass a vast departure from the day-to-day existence of young women. Intensive preparation efforts are required, and the initiate is essentially the focal point of her social network before, during, and after the ceremony. Furthermore, the performance of rituals during the four days serves as powerful connectors between less rigorous skill mastery in childhood to the expectation of more serious role adoption and performance in adulthood" (p. 419). It is recognized that her puberty ceremony is the first major step toward adulthood, and the lessons acquired at this time will be reinforced over the next several years by her relatives who constitute her new support group (reincorporation phase of the RPP). Anxieties can again emerge due to the freedom of this new status and her attempts to try out a new identity, but the psychosocial discomfort is perhaps softened by the support of her social group (see Markstrom & Iborra, 2003).

The Future of Coming-of-Age Ceremonies

It is impressive that the cultures reviewed in the previous three chapters continue their coming-of-age practices for girls into the present day. The

Sunrise Dance has emerged as the most important ceremony of Apache culture, and the Kinaaldá has been stated to be the best-understood and perhaps most frequently practiced ceremony in Navajo culture (Frisbie, 1993). Efforts have been taken among the Sioux groups (i.e., Lakota, Nakota, and Dakota) to reinstitute coming-of-age practices. There was recognition that coming-of-age rites are practiced, in some forms, among bands of Ojibwas. Other groups not addressed in this work have revived customs that had waned from earlier times, and this appears to be a growing trend. What factors account for such commitments to these ancient ceremonies in the technological global context of the 21st century? Relative to the case studies of this book, the matrilineal and matrilocal characteristics of Apache and Navajo cultures speak to the importance of the female lineage to the expectation for the initiate's transformation into White Painted Woman or Changing Woman. As well, Lakota culture was traditionally matrilineal, and the female coming-of-age rites serve to connect the initiate to White Buffalo Calf Woman. The matrilocal nature of traditional Ojibwa culture is also a characteristic that provided a certain degree of power to women. These points reinforce the arguments in chapter 4 that females and the feminine are valued in North American Indian cultures, as are the female personages in the cosmological structures of their belief systems. Additionally, Native cultures have traditionally valued life in multiple forms and levels, and the pubescent girl is a visible reminder of the cycle of life.

Clearly, the data presented in this book give evidence to the value of coming-of-age rites for girls in contemporary North American Indian societies and are suggestive that these events will continue into the future. The proper performances of ancient rituals are regarded as critical components of the life journey, and, at least in Apache, Navajo, and Lakota cultures, the initiate's transcendence to the primary supernatural being of her culture secures all good things to come. A widespread perception is that coming-of-age ceremonies place young people on clear-cut trajectories for life. For instance, in speaking with a group of Navajo students at Diné College on this topic, the unanimous remark to me was that Kinaaldá gives young women needed direction in life. The young women in this college class who had not experienced this event at puberty perceived a deficit, reporting that up to the present time their lives had not been as smooth as they might have been otherwise. One man shared how his wife underwent a Blessing Way Ceremony in adulthood to make up for the absence of a Kinaaldá at puberty. In short, Navajo and Apache informants concur that young women who undergo pubertal rites of passage are somehow better prepared for the challenges of life and that they more readily remain on a level pathway without becoming entangled in the risks of adolescence. The significance of coming-of-age ceremonies to the life course of young women is a theme found in many other North American Indian cultures (e.g., Beck et al., 1996; Bol & Menard, 2000; Hirschfelder & Molin, 2001).

It was suggested in chapter 1 that coming-of-age rites can be construed as protective culturally specific forms of structured activities that facilitate and contribute to positive youth development, including character formation. The protective function of coming-of-age rites was relevant in the past, as in the present, but perhaps the forms of needed protection have altered due to societal changes. North American Indians recognize the challenges posed to contemporary adolescents, and some perceive that their traditional customs have something to offer to the present day as they did in the past. Coming-of-age rituals provide socialization and endorsement of desired cultural values and practices through requirements that initiates perform responsibilities and tasks that teach meaningful lessons. Traditionally, North American Indian societies emphasized character traits such as endurance, honor, responsibility, discipline, and self-control. In my observation of numerous Apache and Navajo coming-of-age ceremonies, it appears that all of these traits continue to be valued and are implicit to ritual activities. For instance, the Apache conviction that life is difficult for women and, therefore, girls must acquire strength, finds expression in rituals that are demanding and physically exhausting for initiates, to both test and extend their limits. With respect to displays of discipline and self-control, one young Apache initiate asked her mother for advice if she had to relieve herself during the long dancing segments of her Sunrise Dance. Her mother's retort of "Just hold it" speaks to the expectation that parents place on their daughters to begin to exhibit more self-controlled, contained behaviors from their puberty rites onward.

In addition to the socialization of important cultural values, pubescent girls are engulfed in atmospheres of support and affirmation prior to, during, and after their coming-of-age rites. Certainly social reinforcement is a contributing factor to character development and serves a protective function relative to the risks of adolescence and the challenges and pressures of adulthood. The gathering of the significant social community on behalf of the initiate is a remarkable experience that must enhance one's sense of personal worth and would be expected to fortify the girl for years to come. Additionally, an ethnic identity is impressed upon the initiate that likely serves to advance pride in her culture, feelings of belongingness, and understanding of her culture's traditions, beliefs, and practice. The female initiate is firmly established within the context of kin and community, and her sense of position and importance is clarified and bolstered in numerous forms through rituals as well as in spontaneous social interaction. Likewise, the association between a female personage of oral tradition, such as White Painted Woman, and all girls and women endows them with significant status in their cultures. When I hear prominent American Indian women speak, such as Henrietta Mann or LaDonna Harris, I am impressed by their strength and assurance, which causes my thoughts to drift to the powerful role models of oral tradition.

In essence, through their coming-of-age ceremonies, it would seem that young women acquire a greater sense of their value and purpose in life through specialized preparations that lead to their engagement in and performance of meaningful rituals that emulate valued roles and responsibilities, the directed instruction they receive including cultural socialization, and the extensive attention and recognition from both family and community members. For example, the ritual during the Apache Sunrise Dance in which girls are approached for prayers and blessings from people of all ages was reported by initiates to be personally gratifying and affirming. It also must be remembered that coming-of-age rites facilitate passage into the spiritual complexities of a culture. Adolescence is frequently regarded as the first time in the life span when the young person possesses the strength to be initiated into such a realm. This statement is made in a general sense, but to acquire full appreciation of the connections between oral traditions, belief systems, and coming-of-age rites and their impacts on contemporary American Indian adolescents, it is necessary to engage in analysis of specific cultures, as occurred in previous chapters. It can be stated overall, however, that in addition to the functions served for adolescent development, coming-of-age ceremonies represent society's hope for the eventual contributions of youth to the social order and in the perpetuation of their cultures. These and other traditional rites offer opportunities to bring something of the past into the present day and perhaps help create a sense of a more ordered, predictable, and secure world.

Notes

1. Contextual and Methodological Considerations

1. Suppression of cultural knowledge and practices was one aim of the European American colonizers in the Western Hemisphere (chapter 2); hence, Indigenous theories that guided proper socialization and ritual activities across the life span were diminished. One aim of this book is to inform readers of these meaningful, viable, and culturally applicable theories.

2. Mexico is part of North America (although it is frequently included with Mesoamerica), and some Indigenous cultures of Mexico practiced puberty customs for girls. For purposes of brevity, the scope of this book is limited to the United States and Canada. However, some cultures addressed in this book were on both sides of what is now known as the U.S./Mexico border (e.g., Apaches).

3. North American Indian Perspectives on Human Development

1. This term is spelled in various ways, and in this instance it is indicated according to the spelling of the cited authors. However, in chapter 8 it is spelled *Ishna Ta Awi Cha Lowan* to be consistent with Black Elk, who related an important story of the girls' puberty ceremony.

2. Libby conducted her fieldwork on puberty rituals among the northern Athabascans in the 1940s, and by then many of her informants were already not practicing the rituals because they failed to perceive their functions. Conflicting sets of values were observed, with the traditional customs associated with puberty, menstruation, and birth disappearing in favor of alternative values and practices brought by Europeans.

4. Menstruation, Cosmology, and Feminism

1. On the other hand, Gill (1987) builds a compelling case for the construction of Mother Earth over the past 200 years. This construction has served both Natives and non-Natives alike, and one should not underestimate the impor-

tance of Mother Earth as an advocate in matters of North American Indian rights and justice, as well as a figurehead in the environmental movement.

2. Corn is an amazing plant with about 300 different races that have developed from centuries of breeding by Indians to improve size, flavor, and pest resistance (Rhoades, 1993). The story of domesticating corn began in 5000 b.c. among the Indians of the Americas. At that time, ears of corn were perhaps 1 inch in length. Centuries of careful genetic cultivation by Indians yielded the product known by the world today. It was the greatest discovery in the New World prior to European contact, and was a major contributing factor to the great Indian civilizations. It truly is an adaptive plant, growing from the Yukon Territory in the far north to Chile in South America. In many Indian cultures of the Americas it serves multiple functions as food, medicine, and an ingredient used in rituals (Kavasch & Baar, 1999).

3. The Iroquois consisted initially of five nations (Mohawk, Oneida, Onondaga, Cayuga, and Seneca) known as the Iroquois Confederacy. The Tuscarora was added as the sixth nation in the early 18th century.

5. Historical Overview of Coming-of-Age Practices

1. To avoid repetitiveness in this chapter, an author(s) is cited only the first time a specific group is discussed. In subsequent mention of practices of the same group, the author's name is not mentioned again unless the information is derived from a different source or it is unclear to which source the statement should be attributed.

2. In the Lakota, Nakota, and Dakota traditions it is stated that White Buffalo Calf Woman imparted to the people seven sacred ceremonies, including the ceremony at the girl's first menses (see chapter 8 for greater discussion of this fascinating rite).

3. As argued in chapter 4, an alternate explanation for covering pubescent girls was to control and manage their power so that it would not interfere with other forms of power required for activities such as hunting.

6. The Apache Sunrise Dance

1. Terms from the Apache language used in this book are predominantly from Basso (1966).

2. As discussed in chapter 3, Schlegel and Barry (1980) found that fertility was not the major theme of girls' puberty ceremonies among North American Indians. Rather, the socialization of responsibility was the major focus, along with the promotion of future physical and spiritual well-being of initiates.

3. This is the scientific explanation for migration patterns of the Southern Athabascans. However, origins, according to Apache oral tradition, are the focus of this chapter.

4. Basso (1966, 1970) wrote of the Cibecue Apache girls' puberty ceremony and identified the primary female supernatural figure as Changing Woman rather than White Painted Woman. Aside from this slight variation, Basso's work is cited throughout this description of the San Carlos Sunrise Dance, because Cibecue and San Carlos are both Western Apache groups with numerous overlaps in culture. Further, Basso's observations of the Sunrise Dance were usually consistent with my own. Indeed, medicine men who conduct Sunrise Dances at San Carlos may come from Cibecue and Whiteriver, both on the Fort Apache Reservation, and San Carlos medicine men may conduct the Sunrise Ceremony among Cibecue and White Moutain groups.

5. While it was not identified as Usen, G. Goodwin (1938) told of White Mountain Apache beliefs and identified the supreme deity as "Rules over Life" or "In Charge of Life." Similarly, the name given for this being by the Chiricahua and Mescalero Apaches is "Giver-of-Life" (Opler, 1935) or "Life Giver" (Opler, 1942). However, Hoijer (1938) observed that the notion of a creator was not sharply defined among the Chiricahuas and that the conception likely emerged through European contact. In contrast, G. Goodwin stated that this concept is likely pre-European among Apaches.

6. Opler wrote of the Chiricahua Apaches. His work and the works of Basso, Goodwin, and Goddard, and Hoijer are classic pieces on the Apache girls' puberty ceremony and are cited throughout this chapter and the next.

7. This research was conducted with the approval of the West Virginia University Institutional Review Board. At San Carlos, I was directed to Mr. Herbert Stevens of the San Carlos Apache Cultural Center, who greatly facilitated this research through providing introductions and access to ceremonies and to participants.

8. Ms. Ellen Big Rope of the Mescalero Apache Cultural Center provided helpful background information and introductions at Mescalero.

9. Two sisters interviewed for this study, who were a year apart in age, experi-

enced a joint Sunrise Dance because their first menses coincided over the period of a few weeks. Their medicine man determined that since the girls' first menses were so close in time, he preferred to perform the dances together.

10. Elizabeth Compton, M.S., accompanied me to five Sunrise Dances. Her insightful observations are very much appreciated.

11. In this respect, the works of Apache authors were particularly sought on this topic, including Goseyun (1991), Nicholas (1939), Quintero (1980), and Talamantez (1991, 2000).

12. Of the camps visited in this study, families typically constructed their camps the weekend prior to the Sunrise Dance. They stayed at their camps the entire week, with the first day of the public ceremony beginning on Friday. On Monday, the final rituals were completed, camps were disassembled, and families returned home.

13. I attended one 2-day ceremony, and Mails (1974/1993) provides a description of such an event.

14. At two Sunrise Dances I attended, the godmothers were not married, so male relatives assumed the roles of godfathers.

15. Turquoise stones, shell beads, and eagle feathers are sacred objects and were used for protective purposes by Slayer of Monsters and Born of Water when they were being tested by their father, the Sun (G. Goodwin, 1939). This is a further illustration of the relevance of oral tradition to the Sunrise Ceremony.

16. At all the dances I attended, the 4-day sequence spanned Friday to Monday. This is the typical schedule, presumably, to facilitate public attendance on the vastly important second and third days (i.e., Saturday and Sunday).

17. In the Apache composite of beliefs, *di yih*, translated as "power," is conceived of as supernatural force that can be obtained under certain conditions from a variety of sources, including objects and the natural environment (Basso, 1966).

18. *Ta chih* refers to sweat bath, a ritual act that occurs for many purposes in Apache culture. *Gish ih zha ha aldeh* is specific to the sweat bath of the girls' puberty ceremony, at which the cane is made.

19. One informant compared cattail pollen to holy water of the Catholics. This informant, a Catholic and also a follower of Apache traditions, stated that the sign of the cross was made with the cattail when it is used on others or oneself. In the purely traditional sense, the cross is symbolic of the four directions (Bourke, 1892).

20. As previously stated and discussed further in the next chapter, informants

confirmed that White Painted Woman and Changing Woman are the same figure. Additionally, Mails (1988) wrote that White Painted Woman, Changing Woman, and White Shell Woman are the same being.

21. All songs are sung in Apache throughout the Sunrise Dance. It was ascertained through interviews that initiates did not have the mastery of the Apache language to understand the meanings of the songs. This point is addressed in the next chapter.

22. Taken together, the four cardinal directions, the four colors, and numerous other practices are implicit to the sacred nature of the ceremony.

23. The Mountain Spirit dancers are sometimes called "crown dancers." A San Carlos Apache cultural expert informed me that the former is the more correct term.

24. According to Opler (1983a), the inclusion of masked impersonators in Apache culture, including clowns, is an influence from Pueblo culture.

25. One medicine man in this study supervised his own team of dancers. This was not always the case, as the dancers may be distinct from the medicine man who conducts the Sunrise Dance. In such a case, the dancers will have their own leader who serves more or less in a manager's role but, more importantly, is their spiritual leader in the construction of masks, painting of designs on their bodies, etc.

26. The name of the sponsor in Mescalero Apache tradition is different from San Carlos practice, in which the girl's parents are the sponsors and the godparents are the co-sponsors.

27. In this respect, one Mescalero informant told how a family from some great distance brought their son with cerebral palsy to be prayed for by a maiden. Her attendant guided her through the performance of the proper rituals she should perform on this boy. The family of the boy reported back at a later date that the boy was walking.

7. Interpretation of the Apache Sunrise Dance

1. The Chiricahua Apaches (the group with which Geronimo and Naiche would eventually be associated) were of the last groups of Apaches to surrender to the U.S. government. As they came under government control, Apaches were removed from the Southwest and experienced forced imprisonment in Florida, Alabama, and ultimately Fort Sill, Oklahoma. Geronimo and his small group of

less than 50 were the last Apaches to surrender to the U.S. military. Geronimo died in captivity at Fort Sill. Four years later, in 1913, the Chiricahua Apaches were allowed to resettle on the Mescalero Apache Reservation in New Mexico.

8. Contemporary Navajo, Lakota, and Ojibwa Puberty Customs

1. In discussing this book with Native colleagues and acquaintances in the United States and Canada, I have been informed of additional illustrations of contemporary coming-of-age practices for Hupa, Oneida, and Seminole girls, and certainly there are others of which I am currently not aware.

2. The number 4 is significant in the puberty ceremonies discussed in this chapter, as it was in the Apache Sunrise Dance discussed in the previous two chapters.

3. The symbolism of the Navajo basket is quite remarkable. For example, the center of the basket reflects the place of emergence; in essence, the spirit of the basket lives there. Circular designs reflect the passage of time and significant components of Navajo beliefs. The white circle around the center represents the Earth. The black segments represent the six sacred mountains, and their exact depiction depends on the size of the basket. It is desirable for the basket to have 12 coils from center to rim, reflecting 12 layers or levels of knowledge. The stitches along the outer rim represent contemporary Navajo people (Schwarz, 1997).

4. Begay (1983) stated that this event occurs on the third night, while Reichard (1977) and Schwarz (1997) indicated the fourth night. Variations in local customs may account for such discrepancies.

5. As explained by W. K. Powers (1977), "*Fireplace* is a term widely used by a number of American Indian tribes as a metaphor for various levels of social and political organization" (p. 3).

6. For a thorough telling of the Lakota creation story, see W. K. Powers (1977, 2000).

9. Broader Perspectives on Coming-of-Age

1. The list of North American Indian women from the past several decades who are recognized for their contributions to the arts, literature, political leadership, and social activism is lengthy and includes such well-known individuals as Ada Deer, Louise Erdrich, Joy Harjo, LaDonna Harris, Winona LaDuke,

Henrietta Mann, Wilma Mankiller, Janet McCloud, Anna Mae Pictou-Aquash, and Buffy Sainte-Marie, among others.

2. Nonetheless, it also must be considered that American youths from low-income backgrounds, regardless of ethnic or European American status, may be attracted to military service because of perceived opportunities for skill development, travel, and adventure that may appear to be unattainable in other ways.

References

Ackerman, L. A. (1995). Complementary but equal: Gender status in the Plateau. In L. F. Klein & L. A. Ackerman (Eds.), *Women and power in Native North America* (pp. 75–100). Norman: University of Oklahoma Press.

Albers, P. C. (2001). Santee. In W. C. Sturtevant (Gen. Ed.) & R. J. DeMallie (Vol. Ed.) *Handbook of North American Indians: Vol. 13, Pt. 2. Plains* (pp. 661–776). Washington DC: Smithsonian Institution.

Alcoff, L. (1995). Cultural feminism versus post-structuralism: The identity crisis in feminist theory. In N. Tuana & R. Tong (Eds.), *Feminism and philosophy: Essential readings in theory, reinterpretation, and application* (pp. 434–456). Boulder CO: Westview Press.

Alford, R. D. (1988). *Naming and identity: A cross-cultural study of personal naming practices*. New Haven CT: HRAF Press.

Allen, P. G. (1986). *The sacred hoop: Recovering the feminine in American Indian traditions*. Boston: Beacon Press.

Allen, P. G. (1991). *Grandmothers of the light: A medicine woman's sourcebook*. Boston: Beacon Press.

American Friends Service Committee. (1998). *Lakota teach their young people new traditions: Renewing a cherished way of life*. Available from <http://www.afsc.org>.

Anderson, M. J., & Ellis, R. (1995). On the reservation. In N. Vacc, S. DeVaney, & J. Wittmer (Eds.), *Experiencing and counseling multicultural and diverse populations* (3rd ed., pp. 179–197). Bristol PA: Taylor & Francis.

Arima, E., & Dewhirst, J. (1990). Nootkans of Vancouver Island. In W. C. Sturtevant (Gen. Ed.) & W. Suttles (Vol. Ed.), *Handbook of North American Indians: Vol. 7. Northwest Coast* (pp. 391–411). Washington DC: Smithsonian Institution.

Asch, M. (1981). Slavey. In W. C. Sturtevant (Gen. Ed.) & J. Helm (Vol. Ed.), *Handbook of North American Indians: Vol. 6. Subarctic* (pp. 338–349). Washington DC: Smithsonian Institution.

Assembly of First Nations. (2000). *First Nations suicide rate*. Available from <http://www.afn.can>.

Awiakta, M. (1993). *Selu: Seeking the Corn-Mother's wisdom*. Golden CO: Fulcrum Publishing.

Bailey, G. A., & Young, G. A. (2001). Kansa. In W. C. Sturtevant (Gen. Ed.) & R. J. DeMallie (Vol. Ed.), *Handbook of North American Indians: Vol. 13, Pt. 1. Plains* (pp. 462–475). Washington DC: Smithsonian Institution.

Barnouw, V. (1950). *Acculturation and personality among the Wisconsin Chippewa*. AAA Memoirs, no. 72.

Barrett, S. M. (Ed.). (1906). *Geronimo's story of his life*. New York: Duffield and Company.

Barry, B., III, & Schlegel, A. (1980). Early childhood precursors of adolescent initiation ceremonies. *Ethos, 8*, 132–145.

Basso, K. H. (1966). The gift of Changing Woman. In Anthropological Papers, No. 76, from *Smithsonian Institution Bureau of American Ethnology Bulletin 196*, pp. 113–173. Washington DC: Government Printing Office.

Basso, K. H. (1970). *The Cibecue Apache*. New York: Holt, Rinehart, and Winston.

Basso, K. H. (1983). Western Apache. In W. C. Sturtevant (Gen. Ed.) & A. Ortiz (Vol. Ed.), *Handbook of North American Indians: Vol. 10. Southwest* (pp. 462–488). Washington DC: Smithsonian Institution.

Beaglehole, E., & Beaglehole, P. (1935). Hopi of the Second Mesa. *Memoirs of the American Anthropological Association, 44*, 5–65.

Bean, L. J., & Shipek, F. C. (1978). Luiseño. In W. C. Sturtevant (Gen. Ed.) & R. F. Heizer (Vol. Ed.), *Handbook of North American Indians: Vol. 8. California* (pp. 550–563). Washington DC: Smithsonian Institution.

Bean, L. J., & Smith, C. R. (1978a). Gabrielino. In W. C. Sturtevant (Gen. Ed.) & R. F. Heizer (Vol. Ed.), *Handbook of North American Indians: Vol. 8. California* (pp. 538–549). Washington DC: Smithsonian Institution.

Bean, L. J., & Smith, C. R. (1978b). Serrano. In W. C. Sturtevant (Gen. Ed.) & R. F. Heizer (Vol. Ed.), *Handbook of North American Indians: Vol. 8. California* (pp. 570–574). Washington DC: Smithsonian Institution.

Bean, L. J., & Theodoratus, D. (1978). Western Pomo and Northeastern Pomo. In W. C. Sturtevant (Gen. Ed.) & R. F. Heizer (Vol. Ed.), *Handbook of North American Indians: Vol. 8. California* (pp. 289–305). Washington DC: Smithsonian Institution.

Beauvais, F. (2000). Indian adolescence: Opportunity and challenge. In R. Montemayor, G. R. Adams, & T. P. Gullotta (Eds.), *Adolescent diversity in ethnic, economic, and cultural contexts* (pp. 110–140). Thousand Oaks CA: Sage.

Beck, P. G., Walters, A. L., & Francisco, N. (1996). *The sacred: Ways of knowledge, sources of life*. Tsaile AZ: Navajo Community College Press.

Begay, S. M. (1983). *Kinaaldá: A Navajo puberty ceremony*. Rough Rock AZ: Rough Rock Demonstration School.

Bell, C. (1997). *Ritual: Perspectives and dimensions*. New York: Oxford University Press.

Bettelheim, B. (1954). *Symbolic wounds: Puberty rites and the envious male*. New York: Collier Books.

Bilharz, J. (1995). First among equals?: The changing status of Seneca women. In L. F. Klein & L. A. Ackerman (Eds.), *Women and power in Native North America* (pp. 101–112). Norman: University of Oklahoma Press.

Blackburn, T. C., & Bean, L. J. (1978). Kitanemuk. In W. C. Sturtevant (Gen. Ed.) & R. F. Heizer (Vol. Ed.), *Handbook of North American Indians: Vol. 8. California* (pp. 564–569). Washington DC: Smithsonian Institution.

Blackman, M. (1990). Haida: Traditional culture. In W. C. Sturtevant (Gen. Ed.) & W. Suttles (Vol. Ed.), *Handbook of North American Indians: Vol. 7. Northwest Coast* (pp. 240–260). Washington DC: Smithsonian Institution.

Boas, F. (1966). *Kwakiutl ethnography*. Chicago: University of Chicago Press.

Bol, M. C., & Menard, N. Z. S. B. (2000). "I saw all that": A Lakota girl puberty ceremony. *American Indian Culture and Research Journal, 24*, 25–42.

Bolt, C. (1987). *American Indian policy and American reform*. Boston: Allen & Unwin.

Boreson, K. (1998). Rock art. In W. C. Sturtevant (Gen. Ed.) & D. E. Walker (Vol. Ed.), *Handbook of North American Indians: Vol. 12. Plateau* (pp. 611–619). Washington DC: Smithsonian Institution.

Bourke, J. G. (1892). The medicine men of the Apache. *Bureau of Ethnology, Ninth Annual Report*, 451–596.

Bowen, T. (1983). Seri. In W. C. Sturtevant (Gen. Ed.) & A. Ortiz (Vol. Ed.), *Handbook of North American Indians: Vol. 10. Southwest* (pp. 230–249). Washington DC: Smithsonian Institution.

Boyce, D. W. (1978). Iroquoian tribes of the Virginia–North Carolina coastal plain. In W. C. Sturtevant (Gen. Ed.) & B. G. Trigger (Vol. Ed.), *Handbook of North American Indians: Vol. 15. Northeast* (pp. 282–289). Washington DC: Smithsonian Institution.

Bright, W. (1978). Karok. In W. C. Sturtevant (Gen. Ed.) & R. F. Heizer (Vol.

Ed.), *Handbook of North American Indians: Vol. 8. California* (pp. 180–189). Washington DC: Smithsonian Institution.

Brightman, R. A. (2004). Chitimacha. In W. C. Sturtevant (Gen. Ed.) & R. D. Fogelson (Vol. Ed.), *Handbook of North American Indians: Vol. 14. Southeast* (pp. 642–652). Washington DC: Smithsonian Institution.

Brightman, R. A., & Wallace, P. S. (2004). Chickasaw. In W. C. Sturtevant (Gen. Ed.) & R. D. Fogelson (Vol. Ed.), *Handbook of North American Indians: Vol. 14. Southeast* (pp. 478–495). Washington DC: Smithsonian Institution.

Brown, D. N., & Irwin, L. (2001). Ponca. In W. C. Sturtevant (Gen. Ed.) & R. J. DeMallie (Vol. Ed.), *Handbook of North American Indians: Vol. 13, Pt. 1. Plains* (pp. 416–431). Washington DC: Smithsonian Institution.

Brown, J. E. (1953/1989). *The sacred pipe: Black Elk's account of the seven rites of the Oglala Sioux*. Norman: University of Oklahoma Press.

Brumbach, H. J., & Jarvenpa, R. (1997). Women the hunter: Ethnoarchaeological lessons from Chipewyan life-cycle dynamics. In C. Claassen & R. A. Joyce (Eds.), *Women in prehistory: North America and Mesoamerica* (pp. 17–32). Philadelphia: University of Pennsylvania Press.

Buckley, T., & Gottlieb, A. (1988). A critical appraisal of theories of menstrual symbolism. In T. Buckley & A. Gottlieb (Eds.), *Blood magic: The anthropology of menstruation* (pp. 3–50). Berkeley: University of California Press.

Callaghan, C. A. (1978). Lake Miwok. In W. C. Sturtevant (Gen. Ed.) & R. F. Heizer (Vol. Ed.), *Handbook of North American Indians: Vol. 8. California* (pp. 264–273). Washington DC: Smithsonian Institution.

Callaway, G., Janetski, C., & Stewart, C. (1986). Ute. In W. C. Sturtevant (Gen. Ed.) & W. L. d'Azevedo (Vol. Ed.), *Handbook of North American Indians: Vol. 11. Great Basin* (pp. 336–367). Washington DC: Smithsonian Institution.

Callender, C. (1978). Illinois. In W. C. Sturtevant (Gen. Ed.) & B. G. Trigger (Vol. Ed.), *Handbook of North American Indians: Vol. 15. Northeast* (pp. 673–680). Washington DC: Smithsonian Institution.

Callender, C., Pope, R., & Pope, S. (1978). Kickapoo. In W. C. Sturtevant (Gen. Ed.) & B. G. Trigger (Vol. Ed.), *Handbook of North American Indians: Vol. 15. Northeast* (pp. 656–667). Washington DC: Smithsonian Institution.

Carmody, D. L., & Carmody, J. T. (1993). *Native American religions: An introduction*. New York: Paulist Press.

Churchill. W. (2002). *Struggle for the land: Native North American resistance to genocide, ecocide, and colonization*. San Francisco: City Lights.

Clark, A. (1981). Koyukon. In W. C. Sturtevant (Gen. Ed.) & J. Helm (Vol. Ed.), *Handbook of North American Indians: Vol. 6. Subarctic* (pp. 582–601). Washington DC: Smithsonian Institution.

Clark, D. W. (1984). Pacific Eskimo: Historical ethnography. In W. C. Sturtevant (Gen. Ed.) & D. Damas (Vol. Ed.) *Handbook of North American Indians: Vol. 5. Arctic* (pp. 185–197). Washington DC: Smithsonian Institution.

Clark, L. H. (1976). The girl's puberty ceremony of the San Carlos Apaches (1). *Journal of Popular Culture, 10*, 431–448.

Coleman, J. S. (1988). Social capital in the creation of human capital. *American Journal of Sociology, 94* (Suppl. 95), s95–s120.

Connors, J. L., & Donellan, A. M. (1998). Walk in beauty: Western perspectives on disability and Navajo family/cultural resilience. In H. I. McCubbin, E. A. Thompson, A. I. Thompson, & J. E. Fromer (Eds.), *Resiliency in Native American and immigrant families* (pp. 159–182). Thousand Oaks CA: Sage.

Cooper, J. M. (1932). The position of women in primitive culture. *Primitive Man, 5*, 32–47.

Cooper, T. W. (1998). *A time before deception: Truth in communication, culture, and ethics.* Sante Fe NM: Clear Light Publishers.

Creswell, J. W. (1998). *Qualitative inquiry and research design: Choosing among five traditions.* Thousand Oaks CA: Sage.

Cross, T. L. (1998). Understanding family resiliency from a relational world view. In H. I. McCubbin, E. A. Thompson, A. I. Thompson, & J. E. Fromer (Eds.), *Resiliency in Native American and immigrant families* (pp. 143–157). Thousand Oaks CA: Sage.

Crow, J. R., & Obley, P. R. (1981). Han. In W. C. Sturtevant (Gen. Ed.) & J. Helm (Vol. Ed.), *Handbook of North American Indians: Vol. 6. Subarctic* (pp. 506–513). Washington DC: Smithsonian Institution.

Csordas, T. J. (1999). Ritual healing and the politics of identity in contemporary Navajo society. *American Ethnologist, 26*, 3–23.

Curtis Collection. (2004). Zuni social customs. *North American Indian* (Vol. 17). Retrieved February 13, 2004, from <http://www.curtis-collection.com>.

Darnell, R. (2001). Plains Cree. In W. C. Sturtevant (Gen. Ed.) & R. J. DeMallie (Vol. Ed.), *Handbook of North American Indians: Vol. 13, Pt. 1. Plains* (pp. 638–651). Washington DC: Smithsonian Institution.

d'Azevedo, L.(1986). Washoe. In W. C. Sturtevant (Gen .Ed.) & W. L. d'Azevedo,

(Vol. Ed.), *Handbook of North American Indians: Vol. 11. Great Basin* (pp. 466–498). Washington DC: Smithsonian Institution.

Debo, A. (1976). *Geronimo: The man, his time, his place*. Norman: University of Oklahoma Press.

de Laguna, F. (1990a). Eyak. In W. C. Sturtevant (Gen. Ed.) & W. Suttles (Vol. Ed.), *Handbook of North American Indians: Vol. 7. Northwest Coast* (pp. 89–196). Washington DC: Smithsonian Institution.

de Laguna, F. (1990b). Tlingit. In W. C. Sturtevant (Gen. Ed.) & W. Suttles (Vol. Ed.), *Handbook of North American Indians: Vol. 7. Northwest Coast* (pp. 203–228). Washington DC: Smithsonian Institution.

de Laguna, F., & McClellan, C. (1981). Ahtna. In W. C. Sturtevant (Gen. Ed.) & J. Helm (Vol. Ed.), *Handbook of North American Indians: Vol. 6. Subarctic* (pp. 641–663). Washington DC: Smithsonian Institution.

Deloria, E. (1944/1979). *Speaking of Indians*. Vermillion SD: Dakota Press.

Deloria, V. (1969). *Custer died for your sins: An Indian manifesto*. New York: Avon.

DeMallie, R. J. (2001a). Sioux until 1850. In W. C. Sturtevant (Gen. Ed.) & R. J. DeMallie (Vol. Ed.) *Handbook of North American Indians: Vol. 13, Pt. 2. Plains* (pp. 718–760). Washington DC: Smithsonian Institution.

DeMallie, R. J. (2001b). Teton. In W. C. Sturtevant (Gen. Ed.) & R. J. DeMallie (Vol. Ed.) *Handbook of North American Indians: Vol. 13, Pt. 2. Plains* (pp. 794–820). Washington DC: Smithsonian Institution.

DeMallie, R. J., & Miller, D. R. (2001). Assiniboine. In W. C. Sturtevant (Gen. Ed.) & R. J. DeMallie (Vol. Ed.) *Handbook of North American Indians: Vol. 13, Pt. 1. Plains* (pp. 572–596). Washington DC: Smithsonian Institution.

Dempsey, H. A. (2001). Blackfoot. In W. C. Sturtevant (Gen. Ed.) & R. J. DeMallie (Vol. Ed.), *Handbook of North American Indians: Vol. 13, Pt. 1. Plains* (pp. 604–628). Washington DC: Smithsonian Institution.

Denniston, G. (1981). Sekani. In W. C. Sturtevant (Gen. Ed.) & J. Helm (Vol. Ed.) *Handbook of North American Indians: Vol. 6. Subarctic* (pp. 433–441). Washington DC: Smithsonian Institution.

Densmore, F. (1929/1979). *Chippewa customs*. St. Paul: Minnesota Historical Society Press.

de Williams, A. A. (1983). Cocopa. In W. C. Sturtevant (Gen. Ed.) & A. Ortiz (Vol. Ed.), *Handbook of North American Indians: Vol. 10. Southwest* (pp. 99–112). Washington DC: Smithsonian Institution.

Diamont, A. (1997). *The red tent*. New York: Picador.

Dickinson, W. (2000). *Envisioning Kinaaldá: Navajo magic, mystery, and myth*. Proceedings of the Twenty-fifth Annual SAS Users Group International Conference, April 9–12, 2000, Indianapolis, Indiana.

Driver, H. E. (1941). Culture element distributions: XVI—Girls' puberty rites in Western North America. *Anthropological Records, 6*, 21–90.

Du Bois, C. (1935). *Wintu ethnography*. University of California Publications in American Archaeology and Ethnology, 36.

Dunham, R. M., Kidwell, J. S., & Wilson, S. M. (1986). Rites of passage at adolescence: A ritual process paradigm. *Journal of Adolescent Research, 1*, 139–154.

Duran, B., Duran, E., & Brave Heart, M. Y. H. (1998). Native Americans and the trauma of history. In R. Thornton (Ed.), *Studying Native America* (pp. 60–76). Madison: University of Wisconsin Press.

Dutton, B. P. (1983). *American Indians of the Southwest*. Albuquerque: University of New Mexico Press.

Eastman, C. A. (Ohiyesa). (1911). *The soul of the Indian*. Lincoln: University of Nebraska Press.

Eggan, F. (Ed.). (1937). *Social anthropology of North American tribes*. Chicago: University of Chicago Press.

Eichstaedt, P. H. (1994). *If you poison us: Uranium and Native Americans*. Santa Fe NM: Red Crane Books.

Elsasser, A. B. (1978a). Mattole, Nongatl, Sinkyone, Lassik, and Wailaki. In W. C. Sturtevant (Gen. Ed.) & R. F. Heizer (Vol. Ed.), *Handbook of North American Indians: Vol. 8. California* (pp. 190–204). Washington DC: Smithsonian Institution

Elsasser, A. B. (1978b). Wiyot. In W. C. Sturtevant (Gen. Ed.) & R. F. Heizer (Vol. Ed.), *Handbook of North American Indians: Vol. 8. California* (pp. 155–163). Washington DC: Smithsonian Institution.

Erikson, E. H. (1968). *Identity: Youth and crisis*. New York: Norton.

Erikson, E. H. (1987). Late adolescence (1959). In S. Schlein (Ed.), *A way of looking at things* (pp. 631–643). New York: Norton.

Erikson, V. O. (1978). Maliseet-Passamaquoddy. In W. C. Sturtevant (Gen. Ed.) & B. G. Trigger (Vol. Ed.), *Handbook of North American Indians: Vol. 15. Northeast* (pp. 123–136). Washington DC: Smithsonian Institution.

Farrer, C. R. (1980). Singing for life: The Mescalero Apache girls' puberty ceremony. In C. J. Frisbie (Ed.), *Southwestern Indian ritual drama* (pp. 125–159). Albuquerque: University of New Mexico Press.

Fasick, F. (1988). Patterns of formal education in high school as *Rites de Passage. Adolescence, 23,* 457–468.

Feest, C. F. (1978). *Virginia Algonquians.* In W. C. Sturtevant (Gen. Ed.) & B. G. Trigger (Vol. Ed.), *Handbook of North American Indians: Vol. 15. Northeast* (pp. 253–270). Washington DC: Smithsonian Institution.

First Nations and Inuit Regional Health Survey National Steering Committee. (1999). *National Report 1999.* St. Regis, Quebec: Author.

Flach, F. (1988). *Resilience: Discovering a new strength at times of stress.* New York: Fawcett Columbine.

Fogelson, R. D. (2004). Cherokee in the East. In W. C. Sturtevant (Gen. Ed.) & R. D. Fogelson (Vol. Ed.), *Handbook of North American Indians: Vol. 14. Southeast* (pp. 337–353). Washington DC: Smithsonian Institution.

Forde, C. D. (1931). Ethnography of the Yuma Indians. *American Archaeology and Ethnology, 28,* 83–278.

Foster, S., & Little, M. (1987). The vision quest: Passing from childhood to adulthood. In L. C. Mahdi, S. Foster, & M. Little (Eds.), *Betwixt & between: Patterns of masculine and feminine initiation* (pp. 79–110). LaSalle IL: Open Court.

Fowler, C. S., & Liljeblad, S. (1986). Northern Paiute. In W. C. Sturtevant (Gen. Ed.) & W. L. d'Azevedo (Vol. Ed.) *Handbook of North American Indians: Vol. 11. Great Basin* (pp. 434–465). Washington DC: Smithsonian Institution.

Fox, M. J. T. (1999). Native women in ancient North America: Ojibway and Iroquois. In B. Vivante (Ed.), *Women's roles in ancient civilizations: A reference guide* (pp. 338–362). Westport CT: Greenwood Press.

French, D. H., & French, K. S. (1998). Wasco, Wishram, and Cascades. In W. C. Sturtevant (Gen. Ed.) & D. E. Walker (Vol. Ed.), *Handbook of North American Indians: Vol. 12. Plateau* (pp. 360–377). Washington DC: Smithsonian Institution.

Fried, M. N., & Fried, M. H. (1980). *Transitions: Four rituals in eight cultures.* New York: Norton.

Frisbie, C. J. (1993). *Kinaaldá: A study of the Navajo girl's puberty ceremony.* Salt Lake City: University of Utah Press.

Frisch, R. E. (1975). Demographic implications of the biological determinants of female fecundity. *Social Biology, 22,* 17–22.

Furstenberg, F. F., & Hughes, M. E. (1995). Social capital and successful development among at-risk youth. *Journal of Marriage and the Family, 57*, 580–592.

Gall, M. D., Borg, W. R., & Gall, J. P. (1996). *Educational research: An introduction* (6th ed.). Addison-Wesley.

Galloway, P. (1997). Where have all the menstrual huts gone? The invisibility of menstrual seclusion in the late prehistoric Southeast. In C. Claassen & R. A. Joyce (Eds.), *Women in prehistory: North America and Mesoamerica* (pp. 47–62). Philadelphia: University of Pennsylvania Press.

Galloway, P., & Kidwell, C. S. (2004). Choctaw in the East. In W. C. Sturtevant (Gen. Ed.) & R. D. Fogelson (Vol. Ed.), *Handbook of North American Indians: Vol. 14. Southeast* (pp. 499–519). Washington DC: Smithsonian Institution.

Ganteaume, C. R. (1992). White Mountain Apache dance: Expressions of spirituality. In C. Heth (Ed.), *Native American dance: Ceremonies and social traditions* (pp. 65–81). Washington DC: Smithsonian.

Garrow, P. H. (1974). An ethnohistorical study of the Powhatan tribes. *The Chesopiean: A Journal of North American Archaeology, 12*, 30–31.

Garth, T. R. (1978). Atsugewi. In W. C. Sturtevant (Gen. Ed.) & R. F. Heizer (Vol. Ed.), *Handbook of North American Indians: Vol. 8. California* (pp. 236–248). Washington DC: Smithsonian Institution.

Gattuso, J. (Ed.). (1991). *Native America*. Singapore: APA Publications.

Gill, S. D. (1987). *Mother Earth: An American story*. Chicago: University of Chicago Press.

Gillespie, B. (1981). Mountain Indians. In W. C. Sturtevant (Gen. Ed.) & J. Helm (Vol. Ed.), *Handbook of North American Indians: Vol. 6. Subarctic* (pp. 326–337). Washington DC: Smithsonian Institution.

Goddard, I. (1978). Delaware. In W. C. Sturtevant (Gen. Ed.) & B. G. Trigger (Vol. Ed.), *Handbook of North American Indians: Vol. 15. Northeast* (pp. 213–239). Washington DC: Smithsonian Institution.

Goddard, P. E. (1909). Gotal—A Mescalero Apache ceremony. In F. Boas (Ed.), *Putnam anniversary volume: Anthropological essays presented to Frederick Ward Putnam in honor of his seventieth birthday, April 6, 1909, by his friends and associates* (pp. 385–394). New York: G. E. Stechert.

Goddard, P. E. (1918). Myths and tales from the San Carlos Apache. *Anthropological Papers of the American Museum of Natural History, 24*, pt. 1. New York.

Goddard, P. E. (1919a). Myths and tales from the White Mountain Apache. *Anthropological papers of the American Museum of Natural History, 24*, 89–139.

Goddard, P. E. (1919b). White Mountain Apache texts. *Anthropological papers of the American Museum of Natural History, 24*, 369–527.

Goldschmidt, W. (1978). Nomlaki. (1978). In W. C. Sturtevant (Gen. Ed.) & R. F. Heizer (Vol. Ed.), *Handbook of North American Indians: Vol. 8. California* (pp. 341–349). Washington DC: Smithsonian Institution.

Golston, S. E. (1996). *Changing Woman of the Apache: Women's lives in past and present*. New York: Franklin Watts.

Goodwin, G. (1938). White Mountain Apache religion. *American Anthropologist, 40*, 24–37.

Goodwin, G. (1939). Myths and tales of the White Mountain Apache. *Memoirs of the American Folklore Society, 33*. New York: J. J. Augustin.

Goodwin, G. (1942). *The social organization of the Western Apache*. Chicago: University of Chicago Press.

Goodwin, N. (2001). Like a brother: Grenville Goodwin's Apache years, 1928–1939. *Journal of the Southwest, 43*, 131–188.

Gordon, D. E. (1988). Formal operations and interpersonal and affective disturbances in adolescents. *New Directions for Child Development, 39*, 51–73.

Goseyun, A. E. (1991). Carla's sunrise. *Native Peoples, 4*, 8–16.

Gould, R. A. (1978). Tolowa. In W. C. Sturtevant (Gen. Ed.) & R. F. Heizer (Vol. Ed.), *Handbook of North American Indians: Vol. 8. California* (pp. 128–136). Washington DC: Smithsonian Institution.

Grant, C. (1978). Eastern Coast Salish. In W. C. Sturtevant (Gen. Ed.) & R. F. Heizer (Vol. Ed.), *Handbook of North American Indians: Vol. 8. California* (pp. 509–519). Washington DC: Smithsonian Institution.

Greene, C. S. (2001). Art until 1900. In W. C. Sturtevant (Gen. Ed.) & R. J. DeMallie (Vol. Ed.) *Handbook of North American Indians: Vol. 13, Pt. 2. Plains* (pp. 1039–1054). Washington DC: Smithsonian Institution.

Griffin-Pierce, T. (2000). The continuous renewal of sacred relations: Navajo religion. In L. E. Sullivan (Ed.), *Native Religions and cultures of North America: Anthropology of the sacred* (pp. 121–141). New York: Continuum.

Grimes, R. L. (1985). *Research in ritual studies*. Metuchen NJ: Scarecrow Press.

Guemple, L. (1995). Gender in Inuit society. In L. F. Klein & L. A. Ackerman (Eds.), *Women and power in Native North America* (pp. 17–27). Norman: University of Oklahoma Press.

Hall, G. S. (1904). *Adolescence* (Vols. 1 & 2). Englewood Cliffs NJ: Prentice Hall.

Halpin, M., & Sequin, M. (1990). Tsimshian peoples: Southern Tsimshian, Coast Tsimshian, Nishga, and Gitksan. In W. C. Sturtevant (Gen. Ed.) & W. Suttles (Vol. Ed.), *Handbook of North American Indians: Vol. 7. Northwest Coast* (pp. 267–284). Washington DC: Smithsonian Institution.

Harvey, A., & Baring, A. (1996). *The divine feminine: Exploring the feminine face of God throughout the world.* Berkeley CA: Conari Press.

Harwell, H., & Kelly, M. (1983). Maricopa. In W. C. Sturtevant (Gen. Ed.) & A. Ortiz (Vol. Ed.), *Handbook of North American Indians: Vol. 10. Southwest* (pp. 71–85). Washington DC: Smithsonian Institution.

Health Canada. (2003). *A statistical profile on the health of First Nations in Canada.* Ottawa, Ontario: Author.

Helm, J. (1981). Dogrib. In W. C. Sturtevant (Gen. Ed.) & J. Helm (Vol. Ed.), *Handbook of North American Indians: Vol. 6. Subarctic* (pp. 217–230). Washington DC: Smithsonian Institution.

Hester, T. R. (1978). Salinan. In W. C. Sturtevant (Gen. Ed.) & R. F. Heizer (Vol. Ed.), *Handbook of North American Indians: Vol. 8. California* (pp. 500–504). Washington DC: Smithsonian Institution.

Hilger, M. I. (1951/1992). *Chippewa child life and its cultural background.* St. Paul: Minnesota Historical Society Press.

Hirschfelder, A. B., & Molin, P. F. (2001). *Encyclopedia of Native American religions: An introduction* (2nd ed.). New York: Facts on File.

Hodge, F. W. (1912). *Handbook of American Indians north of Mexico.* Washington DC: Smithsonian Institution, Bureau of Ethnology.

Hoijer, H. (1938). Chiricahua and Mescalero Apache texts. With ethnological notes by Morris Edward Opler. *University of Chicago Publications in Anthropology.* Chicago: University of Chicago Press.

Honigmann, J. J. (1981a). Expressive aspects of subarctic Indian culture. In W. C. Sturtevant (Gen. Ed.) & J. Helm (Vol. Ed.), *Handbook of North American Indians: Vol. 6. Subarctic* (pp. 718–739). Washington DC: Smithsonian Institution.

Honigmann, J. J. (1981b). Kaska. In W. C. Sturtevant (Gen. Ed.) & J. Helm (Vol. Ed.), *Handbook of North American Indians: Vol. 6. Subarctic* (pp. 442–450). Washington DC: Smithsonian Institution.

Honigmann, J. J. (1981c). West Main Cree. In W. C. Sturtevant (Gen. Ed.) & J. Helm (Vol. Ed.), *Handbook of North American Indians: Vol. 6. Subarctic* (pp. 217–230). Washington DC: Smithsonian Institution.

Hood, E. F. (1984). Feminism and women of color: The inseparability of gender, class, and racial oppression. In A. M. Jaggar & P. S. Rothenberg (Eds.), *Feminist frameworks: Alternative theoretical accounts of the relations between men and women* (2nd ed., pp. 189–202). New York: McGraw Hill.

Hughes, C. C. (1960). *An Eskimo village in the modern world.* Ithaca NY: Cornell University Press.

Hultkrantz, A. (1980). *The religions of the American Indians.* Berkeley: University of California Press.

Hunn, E. S., & French, D. H. (1998). Western Columbia River Sahaptins. (1998). In W. C. Sturtevant (Gen. Ed.) & D. E. Walker (Vol. Ed.), *Handbook of North American Indians: Vol. 12. Plateau* (pp. 378–394). Washington DC: Smithsonian Institution.

Ignace, M. B. (1998). Shuswap. In W. C. Sturtevant (Gen. Ed.) & D. E. Walker (Vol. Ed.), *Handbook of North American Indians: Vol. 12. Plateau* (pp. 203–219). Washington DC: Smithsonian Institution.

Indian and Northern Affairs Canada [INAC]. (1996). *Report of the Royal Commission on Aboriginal Peoples.* Available from <http://www.ainc>.

Indian and Northern Affairs Canada [INAC]. (2000). *Backgrounder: Income security reform (ISR) demonstration projects.* Available from <http://www.ainc>.

Indian and Northern Affairs Canada [INAC]. (2004). *From time immemorial: A demographic profile.* Available from <http://www.ainc.gc.ca>.

Indian Health Service. (1998/99). *Indian health focus: Youth.* Available from <http://www.ihs.gov>.

Inhelder, B., & Piaget, J. (1958). *The growth of logical thinking from childhood to adolescence.* New York: Basic Books.

Jackson, J. B., Fogelson, R. D., & Sturtevant, W. C. (2004). History of ethnological and linguistic research. In W. C. Sturtevant (Gen. Ed.) & R. D. Fogelson (Vol. Ed.), *Handbook of North American Indians: Vol. 14. Southeast* (pp. 31–47). Washington DC: Smithsonian Institution.

Jaimes, M. A., & Halsey, T. (1992). American Indian women at the center of indigenous resistance in contemporary North America. In M. A. Jaimes (Ed.), *The state of Native America: Genocide, colonization, and resistance* (pp. 311–344). Boston: South End Press.

Jessor, R. (1993). Successful adolescent development among youth in high-risk settings. *American Psychologist, 48,* 117–126.

Johnson, J. J. (1978). Yana. In W. C. Sturtevant (Gen. Ed.) & R. F. Heizer (Vol.

Ed.), *Handbook of North American Indians: Vol. 8. California* (pp. 361–369). Washington DC: Smithsonian Institution.

Johnson, M. K., Beebe, T., Mortimer, J. T., & Snyder, M. (1998). Volunteerism in adolescence: A process perspective. *Journal of Research on Adolescence, 8,* 309–332.

Johnson, P. J. (1978). Patwin. In W. C. Sturtevant (Gen. Ed.) & R. F. Heizer (Vol. Ed.), *Handbook of North American Indians: Vol. 8. California* (pp. 350–360). Washington DC: Smithsonian Institution.

Jorgensen, G. (1986). Ghost Dance, Bear Dance, and Sun Dance. In W. C. Sturtevant (Gen. Ed.) & W. L. d'Azevedo (Vol. Ed.) *Handbook of North American Indians: Vol. 11. Great Basin* (pp. 660–672). Washington DC: Smithsonian Institution.

Joseph, A., Spicer, R. B., & Chesky, J. (1949). *The desert people: A study of the Papago Indians.* Chicago: University of Chicago Press.

Kavanagh, T. W. (2001). Comanche. In W. C. Sturtevant (Gen. Ed.) & R. J. DeMallie (Vol. Ed.), *Handbook of North American Indians: Vol. 13, Pt. 2. Plains* (pp. 886–906). Washington DC: Smithsonian Institution.

Kavasch, E. B., & Baar, K. (1999). *American Indian healing arts: Herbs, rituals, and remedies for every season of life.* New York: Bantam Books.

Keating, D. P. (1980). Thinking processes in adolescence. In J. Adelson (Ed.), *Handbook of adolescent psychology* (pp. 211–246). New York: Wiley.

Kehoe, A. B. (1995). Blackfoot persons. In L. F. Klein & L. A. Ackerman (Eds.), *Women and power in Native North America* (pp. 113–125). Norman: University of Oklahoma Press.

Keith, A. B. (1964). The Navajo girls' puberty ceremony: Function and meaning for the adolescent. *El Palacio, 71,* 27–36.

Kelly, I. (1978). Coast Miwok. In W. C. Sturtevant (Gen. Ed.) & R. F. Heizer (Vol. Ed.), *Handbook of North American Indians: Vol. 8. California* (pp. 414–425). Washington DC: Smithsonian Institution.

Kelly, T., & Fowler, S. (1986). Southern Paiute. In W. C. Sturtevant (Gen. Ed.) & W. L. d'Azevedo (Vol. Ed.) *Handbook of North American Indians: Vol. 11. Great Basin* (pp. 368–397). Washington DC: Smithsonian Institution.

Kennedy, D., & Bouchard, R. (1990a). Bella Coola. In W. C. Sturtevant (Gen. Ed.) & W. Suttles (Vol. Ed.), *Handbook of North American Indians: Vol. 7. Northwest Coast* (pp. 323–339). Washington DC: Smithsonian Institution.

Kennedy, D., & Bouchard, R. (1990b). Northern Coast Salish. In W. C. Sturtevant (Gen. Ed.) & W. Suttles (Vol. Ed.), *Handbook of North American Indians: Vol. 7. Northwest Coast* (pp. 441–452). Washington DC: Smithsonian Institution.

Kennedy, D., & Bouchard, R. (1998a). Lillooet. In W. C. Sturtevant (Gen. Ed.) & D. E. Walker (Vol. Ed.), *Handbook of North American Indians: Vol. 12. Plateau* (pp. 174–190). Washington DC: Smithsonian Institution.

Kennedy, D., & Bouchard, R. (1998b). Northern Okanagan, Lakes, and Colville. In W. C. Sturtevant (Gen. Ed.) & D. E. Walker (Vol. Ed.), *Handbook of North American Indians: Vol. 12. Plateau* (pp. 238–252). Washington DC: Smithsonian Institution.

Khera, S., & Mariella, P. S. (1983). Yavapai. In W. C. Sturtevant (Gen. Ed.) & A. Ortiz (Vol. Ed.), *Handbook of North American Indians: Vol. 10. Southwest* (pp. 38–54). Washington DC: Smithsonian Institution.

Kidwell, C. S., Noley, H., & Tinker, G. E. (2001). *A Native American theology.* Maryknoll NY: Orbis Books.

Klein, L. F. (1995). Mother as clanswoman: Rank and gender in Tlingit society. In L. F. Klein & L. A. Ackerman (Eds.), *Women and power in Native North America* (pp. 28–45). Norman: University of Oklahoma Press.

Klein, L. F., & Ackerman, L. A. (Eds.). (1995). *Women and power in Native North America.* Norman: University of Oklahoma Press.

Kleivan, I. (1984). West Greenland before 1950. In W. C. Sturtevant (Gen. Ed.) & D. Damas (Vol. Ed.), *Handbook of North American Indians: Vol. 5. Arctic* (pp. 595–621). Washington DC: Smithsonian Institution.

Kluckhohn, C., & Leighton, D. (1948). *The Navajo.* Cambridge: Harvard University Press.

Kniffen, F., MacGregor, G., McKennan, R., Mekeel, S., & Mook, M. (1935). Walapai ethnography. *Memoirs of the American Anthropological Association, 42,* 7–293.

Knight, C. (1991). *Blood relations: Menstruation and origins of culture.* New Haven CT: Yale University Press.

Koehler, L. (1997). Earth mothers, warriors, horticulturists, artists, and chiefs: Women among the Mississippian and Mississippian-Oneota peoples. In C. Claassen & R. A. Joyce (Eds.), *Women in prehistory: North America and Mesoamerica* (pp. 211–226). Philadelphia: University of Pennsylvania Press.

Kroeber, A. L. (1922). Elements of culture in Native California. *American Archaeology and Ethnology, 13,* 259–328.

Kroeber, A. L. (1923). *Anthropology*. New York: Harcourt, Brace.

Kroeber, A. L. (1925). *Handbook of the Indians of California*. Washington DC: Government Printing Office.

Kroeber, A. L. (1932). The Patwin and their neighbors. *American Archaeology and Ethnology, 29*, 253–423.

LaFromboise, T. D., & Low, K. G. (1998). American Indian children and adolescents. In J. T. Gibb, L. N. Huang, & Associates (Eds.), *Children of color: Psychological interventions with minority youth* (pp. 112–142). San Francisco: Jossey-Bass.

Lahren, S. L. (1998). Kalispel. In W. C. Sturtevant (Gen. Ed.) & D. E. Walker (Vol. Ed.), *Handbook of North American Indians: Vol. 12. Plateau* (pp. 283–296). Washington DC: Smithsonian Institution.

Lambert, B. G., Rothschild, B. F., Atland, R., & Green, L. B. (1978). *Adolescence: Transition from childhood to maturity*. Monterey CA: Brooks/Cole.

Lame Deer, J., & Erdoes, R. (1972). *Lame Deer: Seeker of visions*. New York: Simon and Schuster.

Lamphere, L. (1983). Southwestern ceremonialism. In W. C. Sturtevant (Gen. Ed.) & A. Ortiz (Vol. Ed.), *Handbook of North American Indians: Vol. 10. Southwest* (pp. 743–763). Washington DC: Smithsonian Institution.

Lane, R. (1981). Chilcotin. In W. C. Sturtevant (Gen. Ed.) & J. Helm (Vol. Ed.), *Handbook of North American Indians: Vol. 6. Subarctic* (pp. 402–412). Washington DC: Smithsonian Institution.

Lantis, M. (1984a). Aleut. In W. C. Sturtevant (Gen. Ed.) & D. Damas (Vol. Ed.), *Handbook of North American Indians: Vol. 5. Arctic* (pp. 161–184). Washington DC: Smithsonian Institution.

Lantis, M. (1984b). Nunivak Eskimo. In W. C. Sturtevant (Gen. Ed.) & D. Damas (Vol.Ed.), *Handbook of North American Indians: Vol. 5. Arctic* (pp. 209–223). Washington DC: Smithsonian Institution.

LaPena, F. R. (1978). Wintu. In W. C. Sturtevant (Gen. Ed.) & R. F. Heizer (Vol. Ed.), *Handbook of North American Indians: Vol. 8. California* (pp. 324–340). Washington DC: Smithsonian Institution.

Larson, R. W. (2000). Toward a psychology of positive youth development. *American Psychologist, 55*, 170–183.

Lawrence, J. (2000). The Indian Health Service and the sterilization of Native American women. *American Indian Quarterly, 24*, 400–419.

Lee, J. R. (2001, July 8). *Natives revive Isnati, hope it aids survival in today's world.*

Lincoln NE: Lincoln Journal Star. Available from <http://www.journalstar .com>.

Lee, J. W., & Cartledge, G. (1996). Native Americans. In G. Cartledge with contributions by J. F. Milburn (Eds.), *Cultural diversity and social skills instruction: Understanding ethnic and gender differences* (pp. 205–243). Champaign IL: Research Press.

Leeming, D. A., & Leeming, M. A. (1994). *Encyclopedia of creation myths*. Santa Barbara CA: ABC-CLIO.

Leighton, D., & Kluckhohn, C. (1947). *Children of the People*. Cambridge: Harvard University Press.

Levy, R. (1978). Costanoan. In W. C. Sturtevant (Gen. Ed.) & R. F. Heizer (Vol. Ed.), *Handbook of North American Indians: Vol. 8. California* (pp. 485–495). Washington DC: Smithsonian Institution.

Libby, D. (1952). *Girls' puberty observances among Northern Athabascans*. Unpublished doctoral dissertation, University of California.

Lincoln, B. (1991). *Emerging from the chrysalis: Rituals of women's initiations*. New York: Oxford University Press.

Locke, R. F. (1992). *The book of the Navajo* (5th ed.). Los Angeles: Mankind Publishing Company.

Lum, D. (1996). *Social work practice & people of color: A process-stage approach* (3rd ed.). Pacific Grove CA: Brooks/Cole.

Luomala, K. (1978). Tipai and Ipai. In W. C. Sturtevant (Gen. Ed.) & R. F. Heizer (Vol. Ed.), *Handbook of North American Indians: Vol. 8. California* (pp. 592–609). Washington DC: Smithsonian Institution.

Lutkehaus, N. C. (1995). Feminist anthropology and female initiation in Melanesia. In N. C. Lutkehaus & P. B. Roscoe (Eds.), *Gender rituals: Female initiation in Melanesia* (pp. 1–29). New York: Routledge.

Mails, T. E. (1974/1993). *The people called Apache*. New York: BDD Illustrated Books.

Mails, T. E. (1983). *The Pueblo Children of the Earth Mother* (Vol. 2). Garden City NY: Doubleday.

Mails, T. E. (1988). *Secret American pathways: A guide to inner peace*. Tulsa OK: Council Oak Books.

Mails, T. E. (1996). *The Cherokee people: The story of the Cherokees from earliest origins to contemporary times*. New York: Marlowe.

Maltz, D., & Archambault, J. (1995). Gender and power in Native North America. In L. F. Klein & L. A. Ackerman (Eds.), *Women and power in Native North America* (pp. 230–249). Norman: University of Oklahoma Press.

Markstrom, C. A. (2002). The Indian Child Welfare Act of 1978: Barriers to implementation and recommendations for the future. In D. Grinde (Ed.), *Native Americans* (pp. 101–106). Washington DC: Congressional Quarterly Press.

Markstrom, C. A., & Charley, P. H. (2003). Psychological effects of human caused environmental disasters: Examination of the Navajo and uranium. *American Indian and Alaska Native Mental Health Research: The Journal of the National Center, 11*, 19–45.

Markstrom, C. A., & Iborra, A. (2003). Adolescent identity formation and rites of passage: The Navajo Kinaaldá ceremony for girls. *Journal of Research on Adolescence, 13*, 399–425.

Martin, J. W. (2001). *The land looks after us.* New York: Oxford University Press.

Mary-Rousselière, G. (1984). Iglulik. In W. C. Sturtevant (Gen. Ed.) & D. Damas (Vol. Ed.), *Handbook of North American Indians: Vol. 5. Arctic* (pp. 431–446). Washington DC: Smithsonian Institution.

McClellan, C. (1981a). Inland Tlingit. In W. C. Sturtevant (Gen. Ed.) & J. Helm (Vol. Ed.), *Handbook of North American Indians: Vol. 6. Subarctic* (pp. 469–480). Washington DC: Smithsonian Institution.

McClellan, C. (1981b). Intercultural relations and cultural change in the Cordillera. In W. C. Sturtevant (Gen. Ed.) & J. Helm (Vol. Ed.), *Handbook of North American Indians: Vol. 6. Subarctic* (pp. 387–401). Washington DC: Smithsonian Institution.

McClellan, C. (1981c). Tagish. In W. C. Sturtevant (Gen. Ed.) & J. Helm (Vol. Ed.), *Handbook of North American Indians: Vol. 6. Subarctic* (pp. 481–492). Washington DC: Smithsonian Institution.

McClellan, C. (1981d). Tutchone. In W. C. Sturtevant (Gen. Ed.) & J. Helm (Vol. Ed.), *Handbook of North American Indians: Vol. 6. Subarctic* (pp. 493–505). Washington DC: Smithsonian Institution.

McGuire, T. R. (1983). Walapai. In W. C. Sturtevant (Gen. Ed.) & A. Ortiz (Vol. Ed.), *Handbook of North American Indians: Vol. 10. Southwest* (pp. 25–37). Washington DC: Smithsonian Institution.

McIlwraith, T. F. (1948). *The Bella Coola Indians.* Toronto: University of Toronto Press.

McKee, C. (1989). Feminism: A vision of love. In S. Nicholson (Ed.), *The Goddess re-awakening: The feminine principle today* (pp. 249–267). Wheaton IL: Theosophical Publishing House.

McKennan, R. A. (1959). The Upper Tanana Indians. *Yale University Publications in Anthropology, 55.*

McLendon, S., & Lowy, M. J. (1978). Eastern Pomo and Southeastern Pomo. In W. C. Sturtevant (Gen. Ed.) & R. F. Heizer (Vol. Ed.), *Handbook of North American Indians: Vol. 8. California* (pp. 306–323). Washington DC: Smithsonian Institution.

McMillan, A. D. (1988). *Native peoples and cultures of Canada.* Vancouver: Douglas & McIntyre.

Mihesuah, D. A. (2003). *Indigenous American women: Decolonization, empowerment, activism.* Lincoln: University of Nebraska Press.

Miller, J. (1998). Middle Columbia River Salishans. In W. C. Sturtevant (Gen. Ed.) & D. E. Walker (Vol. Ed.) *Handbook of North American Indians: Vol. 12. Plateau* (pp. 253–270). Washington DC: Smithsonian Institution.

Miller, J., & Seaburg, W. R. (1990). Athapaskans of southwestern Oregon. In W. C. Sturtevant (Gen. Ed.) & W. Suttles (Vol. Ed.), *Handbook of North American Indians: Vol. 7. Northwest Coast* (pp. 580–588). Washington DC: Smithsonian Institution.

Miller, V. P. (1978). Yuki, Huchnom, and Coast Yuki. In W. C. Sturtevant (Gen. Ed.) & R. F. Heizer (Vol. Ed.), *Handbook of North American Indians: Vol. 8. California* (pp. 249–255). Washington DC: Smithsonian Institution.

Moon, S. (1984). *Changing Woman and her sisters.* San Francisco: Guild for Psychological Studies.

Moore, J. H., Liberty, M. P., & Straus, A. T. (2001). Cheyenne. In W. C. Sturtevant (Gen. Ed.) & R. J. DeMallie (Vol. Ed.), *Handbook of North American Indians: Vol. 13, Pt. 2. Plains* (pp. 863–885). Washington DC: Smithsonian Institution.

Muckle, R. J. (1998). *The First Nations of British Columbia.* Vancouver: UBC Press.

Murdock, G. P., & White, D. R. (1969). Standard cross-cultural sample. *Ethnology, 13,* 329–369.

Murphy, M. E. (1993). *The role of music in girls' puberty ceremonies of southwest Native American cultures.* MA thesis, Arizona State University.

Muuss, R. E. (1988). *Theories of adolescence* (5th ed.). New York: Random House.

Myers, J. E. (1978). Cahto. In W. C. Sturtevant (Gen. Ed.) & R. F. Heizer (Vol. Ed.), *Handbook of North American Indians: Vol. 8. California* (pp. 244–248). Washington DC: Smithsonian Institution.

Nabokov, P. (Ed.). (1999). *Native American testimony: A chronicle of Indian-white relations from prophecy to the present, 1492–2000* (Rev. ed.). New York: Penguin Books.

National Center for Education Statistics. (2003). *Status and trends in the education of American Indians and Alaska Natives: Indicator 8.2: Unemployment rates.* Available from <http://nces.ed.gov/>.

Neihardt, J. G. (1932/1959). *Black Elk speaks: Being the life of a holy man of the Oglala Sioux.* New York: Pocket Books.

Newcomb, W. W. (1983). Karankawa. In W. C. Sturtevant (Gen. Ed.) & A. Ortiz (Vol. Ed.), *Handbook of North American Indians: Vol. 10. Southwest* (pp. 359–367). Washington DC: Smithsonian Institution.

Newcomb, W. W. (2001). Wichita. In W. C. Sturtevant (Gen. Ed.) & R. J. De-Mallie (Vol. Ed.), *Handbook of North American Indians: Vol. 13, Pt. 1. Plains* (pp. 548–566). Washington DC: Smithsonian Institution.

Newton, K. (1997). Social capital and democracy. *American Behavioral Scientist, 40,* 575–586.

Nicholas, D. (1939). Mescalero Apache girls' puberty ceremony. *El Palacio, 46,* 193–204.

Nichols, J. (2002, July 7). Inside Apache rite of passage. *The Arizona Republic,* B1, B4.

Niethammer, C. (1977). *Daughters of the Earth: The lives and legends of American Indian women.* New York: Simon and Schuster.

Nomland, G. A. (1935). Sinkyone notes. University of California *Publications in American Archaeology and Ethnology, 36.*

Norelli, G. (Writer/Producer). (1994). *The Sunrise Dance* (Video Recording). Watertown MA: Documentary Educational Resources.

Noriega, J. (1992). American Indian education in the United States: Indoctrination for subordination to colonialism. In M. A. Jaimes (Ed.), *The state of Native America: Genocide, colonization, and resistance* (pp. 371–402). Boston: South End Press.

Olmsted, D. L., & Stewart, O. C. (1978). Achumawi. In W. C. Sturtevant (Gen. Ed.) & R. F. Heizer (Vol. Ed.), *Handbook of North American Indians: Vol. 8. California* (pp. 225–235). Washington DC: Smithsonian Institution.

Olsen, L. (1998). Music and dance. In W. C. Sturtevant (Gen. Ed.) & D. E. Walker (Vol. Ed.), *Handbook of North American Indians: Vol. 12. Plateau* (pp. 546–572). Washington DC: Smithsonian Institution.

Opler, M. E. (1935). The concept of supernatural power among the Chiricahua and Mescalero Apaches. *American Anthropologist, 37,* 65–70.

Opler, M. E. (1936). A summary of Jicarilla Apache culture. *American Anthropologist, 38,* 202–223.

Opler, M. E. (1938). Myths and tales of the Jicarilla Indians. *Memoirs of the American Folklore Society, 31.* New York.

Opler, M. E. (1941). *An Apache life-way: The economic, social, and religious institutions of the Chiricahua Indians.* Chicago: University of Chicago Press.

Opler, M. E. (1942). Myths and tales of the Chiricahua Apache Indians. *Memoirs of the American Folk-Lore Society* (Vol. 7). Menasha WI.

Opler, M. E. (1946). Childhood and youth in Jicarilla Apache society. *Publications of the Frederick Webb Hodge Anniversary Publication Fund* (Vol. 5). Los Angeles: Southwest Museum Administrator of the Fund.

Opler, M. E. (1983a). The Apachean culture pattern and its origins. In W. C. Sturtevant (Gen. Ed.) & A. Ortiz (Vol. Ed.), *Handbook of North American Indians: Vol. 10. Southwest* (pp. 368–392). Washington DC: Smithsonian Institution.

Opler, M. E. (1983b). Chiricahua Apache. In W. C. Sturtevant (Gen. Ed.) & A. Ortiz (Vol. Ed.), *Handbook of North American Indians: Vol. 10. Southwest* (pp. 401–418). Washington DC: Smithsonian Institution.

Opler, M. E. (1983c). Mescalero Apache. In W. C. Sturtevant (Gen. Ed.) & A. Ortiz (Vol. Ed.), *Handbook of North American Indians: Vol. 10. Southwest* (pp. 419–439). Washington DC: Smithsonian Institution.

Opler, M. E. (2001). Lipan Apache. In W. C. Sturtevant (Gen. Ed.) & R. J. DeMallie (Vol. Ed.), *Handbook of North American Indians: Vol. 13, Pt. 2. Plains* (pp. 941–952). Washington DC: Smithsonian Institution.

Osgood, C. (1936/1970). Contributions to the ethnography of the Kutchin. *Yale University Publications in Anthropology, 14.* New Haven: Human Relations Area Files Press.

Osgood, C. (1937). The ethnography of the Tanaina. *Yale University Publications in Anthropology, 16.* New Haven: Yale University Press.

Osgood, C. (1940). Ingalik material culture. *Yale University Publications in Anthropology, 22.* New Haven: Yale University Press.

Osgood, C. (1958). Ingalik social culture. *Yale University Publications in Anthropology, 53*. New Haven: Yale University Press.

Osgood, C. (1971). The Han Indians: A compilation of ethnographic and historical data on the Alaska-Yukon boundary area. *Yale University Publications in Anthropology, 74*. New Haven: Yale University Press.

Osmond, M. W., & Thorne, B. (1993). Feminist theories: The social construction of gender in families and societies. In P. Boss, W. Doherty, R. LaRossa, W. Schumm, & S. Steinmetz (Eds.), *Sourcebook of families theories and methods: A contextual approach* (pp. 591–623). New York: Plenum.

Oswalt, W. H. (2006). *This land was theirs: A study of Native North Americans* (8th ed.). New York: Oxford University Press.

Palmer, G. B. (1998). Coeur d'Alene. In W. C. Sturtevant (Gen. Ed.) & D. E. Walker (Vol. Ed.) *Handbook of North American Indians: Vol. 12. Plateau* (pp. 313–326). Washington DC: Smithsonian Institution.

Parks, D. R. (2001). Pawnee. In W. C. Sturtevant (Gen. Ed.) & R. J. DeMallie (Vol. Ed.), *Handbook of North American Indians: Vol. 13, Pt. 1. Plains* (pp. 515–547). Washington DC: Smithsonian Institution.

Patterson, V. D. (1995). Evolving gender roles in Pomo society. In L. F. Klein & L. A. Ackerman (Eds.), *Women and power in Native North America* (pp. 126–145). Norman: University of Oklahoma Press.

Patton, M. Q. (2002). *Qualitative research and evaluation methods*. Thousand Oaks CA: Sage.

Petersen, A. C., Leffert, N., & Graham, B. L. (1995). Adolescent development and the emergence of sexuality. *Suicide and Life-Threatening Behavior, 25*, 4–17.

Petersen, A. C., Leffert, N., Graham, B., Alwin, J., & Ding, S. (1997). Promoting mental health during the transition into adolescence. In J. Schulenbert, J. L. Maggs, & K. Hurrelmann (Eds.), *Health risks and developmental transitions during adolescence* (pp. 471–497). Cambridge UK: Cambridge University Press.

Phinney, J. (1992). The Multigroup Ethnic Identity Measure: A new scale for use with adolescents and young adults from diverse groups. *Journal of Adolescent Research, 2*, 156–176.

Phinney, J. (1995). Ethnic identity and self-esteem. In A. M. Padilla (Ed.), *Hispanic psychology: Critical issues in theory and research* (pp. 57–70). Thousand Oaks CA: Sage.

Phinney, J. S., Lochner, B. T., & Murphy, R. (1990). Ethnic identity development and psychological adjustment in adolescence. In A. R. Stiffman & L. E. Davis (Eds.), *Ethnic issues in adolescent mental health* (pp. 53–72). Newbury Park CA: Sage.

Piaget, J. (1952). *The origins of intelligence in children.* New York: International Universities Press.

Piaget, J. (1972). Intellectual evolution from childhood to adulthood. *Human Development, 15,* 1–12.

Powers, M. N. (1980). Menstruation and reproduction: An Oglala case. *Signs: Journal of Women and Culture, 6,* 54–65.

Powers, M. N. (1986). *Oglala women: Myth, ritual, and reality.* Chicago: University of Chicago Press.

Powers, W. K. (1977). *Oglala religion.* Lincoln: University of Nebraska Press.

Powers, W. K. (2000). Wiping the tears: Lakota religion in the twenty-first century. In L. E. Sullivan (Ed.), *Native religions and cultures in North America* (pp. 104–120). New York: Continuum.

Prezzano, S. C. (1997). Warfare, women, and households: The development of Iroquois culture. In C. Claassen & R. A. Joyce (Eds.), *Women in prehistory: North America and Mesoamerica* (pp. 88–99). Philadelphia: University of Pennsylvania Press.

Pritzker, B. M. (1998). *Native Americans: An encyclopedia of history, culture, and peoples* (Vols. 1 & 2). Santa Barbara CA: ABC-CLIO.

Quintero, N. (1980). A maiden comes of age. *National Geographic, 157,* 262–271.

Radin, P. (1936). Ojibwa and Ottawa puberty dreams. In *Essays in anthropology presented to A. L. Kroeber in celebration of his sixtieth birthday, June 11, 1936.* Berkeley: University of California Press.

Reagan, A. B. (1931). Notes on the Indians of the Fort Apache region. *Anthropological papers of the American Museum of Natural History, 31.* New York: American Museum Press.

Reichard, G. A. (1977). *Navajo religion: A study of symbolism.* Princeton NJ: Princeton University Press.

Reyhner, J., & Eder, J. (1992). A history of Indian education. In J. Reyhner (Ed.), *Teaching American Indian students* (pp. 33–58). Norman: University of Oklahoma Press.

Rhoades, R. E. (1993). Corn, the golden grain. *National Geographic, 183,* 92–117.

Riddell, F. A. (1978). Maidu and Konkow. In W. C. Sturtevant (Gen. Ed.) & R. F. Heizer (Vol. Ed.), *Handbook of North American Indians: Vol. 8. California* (pp. 370–386). Washington DC: Smithsonian Institution.

Risling, D., & Boyer, P. (1994). Don't forget who you are. *Tribal College Journal, 6*, 20–22.

Ritzenthaler, R. (1978). Southwestern Chippewa. In W. C. Sturtevant (Gen. Ed.) & B. G. Trigger (Vol. Ed.), *Handbook of North American Indians: Vol. 15. Northeast* (pp. 743–759). Washington DC: Smithsonian Institution.

Roessel, R. (1981). *Women in Navajo society*. Rough Rock AZ: Rough Rock Demonstration School.

Rogers, E. S. (1978). Southeastern Chippewa. In W. C. Sturtevant (Gen. Ed.) & B. G. Trigger (Vol. Ed.), *Handbook of North American Indians: Vol. 15. Northeast* (pp. 760–771). Washington DC: Smithsonian Institution.

Rogol, A. D., Roemmich, J. N., & Clark, P. A. (2002). Growth at puberty. *Journal of Adolescent Health, 31*, 192–200.

Ross, J. A. (1998). Spokane. In W. C. Sturtevant (Gen. Ed.) & D. E. Walker (Vol. Ed.), *Handbook of North American Indians: Vol. 12. Plateau* (pp. 271–282). Washington DC: Smithsonian Institution.

Rountree, H. C. (1989). *The Powhatan Indians of Virginia: Their traditional culture*. Norman: University of Oklahoma Press.

Saladin d'Anglure, B. (1984). Inuit of Quebec. In W. C. Sturtevant (Gen. Ed.) & D. Damas (Vol. Ed.), *Handbook of North American Indians: Vol. 5. Arctic* (pp. 476–507). Washington DC: Smithsonian Institution.

Savishinsky, J., & Hara, H. (1981). Hare. In W. C. Sturtevant (Gen. Ed.) & J. Helm (Vol. Ed.), *Handbook of North American Indians: Vol. 6. Subarctic* (pp. 314–325). Washington DC: Smithsonian Institution.

Sawyer, J. O. (1978). Wappo. In W. C. Sturtevant (Gen. Ed.) & R. F. Heizer (Vol. Ed.), *Handbook of North American Indians: Vol. 8. California* (pp. 256–263). Washington DC: Smithsonian Institution.

Schaafsma, P. (1986). Rock art. In W. C. Sturtevant (Gen. Ed.) & W. L. d'Azevedo (Vol. Ed.), *Handbook of North American Indians: Vol. 11. Great Basin* (pp. 215–226). Washington DC: Smithsonian Institution.

Schlegel, A. (1972). *Male dominance and female autonomy: Domestic authority in matrilineal societies*. New Haven CT: Human Relations Area Files Press.

Schlegel, A. (1973). The adolescent socialization of the Hopi girl. *Ethnology: An International Journal of Cultural and Social Anthropology, 12*, 449–462.

Schlegel, A., & Barry, H., III. (1980). The evolutionary significance of adolescent initiation ceremonies. *American Ethnologist, 7,* 696–715.

Schlegel, A., & Barry, H., III. (1986). The cultural consequences of female contribution to subsistence. *American Anthropologist, 88,* 142–150.

Schlegel, A., & Barry, H., III. (1991). *Adolescence: An anthropological inquiry.* New York: The Free Press.

Schulenberg, J. Maggs, J. L., & Hurrelmann, K. (1997). Negotiating developmental transitions during adolescence and young adulthood: Health risks and opportunities. In J. Schulenberg, J. L. Maggs, & K. Hurrelmann (Eds.), *Health risks and developmental transitions during adolescence* (pp. 1–19). Cambridge UK: Cambridge University Press.

Schuster, H. H. (1998). Yakima and neighboring groups. In W. C. Sturtevant (Gen. Ed.) & D. E. Walker (Vol. Ed.), *Handbook of North American Indians: Vol. 12. Plateau* (pp. 327–351). Washington DC: Smithsonian Institution.

Schwartz, D. W. (1983). Havasupai. In W. C. Sturtevant (Gen. Ed.) & A. Ortiz (Vol. Ed.), *Handbook of North American Indians: Vol. 10. Southwest* (pp. 13–24). Washington DC: Smithsonian Institution.

Schwarz, M. T. (1997). *Molded in the image of Changing Woman.* Tucson: University of Arizona Press.

Schweitzer, M. M. (2001). Otoe and Missouria. In W. C. Sturtevant (Gen. Ed.) & R. J. DeMallie (Vol. Ed.) *Handbook of North American Indians: Vol. 13, Pt. 1. Plains* (pp. 447–461). Washington DC: Smithsonian Institution.

Scott, D. G. (1998). Rites of passage in adolescent development: A reappreciation. *Child & Youth Care Forum, 27,* 317–335.

Seaburg, W. R., & Miller, J. (1990). Tillamook. In W. C. Sturtevant (Gen. Ed.) & W. Suttles (Vol. Ed.), *Handbook of North American Indians: Vol. 7. Northwest Coast* (pp. 560–567). Washington DC: Smithsonian Institution.

Sebald, H. (1992). *Adolescence: A social psychological analysis* (4th ed.). Englewood Cliffs NJ: Prentice-Hall.

Select Committee on Indian Affairs. (1977). *Indian Child Welfare Act of 1977: Hearing before the United States Senate Select Committee on Indian Affairs, Ninety-fifth Congress, First Session on S. 1214.* Washington DC: Government Printing Office.

Sharp, H. S. (1995). Asymmetric equals: Women and men among the Chipewyan. In L. F. Klein & L. A. Ackerman (Eds.), *Women and power in Native North America* (pp. 46–74). Norman: University of Oklahoma Press.

Shepardson, M. (1995). The gender status of Navajo women. In L. F. Klein & L. A. Ackerman (Eds.), *Women and power in Native North America* (pp. 159–176). Norman: University of Oklahoma Press.

Shimkin, D. B. (1986). Eastern Shoshone. In W. C. Sturtevant (Gen. Ed.) & W. L. d'Azevedo (Vol. Ed.), *Handbook of North American Indians: Vol. 11. Great Basin* (pp. 308–335). Washington DC: Smithsonian Institution.

Shortridge, F. (1913). The life of a Chilkat Indian girl. *Museum Journal of the University of Pennsylvania, 4,* 101–103.

Silver, S. (1978a). Chimariko. In W. C. Sturtevant (Gen. Ed.) & R. F. Heizer (Vol. Ed), *Handbook of North American Indians: Vol. 8. California* (pp. 205–210). Washington DC: Smithsonian Institution.

Silver, S. (1978b). Shastan peoples. In W. C. Sturtevant (Gen. Ed.) & R. F. Heizer (Vol. Ed.), *Handbook of North American Indians: Vol. 8. California* (pp. 211–224). Washington DC: Smithsonian Institution.

Silverstein, M. (1990). Chinookans of the Lower Columbia. In W. C. Sturtevant (Gen. Ed.) & W. Suttles (Vol. Ed.), *Handbook of North American Indians: Vol. 7. Northwest Coast* (pp. 533–546). Washington DC: Smithsonian Institution.

Silvey, L. A. E. (1999). Firstborn American Indian daughters: Struggles to reclaim cultural and self-identity. In H. P. McAdoo, *Family ethnicity: Strength in diversity* (2nd ed., pp. 72–93). Thousand Oaks CA: Sage.

Slobodin, R. (1981). Kutchin. In W. C. Sturtevant (Gen. Ed.) & J. Helm (Vol. Ed.), *Handbook of North American Indians: Vol. 6. Subarctic* (pp. 514–532). Washington DC: Smithsonian Institution.

Smith, C. R. (1978). Tubatulabal. In W. C. Sturtevant (Gen. Ed.) & R. F. Heizer (Vol. Ed.), *Handbook of North American Indians: Vol. 8. California* (pp. 437–445). Washington DC: Smithsonian Institution.

Smith, D. (1984). Mackenzie Delta Eskimo. In W. C. Sturtevant (Gen. Ed.) & D. Damas (Vol. Ed.), *Handbook of North American Indians: Vol. 5. Arctic* (pp. 347–358). Washington DC: Smithsonian Institution.

Smith, J. G. E. (1981a). Chipewyan. In W. C. Sturtevant (Gen. Ed.) & J. Helm (Vol. Ed.), *Handbook of North American Indians: Vol. 6. Subarctic* (pp. 271–284). Washington DC: Smithsonian Institution.

Smith, J. G. E. (1981b). Western Woods Cree. In W. C. Sturtevant (Gen. Ed.) & J. Helm (Vol. Ed.) *Handbook of North American Indians: Vol. 6. Subarctic* (pp. 256–270). Washington DC: Smithsonian Institution.

Spear, B. (2000). Adolescent nutrition: General. In B. S. Worthington-Roberts & S. R. Williams (Eds.), *Nutrition throughout the life cycle* (pp. 262–287). Boston: McGraw-Hill.

Speck, F. G. (1909/1979). Ethnology of the Yuchi Indians. *University of Pennsylvania Anthropological Publications of the University Museum, 1*. Atlantic Highlands NY: Humanities Press.

Spencer, R. F., & Jennings, J. D. (1965). *The Native Americans: Prehistory and Ethnology of the North American Indians*. New York: Harper and Row.

Spier, L. (1930). Klamath ethnography. *American Archeology and Ethnology, 30*.

Spier, R. F. G. (1978a). Foothill Yokuts. In W. C. Sturtevant (Gen. Ed.) & R. F. Heizer (Vol. Ed.), *Handbook of North American Indians: Vol. 8. California* (pp. 471–484). Washington DC: Smithsonian Institution.

Spier, R. F. G. (1978b). Monache. In W. C. Sturtevant (Gen. Ed.) & R. F. Heizer (Vol. Ed.), *Handbook of North American Indians: Vol. 8. California* (pp. 426–436). Washington DC: Smithsonian Institution.

Spindler, L. (1978). Menominee. In W. C. Sturtevant (Gen. Ed.), B. G. Trigger (Vol. Ed.), *Handbook of North American Indians: Vol. 15. Northeast* (pp. 708–724). Washington DC: Smithsonian Institution.

Stanislawski, M. B. (1979). Hopi-Tewa. In W. C. Sturtevant (Gen. Ed.) & A. Ortiz (Vol. Ed.), *Handbook of North American Indians: Vol. 9. Southwest* (pp. 587–602). Washington DC: Smithsonian Institution.

Statistics Canada. (2001a). *Aboriginal peoples of Canada: A demographic profile*. Available from <http://www.statcan.ca>.

Statistics Canada. (2001b). *Unemployment data: Selected Labour Force Characteristics (50), Aboriginal Origin (14), Age Groups (5A) and Sex (3) for Population 15 Years and Over, for Canada, Provinces, Territories and Census Metropolitan Areas ÊιÊ, 2001 Census—20% Sample Data*. Available from <http://www.statcan.ca>.

Statistics Canada. (2002a). *2001 census Aboriginal population profiles*. Released June 17, 2003. Last modified: 2005–11–31. Statistics Canada Catalogue no. 93F0043XIE.

Statistics Canada. (2002b). *2001 census community profiles*. Released June 27, 2002. Last modified: 2005–11–30. Statistics Canada Catalogue no. 93F0053XIE.

Stephens, W. N. (1962). *The Oedipus complex: Cross-cultural evidence*. New York: Free Press.

Stern, T. (1998a). Cayuse, Umatilla, and Walla Walla. In W. C. Sturtevant (Gen. Ed.) & D. E. Walker (Vol. Ed.), *Handbook of North American Indians: Vol. 12. Plateau* (pp. 395–419). Washington DC: Smithsonian Institution.

Stern, T. (1998b). Klamath and Modoc. In W. C. Sturtevant (Gen. Ed.) & D. E. Walker (Vol. Ed.), *Handbook of North American Indians: Vol. 12. Plateau* (pp. 446–466). Washington DC: Smithsonian Institution.

Stockel, H. H. (1991). *Women of the Apache nation*. Reno: University of Nevada Press.

St. Pierre, M., & Long Soldier, T. (1995). *Walking in the sacred manner*. New York: Simon and Schuster.

Striegel-Moore, R. H., & Cachelin, F. M. (1999). Body image concerns and disordered eating in adolescent girls: Risk and protective factors. In N. G. Johnson, M. C. Roberts, & J. Worell (Eds.), *Beyond appearance: A new look at adolescent girls* (pp. 85–108). Washington DC: American Psychological Assn.

Substance Abuse and Mental Health Services Administration. (2003). *Results from the 2002 National Survey on Drug Use and Health: National Findings* (Office of Applied Studies, NHSDA Series H-22, DHHS Publication No. SMA 03-3836). Rockville, Maryland.

Sullwold, E. (1987). The ritual-maker within at adolescence. In L. C. Mahdi, S. Foster, & M. Little (Eds.), *Betwixt & between: Patterns of masculine and feminine initiation* (pp. 111–131). LaSalle IL: Open Court.

Suttles, W. (1990). Central Coast Salish. In W. C. Sturtevant (Gen. Ed.) & W. Suttles (Vol. Ed.), *Handbook of North American Indians: Vol. 7. Northwest Coast* (pp. 453–475). Washington DC: Smithsonian Institution.

Suttles, W., & Lane, B. (1990). Southern Coast Salish. In W. C. Sturtevant (Gen. Ed.) & W. Suttles (Vol. Ed.), *Handbook of North American Indians: Vol. 7. Northwest Coast* (pp. 485–502). Washington DC: Smithsonian Institution.

Sutton, M. Q. (2004). *An introduction to Native North America* (2nd ed.). Boston: Pearson.

Tafoya, N., & Del Vecchio, A. (1996). Back to the future: An examination of the Native American holocaust experience. In M. McGoldrick, J. Giordano, & J. K. Pearce (Eds.), *Ethnicity and family therapy* (2nd ed., pp. 45–54). New York: Guilford Press.

Talamantez, I. (1991). Images of the feminine in Apache religious tradition. In P. M. Cooey, W. R. Eakin, & J. B. McDaniel (Eds.), *After patriarchy: Feminist transformations of the world religions* (pp. 131–145). Maryknoll NY: Orbis Books.

Talamantez, I. (2000). In the space between earth and sky: Contemporary Mescalero Apache ceremonialism. In L. E. Sullivan (Ed.), *Native religions and cultures of North America* (pp. 142–159). New York: Continuum. ·

Thomas, H., Pendleton, S. A., & Cappannari, C. (1986). Western Shoshone. In W. C. Sturtevant (Gen. Ed.) & W. L. d'Azevedo (Vol. Ed.), *Handbook of North American Indians: Vol. 11. Great Basin* (pp. 262–283). Washington DC: Smithsonian Institution.

Tiller, V. E. (1983). Jicarilla Apache. In W. C. Sturtevant (Gen. Ed.) & A. Ortiz (Vol. Ed.), *Handbook of North American Indians: Vol. 10. Southwest* (pp. 440–461). Washington DC: Smithsonian Institution.

Tiller, V. E. (1996a). *American Indian reservation and Indian trust areas: Mescalero Reservation.* Available from <http://www.commerce.gov>.

Tiller, V. E. (1996b). *American Indian reservation and Indian trust areas: San Carlos Apache Reservation.* Available from <http://www.commerce.gov>.

Tinker, G. (1998). Jesus, Corn Mother, and conquest: Christology and colonialism. In J. Weaver (Ed.), *Native American religious identity: Unforgotten gods* (pp. 134–154). Maryknoll NY: Orbis Books.

Tippeconnic, J. W. (1999). Tribal control of American Indian education: Observations since the 1960s with implications for the future. In K. C. Swisher & J. W. Tippeconnic (Eds.), *Next steps: Research and practice to advance American Indian education* (pp. 33–53). Charleston WV: Clearinghouse on Rural Education and Small Schools.

Tobey, M. (1981). Carrier. In W. C. Sturtevant (Gen. Ed.) & J. Helm (Vol. Ed.), *Handbook of North American Indians: Vol. 6. Subarctic* (pp. 413–432). Washington DC: Smithsonian Institution.

Torrance, R. M. (1994). *The spiritual quest: Transcendence in myth, religion, and science.* Berkeley: University of California Press.

Trebilcot, J. (1984). Sex roles: The argument from nature. In A. M. Jaggar & P. S. Rothenberg (Eds.), *Feminist frameworks: Alternative theoretical accounts of the relations between men and women* (2nd ed., pp. 114–120). New York: McGraw Hill.

Trimble, J. E. (2000). Social psychological perspectives on changing self-identification among American Indians and Alaska Natives. In R. H. Dana (Ed.), *Handbook of cross-cultural and multicultural personality assessment* (pp. 197–222). Mahwah NJ: Lawrence Erlbaum.

Turner, V. (1967). *The forest of symbols: Aspects of Ndembu ritual.* Ithaca NY: Cornell University Press.

U.S. Census Bureau. (2000a). *DP-3. Profile of Selected Economic Characteristics: 2000. Geographic Area: Mescalero Reservation, NM.* Available from <http://factfinder.census.gov>.

U.S. Census Bureau. (2000b). *DP-3. Profile of Selected Economic Characteristics: 2000. Geographic Area: San Carlos Reservation, AZ.* Available from <http://factfinder.census.gov>.

U.S. Census Bureau. (2000c). *GCT-PH1. Population, housing units, area, and density: 2000. Data set: Census 2000 summary file 1 (SF 1) 100–percent data. Geographic area: United States—American Indian and Alaska Native area, and Alaska Native regional corporation.* Available from <http://factfinder.census .gov>.

U.S. Census Bureau. (2001a). *Poverty 2001. Three-year-average median household income and poverty rate by race and Hispanic Origin: 1999–2001.* Available from <http://www.census.gov/hhes/income/income01/prs02asc.html>.

U.S. Census Bureau. (2001b). *Resident Population Estimates of the United States by Sex, Race, and Hispanic Origin: April 1, 1990 to July 1, 1999, with Short-Term Projection to November 1, 2000.* Available from <http://factfinder.census.gov>.

U.S. Census Bureau. (2002). *The American Indian and Alaska Native population: 2000.* Washington DC: Department of Commerce.

U.S. Department of Health and Human Services. (1999). *National Clearinghouse for Alcohol and Drug Information (NCAID): National Household Survey on Drug Abuse (NHSDA).* Available from <http://www.health.org/govstudy/bkd376/TableofContents.aspx#TopOfPage>.

van Gennep, A. (1908/1960). *The rites of passage* (M. Vizedom & G. Caffe, Trans.). Chicago: Chicago University Press. (Original work published 1908)

Waldram, J. B. (1994). Aboriginal spirituality in corrections: A Canadian case study in religion and therapy. *American Indian Quarterly, 18,* 197–21.

Walker, D. E. (1998a). Introduction. In W. C. Sturtevant (Gen. Ed.) & D. E. Walker (Vol. Ed.), *Handbook of North American Indians: Vol. 12. Plateau* (pp. 1–7). Washington DC: Smithsonian Institution.

Walker, D. E. (1998b). Nez Perce. In W. C. Sturtevant (Gen. Ed.) & D. E. Walker (Vol. Ed.), *Handbook of North American Indians: Vol. 12. Plateau* (pp. 420–438). Washington DC: Smithsonian Institution.

Wallace, E. (1978). Sexual status and role differentiation. In W. C. Sturtevant (Gen. Ed.) & R. F. Heizer (Vol. Ed.), *Handbook of North American Indians: Vol. 8. California* (pp. 683–689). Washington DC: Smithsonian Institution.

Wallace, W. J. (1978a). Hupa, Chilula, and Whilkut. In W. C. Sturtevant (Gen. Ed.) & R. F. Heizer (Vol. Ed), *Handbook of North American Indians: Vol. 8. California* (pp. 164–179). Washington DC: Smithsonian Institution.

Wallace, W. J. (1978b). Southern Valley Yokuts. In W. C. Sturtevant (Gen. Ed.) & R. F. Heizer (Vol. Ed), *Handbook of North American Indians: Vol. 8. California* (pp. 448–461). Washington DC: Smithsonian Institution.

Warner, L. D. (1999). Education and the law: Implications for American Indian/ Alaska Native students. In K. C. Swisher & J. W. Tippeconnic (Eds.), *Next steps: Research and practice to advance American Indian education* (pp. 53–80). Charleston WV: Clearinghouse on Rural Education and Small Schools.

Webster, G. (1990). Kwakiutl since 1980. In W. C. Sturtevant (Gen. Ed.) & W. Suttles (Vol. Ed.), *Handbook of North American Indians: Vol. 7. Northwest Coast* (pp. 387–390). Washington DC: Smithsonian Institution.

Weisfeld, G. (1997). Puberty rites as clues to the nature of human adolescence. *Cross-Cultural Psychology, 31,* 27–54.

Werner, E. E., & Smith, R. S. (1982). *Vulnerable but invincible: A longitudinal study of resilient children and youth.* New York: Adams.

Whitaker, K. (1971). The Sunrise Dance: An Apache puberty ceremony. *The Masterkey, 45,* 4–12.

White, J. M., & Klein, D. M. (2002). *Family theories* (2nd ed.). Thousand Oaks CA: Sage.

White, L. A. (1935). The Pueblo of Santo Domingo, New Mexico. *Memoirs of the American Anthropological Association, 43,* 1–210.

Whitman, W. (1937). The Oto. *Columbia University Contributions to Anthropology, 28.* New York.

Wilson, J. (1998). *The Earth shall weep: A history of Native America.* New York: Grove Press.

Wilson, N. L., & Towne, A. H. (1978). Nisenan. In W. C. Sturtevant (Gen. Ed.) & R. F. Heizer (Vol. Ed.), *Handbook of North American Indians: Vol. 8. California* (pp. 387–397). Washington DC: Smithsonian Institution.

Witherspoon, G. (1977). *Language and art in the Navajo universe.* Ann Arbor: University of Michigan Press.

Witt, S. H. (1984). Native women today: Sexism and the Indian women. In A. M. Jaggar & P. S. Rothenberg (Eds.), *Feminist frameworks: Alternative theoretical accounts of the relations between men and women* (2nd ed., pp. 23–31). New York: McGraw Hill.

Woody, R. L., Jack, B., & Bizahaloni, V. (1981). *Social impact of the uranium industry on two Navajo communities.* Tsaile AZ: Navajo Community College.

Wyatt, D. (1998a). Nicola. In W. C. Sturtevant (Gen. Ed.) & D. E. Walker (Vol. Ed.) *Handbook of North American Indians: Vol. 12. Plateau* (pp. 220–222). Washington DC: Smithsonian Institution.

Wyatt, D. (1998b). Thompson. In W. C. Sturtevant (Gen. Ed.) & D. E. Walker (Vol. Ed.) *Handbook of North American Indians: Vol. 12. Plateau* (pp. 191–202). Washington DC: Smithsonian Institution.

Young, G. A., & Gooding, E. D. (2001). Celebrations and giveaways. In W. C. Sturtevant (Gen. Ed.) & R. J. DeMallie (Vol. Ed.), *Handbook of North American Indians: Vol. 13, Pt. 2. Plains* (pp. 1011–1025). Washington DC: Smithsonian Institution.

Zak, N. C. (1989). Sacred and legendary women of Native North America. In S. Nicholson (Ed.), *The Goddess re-awakening: The feminine principle today* (pp. 232–245). Wheaton IL: Theosophical Publishing House.

Zenk, H. B. (1990a). Kalapuyans. In W. C. Sturtevant (Gen. Ed.) & W. Suttles (Vol. Ed.), *Handbook of North American Indians: Vol. 7. Northwest Coast* (pp. 547–553). Washington DC: Smithsonian Institution.

Zenk, H. B. (1990b). Siuslawans and Coosans. In W. C. Sturtevant (Gen. Ed.) & W. Suttles (Vol. Ed.), *Handbook of North American Indians: Vol. 7. Northwest Coast* (pp. 572–579). Washington DC: Smithsonian Institution.

Zenk, H. B., & Rigsby, B. (1998). Molala. In W. C. Sturtevant (Gen. Ed.) & D. E. Walker (Vol. Ed.), *Handbook of North American Indians: Vol. 12. Plateau* (pp. 439–445). Washington DC: Smithsonian Institution.

Zigmond, M. (1986). Kawaiisu. In W. C. Sturtevant (Gen. Ed.) & W. L. d'Azevedo (Vol. Ed.), *Handbook of North American Indians: Vol. 11. Great Basin* (pp. 398–411). Washington DC: Smithsonian Institution.

Index